Elite Deviance

Elite Deviance

SEVENTH EDITION

David R. Simon

University of California, Berkeley/San Jose State University

Allyn and Bacon

Boston • London • Toronto • Sydney • Tokyo • Singapore

Series Editor: Jennifer Jacobson
Editorial Assistant: Tom Jefferies
Marketing Manager: Judeth Hall
Editorial Production Service: Whitney Acres Editorial
Manufacturing Buyer: Joanne Sweeney
Cover Administrator: Joel Gendron
Electronic Composition: Omegatype Typography, Inc.

Internet: www.ablongman.com

Between the time Website information is gathered and published, some sites may have closed. Also, the transcription of URLs can result in typographical errors. The publisher would appreciate notification where these occur so that they may be corrected in subsequent editions.

Library of Congress Cataloging-in-Publication Data

Simon, David R., 1944–
      Elite deviance / David R. Simon. — 7th ed.
          p.   cm.
      Includes bibliographical references and index.
      ISBN 0-205-32176-3 (pbk.)
          1. White collar crimes—United States.   2. Deviant behavior—United
States.   3. Elite (Social sciences)—United States.   4. Corporations—United
States—Corrupt practices.   5. United States—Moral conditions.   I. Title.
      HV6769 .S56   2001
      364.16'8'0973—dc21
2001022338

Printed in the United States of America
10   9   8   7   6   5   4   3   2   1   05   04   03   02   01

Contents

Preface

This seventh edition marks the 20th anniversary of the publication of *Elite Deviance*. Since its initial publication, the book has never waivered in its approach to its subject, namely, that the intense maldistribution of power and wealth amongst the nation's power elite has given rise to a set of criminal and deviant practices that C. Wright Mills termed the higher immorality. As the new millennium dawned, it became crystal clear that these practices, described in depth in this seventh edition, are now global in scope.

These global deviant practices have come to include such crimes as international money laundering, global environmental pollution, illegal wars, which include alliances with known arms smugglers, drug traffickers, and global crime syndicates, export of toxic waste and products that have been banned for sale in the United States because they endanger the public health and safety, and the like.

Likewise, the new millennium has brought absolutely no improvement in the political system in the United States. Hundreds of millions of dollars were spent in the 2000 election by political action committees and super-rich candidates, excluding meaningful third-party candidates from offering alternative policies to the nation's pressing problems. The chaos in Florida demonstrated that the right to vote might be abridged at any time in the United States and in any number of ways. As discussed throughout the text, corruption is a way of life in American politics and has been since the nation was founded. Knowledge of improprieties is but one reason why the voter turnout in America is the lowest of any modern democratic nation.

Elite Deviance and the New Millennium

This seventh edition of *Elite Deviance* appears at the dawn of a new millennium, an era characterized by new global realities. The global nature of elite deviance and its consequences are noted throughout this edition.

- Chapter 1 introduces readers to both the concept of elite deviance and a description of the environment in which these acts of great harm take place. Within the United States as well as globally, the distribution of power and wealth is becoming ever more concentrated, making it more and more difficult to exercise any control over what elites do.

- Chapter 2 presents the higher immorality—an institutionalized set of deviant practices that are now global in scope. This is especially true of elite cooperation with global crime syndicates involved in the $850 billion global narcotics trade and the vast amount of money laundered by legitimate financial institutions, lawyers, and other elite professionals.

- Chapters 3 and 4 discuss the contemporary nature of corporate deviance. The $260 billion price tag and hundreds of thousands of lives taken by global corporate crime make this form of deviance one of the world's most serious social problems. Add to these figures the pollution and resource depletion that are a result of global mass consumption and the gravity of these practices becomes truly immense.

- Chapter 5 is devoted to various types of global elite deviance. International arms smuggling, the dumping of toxic wastes, and the sale of products banned for sale in the United States because of their toxic nature constitute yet another scandal. The chapter also contains an examination of human rights violations by regimes receiving U.S. foreign and military aid.

- Chapters 6, 7, and 9 detail the nature of modern graft and corruption. Scandal in our era has become an institutionalized feature of America's power elite, one as noted, with global ramifications.

- Chapter 8 contains an analysis of the causes of elite deviance and argues that a genuine sociological theory of such deviance must account for causal factors on the macro, immediate milieu, and individual levels of analysis. The chapter discusses how these various causes interrelate, as well as how elite deviance is interrelated with other types of wrongdoing.

- Finally, the epilogue examines the types of policy changes viewed as necessary for the reduction of elite deviance. This section also contains solid suggestions for becoming more informed about and involved in the struggle against the social injustices embodied in elite deviance.

Acknowledgments

Many family members and colleagues have my sincere thanks for the roles they have played in this new edition. Several reviewers made useful suggestions in reorienting some of the theoretical and other discussions in the book: Polly Radosh, Western Illinois University; Paul Camacho, University of Massachusetts, Boston; and William Farrell, University of Michigan, Flint. My pastor, Max Lopez-Cepero alerted me to the religious and moral implications of these great collective sins. Finally, I would like to thank my colleagues at Berkeley, especially Troy Duster, Neil Fligstein, and Ann Swidler, for their stimulating ideas and willingness to discuss these issues. Likewise, my new colleagues at San Jose State deserve my heartfelt appreciation for their encouragement in completing this new edition.

1

The Nature
of Elite Deviance

Scandal-Plagued America:
The Clinton Years as Metaphor

On February 12, 1999, the U.S. Senate acquitted President William Jefferson Clinton of charges that he committed perjury and obstruction of justice in order to hide sexual indiscretions with a one-time White House intern, Monica Lewinsky, thus permitting the forty-second president to complete the remaining 708 days of his term.[1]

During the scandal, many commentators argued that the president had violated his oath of office as the chief law enforcement officer in the land. Under the U.S. Constitution, the president is specifically charged to take care that the laws be faithfully executed, and many critics believed that Clinton not only lied to the American public ("I did not have sex with that woman"), but lied under oath to a federal grand jury and obstructed justice as well. Clinton's supporters, however, claimed that it was the criminal justice system itself that was out of control.

The special counsel, Judge Kenneth Starr, had spent nearly $50 million and four years trying to nail the president on everything from the land deal Whitewater, made in the 1980s, to campaign contribution violations while president. Charges against Starr's investigative tactics were levied over and over by President Clinton's defenders.

On February 23, 1999, the judges who appointed Starr briefly stepped into a dispute between the independent prosecutor and the Justice Department over the conduct of the Monica Lewinsky investigation. The three appeals judges directed Attorney General Janet Reno and Starr to submit written arguments concerning whether the Justice Department has the authority to

1

investigate the independent counsel. The issues involved in a possible investigation were numerous:

- Whether Starr's deputies acted improperly on January 16, 1998, by offering Ms. Lewinsky an immunity deal conditioned on her not discussing the deal with her lawyer. Justice Department rules prohibit prosecutors from discussing immunity deals with defendants unless their lawyers are present.
- Whether Starr or his aides had contacts with lawyers for Paula Jones, who was suing Clinton on sexual harassment charges, that were not disclosed when Starr obtained Reno's approval to investigate the Lewinsky case.
- Whether a law partner of Starr's who allegedly did secret legal work for Mrs. Jones could be said to have represented her. If so, Starr, who had not taken a leave of absence from his law firm, might have been barred by law from handling the Lewinsky case.
- Whether Starr lied under oath in House Judiciary Committee testimony on November 1998 when he denied that court proceedings concerning alleged grand jury leaks by his office were sealed at his request.[2]

Reactions to the president's acquittal and Judge Starr's conduct typified the moral confusion in American life. Members of the clergy decried the death of moral values in America. Members of the military despaired over the troops' low morale and their apparent distrust of their commander in chief. Public opinion polls demonstrated that, for the first time, members of Congress were held in lower esteem than used-car salesmen and prostitutes.[3]

Much more will be said about scandals during the Clinton years (below), but the Lewinsky scandal is something of a metaphor for the scandals of our postmodern age. In many respects, both sad and farcical, the impeachment of President Clinton by the House Judiciary Committee and his acquittal by the Senate were a sham.

1. The offenses with which the president was charged were never regarded as serious enough to warrant removal from office by the vast majority of constitutional scholars. Moreover, public opinion polls from beginning to end made clear that only about one-third of the public thought that the president should be removed from office.
2. The impeachment hearings by the House Judiciary Committee quickly degenerated into an irrelevant circus. Witnesses who had been convicted of perjury by lying about having sex with clients were suddenly converted into experts on perjury and were asked whether they thought perjury was prudent behavior for people in responsible positions. Members of the military were sworn in and asked whether Clinton was ad-

mired by people in the military, as if being an unpopular commander in chief was an impeachable offense.

3. Both Republicans and Democrats papered the public with a constant stream of contradictory messages, a type of propaganda that George Orwell described in his classic *1984* as doublespeak, which gives way to doublethink (holding both sides of a contradiction in one's head and believing both arguments). For example, Clinton claimed that Lewinsky had had sex with him, but that he had not had sex with her. Hillary Clinton claimed that the prosecution of the Lewinsky episode was the result of a right-wing conspiracy, but no one had forced Ms. Lewinsky's favors, including pizza slices, on Clinton; it was the president himself who had invited her into the map room for a private tryst. Moreover, the White House never accused the twenty-one-year-old intern of being a right-wing plant.[4]

The chair of the House Judiciary Committee, Henry Hyde, admitted to having an affair with a married woman himself when he was in his forties. He described it as a "youthful indiscretion," prompting some people to wonder whether Washington politicians ever grow up.

Many Republicans criticized the president for having an affair in the White House map room, where President Roosevelt and Prime Minister Churchill had planned some of World War II's great victories. Can you imagine what these critics would have said if Mr. Clinton had evaded Secret Service protection and taken Ms. Lewinsky to a motel or other cheap rendezvous?

As with all other investigations of major scandals on the federal level since 1963, the real impeachable offenses were overlooked and their origins and causes neglected. The great scandal of the Clinton era is one that has haunted American politics almost since its beginnings and continues to poison the body politic today: campaign financing. This issue surfaced for about 36 hours during the Lewinsky scandal and impeachment hearings but was summarily dropped even by the Republicans, allegedly for lack of evidence. The real problem was that there was plenty of evidence that both Republicans and Democrats routinely accept all kinds of questionable and sometimes illegal contributions from foreign corporations and governments. Both sides pay lip service to the idea of campaign finance reform, but neither is serious about it. Both sides know that money is what it takes to get elected and reelected and that to in any way level the playing field by giving new candidates an equal chance is the last thing entrenched politicians really want. The entire Clinton impeachment charade and the campaign finance scandal are, of course, merely two in a sea of symptoms indicating that the American political system is both corrupt and corrupting to the core.

Consider the following: When President Kennedy was assassinated in Dallas, Texas, on November 22, 1963, a cover-up of the investigation into the crime was personally ordered by President Lyndon Johnson, Assistant Attorney General Katzenbach, and FBI Director J. Edgar Hoover. They allegedly believed that Communist elements from either Cuba or the Soviet Union (or both) might have been involved and feared that a war would result. These officials agreed that the public must be convinced that Lee Harvey Oswald acted alone in killing the president. This was President Johnson's motive in setting up the Warren Commission in December 1963. Moreover, the Warren Commission did indeed find that Oswald had acted alone in killing the president and that Dallas nightclub owner Jack Ruby had acted alone in killing Oswald (who at the time was surrounded by nearly 200 armed law enforcement officers) in a Dallas police station.

Subsequent investigations into the crime by the House Special Committee on Assassinations (HSCA) from 1975 to 1978 found numerous inconsistencies in the case. The HSCA found that President Kennedy was probably assassinated as a result of a conspiracy.[5] Probable suspects included members of organized crime.

The precise nature of a conspiracy in the assassination and those persons or organizations involved have never been determined; consequently, numerous theories have been advanced. Between 1966 and 1993, more than 600 books and 2,000 articles were written about the Kennedy assassination. The dominant view in these writings is that government agencies killed their own president because he was going to make peace with the Soviet Union and end the Cold War. There is also speculation that Kennedy was going to disengage the United States from its involvement in Vietnam. The Kennedy assassination is important because it marks not only the first major postwar scandal but the beginning of a drastic decline in public confidence in government agencies and politicians.

Between 1860 and 1920, the United States suffered only two major crises involving corruption on the federal level, that is, about one scandal every fifty years. However, beginning in 1963 with the investigation into the assassination of President Kennedy, the U.S. federal government has experienced repeated scandals. The scandals themselves are serious social problems and cause all manner of social harm.

Following President Kennedy's death, the United States escalated its presence in Vietnam. The Vietnam War produced a number of scandalous incidents that divided American public opinion and ultimately contributed to public distrust in government. Vietnam was followed by the Watergate scandal, which caused public trust to decline even further. Thus, politicians and governmental agencies have been involved in a number of incidents that have contributed to a deep public distrust of government.

Most significant was the conduct of the government during the Vietnam War (1964–1975). The Pentagon Papers, investigative reporting, and leaks from within the government had the effect of turning public opinion against the war and the government. A number of governmental transgressions were revealed, including the following:

- The manipulation of Congress by President Johnson with the Gulf of Tonkin incident
- The indictment of high-ranking officers for war crimes similar to those committed by the Germans and Japanese during World War II
- The deliberate destruction of civilian targets by U.S. forces
- Intelligence agency suppression of information regarding enemy troop strength and sympathizers in South Vietnam
- Falsified reports by U.S. field commanders regarding the destruction of enemy targets
- The spraying of more than 5 million acres of South Vietnam with defoliating chemicals
- The execution of more than 40,000 so-called enemy agents by the Central Intelligence Agency (CIA) under the Phoenix Program (most without trial)
- Unauthorized bombing raids against North Vietnam

From early 1969 until May 1970, President Richard Nixon assured the American people that the neutrality of Cambodia was being respected. However, Nixon had secretly ordered the bombing of so-called enemy sanctuaries in Cambodia during that period. He was able to keep the bombings secret through the use of a double-entry bookkeeping system arranged between the White House and the Department of Defense.

In 1975, governmental investigations revealed that the CIA had violated its charter by engaging in domestic intelligence by opening the mail of U.S. citizens and spying on members of Congress and newspaper reporters. Moreover, the CIA plotted the assassinations of a number of foreign political officials.[6]

Most significant, the Senate Intelligence Committee revealed that every U.S. president from Eisenhower to Nixon had lied to the American people about the activities of the CIA. Public confidence in government was also lowered when it became known that every president since Franklin Roosevelt had used the Federal Bureau of Investigation (FBI) for political and sometimes illegal purposes. After J. Edgar Hoover's death, we found out how the FBI had been used by its longtime chief to silence his and the bureau's critics. Hoover had also involved the FBI in a number of illegal acts to defeat or neutralize those domestic groups that he thought were subversive.[7]

The Watergate scandal and its aftermath (1972–1974) brought down the Nixon administration. Watergate was a most significant contributor to low public confidence in government in the last quarter of the twentieth century. Illegal acts by governmental officials and/or their agents in Watergate included securing illegal campaign contributions, dirty tricks to discredit political opponents, burglary, bribery, perjury, wiretapping, harassment of administration opponents with tax audits, and the like. By 1975, after these revelations became public and just after the end of the Watergate scandal, public confidence in government was understandably low. One poll revealed that 68 percent of Americans believed that the government regularly lies to them.[8]

The effect of these developments is hardly surprising. In 1980, law professor Arthur S. Miller declared that, in 1978, two years after President Jimmy Carter's election, distrust of government was actually higher than it was during the Watergate period. Nearly two-thirds of voting-age Americans expressed distrust in government, and 70 percent expressed distrust in Congress. Thus, despite the removal of corrupt figures from office, trust in government had not increased. The result, claims Miller, may be a permanent erosion of political trust and the eventual undermining of the respect that citizens have for political institutions themselves.[9]

The Reagan administration did virtually nothing to increase public confidence in the ethical conduct of government officials. In 1987, news broke concerning what was to be the most damaging scandal of the Reagan administration, the Iran–Contra affair. The root of the scandal involved the diversion of funds from profits on missiles sold to the Iranian government. The profits were diverted to the Nicaraguan Contras, a counterrevolutionary force virtually created by the CIA.[10]

At first the entire episode was blamed on Marine Lieutenant Colonel Oliver North. Virtually all high-ranking officials of the Reagan administration claimed that they were "out of the loop" concerning any knowledge of the events. Subsequent investigations and trial testimony, however, pointed to a massive cover-up by White House aides and others.

- **Item:** North's 1989 trial revealed that a 1984 national security group meeting composed of Vice President George Bush, the Joint Chiefs of Staff, several cabinet officers, and President Reagan discussed Contra aid based on solicitation of "third" parties (foreign governments). This was adopted as a strategy of getting around the Boland Amendment that forbid further military aid to the Contras.[11]
- **Item:** President Reagan personally solicited the largest contributions for Contra aid from foreign nations, and a number of Latin American governments were requested to cooperate by falsifying arms sales transactions so that knowledge that the weapons were for the Contras could be hidden. Nations agreeing to falsify such documents were promised increased U.S. foreign aid.

Both the illegal arms sales and illegal solicitation of funds were orchestrated by a secret group, the Enterprise, set up apart from the CIA and other

governmental agencies to ensure secrecy. The Enterprise was composed of retired military and intelligence personnel, arms dealers, and drug smugglers.

A report issued in 1994 by Special Council Lawrence Walsh indicated
that Reagan administration officials covered up many aspects of the scandal
to ensure plausible denial of knowledge of the scandal by President Reagan.
Walsh's report also concluded that former President George Bush had lied to
the press and the American people concerning his knowledge of various aspects of Iran–Contra.

The Clinton administration began suffering from the effects of scandal
almost immediately upon taking office:

- Two nominees for attorney general, Zoe Baird and Judge Kimba Wood,
  had both employed illegal aliens in violation of a 1986 immigration
  law, and their nominations had to be withdrawn.
- A special prosecutor was appointed in 1994 to investigate the connection of the president and Mrs. Clinton to the failed Whitewater savings
  and loan in Arkansas. Soon after, the president established his own
  legal defense fund, hoping to raise $2 million to ward off his increasing
  legal costs. The president was also sued for sexual harassment by a
  former employee of the state of Arkansas, and Mr. Clinton was in a position requiring constant defense of his moral character.
- One hundred agents of the Bureau of Alcohol, Tobacco, and Firearms
  burned the Waco, Texas, compound of the extremist Branch Davidians
  cult in 1993. At least 72 cult members died in the fire and gun battle.
  The agents in charge significantly altered written plans for the raid
  after the 100 deaths and then tried to conceal the changes from officials
  investigating the raid.[12]

The U.S. Congress has also suffered its share of scandals, and these
have badly damaged its credibility.

- **Item:** In 1993, the former House Postmaster Robert Rota and three
  House Post Office employees pled guilty to stealing cash and stamps.
  Rota claimed that he gave two House members, Dan Rostenkowski (D,
  IL) and Joe Kolter (D, PA), $30,000 in Post Office funds.[13] Rosten-
  kowski, powerful head of the House Ways and Means Committee, was
  under indictment but has since been pardoned.[14]

These incidents and numerous others documented throughout this
book are symbolic of the major scandals that have made elite wrongdoing of
major concern in America. According to an opinion study done in late 1990,
public confidence in major institutions is now at an all-time low.

Thirty percent of employees have personally witnessed violations of
criminal or ethics codes by their bosses, including making dangerous products, engaging in criminal activity, practicing discrimination, and/or breaking

job safety laws. Only one in ten Americans is satisfied with his or her job. Only three in ten feel any loyalty to their company, and 43 percent claim that they cannot trust their co-workers.

Seventy percent of Americans now claim that there are no living heroes, and 80 percent believe that morals and ethics need to be taught in schools. Moreover, the public now believes that the leading cause of U.S. economic decline is unethical behavior by business executives.

The lowest-rated occupations for honesty and integrity include Congress member and local politician, TV evangelist, lawyer, stockbroker, oil company and TV network executive, union leader, and insurance and car salesperson.[15]

A 1991 study by the Kettering Foundation indicates that the American people are highly alienated from political life. They feel excluded from the political process by politicians, journalists, and lobbyists and that money and privilege have replaced votes such that there is no point in political participation. Underscoring this is the fact that only 36 percent of eligible voters voted in the 1998 election. Voter turnout reached a century low in 1998 and shows no sign of improving. The 1998 figure represents the lowest turnout in a nonpresidential election of any industrial democracy in the world. A 1999 poll revealed that only 13 percent of the electorate stated that they were interested in the presidential campaign.

The public believes that money has a pervasive influence in political campaigns, wherein candidates often spend millions of dollars to secure $100,000-a-year positions. The 1991 study also found that media (especially television) coverage of campaigns further alienates voters, due in part to the use of the sound bite, which reduces complex issues to slogans lasting only a few seconds.[16]

These findings closely resemble those presented by pollster Lou Harris in his 1987 book *Inside America*. Harris found that, by 1988, 82 percent of the public expressed the belief that business is motivated primarily by greed. Moreover, 60 percent revealed a profound political alienation, believing that their interests are not represented by politicians. Rather, they believe that the political system serves the concerns of rich and powerful interest groups. In a 1987 Harris poll, 81 percent of Americans felt that the rich get richer and the poor get poorer. (This is the highest percentage recorded in response to this question since Harris first asked it in 1966.) Sixty-six percent felt that the number of people expressing a great deal of confidence in institutions, professions, and leaders continues to decline, compared to public confidence two decades ago.

The crisis of confidence continued into the 1990s. As Vice President Al Gore states, "Public confidence in the federal government has never been lower. The average American believes we waste 48 cents of every tax dollar. Five of every six want 'fundamental change in Washington. Only 20 percent of Americans trust the federal government to do the right thing most of the time, down from 76 percent 30 years ago.'"[17] A 1994 poll indicated that less than 30 percent of Americans trust Congress.[18]

> Likewise, a 1992 American National Elections Study found that almost 70 percent of the public believes that government is untrustworthy, the highest percentage since the question was first asked in 1964. Moreover, over two-thirds of the public believes the government wastes a lot of money, and nearly 75 percent believe that the government is run "for a few big interests." Over 45 percent of the public believes that "quite a few of the people" running the government are corrupt. Again, all the responses represent record levels of public distrust [and] contempt for government.[19]
>
> Finally, a 1994 *Newsweek* poll found that 76 percent of the American people believe their country is in a state of "moral and spiritual decline," and 55 percent of the public blame government and political leaders "for the problem of low morals and lack of personal character in the" country.[20]

In addition, Lou Harris discerned that public alienation is "deep seated in modern American life," is "profoundly disturbing for the nation," and that unless something is done to reverse it, the nation faces certain trauma with a price that could be "enormous."[21] While numerous social critics have recently expressed alarm over the decline of ethics and honesty and the rise of greed and corruption among the nation's elite, it is important to realize that the latest round of wrongdoing is merely part of a process that has been consistent with American life for the past four decades. Moreover, large corporations have proved every bit as deviant as political organizations.

Scandals within the Economic Sphere

The public's sagging confidence in major U.S. institutions extends beyond government. Increasingly, big business has come to be viewed with distrust and cynicism. Indeed, by 1979, big business tied with Congress as "least trusted" from a list of ten major institutions.[22] Let's review some of the incidents that have contributed to these negative feelings.

Since the 1960s, when Ralph Nader launched the consumer movement, consumer unhappiness with the quality of goods and services provided by business has grown dramatically. By 1978, it was estimated that the federal government alone received about 10 million consumer complaints annually.[23]

Some corporations have willfully marketed products known to be dangerous. There are numerous examples of this problem, the most notorious being the marketing of the Pinto by the Ford Motor Company. Ford knew that this car had a defective gasoline tank that would ignite even in low-speed rear-end collisions. Ironically and tragically, Ford continued to sell this defective and dangerous car, even though the problem could have been solved for a cost of $11 per vehicle.[24]

In 1978, the Senate revealed that, between 1945 and 1976, approximately 350 U.S. corporations admitted to making bribes of some $750 million to officials of foreign governments. Many of these companies made such payments without informing their stockholders.[25] Moreover, the Watergate investigation revealed that more than 300 corporations illegally contributed to President Nixon's 1972 reelection campaign.[26] No corporate executives were sent to prison for their involvement in concealing or making such payments. Advertising is full of examples of fraudulent claims for products. And the stock market has been manipulated to defraud clients, as was revealed in 1975, when officials of the Equity Life Insurance Company were indicted for manipulating the price of shares by inventing thousands of nonexistent insurance policies. Between $2 and $3 billion was lost by thousands of investors, making this the largest investment fraud to date. Equity's chairman, along with several other company officials, was convicted of the crime, but received suspended sentences or prison terms that varied from only two to eight years.[27] By 1982, it was estimated that price fixing among corporations cost the consumer $60 billion per year. In addition, between 1970 and 1980, 117 of 1,043 major corporations (11 percent) had committed at least one serious criminal offense, including twenty-eight cases of bribery, kickback, or illegal rebates; twenty-one cases of illegal campaign contributions; eleven cases of fraud; and five cases of tax evasion. In all, fifty executives were sent to jail, and thirteen fines were levied in excess of $550,000 (ranging to a high of $4 million).[28]

Perhaps the largest energizer of negative feelings toward big business has been the realization that corporations are guilty of what we might call "chemical crimes." Through dumping of waste products into the air, water, and landfills and the production of products that pollute unnecessarily, businesses have assaulted the public with pollutants, with dangerous implications for the health of present and future generations. Of the many examples of this chemical assault, we will describe one in some detail, Love Canal.

From 1942 to 1953, the Hooker Chemical Company dumped more than 20,000 tons of toxic chemical waste into the Love Canal near Niagara Falls, New York. After Hooker sold the dump site to the local board of education in 1953 for one dollar, an elementary school and playground were built on the site, followed by a housing development. For at least twenty years prior to 1977, toxic chemicals had been seeping through to the land surface. However, in 1977, highly toxic black sludge began seeping into the cellars of the school and nearby residences. Tests showed the presence of eighty-two chemicals in the air, water, and soil of Love Canal; among them were twelve known carcinogens, including dioxin, one of the deadliest substances ever synthesized. There is evidence that Hooker Chemical knew of the problem as far back as 1958 but chose not to warn local health officials of any potential problems because cleanup costs would have increased from $4 million to $50 million.

Knowledge of the existence of toxic chemicals in the area caused a financial hardship for the residents. Once word of the contamination got out, their homes became worthless. But much more important, tests revealed that the inhabitants of this area had disproportionately high rates of birth defects, miscarriages, chromosomal abnormalities, liver disorders, respiratory and urinary disease, epilepsy, and suicide. In one neighborhood a few blocks from Love Canal, a survey by the homeowners' association revealed that only one of the fifteen pregnancies begun in 1979 ended in the birth of a healthy baby; four ended in miscarriages, two babies were stillborn, and nine others were born deformed.[29]

Today, it is now clear: Love Canal is merely the tip of the U.S. waste iceberg.

- **Item:** In 1993, the Environmental Protection Agency (EPA) and Harvard School of Public Health estimated that particle pollution from factories causes 50,000 to 60,000 deaths each year. Most vulnerable are children with respiratory diseases, asthmatics of all ages, and elderly people with ailments like bronchitis. The poor and working class, who tend to live closest to chemical factories, suffer the highest rates of pollution-caused cancer. Indoor pollution, including secondhand cigarette smoke and radon gas, causes 5,000 or more cancer cases annually.[30]
- **Item:** Answering a congressional inquiry in 1990, the EPA identified 149 industrial plants in thirty-three states where the surrounding air was known to be "quite dangerous."[31] At one facility in Port Neches, Texas, the lifetime risk of contracting cancer was 1 in 10. A risk of 1 in 1 million is considered unacceptable by EPA standards. Yet, at another forty-five of these plants, the risk of contracting cancer was less than 1 in 100, and at all the others the risk was greater than 1 in 10,000.
- **Item:** By 1985, the EPA had recognized 19,000 hazardous waste dump sites. Eight hundred of these sites had been placed on a priority list, but only 10 had been cleaned up.[32]
- **Item:** In the summer of 1988, beaches from Long Island to New Jersey were covered by a "nauseating array of waste": plastic tampon applicators, balls of sewage two inches thick, and a host of drug paraphernalia and medical waste, including needles, syringes, crack (rock cocaine) vials, stained bandages, containers of surgical stitches, prescription bottles, and vials of blood (some of which tested positive for hepatitis B and HIV viruses).[33]
- **Item:** Since 1986, 10 million tons of sludge processed in local sewage treatment plants in New York and New Jersey have been transported on barges beyond the continental shelf and released underwater, threatening fishing industries from South Carolina to Maine. The deaths of thousands of dolphins, seals, birds, and fish along U.S. coasts have

reached alarming proportions, prompting local cleanup campaigns and protests.[34]

- **Item:** The Department of Energy is also experiencing environmental scandal. In 1991, it was learned that the companies that operated the department's Savannah River nuclear reactor, Westinghouse and Bechtel subsidiaries, hid huge cost overruns by illegally transferring tens of millions of dollars in and out of construction accounts. The illegal transfers also went to pay Bechtel's expensive management fees, to construct unauthorized new projects, and to hide other cost increases from both Congress and the Department of Energy. The scandal followed news by the General Accounting Office that the cleanup of the Department of Energy's radioactive poisons would cost $200 billion or more and would take up to fifty years. The department has spent $3 billion trying to repair three nuclear reactors at its Savannah River plant, only one of which will be reopened. Moreover, it has shut down its plutonium machining and processing plant in Colorado and a nuclear repository in New Mexico because of safety and environmental problems.[35]

The list of acts involving the most powerful U.S. political and business organizations and their leaders could be extended almost indefinitely. Similarly, scores of additional opinion polls registering mounting public distrust, cynicism, and alienation regarding the most powerful U.S. economic and political institutions and the individuals who head them could be discussed. What is most important for our purposes, however, is that the characteristics that these incidents share are what we call *elite deviance*. These characteristics include the following:

1. The acts are committed by persons from the highest strata of society: members of the upper and upper-middle classes. Some of the deeds mentioned earlier were committed by the heads of corporate and governmental organizations; others were committed by their employees on behalf of the employers.
2. Some of the acts are crimes in that they violate criminal statutes and carry penalties such as fines and imprisonment.[36] Other acts violate administrative or civil laws, which may also involve punishment. Included are both acts of commission and omission.[37] Other acts, such as U.S. presidents lying to the public about the Vietnam War, although not illegal, are regarded by most Americans as unethical or immoral (that is, deviant). Thus, elite deviance may be either criminal or noncriminal in nature.
3. Some of the actions described previously were committed by elites for personal gain (for example, members of Congress who accepted bribes), or they were committed by the elites or their employees for purposes of enhancing the power, profitability, or influence of the orga-

nizations involved (for example, when corporations made bribes overseas for the purpose of securing business deals).

4. The acts were committed with relatively little risk. When and if the elites were apprehended, the punishments inflicted were in general very lenient compared to those given common criminals.[38]

5. Some of the incidents posed great danger to the public's safety, health, and financial well-being.

6. In many cases, the elites in charge of the organizations mentioned were able to conceal their illegal or unethical actions for years before they became public knowledge (for example, Hooker Chemical's dumping of poisonous chemicals and the presidential misuses of the FBI and CIA). Yet the actions mentioned were seemingly compatible with the goals of such organizations (that is, the maintenance or enhancement of the organization's power and/or profitability).[39]

A Theory of Elite Deviance

Elite deviance, in all its forms, now constitutes a major social problem for American society and, as will be explored, much of the world as well. This does not mean, however, that there is a consensus concerning what constitutes deviance. Notions of elite wrongdoing, white-collar crime, and related concepts are now the focus of intense debate in the social sciences. In this regard, the conflict perspective and the evidence amassed in support of it offer the best starting point concerning a causal theory of elite deviance.

Criminologists and students of criminal justice tend to focus on the study of individual criminals in their research. The criminal justice system itself was originally established to protect the rights of accused persons, not to discover the causes of or ways to prevent criminal activity. As a result of this bias in American society, the social sciences focus heavily on individual crimes, individual rights, and individual cases. This is especially the case with street crimes (for example, homicide, robbery, burglary, and rape), which receive the lion's share of attention and resources in law enforcement, the courts, and correctional institutions. Street crimes are also the major preoccupation of both the criminology and criminal justice fields.

This is not to say that the street crime problem is unimportant. Indeed, as we will examine later in this book, street crime, organized crime, and elite deviance are interrelated in numerous ways (see Chapter 8). In fact, the crime problem in the United States is actually rooted in a system in which lower-class criminals, organized crime, a corrupt public sector, and deviant corporations cooperate for purposes of profit and power.

Thus, our examination begins with the proposition that crime and deviance are societally patterned. This means that certain sociological factors cause crimes to be committed by both individuals and organizations.

Among the most important of these factors in American society is the U.S. power structure itself.

The U.S. Social Structure: The Power Elite

The view of the U.S. social structure that we support is the one advocated by the late C. Wright Mills.[40] Mills proposed that the dominant institutional structures of American life comprise a power elite of the largest corporations, the federal government, and the military. These dominant institutions are headed by elites, people whose positions within organizations have provided them the greatest amounts of wealth, power, and often prestige of any such positions in the nation. Immediately below this power elite is a subgroup of corporations that comprise the mass media. The source of their power is communications, which clearly differentiates elites from nonelites in American society. A sizable Washington press core waits for the daily pronouncements of political elites. Moreover, 90 percent of the commercials on prime-time television are sponsored by the nation's 500 largest corporations.[41]

The corporate, political, and military worlds are interrelated in numerous ways. Most members of the president's cabinet come from the ranks of big business and return there when their government service ends; numerous Pentagon employees, civilian and military, are employed by weapons industry firms upon retirement.

These interrelationships mean that the deviance within this elite often involves two or more organizations: one or more corporations and one or more government agencies. Power and private wealth are concentrated in the hands of the elite. Together, these institutions determine primary societal objectives, priorities, and policies and thus greatly influence the so-called lesser institutions (that is, the family, religion, and education). The elite dominate these lesser socializing institutions and thus shape the American social character.

The Evidence for a Power Elite. In the United States, elites possess not only great riches and the ability to make decisions that affect the conduct of nonelites (political power), but studies reveal that they also exert a great deal of control over such resources as education, prestige, status, skills of leadership, information, knowledge of political processes, ability to communicate, and organization. "Moreover, elites [in America] are drawn disproportionately from...society's upper classes, which are made up of those persons...who own or control a disproportionate share of the societal institutions industry, commerce, finance, education, the military, communications, civic affairs, and law."[42]

One recent study concludes that there are 5,416 positions within the nation's most powerful economic, governmental, military, media, legal, civic, and educational institutions. These positions constitute a few ten thousandths of 1 percent of the population.[43] Yet the amount of resources that they control is immense. Consider these data for the early 1990s:

- In industry, 100 out of 200,000 corporations control 55 percent of all industrial assets. The largest 500 industrial corporations control three-quarters of manufacturing assets. The largest 800 corporations employ one of every five workers in the civilian labor force.[44]
- In transportation and utilities, 50 out of 67,000 companies control two-thirds of the assets in the airline, railroad, communications, electricity, and gas industries.[45]
- In banking, 50 out of 14,763 banks control 64 percent of all banking assets. Three of these banks, Bank America, Citicorp, and Chase Manhattan, control almost 20 percent of such assets.
- In insurance, 50 out of 2,048 firms control 80 percent of all insurance assets. Two insurance companies, Prudential and Metropolitan Life, control nearly one-quarter of such assets.[46]
- In the mass media, a mere fifty corporations are in control. Twenty companies own half the 61 million newspapers sold daily in the United States, and another twenty companies receive over half the revenues from the 61,000 U.S. magazines published. Three firms control most of the revenues and audiences in television, while ten control radio, eleven control book publishing, and four control movies.[47]

One basis of this great concentration of power and resources is the income and wealth possessed by the elite, that is, its economic power. Such wealth is owned by relatively few individuals in families and corporations.

International data now indicate that wealth is more unequally distributed in the United States than in other modern democracies. Thus, by the 1990s, the top 1 percent of wealth holders owned 42 percent of America's wealth. Moreover, from 1983 to 1989, the share of the nation's income held by the top 20 percent increased from 52 to 56 percent while that of the remaining 80 percent decreased from 48.1 to 44.5 percent.[48]

Collectively, economic power is centralized in a relatively few major corporations and financial institutions. "Out of the 2 million or so corporations, some 200 nonfinancial companies account for 80 percent of all resources used in manufacturing; 60 percent of all assets, three-fifths of all buildings, equipment, and land are owned by nonfinancial companies."[49]

The top 100 industrial corporations now control 75 percent of the assets of Fortune 500 corporations.[50] One study of the 250 largest U.S. corporations found that all but a handful (17) had at least one of their chief executives sitting on the board of at least 1 additional corporation in the top 250. Some of them even held seats on competing companies, a practice that has been illegal since 1914 with the passage of the Clayton Antitrust Act. Moreover, even people who serve on the board of directors of one company may serve as an executive of another company. This situation has been found to exist for more than 250 directors of the top 500 corporations.[51]

- More important than such interlocks is the shared ownership that characterizes U.S. corporate capitalism, concentrated among large banks and wealthy families. Of the 14,000 commercial banks in the United States, 100 control half of all bank deposits.[52] Many of these banks administer the trust funds of wealthy individuals or other sources of capital with which they purchase stock. One study done in the 1980s observed that people who sit on the board of directors of General Motors also have seats on 29 other corporate boards, including Gulf Oil, Anaconda Copper, Proctor & Gamble, Chase Manhattan Bank, and American Express. Collectively, the number of boards interlocked by members of these corporations includes 700 companies. Most important, these networks of interlocking directorates tend to remain stable over time.

What do all these facts mean? The largest 500 or so manufacturing firms and some 50 financial institutions, controlling two-thirds of all business income and half the nation's bank deposits, are interlocked by directorships and controlled by less than 0.5 percent of the population. Put simply, U.S. corporate assets reside in a few hands. More specifically, half of all assets in industry, banking, insurance, utilities, transportation, telecommunications, and the mass media is controlled by a mere 4,500 individual presidents and directors.[53] This concentration allows a very small corporate community to exercise power over one-third of the nation's gross national product and considerable indirect influence over the remainder of the nation's goods and services.[54] This is true because corporate leaders can invest money where and when they choose; expand, close, or move their factories and offices at a moment's notice; and hire, promote, and fire employees as they see fit. These powers give them direct influence over the great majority of Americans who depend on wages and salaries for their incomes. They also give the corporate rich indirect influence over elected and appointed officials because the growth and stability of a city, state, or the country as a whole can be jeopardized by a lack of business confidence in government.[55]

The Political Elite.   Aside from the economic elite, the nation also possesses a political elite. The political elite, to a significant extent, overlaps with, yet is independent from, the economic elite. The corporate managers, owners (super-rich individuals and families), and directors are, for the most part, members of the American upper class. Membership in the upper class is typically measured by such indicators as (1) one's name in the *Social Register*, an exclusive list of influential persons published in major U.S. cities and containing the names of about 138,000 persons; (2) attendance at elite private secondary schools and universities; (3) membership in exclusive social clubs and annual attendance at upper-class vacation retreats (e.g., Bohemian Grove, Pacific Union Club, Knickerbocker Club); and, of course, (4) seats on boards of the largest interlocked corporations.[56]

The political elite differs from the corporate or economic elite in that it includes persons occupying "key federal government positions in the executive (presidential), judicial (the Supreme Court and lesser federal courts), and legislative (congressional) branches [and]…the top command positions in the Army, Navy, Air Force, and Marines."[57] Numerous studies reveal that the political elite is composed of persons from both the upper-middle class (lawyers, small businesspeople, doctors, farmers, educators, and other professionals) and the upper class. The upper class tends to dominate the federal branch of the government, while upper-middle-class professionals make up the preponderance of the legislative branch. A study of presidential cabinets, from McKinley to Nixon, examining the degree to which cabinet heads were recruited from the ranks of big business, indicated that, from 1897 to 1973, big business supplied from 60 percent (under McKinley) to 95.7 percent (under Nixon) of presidential cabinet members.[58]

Another study found that 63 percent of the secretaries of state, 62 percent of the secretaries of defense, and 63 percent of the treasury secretaries have been members of the national upper class.[59] A few examples of the members of the power elite include the following:

- John Foster Dulles was secretary of state from 1953 to 1960. Before his appointment he was senior partner in a prestigious law firm, Sullivan and Cromwell, and sat on the boards of numerous corporations: Bank of New York, American Bank Note Company, United Railroad, International Nickel of Canada, American Cotton Corporation, and European Textile Corporation. Dulles was also a trustee of leading civic organizations: the New York Public Library, the Rockefeller Foundation, and the Carnegie Endowment for International Peace. His brother, Allen, was director of the CIA (1953–1961) and a member of the Warren Commission, the panel set up by President Johnson to investigate the assassination of President Kennedy.
- Alexander Haig, secretary of state in 1981–1982, is currently president of United Technologies Corporation, a major defense contractor. Haig is a former four-star U.S. Army general; former Supreme Commander of NATO forces in Europe; former assistant to President Nixon; former deputy commander of the U.S. Military Academy in West Point, New York; and former deputy secretary of defense. He is the man most responsible for the terms set down in the pardon of President Nixon following the Watergate scandal.

Corporate position has rarely been better represented in government than it is by the position of secretary of the treasury.

- George Bush's treasury secretary, Nicholas Brady, was a former chairman of Dillion Read & Company, a major Wall Street investment firm, and member of the board of directors of Purolator, National Cash Register, Georgia International, and Media General.
- Jimmy Carter's treasury head, Michael Blumenthal, is president of the Bendix Corporation, former vice president of Crown Cork Company, and trustee of the Council on Foreign Relations.

President Clinton promised the American people a cabinet that looks like America, meaning there would be more women and minorities. However, he did not promise us a cabinet that resembled America's social class makeup. President Clinton appointed more millionaires to cabinet posts than Reagan or Bush.[60] Among the examples are these:

- Treasury Secretary Lloyd Bentsen was a champion of tax breaks for corporations during his Senate career, and 89 percent of Bentsen's $2.5 million campaign fund in his last Senate bid came from corporate political action committees (PACs). Bentsen's personal worth exceeds $10 million, and he possesses holdings in a number of businesses in Texas. His deputy secretary, Roger Altman, comes from a Wall Street investment firm, Blackstone Group. This company has been involved in the four largest American acquisitions made by Japanese firms, including Sony's takeover of Columbia Pictures and CBS Records.
- Commerce Secretary Ron Brown, former head of the Democratic National Committee, hails from an elite law firm, Patton, Boggs, and Blow. Brown has represented many major corporations, including Japan Airlines and American Express, and his firm represents such clients as Mutual Life Insurance, New York Life, and the former dictator of Haiti, "Baby Doc" Duvalier.
- Trade Representative Mickey Kantor was law partner in Manatt, Phelps, Phillips, & Kantor, which has represented Occidental Petroleum, Atlantic Richfield Coal and Oil, Martin Marietta, and Philip Morris Tobacco Company. Kantor represented tobacco industry groups trying to prevent passage of a smoke-free restaurant bill in Beverly Hills, California.
- Secretary of State Warren Christopher, a lawyer from O'Melveny and Meyers, represented Exxon oil corporation in its pollution of Prince William Sound, Alaska. He also represented E.F. Hutton after its check-floating scandal in which Hutton took advantage of the lag between the time checks were written and the time that they actually cleared, earning millions in extra interest. Christopher has also served on the board of Southern California Edison, Lockheed, United Airlines, Banker's Trust (New York), Occidental Petroleum, and Japan's Fuji Bank and Mitsubishi Corporation.

Thus, it makes little difference whether the White House is run by Republicans or Democrats; those who run the government largely tend to come from corporate backgrounds and share remarkably similar educational and cultural experiences and affiliations.

In the 99th Congress, 251 members were lawyers (the most common profession), and the next largest share were in business, especially service industries (publishing, broadcasting, and real estate). Fifty members spent all or part of their careers in education, and thirty were in communications. Perhaps more important is the legislators' economic status.

> An estimated one-third of all senators were millionaires, and two-thirds of all senators supplemented their salaries with outside incomes of $20,000 or more. The House [was] more middle class economically speaking, but…at least 30 of their members are millionaires, and more than 100 report incomes of $20,000 or more annually beyond their congressional salaries.[61]

While it is true that economic power and state or government power are interlinked, they are not related in a conspiratorial fashion. This is an important point because a number of people who have written on the subjects of elite power and political corruption do believe in conspiracies.[62] A second distorted view of the elite has been put forth by certain muckraking journalists, who hold that while the state and the upper class are relatively independent, certain "moral and legal lapses in this independence" occur.[63] This view purports that the business class gets what it desires from government by engaging in all manner of corruption, lobbying, and other forms of illegal or unethical behavior.

The view expressed in this book is that the conspiratorial view of elite behavior is simplistic. Even though conspiracies do occur from time to time and always will, such explanations do a disservice to the complex nature of elite power and elite deviance.

The conspiratorial view of the elite is unrealistic for a number of reasons. First, not only are the elite somewhat diverse as to class background, but they are ideologically diverse, as well. That is, political opinions among elites range from conservative to social democrat. Although it is true that the elites agree on the basic rules of politics (that is, free elections, the court system, and the rule of law) and believe in the capitalist economic system, they disagree considerably about such issues as the power of business, civil rights, welfare, and foreign policy.[64]

Second, elites do not control the federal government because they do not possess a monopoly of political power. The structure of capitalist society is such that elite rule is faced with economic and other crises (for example, inflation, unemployment, war, racism) that lead nonelite interests to demand changes consistent with their interests (for example, unemployment benefits in periods of high unemployment). As William Chambliss has concluded,

"The persistence of and importance of the conflicts resolved through law necessarily create occasions where well-organized groups representing [non-elite] class interests manage to effect important legislation."[65]

Third, the conspiratorial view relating to elites dominating the state through corruption masks some of the most important unethical patterns that characterize much of elite deviance. For example, during the hearings regarding his appointment as vice-president in the mid-1970s, Nelson Rockefeller was questioned about his gift-giving habits but was not held "accountable for the shootings at Attica (prison) or…for the involvement of Chase Manhattan [Bank] in the repressive system of South African racism."[66]

Likewise, the right wing's conspiratorial view of a capitalist elite plotting to lead the nation into communism hides much of the unethical behavior of corporations that results as a consequence of the structure of corporate capitalism itself. As mentioned, about one-third of the economy is dominated by corporate giants. Such giantism means that, in many manufacturing (for example, cereals, soups, autos, and tires) and financial industries, a handful of firms (often four or less) accounts for more than half the market in a particular industry or service. Such situations are often characterized by artificially high prices due not to secret price-fixing conspiracies but to a practice known as price leadership. This results when one firm decides to raise prices on a given product and is then copied by the other major firms in the same field. The costs of these monopolistic price distortions are discussed in depth in Chapter 3. This and other unethical practices considered in detail in this volume are not accounted for by conspiratorial views of the economy and government and the linkages between them.

Our position is that it is more fruitful to consider deviance within the context of the relationships between business and governmental organizations, the functions performed by government, and the internal organizational structure of both the corporate and political organizations that constitute the elite sectors of society. In sum, we concur with Michael Parenti's view that "elite power is principally systemic and legitimating rather than conspiratorial and secretive."[67]

Economy–State Linkages and the Functions of Government

To understand the interrelationships between the economy and the state is to comprehend how elites attempt to formulate and implement public policy. These interrelationships are based on connections among corporations, large law firms that represent large corporations, elite colleges and universities, the mass media, private philanthropic foundations, major research organizations (think tanks), political parties, and the executive and legislative branches of the federal government. Key examples of these interlocks of moneys, personnel, and policies are pictured in Figure 1.1.

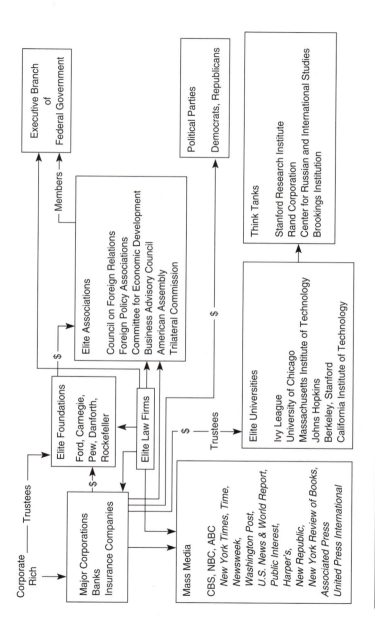

FIGURE 1.1   *The Capitalist Elite: Links among the Ruling Elite*

Source: Adapted from G. William Domhoff, "State and Ruling Class in Corporate America," *The Insurgent Sociologist* 4, Spring 1974, 9. By permission of G. William Domhoff and *The Insurgent Sociologist.*

Aside from the major corporations and the federal government, the rest of the organizations are included for several reasons:

1. Twenty-five universities and colleges listed in Figure 1.1 control 50 percent of all educational endowment funds and include some 656 corporate and other elites as their presidents and trustees. Moreover, only 50 foundations out of 12,000 control 40 percent of all foundation assets.[68] The officers of such foundations often have experience in elite corporations, educational institutions, and/or government.

2. The elite civic associations bring together elites from the corporate, educational, legal, and governmental worlds. Such organizations have been described as "central coordinating mechanisms in national policy making."[69] These organizations issue public position papers and investigative reports on matters of domestic and foreign policy. Membership in one or more of these organizations is sometimes a prerequisite to a high-ranking post within the executive branch of the federal government.

For example, the majority of the Carter cabinet (including Jimmy Carter himself) served on the Trilateral Commission prior to assuming office. The commission was formed by David Rockefeller, chairman of the board of the Chase Manhattan Bank; heir to the Exxon fortune; graduate of Harvard; member of the boards of directors of B. F. Goodrich, Rockefeller Brothers, Inc., and Equitable Life Insurance; and trustee of Harvard. Rockefeller is also the chairman of the Council of Foreign Relations (CFR). Almost all recent secretaries of state, including Cyrus Vance and Henry Kissinger, have been CFR members.[70]

3. The mass media are concentrated in that there are three major television and radio networks, NBC, ABC, and CBS. These networks are also multinational corporations that own or are owned by other corporations. For example, NBC is owned by General Electric, a major manufacturer of appliances and weapons systems components. Controlling shares in the three television networks are owned by five New York commercial banks: Chase Manhattan, Morgan Guaranty, Citibank, Bankers Trust, and the Bank of New York.[71]

The media also include the major wire services, Associated Press and United Press International, from which most national and international news make their way into U.S. radio, television, and newspapers. Regarding newspapers and news weeklies, the *New York Times,* the *Washington Post, Time, Newsweek* (owned by the *Washington Post*), and *U.S. News & World Report* are regarded as the most influential publications in their field.[72] Most cable TV networks are also owned by media conglomerates. One exception is the holdings of Ted Turner, which include the Cable News Network (CNN), stations WTBS and TNT, and the Atlanta Braves, Hawks, and Falcons sports teams.

Moreover, the major sponsors of television programs on the three networks are other large corporations. The media tend to portray deviant behavior as violent behavior that is perpetrated by poor nonelites. As one recent study concludes, the crime reported in television news and newsmagazines includes kidnappings and particularly gruesome murders. "Ordinary people who carry out nonviolent crimes or violate the mores rarely appear in national news."[73] However, "the economically powerful, such as officers of large corporations and holders of great wealth, are filmed or written about rarely, and then usually for reasons having little to do with their economic power, [except] when they are involved in some conflict with the federal government or are having legal difficulties."[74]

Overall, the media function to portray crime and deviance as a problem created by nonelites and to describe corporate capitalism as a system characterized by competition, freedom, and, while flawed, the best of all existing worlds. As a *Time* magazine profile put it: "Plainly capitalism is not working well enough. But there is no evidence to show the fault is in the system—or that there is a better alternative.... For all its blemishes capitalism still holds out the most creative and dynamic force that any civilization has ever discovered: the power of the free ambitious individual."[75]

Such propagandistic exercises are also characteristic of numerous television commercials and public service announcements (often prepared by the elite National Advertising Council) that insist that the oil companies are "working to keep your trust" or that our "economics quotients" (knowledge about the U.S. economic system) could stand improvement. Thus, one overall function of the mass media is to ensure the continuation and growth of the system of corporate capitalism.

4. Twenty-eight super law firms do much of the legal work for the corporations, mass media, and educational and civic foundations. In addition, senior lawyers in such firms often fill posts on various foundations and civic and educational institutions and from time to time assume various posts within the executive branch of the federal government. A good example of one such super lawyer is Paul Warnke, President Carter's chief negotiator in the Strategic Arms Limitation Talks. Warnke is also a member of the Trilateral Commission, a director of the CFR, a former assistant secretary of defense, and partner in a Washington law firm that included former Defense Secretary Clark Clifford.[76]

5. Finally, there are numerous elite-related think tanks, primarily research institutes. In general, these operations receive moneys from both public and private sources, depending on the type of research that they do. For example, about 5 percent of the Department of Defense's research and development budget in the 1960s and early 1970s went to such research organizations.[77]

Think tanks perform a very wide variety of research tasks and are closely allied with the business arm of the American power elite. For instance, the

American Enterprise Institute is allied with the conservative wing of the Republican party and Southern Democrats. Its activities primarily involve studies, the end products of which are policy proposals aimed at enhancing the profitability and power of its corporate clients.[78]

- **Item:** In the 1970s new "think tanks," especially the American Enterprise Institute (AEI) and the Heritage Foundation, were established and richly endowed by corporate money. The right-wing Heritage Foundation was started with a $250,000 donation from Colorado beer tycoon Joseph Coors. AEI's patrons included AT&T ($125,000), Chase Manhattan Bank ($125,000), Exxon ($130,000), General Electric ($65,000), General Motors ($100,000), and Proctor & Gamble ($165,000). AEI quickly became a "primary source of Washington opinion" shaping the policy positions of Washington politicians and the mass media.[79]

The American Enterprise Institute and other think tanks also prepare studies for influential big business lobby groups, such as the National Association of Manufacturers and the United States Chamber of Commerce. In short, think tanks provide valuable research aid in achieving the policy aims of elites, both inside and outside of government. Figure 1.1 on page 21 depicts the structures that supply personnel, money, and policy to the federal government but does not describe the processes used by or the benefits from the state sought by elites. Such means and benefits are important in that when they are abused, they constitute forms of elite deviance. These benefits will be discussed in following sections.

Lobbying.   The principle of majority rule is sometimes violated by special interests, which, by deals, propaganda, and the financial support of political candidates, attempt to deflect the political process for their own benefit. Individuals, families, corporations, and various organizations use a variety of means to obtain numerous benefits from congressional committees, regulatory agencies, and executive bureaucracies. To accomplish their goals, lobbyists for the special interests "along with the slick brochures, expert testimonies, and technical reports,... still have the slush fund, the kickback, the stock award, the high paying job offer from industry, the lavish parties and prostitutes, the meals, transportation, housing and vacation accommodations, and the many other hustling enticements of money."[80]

The existence of lobbyists does not ensure that the national interests will be served or that the concerns of all groups will be heard. Who, for example, speaks for the interests of schoolchildren, minority groups, the poor, people who are mentally retarded, renters, migrant workers, in short for the relatively powerless? And if there is a voice for these people, does it match the clout of lobbyists backed by the fantastic financial resources of the elite?

In fairness, it must be stressed that the success of such lobbies is not ensured.

> Big economic interests don't always win. The cargo preference bill was defeated. So was the 1979 sugar quota. The Consumer Cooperative Bank bill passed the House by one vote and became law. Sometimes scandal or the weight of evidence can push Congress in the right direction. And it must be noted that when a congressman from Michigan votes to bail out Chrysler, or a congressman from Wisconsin votes for dairy price supports, he is also voting to benefit his own constituents. This may not favor the public interest, but it is predictable politics, not personal corruption.... To receive money from an interest doesn't mean a member of Congress is controlled, per se. There are indentured politicians and there are principled conservatives; the former virtually auction their souls to the highest bidder while the latter may truly believe that the government shouldn't be forcing pharmaceutical firms to pre-market test their drugs.[81]

Nevertheless, corporate lobbies usually do exert a significant influence.

Financing Political Campaigns.   Perhaps one of the most elite-dominated and undemocratic features (at least in its consequences) of the U.S. political system is a result of the manner in which campaigns are financed. Political campaigns are expensive, with statewide campaigns sometimes costing hundreds of thousands of dollars and national campaigns running into the millions. This money is raised from contributions, and campaign contributions now represent a major scandal for both political parties. In the 1996 presidential elections the Democratic party attempted to raise $200 million for the Clinton–Gore reelection campaign. Some of the tactics used involved clear violations of federal law.

Between 1983 and 1988, 163 savings and loan (S&L) political action committees (PACs) gave $11 million to congressional candidates, with donations increasing 42 percent just before the S&L bailout was authorized by Congress.[82] The campaign donations from the S&L industry resulted in the most massive financial scandal in U.S. history. Members of various S&Ls allowed Democratic Congress members to use S&L-owned yachts for fundraising purposes and even paid for one influential congressman's dinners, which amounted to $20,000 for a single year. S&L lobbyists also contributed to the establishment of a business school for Utah Senator Jake Garn, who co-authored a bill allowing S&Ls to engage in all manner of questionable financial practices. The final cost to the public may be over $1 trillion. (See Chapter 2 for details.)

Thus, the passage of favorable laws or the defeat of unfavorable ones may directly result from the finances of special interests. So, too, may the special interests receive beneficial governmental rulings and the maintenance of tax loopholes. Since these investments pay off, it is only rational for the special interests to donate to the candidates of both parties to ensure that their interests are served. The result is that the wealthy have power, while the less well-to-do and certainly the poor have little influence on office holders.[83]

By law, corporations cannot directly contribute any of their funds to political parties or candidates. However, because corporations apparently find that political contributions help them, many have contributed to political campaigns illegally. This can be done either by giving money to employees, who in turn make individual contributions, or by forcing employees to contribute to a party or candidate as a condition of employment. Watergate showed that many companies engaged in fraudulent bookkeeping practices to cover up their political expenditures.

To counter the potential and real abuses of large contributors, the 1976 presidential campaign was partially financed from public funds; about $20 million was allocated to each of the two major candidates. Congress, however, refused to provide a similar law for its members or potential members. As a result, the moneys contributed to congressional candidates rose sharply. In 1978, the total gifts from all reporting interest groups to candidates for Congress was $35 million, compared to $22.6 million in 1976 and only $12.5 million in 1974. The most discussed phenomenon in campaign financing today is undoubtedly the PAC.

> PACs are "nonparty," "multicandidate" political committees that maintain a separate, segregated fund for political contributions: "nonparty" because they are set up by interest groups, "multicandidate" because they distribute their largesse to at least five candidates ("political contributions" only; no charity to be mixed in here).[84]

Although some PACs are established by the numerous single-issue groups, such as the National Rifle Association and environmental or anti-abortion causes, the vast majority of PAC money stems from corporate interests. Thus, in the 1981–1982 congressional campaign, corporate PACs spent $50 million of the $83 million given to candidates, a tenfold increase over the amount given to candidates in 1972. Seven million dollars of that money (more than 7 percent) came from oil and gas interests. The chairs of the House and Senate energy committees received funds from thirty-four and thirty-seven energy PACs, respectively.[85]

PAC money is now far and away the largest source of congressional campaign funds, with business PAC contributions favoring Republicans over Democrats by a ratio of two to one. Indeed, in the 1970s there were about 600 PACs in Washington. By the 1992 election, there were 4,585, and all but about 365 of these were corporate in nature. "Candidates have become so dependent on PAC money that they actually visit PAC offices and all but demand contributions."[86] The beer distributors' PAC is called six-PAC. There is also a Beef-PAC, and an Ice Cream-PAC. These PACs may donate up to $5,000 to each congressional candidate in both primary and general election campaigns. During the 1991–1992 political campaign, all Democratic congressional candidates raised $360 million, while Republican candidates raised $293 million. The GOP National Committee raised an additional $85.4 million, while the Democratic National Committee raised $65.7 million. The vast majority of these funds (about 80 percent) came from PACs.

What do PACs expect from the Congress members receiving their funds? Votes on important pieces of legislation. For example, in 1992, Senator David Prior, an Arkansas Democrat, sponsored a bill that would link a huge tax break for establishing factories in Puerto Rico with stable prices for prescription drugs. Nine of the top ten recipients of drug PAC money from 1981 to 1991 voted for tabling (thus killing) this unfavorable legislation. [87]

By the late 1980s, politicians from all sides had become alarmed about the dangers of PACs to democracy. Senator Charles Mathias remarked that the current system of financing congressional elections threatened to "erode public confidence in the electoral process and in government itself."[88] Conservative Barry Goldwater stated that unlimited spending in political campaigns "cuts at the very heart of the democratic process."[89] Despite such pronouncements, in 1988 the ill effects and influence of PACs continued unabated.

- **Item:** The oil industry lobbied for and received the repeal of the windfall profits tax. One leader of the repeal was Senator Lloyd Bentsen, later treasury secretary and owner of an interest in a petroleum distribution company. Oil industry contributions to congressional campaigns in 1988 were $2.35 million.
- **Item:** Fifty-one U.S. senators and 146 members of the House of Representatives are either founders or officers of Washington, D.C., tax-exempt organizations that produce either research statistics or corporate propaganda for lobbying purposes.[90]
- **Item:** In 1960, less than 400 lobbyists were registered with the U.S. Congress. By 1992, 40,000 were registered.[91] These 40,000 people represent mostly American and foreign corporations. Much of this growth came in the 1970s and 1980s when the capitalist class decided it was underrepresented in the nation's capital. Eighty percent of the Fortune 500 corporations established "public-affairs offices" (lobby groups) in Washington.[92]
- **Item:** In 2000, the Republican party insisted that its financial base was primarily small contributors, but research by the *New York Times* revealed that the GOP had received $90 million from a small pool of wealthy individuals, some of whom kept their contributions secret. An elite group of 739 contributors provided two-thirds of the Republicans' $137 million "soft money," the unrestricted donations. Some contributors were directed by GOP officials to make their donations in secret ways. Those people and corporations that gave at least $250,000 between 1999 and

2000 were labeled Platinum Level members. The Federal Election Commission showed only 54 such corporations and individuals because donors were asked to split their funds into smaller checks, thus making their origin harder to trace.[93]

These examples not only illustrate the dangers of PAC influence in Congress but also indicate why many of the laws designed to control corporate crime were so weakened during the Reagan years. (See Chapter 2 for further discussion of these issues.)

Meanwhile, in Congress, one effect of PAC money has been to alter the very structure of power within the institution. Representative Jim Wright of Texas was elected speaker of the House after giving $312,000 of his own campaign funds to 141 members. Moreover, consider that senators now spend 60 to 70 percent of their time raising the money needed to be reelected; during an entire six-year term, as much as $10,000 per week must be raised.[94] Finally, political parties have found loopholes in election laws, laundering moneys through state party committees, which allows them to spend beyond the $54 million limit in presidential campaigns. Such moneys have included massive contributions from individuals (for example, $1 million from Joan Kroc of McDonald's and $503,263 from a former U.S. ambassador) that federal financing of election laws was designed to stop.[95]

Candidate Selection.   Closely related to our discussion of PACs is the process by which political candidates are nominated. Being wealthy or having access to wealth is essential for victory because of the enormous cost of running a successful campaign. It cost up to $5.5 million to elect a senator and/or representative in 1992.[96] This means, then, that the candidates tend to represent a limited constituency, the wealthy. "Recruitment of elective elites remains closely associated, especially for the most important offices in the larger states, with the candidates' wealth or access to large campaign contributions."[97]

The two-party system also works to limit candidates to a rather narrow range. Each party is financed by special interests, especially business.

> When all of these direct and indirect gifts (donations provided directly to candidates or through numerous political action committees of specific corporations and general business organizations) are combined, the power elite can be seen to provide the great bulk of the financial support to both parties at the national level, far outspending the unions and middle-status liberals within the Democrats, and the melange of physicians, dentists, engineers, real-estate operators, and other white-collar conservatives within the right wing of the Republican party.[98]

Since affluent individuals and large corporations dominate each party, they influence the candidate selection process by giving financial aid to those sympathetic with their views and by withholding their support from those who differ. The parties, then, are constrained to choose candidates with views congruent with the elite moneyed interests.

Benefits That Elites Seek from the State

A number of factors about the current historical era bear on the nature of elite deviance. Over the last twenty years, the United States has experienced the most dramatic economic and political change of the post–World War II era. Unfortunately, this unprecedented change has contributed to a wave of elite deviance that is virtually out of control.

Economically, the United States is no longer the dominant power it once was. Its share of the world's income is now half what it was two decades ago. The U.S. manufacturing base has severely declined, and millions of manufacturing jobs located in the nation's Northeast and Midwest have been relocated overseas, where labor is cheaper, taxes are lower, and raw materials are more accessible (see Chapter 5). Two-thirds of the workforce now engages in service-sector positions, and one-quarter of all jobs are now government related.

As a result of these changes, corporations grow not by expanding plants and equipment and thus creating new jobs but by buying other corporations. Another related effect of these economic changes is insider trading scandals on Wall Street.

In addition, the United States experienced an era of inflation accompanied by unemployment from the 1970s to the early 1990s. Although the rate of inflation has slowed in recent years, in real terms, American workers are no better off economically than they were twenty years ago. One result has been an outbreak of criminal and unethical behavior at all levels of society. The unemployment rate has settled at about 7 percent, a level that would have been viewed with some alarm twenty-five years ago. Today, it is viewed as an improvement, which is an indication of just how much economic decline Americans have become accustomed to.

Central to our understanding of elite deviance is the relationship between the corporate and political institutions. Many contemporary conflict theorists believe that the central contradiction of the capitalist order is now focused on the state. The political institution is being asked to perform two contradictory functions. On the one hand, politically influential corporations demand state assistance in capital accumulation (profit expansion) through tax relief, lucrative government contracts, subsidies, loans, and loan guarantees. Corporations also receive military protection of their overseas markets and investments. But, on the other hand, for its legitimacy to be maintained, the state must meet the demands placed on it for public assistance: social programs designed to aid those suffering from poverty, unemployment, homelessness, mental illness and retardation, drug addiction, and other problems arising in modern capitalist societies.

The result is that the state is caught in the middle. The demand for state services and expenditures consistently exceeds state revenues. One consequence of this situation is a massive deficit, which can be reduced in only three ways.

1. Reduce support for corporate programs (for example, defense contracts, subsidies, loans, corporate taxes). This is unlikely, due to corporate influence in the policy-making process.
2. Cut social programs for the unemployed, poor, elderly, and other needy groups. If too much is cut, it will appear that the government is serving the wealthy and powerful at the expense of those in need, which would prompt a massive withdrawal of legitimacy by ordinary people. This in turn might result in mass resistance to fighting additional wars to preserve corporate holdings, a tax revolt that might increase debt, or a new political movement designed to redistribute wealth, income, and political power in a more democratic fashion.
3. Raise taxes for citizens. This is unpopular among those who vote and is thus something that no serious candidate wishing to be elected would propose.[99]

The situation is made worse by the competitive sector of the economy, the 12 million small and medium-sized businesses that suffer the crises of farm foreclosures, bank failures, and bankruptcy. In recent decades, these businesses have struggled against high interest rates and suffered declining demand for their goods and services because corporate America has transferred millions of jobs to places with lower wage scales, both in the United States and overseas.

Corporate deviance also plays a role in these processes. Indeed, Harold Barnet has argued that marketing unsafe products, polluting the environment, and violating health, safety, and labor laws all help to increase corporate profits by transferring various costs to consumers, workers, and the public in general.[100] Moreover, the appalling lack of enforcement of corporate crime laws and the lenient sentences handed down in the few cases that get convictions serve further to indicate that the state functions largely to encourage capital accumulation, not to repress elite wrongdoing.

The Higher Immorality and Links between Various Kinds of Crime

Many have characterized the 1980s and 1990s as a period in which the individual focus was on self-concern, personal survival, and greed.[101] This personal focus was aided and abetted by a conservative, probusiness administration that somehow made greed seem moral and corruption an everyday fact of political life (see Chapter 2). The result was a wave of scandal in the corporate, political, and military worlds. It was spawned by the centralization of power within large organizations composing the elite and covered up by the mass media, which continually provided diversion, distraction, and social-ization to the very norms of the elite.

Mills argued that the power elite had managed to institutionalize devi-ant behavior within its ranks. This is significant, in part because sociologists usually consider deviant behavior as constituting abnormal episodes and characterizing a minority of people. Various chapters ahead contain evi-dence demonstrating that deviance and crime among many segments of the nation's economic, political, and military elite are frequent. Moreover, the deviance within the elite differs markedly from that of other social classes because it involves so much more money, power, and resources than are available to people in other strata.

The higher immorality consists of a group of acts and behaviors in-tended to increase profit and power (see Chapter 2). However, the nature of the higher immorality has changed within recent years. Corporate crime and political scandal are now interrelated not only to each other but also to other types of crime and deviance.

The American drug problem is a central example. More than $200 bil-lion of the world's $750 billion in illegal drugs is consumed in the United States. Drugs can be smuggled into the United States with the cooperation of banks (which launder drug money) and political elites (who accept payoffs), both here and in countries of origin. General Manuel Noriega, one-time leader of Panama, was convicted in 1992 for accepting bribes from the Latin American cocaine cartel. At the same time, Noriega was a longtime em-ployee of the CIA, which for years had known of his involvement in the drug trade. The CIA has also been involved in various aspects of drug trafficking for more than forty years in Europe, Southeast Asia, and most recently Latin America (see Chapter 2).

After being smuggled in, the drugs are often distributed to street gangs and peddlers by organized criminal syndicates, one of whom is the Italian American Mafia. At its lowest level, the American drug problem is directly related to the vast majority of property crimes committed by street criminals who seek money in support of drug habits. Hundreds of murders each year are committed by gangs seeking to control territory in the drug trade. Thus, crime at all levels of American life is now interrelated, as organized crime and supposedly legitimate elites cooperate for a variety of reasons in inter-national drug traffic.[102]

From what we have said about lobbying, election financing, and candi-date selection, it is obvious that much of the higher immorality involves po-litical activities and for good reasons. The state not only regulates the capitalist economy, but also federal, state, and local governments now ac-count for 32.2 percent of the gross national product. Two-thirds of these goods and services stem from spending by the federal government alone.[103] Thus, elites seek favorable legislation (or prevention of unfavorable legisla-tion), as well as tax breaks, subsidies, and lucrative government contracts.

Such contracts include everything from multibillion-dollar weapons systems to office furniture and paint. These contracts not only are influenced by the decisions of congressional members but are also often the charge of various bureaucrats with the federal government.

For example, the Government Services Administration (GSA) is in charge of securing virtually all office supplies for the entire federal government. Thus, favors from lobbyists are also from time to time dispensed to bureaucrats, as well as elected members of Congress. These favors are illegal when they include kickbacks (payments by contractors that usually involve a certain percentage of the contract in which a firm is interested). But other favors may simply include the promise of a job with the company upon completion of government services. While not illegal, these types of deals are unethical.

In addition, many independent regulatory agencies (for example, the Federal Communications Commission, Interstate Commerce Commission, Federal Trade Commission) have some impact on virtually every large and small business in the United States. The personnel in these agencies are not infrequently the target of various lobbying and other efforts (for example, the promise of a job in the industry that they regulate). Often, certain staff members of these agencies come from the industries that they oversee, and in some cases, the industries involved requested the initial regulation.

Finally, it is important to realize the influence that elites possess over the enactment or lack of enactment of legislation that defines what is and is not against the law in the first place. Examples of such influence are legion.

- **Item:** In 1977, the House passed a bill to create a Federal Consumer Protective Agency by a vote of 293 to 94; it was defeated in the Senate by a filibuster. The bill was opposed by the National Association of Manufacturers, the National Association of Feed Chains, and some 300 other companies and trade associations.[104]
- **Item:** The automobile industry got the Justice Department to sign a consent decree that blocked any attempt by public or private means to sue them for damages occurring from air pollution.
- **Item:** Many of the nation's antitrust laws appear, on the surface, to be actions that regulate business. However, many of these laws were actually requested by big business. Such laws, as we will see in Chapter 2, exclude new competitors from the marketplace and have been used to reduce the influence of labor unions. These laws have also functioned to increase public confidence in the quality of food and drugs by having such products certified safe by government inspection. For example, the 1906 Meat Inspection Act received a lot of support because of the muckraking activities of Upton Sinclair, who exposed the bad conditions in the meat processing industry. However, this act also delighted the large meat packers; it helped them to export successfully by meeting the high safety standards required by European countries.

Nonetheless, the action crippled smaller companies. Americans were left with poor-quality meat and low wages.[105]

Such laws often help to create uncompetitive (monopolistic) situations and are usually welcome (even favored) by big business. Moreover, such laws are rarely enforced, and the penalties for breaking them tend to be minuscule. Numerous additional examples could be cited showing how, time and again, corporate officials and politicians have, without penalty, violated laws or prevented acts from being made public that involved the theft of great amounts of money or the taking of many lives.

Another of the great problems in dealing with elite deviance is that all laws are not administered equally. The laws that are administered most seriously tend to be those related to the deviance of the powerless nonelites. This process works in very subtle ways but nevertheless ensures a bias in favor of the more affluent.

One way in which this bias operates is illustrated by examining the priority given the investigation and prosecution of corporate crimes within the federal government. Despite some of the advances noted in recent years, corporate crime remains a low priority.[106] As of 1992, the federal government still possessed no centralized statistical capability to index the extent of elite and other white-collar crimes. Yet for years the FBI, through its Uniform Crime Reports, has monitored street crimes involving both violence and crimes against property (for example, burglary).

Clearly, white-collar crime does not draw the attention of government and law enforcement officials. And for this reason it does not draw the resources. In fact, the Reagan administration cut back funding designated for white-collar prosecutions by the Justice Department. By 1990, the FBI had only 650 agents to investigate 7,000 fraud claims in connection with the massive S&L scandal. The FBI has estimated that it needed a minimum of 1,000 agents to do an adequate job.[107]

The Criminal Justice section of the American Bar Association issued this conclusion: "For the most part within the Federal agencies with direct responsibility in the economic crime offenses area, available resources are unequal to the task of combating economic crime.... In cases where seemingly adequate resources exist, these resources are poorly deployed, underutilized, or frustrated by jurisdictional considerations."[108]

Thus, the bias of the federal law enforcement effort, as well as state and local efforts (see Chapter 2), remains slanted toward the crimes of nonelites.

The Classification of Elite Deviance

The bias of the law enforcement effort in areas other than elite deviance has had dramatic consequences for the scholarly study of such acts. Federal granting agencies and elite foundations have historically provided little funding for the study of elites. The first empirical study of elite deviance was not published until 1940 (Sutherland's *White Collar Crime*), and there has been what Clinard and Yeager describe as "little follow-up research, with only minimal study being carried out on illegal corporate behavior."[109]

With such minimal study devoted to the subject, such terms as white-collar crime have become ambiguous. A former head of the FBI defined white-collar crime as "crimes that are committed by nonphysical means to avoid payment or loss of money or to obtain business or personal advantage where success depends upon guile or concealment."[110] Moreover, he applied the term to crimes committed by persons from every level of society, including both elites and nonelites.

The Justice Department's current definition of white-collar crime is so ambiguous that it is difficult for criminological researchers to determine the targets of FBI investigations in this area. This definition of white-collar criminality includes just about everything that is both illegal and nonviolent, involving "traditional notions of deceit, deception, concealment, manipulation, breach of trust, subterfuge, or illegal circumvention."[111]

> This definition is so nonspecific that it could include everything from welfare cheating by the poor to antitrust violations by upper class business.... What is clear is that the Justice Department has drastically altered and expanded the usual definition of white-collar crime as it has previously been understood by both academic social science and law enforcement.[112]

The view of elite deviance discussed here differs considerably from these definitions. First, our concern is only with persons of the highest socioeconomic status. That is, we have defined the elites of U.S. society as comprising corporate and government officials. We have done this because of the enormous wealth and power that reside in the nation's political economy and the relationship between the economic and political institutions. We have, therefore, not included in our discussion labor unions or organized criminal syndicates, except insofar as there are deviant relationships between these organizations and corporate and governmental entities (for example, the CIA hired Mafia members to assassinate Castro).

Second, unethical and immoral acts are an important category of elite deviance, a view that is not shared by all students of the subject. One criminologist described a similar classification as "definitional quicksand."[113] In a way, this is true. What is criminal is often easily understood by studying only those acts that are codified in criminal statutes. This would make our task relatively easy. But such an approach overlooks many complexities. For example, in most instances, "only a short step separates unethical tactics from violations of law. Many practices that were formerly considered unethical have now been made illegal and [are] punished by government."[114] Such acts include air and water pollution, bribes made overseas by multinational corporations, the disregard of safety and health standards, and false advertising. Thus, what is considered unethical at one time often becomes illegal later.

Let us concede that the definition of what is unethical is, like deviance itself, often in the eye of the beholder and thus subject to intense debate. Nevertheless, as one observer states: "It is all too human to bracket law breaking with immorality, to assume that a person who offends against the law is ipso facto less moral than one whose activities remain within the legally permitted. Yet a few moments' honest reflection will convince us that the mere fact of transgressing the legal code or not tells us very little about our spiritual condition."[115]

The position taken herein is that it is unavoidable and indeed desirable that students of deviance concern themselves with our spiritual condition. As Galliher and McCartney, two criminologists, have pointed out:

> [If] sociology makes no moral judgment independent of criminal statutes, it becomes sterile and inhuman, the work of moral eunuchs or legal technicians. … If moral judgments above and beyond criminal law were not made, the laws of Nazi Germany would be indistinguishable from the laws of many other nations. Yet the Nuremberg trials after World War II advanced the position that numerous officials of the Nazi government, although admittedly acting in accordance with German laws, were behaving in such a grossly immoral fashion as to be criminally responsible.… In the Nuremberg trials, representatives of the Allied governments, France, England, the Soviet Union, and the United States, explicitly and publicly supported the idea of a moral order and moral judgments independent of written law.…

However, defining elite deviance need not be so controversial or so subjective. There is an objective definition of such deviance that can be scientific, if by scientific one means concepts that can be measured. One such concept is harm. In this book, elite deviance refers to acts by elites and or the organizations that they head that result in any of the following types of harms:[116]

1. *Physical harms* include death and/or physical injury or illness.
2. *Financial harms* include robbery, fraud, and various scams not legally defined as fraud but which, nevertheless, result in consumers and investors being deprived of their funds without receiving goods or services for which they contracted.
3. *Moral harms* are the deviant behavior of elites (people who head governmental or corporate institutions) that forms a negative role model that encourages deviance, distrust, cynicism, and/or alienation among nonelites (members of the middle and lower classes).

For example, President Nixon resigned from office in 1974 because of the Watergate scandal. Following this, confidence in government fell dramatically and has never recovered.

Not all harmful conditions are social problems. Harms become social problems only if they are socially patterned. Socially patterned harms are traits, characteristics, or behaviors exhibited by groups of people or institutions. Thus, the inclusion of unethical acts in the study of elite deviance represents not merely a residual category but also the cutting edge of a neglected and important field of inquiry.

Third, our view of white-collar crime differentiates acts of personal enrichment from acts that are committed on behalf of one's employer.[117] This often becomes a difficult distinction to maintain when studying the deviance of elites because some elites own the organizations in which (and on behalf of whom) they commit such acts. This distinction is probably easier to maintain when discussing political corruption than it is when discussing economic deviance. However, many politicians receive illegal payments or campaign contributions for the purpose of winning elections, not necessarily for the purpose of hiding such moneys in secret bank accounts or making other personally enriching expenditures.

Also, some acts of employees committed on behalf of employers are indirectly personally enriching and committed for the purpose of ensuring job security or obtaining a promotion within the organization. This is not to say that employees never embezzle funds for personal use or that politicians do not take graft for the purpose of adding to their personal bank accounts. The point is simply that the distinction between acts that are personally enriching and acts committed on behalf of maintaining and/or increasing the profitability or power of an organization in which one is an owner or employer is difficult to maintain.

Therefore, our view of elite deviance includes three types of acts: (1) economic domination, (2) government and governmental control, and (3) denial of basic human rights.[118]

Acts of Economic Domination

Acts of economic domination include crimes and unethical deeds that are usually committed by single corporations or by corporations in league with other organizations (for example, the CIA). Typically, such crimes include violations of antitrust laws, which prohibit the formation of monopolies, price-fixing, and false advertising. These crimes also involve defrauding consumers, polluting the environment, and bribing politicians, both at home and overseas. Acts of economic domination also include crimes committed by business such as not correcting unsafe working conditions and deliberately manufacturing unsafe goods and hazardous medicines and foods. And in some instances corporations illegally enter into business ventures with organized criminal syndicates.

However, some acts of economic deviance that are illegal in the United States are legal abroad. For example, an organic mercury fungicide, banned by law for sale in the United States, was used in Iraq to coat by-products of 8,000 tons of wheat and barley. This resulted in 400 deaths and 5,000 hospitalizations among Iraqi customers.[119]

Dumping of unsafe products is a $1.2 billion per year business. It is perceived as being unethical by journalists, government officials, and certain businesspeople. Nonetheless, it is not illegal.

Crimes of Government and Governmental Control

This category includes tax loopholes and other forms of "corporate welfare," including subsidies and certain special favors granted in doing business with the government and numerous acts involving the usurpation of power. Involved here are the Watergate crimes, crimes of electioneering, and other acts involving violations of civil liberties, graft, and corruption and designed to perpetuate a given administration and to enrich its members. Also included are crimes committed by the government against persons and groups that are supposed threats to national security, such as crimes of warfare and political assassination.[120]

Related to offenses viewed as threats to national security are violations of individual civil rights, including illegal surveillance by law enforcement agencies, infiltration of law-abiding political groups by government agents, and denials of due process of law.

Many unethical acts are also committed by governmental organizations and officials. Some examples include classifying certain types of information as secret simply to cover up embarrassing incidents, making campaign promises that candidates know that they cannot or will not keep, defining a situation as a genuine crisis when no real crisis exists, letting out government contracts without competitive bidding, and allowing cost overruns on such contracts.

Elite Deviance as a Denial of Basic Human Rights

Related to both deviance by corporations and deviance by governments are actions that contribute to various types of social injuries. Included here are threats to the dignity and quality of life for specific groups and humanity as a whole. Such practices as racism and sexism, especially sexual harassment, either political or economic, fall into this category. In addition is the threat to the human race posed by nuclear arms. While such notions of humanity are not always part of a nation's laws, they should enter into any value judgments made concerning the worth and dignity of individuals.

A body of international agreement and law contains basic notions concerning human rights. Most nations of the world, including undemocratic nations, now agree that such rights should include the provision of basic material needs and freedom from torture, arbitrary arrest and detention, assassination, and kidnapping.

Thus, the criminal and unethical acts of corporations and government and the violations of basic human rights that are part of certain bodies of international agreements subscribed to by the United States constitute the subject matter of elite deviance.

Conditions Leading to Elite Deviance

In the remainder of our inquiry into the various types of elite deviance, several assumptions will be made regarding the causes, costs, and consequences of such actions. First, organizations are often characterized by what has been termed "the shield of elitist invisibility."[121] This refers to their actions as well as the heads of political organizations and governmental agencies frequently being shrouded in secrecy. Corporate management and government officials are often shielded from the press, government investigators, and boards of directors (in the case of corporations) by virtue of the power that they possess over information. For example, the illegal payments made by the Gulf Oil Company during the 1970s were kept secret from the board of directors by Gulf's chief executive officer for more than eighteen months after the scandal made headlines.

Such deceptions are possible in huge organizations. Corporations are often international organizations, characterized by "complex and varied sets of structural relationships between the boards of directors, executives, managers, and other employees on the one hand, and between parent corporations, corporate divisions, and subsidiaries on the other."[122] These complex relationships often make it impossible for outsiders and many insiders to determine who is responsible for what. Such structural complexities make it relatively easy to perform numerous acts that corporate managers wish to be kept secret. Next, the benefits involved in such deviance far outweigh the risks of apprehension and penalty. Although estimates of the cost of corporate crime are made infrequently and most date back to the 1970s and early 1980s, two congressional studies have put the figure between $174 and $200 billion annually.[123] This is more than the cost of all other types of crime plus the cost of running the entire criminal justice system combined. No source can give exact estimates concerning the costs of political corruption and various kickbacks, but the *New York Times* estimated that business bribery and kickbacks, at least a portion of which goes to politicians, may run as high as $15 billion per year.[124] Thus, the monetary rewards of corporate and political crime are without parallel.

Coupled with these rewards are minimal risks. From 1890 to 1970, only three businesspeople were sent to jail for violations of the Sherman Antitrust Act (see Chapter 2 for details), and from 1946 to 1953, the average fine levied in such cases was $2,600 (with $5,000 being the maximum possible).[125] Thus, there is very little incentive not to violate some laws. And as criminologist

Donald Cressey has stated, "Some businessmen have so little respect for the law that they would prefer an antitrust indictment to being caught wearing argyle socks.... They do so because they do not believe in these laws. This is another way of saying that they consider such laws...illegitimate."[126]

The prime goal of business is to make a profit, and, according to the business ideology, government regulation is often viewed as meddling (see Chapter 2). In summary, organizational structure, complexity, and primary goals (autonomy and profit) all help to shield top-level officials from the scrutiny of the press and the law. In addition, the lenient penalties established for much elite deviance are ineffectual deterrents.

Consequences of Elite Deviance

The consequences of elite deviance to U.S. society are thought to be monumental by most experts. Consider the following:

1. It is estimated that five times as many persons die each year from illnesses and injuries contracted on the job (100,000 to 200,000 persons) than are murdered by all street criminals.[127] (See Chapters 3 and 4 for details.)
2. We have observed that public confidence in U.S. economic and political elites has drastically declined with revelations of elite deviance. In addition, many criminologists believe that deviance by elites provides either motivation or rationalization for nonelites to commit profit-oriented crimes.[128]
3. The power of elites to help shape criminal law and its enforcement raises serious questions regarding the racial and class biases of the criminal justice system's traditional equating of the crime problem in the United States with street crime.
4. The monetary costs of elite deviance are thought to contribute substantially to inflation. Estimates range from $17.7 to $231 billion a year in the prices added to goods and services. (See also Chapter 8.)
5. It will be demonstrated that elite deviance has been an important cause of the persistence and growth of organized crime in the United States. This assistance has been provided by both economic and political elites (see Chapter 2).

One sociologist has argued that there exists a symbiotic (mutually interdependent) relationship between deviance by elites and deviance by nonelites because elite deviance greatly affects the distribution of power in society. Much elite deviance is aimed at maintaining or increasing the proportion of wealth and power that rests in elite hands. Given the inequitable distribution of such resources, the most powerless and economically deprived members of society suffer from social conditions "that tend to provoke powerless individuals into criminality."[129] Likewise, it is possible that elites, who view themselves as respectable members of society, view the deviance of the powerless as the genuinely dangerous type of crime faced by society. Such attitudes result in elites viewing themselves as morally superior to nonelites and the crimes that elites commit as not really criminal. Thus, elites may be even more likely to violate legal and ethical standards because of the deviance of nonelites, which is in part caused by the inequitable distribution of resources, the existence of which is in turn related to elite power.

Finally, the consequences listed previously regarding elite deviance constitute a mere beginning. The relationship between the acts of the powerful and those of the powerless, especially deviant acts, has not been well investigated by scholars. Moreover, the behavior of elites, insofar as it effects an alienation and loss of confidence among nonelites, undoubtedly has additional negative consequences about which we have much to learn. What is clear is that elite deviance possesses numerous important social, economic, and political consequences for all society. Only a few of the most dramatic of these consequences will be examined in this volume.

Conclusion

This chapter has introduced the topic of elite deviance. Because of the Vietnam conflict, Watergate, the Iran–Contra scandal, the S&L bailout, and numerous recent incidents involving corporate and governmental wrongdoings, elite deviance has become a major public concern. Closer examination reveals that the deviant acts of economic and political elites are not random events. They are related to the structure of wealth and power in the United States and to the processes that maintain such structures.

Moreover, aside from being illegal or unethical (at least according to the norms maintained by persons outside the organization committing the deviant act), elite deviance has several basic characteristics:

1. It occurs because it furthers the goals of economic and political organizations, that is, the maintenance or increase of profit and/or power.
2. It is committed with the support of the elites who head such organizations. Such support may be open and active or covert and implied.
3. It may be committed by elites and/or employees acting on their behalf.[130]

Such deviance is important because it holds many negative consequences for society, including high prices, dangerous products, and the increased motivation to commit deviance on the part of nonelites.

Despite all the public attention recently devoted to elite deviance, it remains a poorly understood and hence unresolved social problem in U.S. society. Since corporations and government now touch nearly every aspect of our daily lives, it behooves us all to learn as much as possible about the dimensions of and possible solutions to this type of deviant behavior.

Critical Thinking Exercise 1.1: Researching the Power Elite

Obtain a list of the members of the Clinton cabinet from *The World Almanac* or *The World Almanac of U.S. Politics*. Then look up and tabulate the backgrounds of the cabinet members in *Who's Who?* or other references using the criteria for upper-class membership given in this chapter. These criteria include:

1. Having one's name in the *Social Register*
2. Attendance at private elite preparatory schools and universities (the elite universities are listed in Figure 1.1)
3. Membership in exclusive social clubs and annual attendance at upper-class vacation retreats (for example, Bohemian Grove)
4. Membership on board of directors of the nation's largest corporations
5. Upper-class income—typically in the millions of dollars per year—and upper-class wealth—typically in the tens of millions of dollars

Show your results in a table that distinguishes between upper-class and non–upper-class cabinet members. You may also wish to examine some of the backgrounds of undersecretaries in various cabinet posts.

Endnotes

1. Peter Baker and Helen Dewar, "The Senate Acquits President Clinton," *Washington Post,* February 13, 1999, A1.
2. Associated Press, February 23, 1999.
3. See David Simon and Frank Hagen, *White Collar Deviance* (Needham Heights, MA: Allyn & Bacon, 1999), 50–54.
4. See David Simon, *Criminal Justice Ethics* (Needham Heights, MA: Allyn & Bacon, in press), Chapter 8.
5. Anthony Summers, *Conspiracy* (New York: Paragon House, 1980), 14. Summers's readable treatise remains one of the best guides to the unanswered questions concerning the Kennedy assassination.
6. See Sam Adams, "Vietnam Cover-up Playing War with Numbers," in *Focus: Unexplored Deviance,* ed. C. Swanson (Guilford, CT: Dushkin, 1978), 93–105 (article originally appeared in *Harper's,* May 1975); A. Rogow, *The Dying of the Light* (New York: Putnam, 1975), 261–71; and Michael Parenti, *Democracy for the Few,* 3rd ed. (New York: St. Martin's Press, 1980), 15–55.
7. See David R. Simon, "Watergate and the Nixon Presidency: A Comparative Ideological Analysis," in *Watergate and Afterward: The Legacy of Richard M. Nixon,* eds. L. Friedman and W. F. Levantrouser (Westport, CN: Greenwood Press, 1992), 5–22.

8. Alan Wolfe, *The Seamy Side of Democracy*, 2nd ed. (New York: Longman, 1975), vii.

9. Arthur S. Miller, "Declining Faith in Government Institutions," *Society* 17, January/February 1980, 3.

10. See Bill Moyers, *The Secret Government* (Berkeley, CA: Seven Locks, 1977).

11. See T. Draper, "The North Trial," *New York Review of Books*, 1988.

12. *San Francisco Chronicle*, September 30, 1993, A-8.

13. M. Hoffman, *The World Almanac and Book of Facts 1993* (New York: Pharos Books, 1992), 53.

14. R. Ferrighetti, *The World Almanac and Book of Facts 1994* (Mahwah, NJ: Funk & Wagnalls, 1994), 60, 75.

15. James Patterson and Peter Kim, *The Day Americans Told the Truth: What People Believe about Everything That Really Matters* (New York: Prentice Hall, 1991), 143, 150, 155, 207, 231. This is an important study of many public attitudes concerning American life and culture.

16. *Seattle Post Intelligencer*, "Americans Feel Cut Off from Political Process," June 11, 1991, A-3.

17. Vice President Al Gore, *Creating A Government That Works Better & Costs Less: Report of the National Performance Review* (Washington, DC: U.S. Government Printing Office, 1993), 11.

18. *New York Times Magazine*, January 23, 1994, 23.

19. See Stephen Craig, *The Malevolent Leaders: Popular Discontent in America* (Boulder, CO: Westview), 11.

20. See Howard Fineman, "The Virtuecrats," *Newsweek*, June 13, 1994, 31, 36, for poll results.

21. These data are taken from Louis Harris, *Inside America* (New York: Vintage, 1987), 35–37, 346.

22. See "Opinion Roundup," *Public Opinion* 5, October/November 1979, 31.

23. See M. Clinard and P. Yeager, "Corporate Crime: Issues in Research," *Criminology* 2, August 1978, 260.

24. S. Balkan et al., *Crime and Deviance in America: A Critical Approach* (Belmont, CA: Wadsworth, 1980), 170.

25. J. Roebuck and S. C. Weeber, *Political Crime in the United States: Analyzing Crime by and against Government* (New York: Praeger, 1978), 86.

26. Clinard and Yeager, 260.

27. See J. Conyers, Jr., "Corporate and White-Collar Crime: A View by the Chairman of the House Subcommittee on Crime," *American Criminal Law Review* 17, March 1980, 290; and W. E. Blundell, "Equity Funding: I Did It for the Jollies," in *Crime at the Top: Deviance in Business and the Professions*, ed. J. Johnson and J. Douglas (Philadelphia: J. B. Lippincott, 1978), 153–85.

28. Irwin Ross, "How Lawless Are Big Companies," in *Florida 2000: Creative Crime Control*, ed. L. A. Wollan (Tampa: Florida Endowment for the Humanities, 1983), 39–46 (originally appeared in *Fortune*, December 1, 1980).

29. Ralph Nader and Ronald Brownstein, "Beyond the Love Canal," *The Progressive* 44, May 1980, 28, 30.

30. R. Hilts, "50,000 Deaths a Year Blamed on Soot in Air," *San Francisco Chronicle*, December 13, 1993, A-8. *San Francisco Chronicle*, July 19, 1993, A-1, A-15.

31. William Greider, *Who Will Tell the People? The Betrayal of American Democracy* (New York: Simon & Schuster, 1992), 124.

32. "Toxicity," *The People* 95:111, August 31, 1985, 4.

33. "The Dirty Seas," *Time*, August 1, 1988, 44.

34. Ibid., 48.

35. This account is based on Keith Schneider, "Storm-tossed Admiral Rides Scandal at Energy Department," *New York Times*, June 14, 1991, A-13.

36. G. Geis, "Upper World Crime," in *Current Perspectives on Criminal Behavior: Original Essays in Criminology*, ed. A. Blumberg (New York: Knopf, 1974), 114–37.

37. See R. Kramer, "Corporate Criminality: The Development of an Idea," in *Corporations as Criminals*, ed. E. Hochstedler (Beverly Hills: Sage, 1984), 1–38; and C. Little, *Understanding Deviance and Control* (Itasca, IL: Peacock, 1983), 214.

38. See Alex Thio, *Deviant Behavior* (Boston: Houghton Mifflin, 1978), 353.

39. See M. Mintz and J. Cohen, *Power, Inc.* (New York: Viking, 1976), xix.

40. See especially the following by C. Wright Mills: *The Sociological Imagination* (New York: Oxford University Press, 1959); *The Power Elite* (New York: Oxford University Press, 1956); and *Character and Social Structure* (New York: Harcourt, Brace, and World, 1953) (with Hans Gerth). Other useful works include Joseph Simecca, *The Sociological Theory of C. Wright Mills* (Port Washington, NY: Kennikat, 1978); *Society and Freedom: An Introduction to Humanist Sociology* (New York: St. Martin's Press, 1981); and John Eldridge, *C. Wright Mills* (New York: Tavistock, 1983).

41. See Michael Parenti, *Make Believe Media: The Politics of Entertainment* (New York: St. Martin's Press, 1991); and Erick Barnouw, *The Sponsor* (New York: Oxford, 1978).

42. T. Dye and H. Zeigler, *The Irony of Democracy*, 9th ed. (Belmont, CA: Wadsworth, 1993), 4. For an excellent summary of the evidence supporting the existence of an elite, see Harold Kerbo and Richard Della Fave, "The Empirical Side of the Power Elite Debate," *Sociological Quarterly* 20, Winter 1979, 5–220.

43. Ibid., 14, 19, 235.

44. See Douglas Dowd, *U.S. Capitalist Development Since 1776: Of, By, and For Which People?* (New York: M.E. Sharpe, 1993), 113–15.

45. Thomas Dye, *Who's Running America?* 3rd ed. (Englewood Cliffs, NJ: Prentice Hall, 1983), 38.

46. Thomas Dye, *Who's Running America?* 4th ed. (Englewood Cliffs, NJ: Prentice Hall, 1986), 16–19.

47. Ben Bagdikian, *Media Monopoly* (Boston: Beacon Press, 1983), 3; and John Hewitt, "Building Media Empires," in *Media U.S.A.*, ed. A. Asa Berger (New York: Longman, 1991), 396.

48. See Edward N. Wolff, "How the Pie Is Sliced, America's Growing Concentration of Wealth," *American Prospect*, Summer 1995, 58–64.

49. Kevin Phillips, *The Politics of Rich and Poor* (New York: Random House, 1990), 17, 28; and Kevin Phillips, *Boiling Point* (New York: Random House, 1993), Chapter 1.

50. Dowd, 1993, 114.

51. These figures are taken from Peter Evans and Steve Schneider, "The Political Economy of the Corporation," in *Critical Issues in Sociology*, ed. Scott McNall (Chicago: Scott, Foresman, 1980), 221.

52. Evans and Schneider, 222.

53. Dye (4th ed.), 176.

54. G. David Garson, *Power and Politics in the United States* (Lexington, MA: D.C. Heath, 1973), 181, 182, 185.

55. G. William Domhoff, *Who Rules America Now?* (Englewood Cliffs, NJ: Prentice Hall, 1983), 77. Such power also stems from the fact that the U.S. upper class contributes heavily to political parties, campaigns, and PACs (see discussion that follows). Moreover, its media ownership aids it in gaining an "impact on the consciousness of all (social) classes in the nation." From D. Gilbert and J. Kahl, *The American Class Structure* (Homewood, IL: Dorsey Press, 1982), 348–49.

56. See G. William Domhoff, *Who Rules America?* (Englewood Cliffs, NJ: Prentice Hall, 1967), 87–96, *The Power Elite and the State: How Policy Is Made in America* (Hawthorne, NY: Aldine de Gruyter, 1990); and "The American Power Structure," in *Power in Modern Societies*, eds. M. Olsen and M. Marger (Boulder: Westview, 1993), 170–195, for evidence concerning the national upper class and their policy-making role.

57. T. R. Dye and J. W. Pickering, "Governmental and Corporate Elites: Convergence and Differentiation," *Journal of Politics* 36, November 1974, 905.

58. P. Freitag, "The Cabinets and Big Business: A Study of Interlocks," *Social Problems* 23, December 1975, 137–52.

59. H. Kerbo, "Upper Class Power," in Olsen and Marger, 223–237.

60. N. Savio, "The Business of Government: Clinton's Corporate Cabinet," *Multinational Monitor*, January 1993, 24–26, is the source of this and the following examples.

61. Roger H. Davidson and W. J. Oleszak, *Congress and Its Members*, 2nd ed. (Washington, DC: Congressional Quarterly Press, 1985), 110.

62. This point and the discussion that follows are based on R. A. Garner, *Social Change* (Chicago: Rand McNally, 1977) 252–54. For a right-wing conspiratorial view, see Gary Allen, *None Dare Call It Conspiracy* (Rossmor, CA: Concord Press, 1971); and Pat Robertson, *The New World Order* (Dallas: Word, 1991).

63. Garner, 253.

64. For a summary of such differences, see Dye (2nd ed.), 190–95.

65. See William Chambliss (ed.), *Criminal Law in Action* (Santa Barbara, CA: Hamilton, 1975), 230.

66. Garner, 253.

67. Michael Parenti, *Power and the Powerless* (New York: St. Martin's), 22.

68. Dye (4th ed.), 153.

69. Dye (2nd ed.), 126.

70. Dye (2nd ed.), 29.

71. See T. H. White, *The Making of the President 1972* (New York: Atheneum, 1973), Chapter 8; Domhoff, *Who Rules America?* 79–83.

72. Parenti, *Democracy for the Few,* 168. See also Michael Parenti, *Inventing Reality: The Politics of the News Media,* 2nd ed. (New York: St. Martin's Press, 1993), 29.

73. Herbert J. Gans, *Deciding What's News* (New York: Pantheon, 1979), 12.

74. Gans, 14.

75. G. M. Tabor, "Capitalism: Is It Working?" *Time,* April 21, 1980, 55.

76. Dye (2nd ed.), 115–16.

77. Michael T. Klare, *War Without End* (New York: Knopf, 1972), 77.

78. G. William Domhoff, *The Powers That Be: Processes of Ruling Class Domination in America* (New York: Vintage, 1978), 118.

79. Greider, 51 ff. This is one of the best books on the ills of the American political system.

80. Parenti, *Democracy for the Few,* 226.

81. Mark Green and Jack Newfield, "Who Owns Congress?" *Village Voice,* April 21, 1980, 16.

82. Michael Waldman, *Who Robbed America? A Citizen's Guide to the Savings and Loan Scandal* (New York: Random House, 1990), 65.

83. See Warren Weaver, Jr., "What Is a Campaign Contributor Buying?" *New York Times,* March 13, 1977, E-2.

84. A. Etzioni, *Capital Corruption* (New York: Harcourt, Brace, and Jovanovich, 1984), 3.

85. W. C. Cooper, "Take Back Your Dirty PAC Money," *The Nation,* May 7, 1983, 565; Green, *Who Runs Congress?* 30–31.

86. R. Wagman (ed.), *The World Almanac of U.S. Politics* (Mahwah, NJ: Funk & Wagnalls, 1993), 19.

87. D. Drake and M. Uhlman, *Making Drugs Making Money* (Kansas City, MO: Andrews & McMeel, 1993), 41.

88. Charles Mathias, "Should There Be Financing of Congressional Campaigns?" *Annals of the American Academy of Political and Social Science* 486, July 1986, 65.

89. Ibid., 66. See also Richard Bolling, "Money in Politics," *Annals of the American Academy of Political and Social Science* 486, July 1986, 76–80, for additional comments by a leading federal politician.

90. See Greider, 51.

91. Ross Perot, *Not for Sale at Any Price* (New York: Hyperion, 1992), 140.

92. Greider, 52 ff.

93. Don Van Natta, Jr., and John M. Broder, "The Few, the Rich, and the Rewarded Donate the Bulk of G.O.P. Gifts," *New York Times,* August 1, 2000, A-1.

94. Robert Sherrill, "Deep Pockets," *The Nation* 247, August 27, September 3, 1988, 170.

95. Liz Galtney, "A Case of Legal Corruption," *U.S. News & World Report* 7, November 1988, 20, 21–23.

96. R. Wagman (ed.), 17. See also Ed Garvey, "Campaign Reform? Get Real," *The Progressive,* September 1993, 18–20. Garvey notes that the average cost of a Senate seat in 1992 was $3.5 million, and the average House seat cost $555,000.

97. Walter D. Burnham, "Party System and the Political Process," in *The American Party System,* 2nd ed., ed. William N. Chambers and Walter D. Burnham (New York: Oxford University Press, 1975), 277.

98. Domhoff, *The Powers That Be,* 148.

99. This perspective is discussed in James O'Conner, *The Fiscal Crisis of the State* (New York: St. Martin's Press, 1973); Harold Barnet, "Corporate Capitalism, Corporate Crime," *Crime and Delinquency,* January 27, 1981, 4–23; and F. T. Cullen et al., *Corporate Crime Under Attack: The Ford Pinto Case and Beyond* (Cincinnati: Anderson, 1987), Chapter 2.

100. Barnet, 4–6.

101. Two of the most interesting works on this topic are Charles Derber, *Money, Murder, and the American Dream: Winding from Wall Street to Main Street* (Boston: Faber & Faber, 1992); and Steven Messner and Richard Rosenfeld, *Crime and the American Dream,* 3rd ed. (Belmont, CA: Wadsworth, 2001).

102. James Mills, *The Underground Empire* (New York: Dell, 1986).

103. Morton Paulson, "What Is Business Afraid Of?" *National Observer,* October 5, 1974, 14.

104. Currie and Skolnick, *Crisis in American Institutions* (New York: Harper Collins, 1996), 25.

105. See Stuart Hills (ed.), *Corporate Violence: Injury and Death for Profit* (Totowa, NJ: Roman & Littlefield, 1988); and David R. Simon, "Book Review Essay: White-Collar Crime and Its Future," *Justice Quarterly* 5, March 1988, 157, 159.

106. See Conyers, 291, 299, and Chapter 2 of this volume.

107. Steve Hedges and Gordon Witkins, "The Bulletproof Villains," *U.S. News & World Report,* July 23, 1990, 18.

108. ABA Section on Criminal Justice, Committee on Economic Offenses, March 1977, 6–7, cited in Conyers, 290.

109. Clinard and Yeager, 256.

110. William Webster, "Examination of FBI Theory and Methodology," in Conyers, 276.

111. Attorney General of the United States, *National Priorities for the Investigation and Prosecution of White-Collar Crime* (Washington, DC: Government Printing Office, 1980), ii.

112. David R. Simon and Stanley L. Swart, "The FBI Focuses on White-Collar Crime: Promises and Pitfalls," *Crime and Delinquency* 30, January 1984, 109.

113. See Geis, 117.

114. Clinard and Yeager, 107, 204.

115. John B. Mays, *Crime and the Social Structure* (London: Faber & Faber, 1967), 39.

116. The following discussion is based on Laura Schrager and James F. Short, "Toward a Sociology of Organizational Crime," *Social Problems* 25, February, 407–419; and David R. Simon, *Social Problems and the Sociological Imagination* (New York: McGraw-Hill, 1995), 13–18.

117. See H. Edelhertz et al., *The Investigation of White-Collar Crime* (U.S. Government Printing Office: Washington, DC, 1977), 7.

118. For an extended discussion of this typology, see Richard Quinney, *Class, State and Crime* (New York: McKay/Longman, 1977), 50–52.

119. See Mark Dowie, "The Corporate Crime of the Century," *Mother Jones* 9, November 1979, 24.

120. Quinney, 51.

121. W. C. Scott and David K. Hart, *Organizational America* (Boston: Houghton Mifflin, 1979), 40.

122. Clinard and Yeager, 265.

123. Ovid Demaris, *Dirty Business* (New York: Harper's Magazine Press, 1974), 12. See also James W. Coleman, *The Criminal Elite,* 3rd ed. (New York: St. Martin's Press, 1992), 6–8.

124. See "Companies' Payoffs in U.S. Come under New Scrutiny," *New York Times,* March 16, 1976, A-1.

125. See Ralph Nader and Mark Green, "Crime in the Suites," *New Republic,* April, 29, 1972, 19. The maximum fine was raised to $55,000 in 1955; however, this is still a pittance compared with the multimillion-dollar profits of most large corporations.

126. Donald Cressey, "White Collar Subversives," *Center Magazine* 6, November/December 1978, 44.

127. See "Job Hazards," *Dollars and Sense* 56, April 1980, 9.

128. Thio, 85, 89.

129. Conyers, 293.

130. For further discussion of these issues, see M. David Ermann and Richard J. Lundman (eds.), *Organizational Deviance,* 4th ed. (New York: Oxford University Press, 1993), 7–9.

2

Elite Deviance and the Higher Immorality

The Nature of the Higher Immorality

Sociologist C. Wright Mills once remarked that "as news of higher immoralities breaks [people] often say, 'Well another one got caught today,' thereby implying that the cases disclosed are symptoms of a much more widespread condition."[1] Mills used the term *higher immorality* to describe a *moral insensitivity*[2] among the most wealthy and powerful members of the U.S. corporate, political, and military elite (which he termed the *power elite*). For Mills, the higher immorality translated into a variety of unethical, corrupt, and sometimes illegal practices, which were viewed as a systematic, institutionalized feature of contemporary U.S. society.

In business and in government, Mills felt, many transactions are accomplished by interpersonal manipulation. One type of such manipulation by the successful is using a *false front:* pretending to be interested in what others have to say, attempting to make others feel important, and radiating charm and self-confidence (despite one's own insecurities). Obviously, if social relations are based on insincere feelings, these activities would be characterized by a good deal of alienation on the part of the participants.

In addition, Mills believed that some business and political arrangements include the favors of prostitutes. The sexual favors of these high-priced call girls are often paid for with executive expense account allotments[3] (which will be discussed later). Aside from interpersonal manipulation and the peddling of high-priced vice, the higher immorality also includes the following:

1. Unethical practices relating to executive salaries and expense accounts
2. Unfair executive and corporate tax advantages

3. The deliberate creation of political and/or economic crises by the power elite
4. The manipulation of public opinion
5. The violation of antitrust and other laws relating to political corruption

Since Mills described these various types of deviance in the 1950s, the nation has witnessed scandal after scandal involving these forms of the higher immorality. Thus, an up-to-date analysis of the nature and significance of the higher immorality is in order.

This chapter is concerned with executive salaries and expense accounts, laws relating to the incomes of corporate executives and corporations, the creation of phony crises by the power elite, and violations of antitrust laws. We also consider one form of the higher immorality only hinted at in Mills's provocative analysis: the relationships between the wealthy and powerful and members of organized crime. We begin with a microcosm of the higher immorality, the disastrous savings and loan (S&L) scandal.

Case Study: The Savings and Loan Scandal

The S&L scandal has been termed "the greatest...scandal in American history"[4] and has come to symbolize the greed and corruption that characterized so much of the Reagan era. The failure of savings and loan institutions in the 1980s is remarkable for many reasons, not the least of which is that it exemplifies virtually all aspects of the higher immorality. Before elaborating on the deviant aspects of the crisis, it would be useful to discuss the basic events leading up to it. Several key events are viewed by most analysts as being responsible for this crisis.

1. *Tight money supply in 1979:* Paul Volcker, head of the Federal Reserve Board, adopted very tight controls over the nation's money supply, resulting in interest rates increasing to double-digit levels. This produced an increase in the costs of running S&Ls by 9 to 11 percent, with no appreciable increase in revenues. Customers withdrew billions in deposits from S&Ls and invested the money in higher-yield outlets. As a result, by 1980, two-thirds of the nation's S&Ls were losing money, and many were insolvent (that is, had more debts than assets).[5]

2. *Deregulation and Monetary Control Act of 1980:* This act raised deposit insurance on individual accounts from $40,000 to $100,000 per account, lifted the cap on interest rate controls, and allowed S&Ls and banks to pay interest on savings accounts. This last measure created a tremendous problem because while the interest that S&Ls paid on savings accounts increased, the interest paid by loan holders on long-term loans made years earlier remained

low. As a result, S&Ls lost a record $3.3 billion during the first half of 1982.[6] The S&L industry lobbied heavily for relief, which came in the form of the Garn–St. Germain Act.

3. *Garn–St. Germain Act of 1982:* This act contained two key provisions: (a) S&Ls were allowed to offer money-market instruments (for example, "jumbo" certificates of deposit of $100,000 denominations) free of withdrawal penalties and limits on interest rates; and (b) up to 40 percent of an S&L's assets could be invested in nonresidential property (for example, shopping centers and condo and apartment projects).

Additional regulations (c) allowed a single investor to own an S&L (previously, a thrift was required to have at least 400 stockholders, with no one holder owning more than 25 percent) and (d) permitted S&L owners to capitalize (begin) ownership with property or "other 'noncash' assets" instead of money. Finally, (e) thrifts were no longer required to obtain down payments on loans from borrowers. S&Ls could finance up to 100 percent of a deal with borrowers not having paid a penny of their own money on a loan. One of the results of this law was an invasion of real estate developers into S&L ownership. Thus, by 1987, 80 percent of Texas S&Ls were owned by former real estate developers.[7]

These two new acts and accompanying regulations allowed S&L owners to engage in numerous unethical financial tricks that ultimately resulted in the undoing of many owners and their institutions. On a large scale, this actually created the economic catastrophe now associated with the S&L scandal. The unethical activities that led to the S&L failures include much of what Mills described when characterizing the higher immorality.

- **Item:** Realtors instigated *land flips,* whereby a piece of land was repeatedly sold back and forth among executives, each sale at a higher price. This usually required a bribe to a land appraiser each time that the property was resold. On the same day that the 1982 Garn–St. Germain Act was passed, a group of land developers and mortgage brokers associated with Vernon Savings and Loan bought and sold the same land parcels three times, creating $12 million of on-paper profits and a $14.4 million loss to the S&L when the loans that financed the sales could not be repaid.[8]
- **Item:** Prostitutes were used to close business deals. Karen Wilkening of San Diego, the notorious Rolodex Madam, was used by Don Dixon, head of Vernon S&L, to supply prostitutes for the "staff meetings" held in San Diego County. The call girls' fees were paid by the S&L. In April 1991, Dixon was sentenced to three consecutive five-year prison terms and fined $611,000 for using depositors' money to hire prostitutes and to build his California house, where he and his staff partied with the women.[9]

- **Item:** Several S&Ls paid their executives fabulous salaries while losing considerable sums of money. Lincoln S&L, owned by Charles Keating, is a prime example. During one period when the institution lost $300 million, Keating paid himself and his staff, which included several members of his family, some $4 million in salaries.
- **Item:** Impressive episodes of tax relief and subsidies occurred once the Resolutions Trust Corporation (RTC) was formed by Congress to bail out ailing S&Ls. Under the RTC charter, all bad S&L assets were guaranteed profitable for ten years by direct federal subsidy. Among the big winners:

    Arizona businessman James Fall received $1.5 billion in government subsidies to buy fifteen failed S&Ls while putting up only $1,000 of his own money.

    Trammel Crow, a Texas billionaire, and his partners invested $128 million in 1989 and received $3.2 billion in thrift assets and $1.49 billion in federal aid. Interestingly, Trammel donated $128,000 to the 1988 Bush campaign.

    Robert Bass invested $550 million in American Savings and Loan and in return received ownership of a $30 billion S&L, along with $2.5 billion in cash or $1 for every seven cents invested. Bass promptly created a separate S&L branch for the institution's bad loans and utilized $1.5 billion in S&L deposits to finance corporate mergers (see Chapter 3).[10]

- **Item:** John Ellis Bush (Jeb) of Miami, Florida, son of former President George Bush, had received considerable financial support from Miami's Cuban community.[11] Along with business partners, he defaulted on a shared $4.6 million loan from Broward S&L, which later collapsed. Later, federal regulators reduced the estimated amount owed by this group to $500,000, stiffing tax payers for the remaining $4 million. One of his business partners, Camilo Padreda, had previously been accused of and indicted for looting Jefferson S&L (McAllen, Texas). Another partner of Padreda's, Hernandez Cartaya, has been associated with CIA operatives and contractors who had systematically misused ("looted") at least twenty-six S&Ls as part of Iran–Contra operations. In 1989, Padreda pleaded guilty to defrauding HUD of millions of dollars during the 1980s.

While working for Miguel Recarey, Jeb's employer facilitated the largest health maintenance organization Medicare fraud in U.S. history, involving overcharges, false invoicing, and outright embezzlement. Recarey was convicted and has since fled the country. This same medical business is also believed to have been tied to Iran–Contra operations. A Health and Human Services agent who was continually blocked in his investigation by Washington claims that Recarey and his hospital were treating wounded Contras from Nicaragua; part of the $30 million a month given by the government to treat Medicare patients was used to set up field hospitals for the Contras.

Another of former President Bush's sons, George W. Bush, worked in Dallas, Texas. In 1983, George W's failing Spectrum 7 Oil Company was taken over by Harken Energy, which gave him a job with generous stock options and benefits. It was underwritten by Stephens, Inc. (Little Rock, Arkansas), which was heavily involved in both the Nugan Hand Bank scandal (Australia) and international money laundering with Bank of Credit and Commerce International (BCCI). Harken took financial advantage of having been tipped off regarding Persian Gulf troubles.

- **Item:** Several writers dealing with the S&L scandal have noted that if the Reagan administration had allowed the S&Ls to fail in the early 1980s, there would have been no scandal. Losses at that time were a mere $3 billion, and there were enough assets in the government insurance agencies involved to cover them. But by passing the Garn–St. Germain Act, which allowed S&Ls to engage in all sorts of questionable practices, the government created a crisis where none previously existed.

Unfortunately, this atmosphere of crisis creation continues today, thanks in part to the practices of the RTC. In June 1991, the Government Accounting Office (GAO) reported that the RTC's handling of the S&L crisis was so haphazard that the accuracy of its reporting practices was impossible to establish. RTC failed to track billions of dollars' worth of real estate and did a poor job of overseeing contractors handling cash. Examples of RTC's lax practices include the following:

> It awarded a $7.4 million contract to sell real estate that it had already sold.

> It did not question a contractor's bill for $120,000 in miscellaneous expenses.

> It failed to keep any information on three of seventeen accounts checked by GAO and only inadequate information on three others. Moreover, three RTC offices checked by GAO lacked minimal controls to prevent double billing and double payments to vendors and others doing business with them.[12]

- **Item:** There were also some important instances of manipulation of public opinion. News that might have altered the public's voting behavior in the 1986 and 1988 elections was kept under wraps. The

Reagan administration put pressure on S&L regulators to keep quiet until after the elections were held.

- **Item:** It has been estimated that 60 percent of the $1.4 trillion lost in the S&L debacle may be due to fraud. By late 1990, 331 executives, accountants, lawyers, and others connected with the scandal had been found guilty and sentenced to prison. The average prison term was two years. In November 1990, the Federal Bureau of Investigation had some 7,000 S&L-related fraud cases under investigation, 100 of which were selected for priority prosecution. This makes the S&L scandal the largest in American history, based on the amount of money and the number of criminal acts involved.[13]

- **Item:** The S&L scandal is also related to other recent corporate scandals. For instance, the giant investment firm Drexel, Burnham, Lambert utilized bribery, extortion, and other illegal means to defraud more than forty S&Ls by creating a sham junk bond market. The U.S. Justice Department brought a $6.8 billion civil suit against Drexel in 1989. Charles Keating bought $779 million in junk bonds for Lincoln Savings, for which he received an illegal kickback from Drexel.[14] Keating was convicted of fraud and other crimes and is awaiting sentencing. His meeting with five U.S. Senators (Dennis DeConcini, John Glenn, Alan Cranston, Donald Reigle, and John McCain) and head of the Federal Home Loan Bank Board, Edwin Gray, to forestall the closing of his insolvent thrift provoked an ethics scandal in Congress. Only Senator Cranston was formally censured.

- **Item:** Considerable circumstantial evidence shows important links between some S&L executives and other investors and organized crime. What is more disturbing, however, is that many of these same S&L executives are also linked with the Central Intelligence Agency (CIA). A number of writers claim that the CIA laundered drug money through Mafia-linked S&Ls in order to buy arms for the Contras. Much of the information regarding CIA–Mafia activity in the S&L crisis was uncorked by *Houston Post* reporter Pete Brewton. Brewton almost single-handedly discovered that the failure of at least twenty-two S&Ls was linked to Mafia–CIA activity.[15] The pattern in these failures concerns a small group of operatives, men like former casino owner Herman Bebe, who has ties to New Orleans boss Vincent Marcello, and Mario Renda, a financier with ties to Bebe. Some examples:

> Renda and the CIA were involved in the 1984 failure of the Indian Springs State Bank of Kansas City, Kansas. Indian Springs hired Anthony Russo, lawyer for the Civella Mafia family of Kansas City. Russo was also a consultant to Global International Airways, whose owner, Farhad Azima, borrowed $600,000 from Indian Springs in violation of a $349,000 borrower limit. Global

flew missions under contract to the CIA. Indian Springs also lent $400,000 to Las Vegas Dunes casino owner Morris Shenker, former attorney for murdered Teamsters president Jimmy Hoffa and an associate of the Civella family. At the time that loans were made to the Civellas, the family was under indictment for skimming $280,000 from Las Vegas's Tropicana casino.

Bebe also had ties to Neil Bush, son of the president and board member of Silverado Savings of Denver. Bebe borrowed money from Silverado, as did Howard Corson, Houston developer and CIA operative. Some of the funds lent to Corson may have been used to pay for CIA covert operations in Nicaragua.

The president of Indian Springs was killed in 1983 in a mysterious car fire that started in the vehicle's backseat.

Mario Renda also went into business brokering deposits to S&Ls that agreed to loan money to phony companies. In return, Renda and his business associates, who had ties to New York's Lucchese family, received finder's fees of from 2 to 6 percent on the loans. Most of the loans made to individuals with Mafia ties were defaulted on, hastening the demise of a number of S&Ls. Altogether, Renda had ties to 160 S&Ls, 104 of which failed. Subsequently, he and his partners were sued for $60 million by the Federal Deposit Insurance Corporation (FDIC) for skimming $16 million from an S&L and for tax fraud. He received a two-year sentence.

In one trial involving a former Mafia stockbroker, it was revealed that the broker's partner was a CIA pilot. The pilot confessed that the CIA had laundered drug money through unsuspecting S&Ls and obtained S&L loans just before sending money to the Contras, in violation of the Boland Amendment (see Chapter 9). The pilot was indicted in September 1986 for defrauding a Florida S&L and given a thirty-two-year prison sentence and a $1.75 million fine. Renda received a two-year prison sentence and a $100,000 fine in the same case.[16]

In 1991, it was learned that Arab financiers, including Saudi investor Ghaith Pharaon, had used their own Belgium bank, BCCI, to purchase an interest in First American Bank of Washington, D.C. Pharaon also associated with David Paul, chief executive officer of Centrust S&L, and arranged in 1988 for BCCI to buy the $25 million in Centrust bonds that Centrust later repurchased. In 1990, BCCI officials pleaded guilty to laundering $15 million through its Miami and Tampa subsidiaries and paid a record $14.6 million fine. Five BCCI employees were sentenced to prison terms. One of the officials was a former personal banker to General Manuel Noreiga of Panama, a former employee of the CIA (see Chapter 9). Investigations are also underway to determine whether BCCI secretly owned any additional American banks through front investors, such as former secretary of defense Clark Clifford and his law partner, Robert Altman.[17]

BCCI is also being investigated in the United States and a number of foreign countries for a variety of criminal activities. The bank's assets have been seized by regulators in sixty-nine nations, making it the largest fraud case in the history of banking. Estimates show that BCCI may have defrauded investors of at least $5 billion and possibly as much as $15 billion. The scandal may affect the political careers of British Prime Minister John Major and former CIA Director Robert Gates, both of whom are accused of knowing about BCCI's illegalities and doing little about them. Among the chief accusers are Manhattan District Attorney Robert Morganthau, who claims that he received virtually none of the assistance he requested in his own two-year BCCI investigation, and Lloyds of London, which claim that their repeated requests to U.S. attorneys in Miami and New Orleans to seize BCCI records were ignored.

- In July 1991, the Federal Reserve Board fined BCCI $200 million and forbade it from engaging further in any U.S. banking activities. This was BCCI's second conviction in three years in the United States, the first coming in Florida in 1988. In that case, BCCI paid a $14 million fine for laundering illegal funds but was able to negotiate a plea bargain wherein the government agreed not to charge the bank with any additional offenses under investigation or known to investigators. This unusual deal and additional memos have given rise to charges that the Justice Department covered up further BCCI investigations.
- Motives for covering up BCCI activities also involve covert operations by U.S. intelligence agencies. Both the CIA and the National Security Council illegally funneled moneys through BCCI to buy arms for the Nicaraguan Contras and Afghan rebels. BCCI also had its own 1,500-person "black" (secret) network that engaged in a variety of illegal activities, including bribing numerous politicians in various nations, smuggling arms and drugs, furnishing prostitutes, and carrying out acts of terrorism, blackmail, kidnapping, and perhaps murder. Some of these activities may have been committed in cooperation with the CIA.
- BCCI paid millions to a variety of influential politicians, including $8 million to former President Jimmy Carter for his Global 2000 project, and lobbyists to keep from being investigated. BCCI also cultivated close ties with former Carter officials Bert Lance (from whom it purchased the National Bank of Georgia) and Andrew Young. BCCI also kept secret accounts for numerous foreign dictators, such as Manuel

Noreiga, Saddam Hussein, and Ferdinand Marcos, as well as Colombian drug cartel leaders and terrorist Abu Nidal.[18]

The S&L scandal also typifies the lax nature with which corporate crime is prosecuted and punished within the criminal justice system. Between 1987 and 1992, 75 percent of all S&L fraud cases referred to the Justice Department for prosecution were dropped. In prosecuted cases, the average prison term handed down was 2.4 years. The average sentence for bank robbery in the United States is 7.8 years.[19]

Moreover, in February 1993 the GAO criticized the Bush administration for its inaction in investigating bank fraud, particularly as it related to the S&L debacle. The Bush administration created only two of the twenty-six special task forces it had promised and managed to collect just 4.5 percent of the $846 million in fines and judgments imposed in the fraud cases. This was a miserable effort indeed considering that the S&L scandal represents the largest series of white-collar crimes in American history.[20]

The S&L scandal is typical of the scandals that have involved U.S. elite since 1963. Beginning with the assassination of President John F. Kennedy, numerous studies have found links between organized crime, the so-called secret government/team[21] (of which the CIA is a major part), and various business and military interests. These scandals and relationships are explored in depth in Chapters 7 through 9.

The Higher Immorality and the Political Economy

Mills's notion of the higher immorality has rarely been viewed as a theory of elite crime. However, closer examination will reveal that it is indeed a set of theoretical propositions concerning an institutionalized set of behaviors among the U.S. power elite. In this section, we explore the general parameters of the higher immorality within the political economy.

Corporate Compensation: Salaries, Taxes, and Perks

Since the higher immorality involves the pursuit of money, the mechanisms by which money is obtained and retained are very important. As Mills put it, "Higher income taxes have resulted in a whole series of collusions between the big firm and higher employee. There are many ingenious ways to cheat the spirit of the tax laws, and the standards of consumption of many high-priced men are determined more by complicated expense accounts than by simple take-home pay."[22]

The accuracy of Mills's description can be gauged by a study of all the various rewards granted top corporate executives. Perhaps the most innovative scheme used by corporate executives to raise their own salaries concerns the management of General Dynamics (GD), a major defense contractor with a long history of defense fraud convictions (see Chapter 5). In 1991, while GD was busy laying off 30 percent of its workers, its chairman, William Anders, asked stockholders to approve $7.6 million worth of bonuses for GD's top twenty-five executives. The bonuses, tied to the performance of GD stock, were approved by 77 percent of the company's stockholders. In light of the layoffs, the bonuses were the subject of angry worker demonstrations.[23]

The situation at GD is symbolic of a national debate over executive pay. Three-fourths of the American people now believe that corporate executive salaries are too high, and the Securities and Exchange Commission has ruled that executive pay can come before corporate stockholders for a vote. Excessive corporate compensation is a fundamental reason for the great inequality of wealth and income in America (see Chapter 1). As of 1999, 90 percent of all stock is still owned by the richest 10 percent of the population. The wealthiest 5 percent of Americans own three-fourths of all corporate stock, and half of the entire market is owned by the richest 1 percent of Americans, whose annual incomes exceed $250,000 or who have an average net worth of $650,000.[24]

- In 1978, chief executive officers (CEOs) of large corporations made 60 times more than the pay of the average worker. By 1997, the ratio had grown to 189 to 1.
- Today, 28.6 percent of U.S. workers earn less than $7.79 per hour, the amount needed to lift a family of four out of poverty with full-time employment. An additional 14.4 percent earn between $7.80 and $9.99 per hour. A mere 57 percent of the U.S. workforce earns more than $10 per hour.[25]
- Stock options and other benefits push total average executive compensation to between $10 and $78 million per year. Leon Hirsch, CEO of U.S. Surgical, who took home $118 million in 1991, believes that he "is not paid enough."[26]

Why Is Executive Pay So High?   Such increases are rarely tied to company performance. For example, in 1990, Reebok shoes CEO Paul Fireman earned enough to put him in the top-ten list of best-paid chief executives, yet Reebok's yearly profits increased only 1 percent over the 1989 total.[27] Executive compensation is highly correlated with the salaries of committee members in charge of approving executive salaries.[28] Thus, corporate executives possess the power to reward themselves by placing people on corporate boards who are predisposed to vote executive pay increases. CEOs are also likely to get raises if other CEOs are getting them, thus effectively reversing the law of supply and demand.

One of the most widely used and effective devices for amassing corporate wealth is the corporate stock option. A *stock option* is "a right given a corporate executive to buy his company's stock at some time in the future, at a specified price the date the option is granted."[29] For example, suppose that an executive is given an option to buy 100,000 shares of his or her company's stock on January 15, 1991, and on that day the price of such stock is $75 per share. If the executive contracted to buy the stock at $50 per share back in 1989, he or she may still buy at that price. The profit on the stock amounts to $25 per share on 100,000 shares, or $250,000. The executive does not pay income tax on this windfall but does pay capital gains tax. Such taxes, however, are only 40 percent, considerably less than the income tax one would pay on such an amount.

Nonetheless, let us continue with our examination of stock options. Some corporations have plans that allow them to withdraw high-price stock options and publish new ones to reflect lower market prices. Some corporations even provide low-cost or no-interest loans so that stock options may be purchased. Sometimes no repayment of the loan's principal (actual amount of the loan) is required until the executive "dies, retires, quits, or goes bankrupt."[30] And if the stock price falls further, executives are commonly permitted to turn in their shares to the company at the time that the loan is canceled. Hence, executives are not subject to the risks on the market that plague the bulk of the nation's stockholders.

Another innovative plan, called *stock appreciation rights* (SAR), further confirms Mills's claim regarding executive avoidance of taxation. Instead of paying money for stock shares, executives merely collect from the company money or stock shares equal to any increase in the stock's value. Doing this allows executives to escape paying capital gains taxes and any money for the stock option. By 1977, 80 percent of the top 200 industrial corporations had opted for the SAR alternative.

Other advances in tax avoidance have occurred in recent years. One plan, adopted by 29 percent of companies with sales of over $3 million, allows executives to choose options that make stock payments on either a spread-out or lump-sum basis, resulting in more tax savings. Such plans are usually so complex that company stockholders are unable to understand them, especially when the details are hidden in the fine-print sections of stockholder reports. Such practices involve deceiving stockholders and prevent stockholder revolts.

Another stock-option plan permits executives to purchase stock at its book-value price. Rather than buy stock at market prices, executives buy it at a price per share equal to the company's assets minus its liabilities. This price rarely declines and usually increases greatly, regardless of stock market swings. Later, executives are permitted to sell the stock to the company at its new book value. The perks (perquisites) of corporate life are not limited to salaries, bonuses, and stock options. Indeed, the corporate compensation landscape now represents a form of corporate socialism for top executives. Among the tax-exempt perks enjoyed by corporate managers are the following:

> [F]inancial counseling, tax and legal assistance, company automobiles and chauffeur services (for business and sometimes for personal use), company-provided planes, boats, and apartments (for business and sometimes for personal use), company paid or subsidized travel, recreation facilities, club memberships, liberal expense accounts, personal use of business credit cards,... complete medical coverage, including...home, health care, dental, and psychiatric care—all without outlays by the executive...college expenses for children, "social-service sabbaticals," and the best and most complete form of disability, accident, and life insurance.[31]

Today, 75 percent of executive compensation consists of nonsalary bonuses, stock options, and related perks.

All in all, the success of American corporate executives has undermined the public's faith in the U.S. economic system, caused a brain drain of bright people from teaching and public service, and helped to create a "greed is good" attitude among middle- and lower-level managers. The result is an unprecedented cynicism of employees toward companies and bosses.[32]

Other advantages secured by the elite, especially those relating to tax laws and private foundations, are also important because they have, in some instances, facilitated both political and economic crimes.[33] Such advantages deserve a closer look.

Welfare for the Well-Off: Tax Breaks

The U.S. system of government has produced what is known as a dual-welfare system. Programs for the poor are termed *relief, welfare, assistance,* or *charity.*[34] Programs for the rich, however, are called *tax expenditures, subsidies, price supports, parity,* and the like.

The dual-welfare system is an integral part of the higher immorality, allowing the rich to become richer at the expense of the middle class and the poor. Mark Zepezzaur and Arthur Naiman have recently put the costs of corporate welfare at $448 billion, "about 3.5 times as much as the $130 billion we spend yearly for the poor."[35] Such "wealthfare" includes subsidies, tax deductions, tax exemptions, tax-free investments, excessive government pensions, and $172 billion worth of fraud and waste in the Defense Department (see Chapter 5 for details).[36]

One mechanism by which rich individuals and corporations are allowed to retain their wealth is the tax loophole (now called *tax expenditures* by government). In fact, 90,000 corporations paid no federal income taxes whatsoever one year. Since 1981, the maximum corporate tax rates allowed by law have been cut from 46 to 34 percent.[37]

In the 1940s, corporate income taxes accounted for 33 percent of federal income tax receipts. The figure now stands at 15 percent and has remained constant since the late 1980s. All of corporate America now pays less in taxes than those paid by families in just three states, New York, California, and Ohio.[38] Some examples of corporate tax bills in 1991–1992, when the corporate tax rate was 33 percent, include the following:

- Chase Manhattan paid 1.7 percent of its $1.5 billion income in taxes.
- Baxter International paid 5.4 percent of its $1.4 billion earnings in taxes.
- Texico Oil paid 8.8 percent of its $2.7 billion income in taxes.
- Ogden Corporation paid one-tenth of 1 percent of its $217 million earnings in taxes.[39]

Many special deductions keep the tax bills of corporations and the rich below those of average Americans (on a percentage basis). Some of these are discussed next.

The Asset-Depletion Range

Over half the benefits from asset depletion go to the largest 103 U.S. manufacturing corporations.[40] This tax law makes an allowance for wear and tear on equipment by allowing a depreciation deduction. In reality, there is no way of knowing how long a piece of equipment will last; it merely depends on how quickly a given company decides to replace it. Before the asset-depletion allowance, most equipment had to be depreciated over a ten-year period for tax purposes. Now, however, a company is allowed to depreciate equipment over an eight-year period, 20 percent faster than before. Of course, such equipment lasts eight years, ten years, or even longer. The odd thing about the asset-depletion range is that it comes at a time when 25 percent of the nation's plant capacity is already underused. Hence, the need for new equipment is suspect. This and other features of the Reagan plan reduced government revenues by $750 billion between 1981 and 1984 and by $1 trillion between 1984 and 1988. Meanwhile, government deficits zoomed from $40 billion in 1980 to $210 billion in 1987. Indeed, by 1984, corporate tax breaks cost the federal treasury $150 billion and, by 1986, $250 billion a year.

In 1993, the federal Omnibus Budget Reconciliation Act became law. The law gives corporations some of the most confounding deductions in American history.

- A "potato chip" deduction clause allows merging corporations to depreciate their product names and intangible assets. Thus, over a fifteen-year period, companies are allowed to deduct for all manner of secret ingredients in product formulas (for example, floor waxes and deodor-ants), as well as for brand names: Doritos, Quaker, and Kellogg's. Moreover, the law states that past attempts to write off such intangibles are now legal, even if they were previously denied by the Internal Rev-enue Service (IRS) or courts. Thus, corporations can now file for re-funds from previous years.

- The act also contains a variety of special laws. Banks that made bad loans can deduct these as bad debts. Foreign-owned companies are taxed at rates lower than American companies. Poorly run corpora-tions that are losing money can now get refunds from previous years.
- Corporations can now deduct executive salaries and interest payments on borrowed money, much of which has gone for mergers in recent years (as discussed in Chapter 3). The deductions on interest alone total $200 billion. Thus, in 1991–1992, Stone Container paid no federal cor-porate income taxes on its $493 million earnings due to its deduction for interest on its debt. Moreover, the owners of this debt (bondholders) escaped taxes on the part of their individual incomes that Stone paid in interest to them.

The results of these deductions constitute nothing less than a scandal. Money is used for mergers, which, in turn, result in plant closings and the loss of over 2.5 million middle-class jobs in recent years. Corporate taxes de-crease, executive salaries increase, unemployment reaches depression levels, and what's left of the American middle class is saddled with an increased tax bill.[41]

Taxes and Multinational Corporations

Many multinational corporations take advantage of foreign tax credits, which allow a company to pay taxes on profits made overseas, where taxes are usually less, and to pay no taxes on such profits in the United States. This has made some nations, including Liechtenstein, Panama, and Liberia, tax havens for large corporations. The practice of setting up dummy corpora-tions overseas to which items are sold only on paper (for purposes of tax avoidance) is also common.

Misappropriated Charity: Foundations

Despite the tax advantages granted to corporations, individuals who own controlling interests in corporations also tend to do all they can to ensure that their fortunes are passed on to their kin. To escape inheritance and other taxes, a boon to such individuals has been the tax-exempt foundation.

The purpose of a foundation is supposedly to facilitate charitable contri-butions. As of 1987, a mere 2.8 percent of U.S. foundations held $100 million or more in assets, accounting for more than 59 percent of total foundation assets and 45 percent of all foundation giving.[42] Setting up a tax-exempt foundation exempts all assets therein from income and capital-gains taxes, as well as most inheritance taxes. On the surface, this seems morally upright because such funds are, after all, given to worthy causes. Underneath, however, the reality is somewhat different.

Foundations excel at investing money and escaping taxation. A government study of 1,300 foundations found that 180 owned 10 percent or more of a corporation's stock (often enough to gain a controlling interest in a company).[43] Far from being strictly charitable, foundations play a major role in the corporate decisions that affect the private sector of the economy, as well as politics.

Moreover, there have been incidents of government interference by awarding private foundation grants. This has especially been the case with the CIA. In 1966, the CIA disbursed $400,000 through the J. M. Kaplan Fund to a research institute. The institute in turn financed research centers in Latin American countries, which also drew support from the Agency for International Development (a U.S. foreign-aid agency), Brandeis and Harvard universities, and the Ford Foundation. The CIA also sponsored the travel of various social scientists to communist countries. The Kaplan Fund had also been financed by foundations, although it was not even listed with the IRS. This suggests that the foundation was fraudulently created by the CIA. Seven other foundations were discovered to have been CIA-created conduits, but the purposes or amounts of money given have never been made public. Why the CIA went into the charity business, which is a clear violation of its charter, has also gone unexplained.[44]

Foundation money has been used for a number of causes that have nothing whatever to do with charity, which represents one more form of the higher immorality. The Ford Foundation, for example, has lent large sums of money to private corporations, in effect competing with private banks. Howard Hughes created the Hughes Medical Institute to insure the liabilities of a number of Hughes's own companies.

Other foundations have made loans to businesspeople for the purpose of closing business deals. Foundation grants have also been used for the following:

1. Bankrolling political candidates
2. Financing experiments with school decentralization in slums in which African Americans live
3. Supporting militant political organizations, on both the left and right
4. Financing the foreign travels of the staff of U.S. senators
5. Financing activities of moderate (middle-class) civil rights organizations, which have largely failed to understand or alleviate the problems of poor ghetto blacks (who rarely receive such money without strings)[45]

In short, foundations have been used for deviant purposes that have nothing whatever to do with charity.

Royalties for the Rich: Subsidies

In addition to all the tax loopholes created for the rich and the corporations, many more billions of dollars in benefits are paid by the government. These benefits are called subsidies, and they are made in the form of payments, low-interest loans, and/or in-kind benefits (whereby services of various kinds are provided by the government). Such generosity is extended to many different industries. However, it tends to benefit mostly the largest and wealthiest interests.

In agriculture, for example, the lion's share of such payments go to the largest individual and corporate farmers "to limit the production of crops by buying up crop surpluses,…keeping prices (to consumers) and profits high while subsidizing the expansion of giant corporate farms at the expense of family farms."[46] Among others receiving subsidies are oil companies, a bowling alley in Dallas, an Ohio radio station, and the queen of England (for not producing crops on the royal family's Mississippi plantation).[47]

By 1982, farm subsidies had become the nation's largest welfare program, totaling $28 billion, $3 billion more than farm income. Twenty-five percent of subsidies went to just 4.6 percent of U.S. farmers, who produce 80 percent of all farm income, averaging over $100,000 per year. The effect of such subsidies on farm prices is to raise the floor (bottom) price on farm products, making U.S. food exports uncompetitive. As a result, farm exports declined $5 billion from 1982 to 1983. Farm subsidies thus keep food prices from falling and transfer money from consumer to producer at home.[48]

- Among the most suspect of direct subsidies were those given International Telephone and Telegraph (ITT) and General Motors (GM) for damages inflicted on their plants in Germany during World War II. GM collected $33 million for damages to its truck plant, which produced trucks used by the Nazis throughout the war. ITT owned plants that produced bombers for the Nazi Air Force, which were used (among other things) to destroy Allied shipping. Ironically, ITT produced direction finders for the Allies that were designed to protect Allied convoys from enemy attack! ITT received $27 million for damages inflicted by Allied planes on its German plants.[49] Thus, inadvertently, both GM and ITT aided the Nazi war effort and were, in effect, reimbursed by the U.S. government for doing so.

To say the least, "subsidies go to a bewildering array of industries, seemingly without rhyme or reason."[50]

- **Item:** The United States owns power plants in Nevada that produce electricity for about one penny per kilowatt. As a result, the citizens of Las Vegas (with its huge neon signs) pay 5.6 cents per kilowatt for electricity, while residents in the Northeast pay 12 cents per kilowatt for their unsubsidized electricity.
- **Item:** The Farmer's Home Administration (FHA) has lent the nation's farmers $56 billion but is continually unable to collect bad loans. In one instance, forty-three large borrowers owing $79 million ($1.8 million each) had their loans reduced to $64 million when they could not pay. The FHA has already written off some $10 billion in bad loans, and some borrowers are paying as little as 1 percent interest due to government subsidies on loans.
- **Item:** The Government Services Administration owns some 15 million feet of vacant office space. Yet, in 1992 it leased an additional $2 billion in space and spent an additional $5 billion on new construction (including $1.6 billion for a World Trade Center building). Most puzzling is the fact that 10 to 25 percent of federal office space is vacant. Vice President Al Gore recommended suspension of all new federal office space.[51]
- **Item:** The government owns 340,000 nonpostal motor vehicles that cost $3 billion to buy and $915 million a year to maintain. Depreciation costs on these vehicles are estimated at about $600 million annually. The White House alone has a fleet of 29 limousines.
- **Item:** The government also operates a fleet of 1,200 civilian aircraft at an annual cost of $800 million. But it spends another $100 million to lease an additional 5,000 planes. The 2 presidential 747s alone cost $410 million.
- **Item:** The federal government spends somewhere between $676 million and $2 billion a year for office furniture and decorations. The exact amount is not known.
- **Item:** The Department of Interior spends $100,000 a year to train beagles in Hawaii to sniff for brown tree snakes.[52]

The federal government has subsidized a variety of businesses and professions for little apparent reason. Government funds have been spent for the following:

- To build a $6.4 million ski resort in Idaho
- To perform $13 million worth of repairs on a privately owned dam in South Carolina.
- To convert a ferry boat into a $3.1 million crab restaurant in Baltimore
- To refurbish a privately owned museum in Johnstown, Pennsylvania, at a cost of $4.3 million
- To buy a private pleasure boat harbor in Cleveland for $11 million

- To do a $6 million track repair job for the Soo Railroad
- To build a $10 million access ramp at a privately owned Milwaukee stadium
- To pump sand onto privately owned beaches of Miami hotels for $33 million
- To buy former Vice President Dan Quayle's gold-embossed playing cards for $57,000, a great subsidy for the manufacturer[53]

Also:

- Beekeepers have been voted a special subsidy for producing honey. The law involved has resulted in the U.S. government storing away 110 million pounds of honey at a cost of $1 billion while the United States imports 110 million pounds of expensive foreign honey.
- In 1990, Congress allocated $1 billion for the Department of Agriculture to aid in the advertising of U.S. agricultural products overseas. The money was allegedly supposed to help farmers and small, struggling firms, but some of the funds involved went to the nation's largest corporations. Gallo Wines, Sunkist, Blue Diamond Almonds, McDonald's, Ralston-Purina, Dole, Pillsbury (a British-owned firm), Wesson, Campbell Soup, Kraft, and even Newman's Own received from $100,000 to $6.2 million to promote the sale of their products in what amounted to a grant in a strange "corporate welfare" program.[54]
- The Small Business Administration (SBA) is supposed to aid America's 15 million small firms, many of which are struggling to stave off bankruptcy. However, one government investigation revealed that many of the loans go to large businesses, firms worth up to $6 million with 1,500 employees. Moreover, the SBA, as of 1990, had $10 billion in outstanding loans and $1 billion in liquidations (that is, loans in default).[55]
- Officially, the federal government owns the airwaves, meaning that it sells licenses for radio, television, and cellular phone businesses. Recently, it let its cellular phone licenses go for a mere $200 each. These licenses are worth an estimated $232 million.
- The Army Corps of Engineers has been providing services for commercial customers for a song. It has processed 15,000 applications for dredging various lakes, rivers, and streams costing $86 million but has collected only $400,000 in fees.[56] The Food and Drug Administration inspects 1.5 million food products per year for labeling and safety standards. But the government, not food firms, pay for this service. Charging user fees could save an estimated $1.5 billion over a five-year period.[57]

What all this means is that much of what the federal government spends is wasted, and such incidents as those mentioned do considerable moral harm.

Some interesting loans are also made. Such loans have bankrolled much of the nation's hospital and private housing construction through Federal Housing Authority and Veterans Administration (VA) mortgages. Lockheed was guaranteed a $250 million loan in the early 1970s to keep from going bankrupt. The giant firm was later involved in bribery scandals that aided in undermining U.S. foreign policy objectives. At the time that the Lockheed loan was made, the "Federal Government had outstanding…$56 billion in direct loans,…$167 billion in loan guarantees,…a total of $223 billion—twice the sum of all commercial and industrial loans that commercial banks had outstanding."[58] This seemingly nonsensical subsidy parade takes place in part to keep inefficiently managed corporations afloat at the taxpayers' expense.

Businesses whose sole customer is the government commonly receive subsidies. Large defense contractors are often granted free use of government laboratories, equipment, electricity, and so on. One study estimated the amount of government-owned facilities in the hands of various defense contractors at $13 billion.[59] This for an industry with profit margins among the highest in the private sector of the economy! (The consequences of extending such benefits to defense contractors are explored in Chapter 5.)

In sum, the various subsidies and tax breaks in the 1980s totaled $117 to $125 billion a year. In 1988, $618 billion was extended in guaranteed loans and subsidies.[60] Large corporations and wealthy individuals continue to receive such advantages because they are able to manipulate public opinion in their favor. This manipulation is a very important aspect of the higher immorality, as we now discuss.

The Creation of Crisis

One aspect of the higher immorality identified by Mills concerns the concept of *crisis*.

> Crisis is a bankrupted term because so many men in high places have evoked it to cover up their extraordinary policies and deeds. As a matter of fact, it is precisely the absence of genuine crisis that has beset our morality. For such crises involve situations in which men at large are presented with genuine alternatives, the moral meanings of which are clearly open to public debate. Our higher immorality and general weakening of older values have not involved such crises.[61]

Perhaps nothing in our recent experience so confirms Mills's words as the energy crisis of the 1970s.

The oil industry is the giant of the capitalist system. Oil accounts for one-fifth of all profits in the manufacturing sector of the economy, making oil the richest industry in the world.[62] By the early 1970s, however, several situations at home and around the world threatened to reduce oil profits. Let's review these conditions.

At home, the oil-depletion allowance (allowing oil companies to deduct a certain percentage of their income) had been reduced (in 1969) from 27.5 to 23.5 percent. The oil companies thus expanded their overseas operations in order to take advantage of the foreign tax credit, which, between 1971 and 1974, reduced their U.S. tax bills by 75 percent.[63] Also at home, from 1960 to 1972, small, independent oil companies had increased their share of the domestic gasoline market from 10 percent to 25 percent. The number of new oil wells in the United States had steadily declined between 1956 and 1972. Indeed, total drilling had declined from 208 million to 86 million feet per year; 20,000 flowing wells had been capped in California alone. This reduced U.S. oil production by 5 billion barrels a year. Only one new major oil refinery was built in the United States between 1968 and 1972.[64]

Overseas, the large oil companies, which from 1948 until the late 1960s had controlled 42 percent of the oil reserves in the Mideast, began having problems. By 1970, Arab nations began demanding a larger share of control over the production of their own oil.

> In that year the new revolutionary government of Kaddafi in Libya withheld production in order, successfully, to force a price increase on Occidental, an independent whose operations relied on Libyan oil. Because of the better terms offered Arab states by the independents, the Arab "take" had been edging up. But Occidental's capitulation threatened to open the gate to soaring profits for OPEC in the 1970s. In February 1971, the Teheran Conference was called to deal with the rapidly shifting situation. Here the large oil companies tried to press for a united front vis-à-vis OPEC. They sought to avoid the sort of disunity marked by Occidental's caving in to Libyan demands. The oil companies were undercut, however, not only by the independents but also by the U.S. State Department itself. The department, seeking better Arab–American relations, let it be known that the United States was not committed to a single-agreement approach. Failing to reach accord, the oil companies agreed to concessions to the Arab governments.[65]

The excuse to increase profits and ensure their increase for the future came in October 1973. During the Arab–Israeli War, the Arab-dominated OPEC nations announced an embargo on oil exports to the West. They also announced a dramatic increase in the price of crude oil from $2.50 to about $11 per barrel. The oil companies then announced a dramatic shortage of imported oil and stated that the demand for domestic oil could do nothing but increase. Thereupon, the oil companies announced increased prices for domestic crude oil equal to the increases in OPEC oil. The price of oil soon quadrupled.

This was only the beginning of the fabricated crisis. The truth seems to be that there was no embargo (withholding of oil) by OPEC. Imports for the last three months of 1973 were 32 percent above those for the last three months of 1972![66] The withholding of gasoline by the oil companies from the U.S. customer had a large impact.

- **Item:** From 1973 to 1974, oil company profits increased 80 percent. The oil companies claimed that the profits were needed for new exploration for oil. However, the oil companies invested in such things as real estate, entertainment, and a department store chain, as well as coal and uranium. Indeed, by 1975, the oil companies owned 50 percent of U.S. nuclear fuel, 54 percent of the coal reserves, and 45 percent of the uranium reserves.[67]
- **Item:** Oil withheld from independent dealers drove many of them out of business. By May 1973, 1,200 independent gasoline stations had closed, and by the end of the year the number had reached 10,000.[68]
- **Item:** The oil companies also used the artificial crisis to exact concessions from the government. The large companies had contributed a lusty $7 million to the Nixon campaign of 1972. Not surprisingly, they had little problem finding sympathy for their wishes.
- **Item:** A deal was closed with the Soviet Union and Communist China involving the purchase of $45.6 billion of natural gas. This involved sale by the oil companies of $10 billion of pipeline, supertankers, and liquefaction equipment. The Soviet gas was to be sold at prices up to three times higher than domestic natural gas.
- **Item:** Congress granted permission to build the Alaskan pipeline. The pipeline was not to extend across Canada, where it could be integrated into pipelines in the Midwest, but 798 miles across Alaska. The result was, in the late 1970s, a glut of crude oil on the West Coast, some of which was exported to Japan, while shortages of unleaded gasoline developed throughout the United States, sending gasoline prices soaring. The pipeline was constructed by the oil companies themselves, in partnership with the state of Alaska, at a cost overrun that was estimated at 800 percent. Moreover, the oil companies were also granted a profit on the crude oil that flows through the pipeline, on the transporting of the oil, on its refining, and on the final sale of the refined product.
- **Item:** In 1973, President Richard Nixon removed all quotas and tariffs on imported (expensive) oil and substituted scaled license fees of 21 cents a barrel for five years. New oil refineries, however, were allowed to use 75 percent of the imported oil free of such fees. Exxon thereupon announced plans to expand its domestic refining capacity by 30 percent.
- **Item:** By 1977, the annual acreage of federal lands leased for oil exploration on the U.S. continental shelf had tripled.
- **Item:** President Nixon proposed that the oil companies be granted additional tax relief amounting to 12 percent of the cost of producing new wells and a 7 percent increase added to the 90 percent "dry hole" write-off, thus allowing investors to deduct 97 cents of every dollar lost from wells that failed to produce oil.
- **Item:** In December 1973, Nixon classified all oil produced over the amount produced in 1972 as "new crude" and hence free from any price controls. "Old crude" was allowed to rise $1 a barrel to provide a further incentive to the oil companies to raise production.

The final irony in the energy crisis of 1973 was that, in September and October, oil storage tanks in the United States were so full that many tankers were diverted to Europe, where their contents were sold at higher prices. In Holland and Israel, which were also embargoed by the Arabs, there were no lines at gas stations. But in those countries, there were no government price controls that the oil companies had to fight to remove.[69]

The 1973–1974 oil crisis contained elements of the lack of public debate that Mills claimed were characteristic of crisis creation. In June 1973, a report issued by the Federal Trade Commission (FTC) stated that the oil shortage "was the result of anticompetitive practices fostered by government regulations and manipulated by major oil companies to protect their profits."[70] The report accused the oil companies of using tax breaks to make huge profits in drilling for oil, while running their refining, distributing, and marketing operations so cheaply that independent producers were undersold and outcompeted. Moreover, the FTC claimed that the large oil producers had ensured adequate gasoline supplies for their own gasoline stations while refusing to sell gasoline to independent stations. The FTC concluded that the large oil companies obtained profits that were "substantially in excess of those they would have obtained in a competitively structured market."[71]

In response to the FTC report, Treasury Secretary William Simon took to the airwaves to quote a study prepared by his department's Office of Energy advisor, which characterized the FTC report as incorrect. Later, in 1974, Simon in effect censured information that had previously been available through the Commerce Department concerning the amounts of imported oil on the grounds of national security.

In February 1979 came signs that a new energy crisis was being fabricated. A revolution in Iran, whose production accounted for 5 percent of U.S. imports, cut off oil supplies from that nation. Oil companies and pro-oil politicians immediately began threatening rationing and $1-a-gallon gasoline within a year.[72] The government and large oil companies used the crisis atmosphere to propose various plans that would benefit the oil industry in the deregulation of oil prices: repeal of the law forbidding the export of Alaskan oil (making for more Alaskan crude and a return to full oil production in California), exchange of Alaskan oil for Mexican petroleum, easing of environmental regulations on coal burning, and a slowdown of the phaseout of polluting lead additives in gasoline.[73] All this occurred when the world, and especially the United States, had a surplus of oil. The real losers in all this, of course, are the suspicious but nevertheless manipulated and ripped-off U.S. consumers, voters, and taxpayers.[74]

In early 1991, operations Desert Shield and Desert Storm were also manipulated by major oil companies to raise gasoline prices, resulting in an extra million dollars in profits for the largest firms. Meanwhile, independent oil dealers complained about being unable to obtain oil products and made charges of cheating on oil futures by New York Mercantile Exchange commodity firms and record stock sell-offs by the oil companies themselves.[75] So loud was the outcry over perceived oil company deviance that President George Bush, himself a former oil company executive, felt compelled to warn oil corporations against price gouging. President Bush's warning was perhaps too little too late. The consolidation of power by oil multinationals since the 1970s has created an environment ripe for deviance.

- **Item:** In recent years, many of the nation's largest oil companies either have been found guilty of price-fixing or have settled out of court. Among the payments ordered by the courts in 1988 are the following:[76]

    $2.1 billion by Exxon
    $408 million by AMOCO
    $381 million by Atlantic Richfield
    $660 million by Occidental
    $600 million by Cities Services

- **Item:** The oil companies continue to use the gains made during the energy crisis of the 1970s to further consolidate ownership and control within the energy industry. Oil conglomerates have led the way in the merger movement of the 1980s. Standard Oil of California purchased Gulf Oil for $14 billion; Texaco bought Getty Oil; Du Pont purchased CONOCO; Mobil Oil purchased Superior Oil; Royal Dutch Shell obtained Shell Oil; and Occidental purchased Cities Services. Of the largest twenty corporations in the manufacturing sector of the economy, thirteen are now oil companies.[77]
- **Item:** In 1994, a federal court found that Exxon acted recklessly by permitting Captain Joseph Hazlewood to command the *Exxon Valdez* supertanker in 1988. Hazlewood ran aground in Prince William Sound, Alaska, on March 24, 1988, causing the worst tanker oil spill on the North American continent. Exxon, which has already spent $3.4 billion to clean up the spill, may now be liable for up to an additional $1.5 billion in compensatory damages and $15 billion in punitive damages in this civil case.[78] The case is a direct result of the concessions granted the oil companies during the pseudo-oil "crisis" of the 1970s.

Antitrust Laws

Mills believed that much corporate crime results because it is often good business to break the law. As he said, businesses "obey these laws, when they do, not because they feel that it is morally right, but because they are afraid of being caught." Therefore, such laws "exist without the support of firm moral conviction. It is merely illegal to cheat them, but it is often considered smart to get away with it."[79]

There are several reasons why businesses sometimes consider it smart to break the laws that regulate their activity. First, many laws are ambiguous and contain exemptions and exclusions, leaving a great deal of room for interpretation by the courts. Second, many laws regulating business activity are hardly strict in their penalties. Indeed, many items of business laws are settled in civil rather than criminal courts. Imprisonment under such laws is rare, and the fines imposed for breaking them many times amount to no more than a slap on the wrist. Finally, the enforcement of such laws is often lax because government devotes comparatively few resources to catching corporate offenders. This lack of enforcement can be explained by examining the Sherman Act (1890), the Federal Trade Commission Act (1914), and the Robinson–Patman Act (1936).

The Sherman Act prohibits "unreasonable restraints upon and monopolization of trade."[80] The act also outlaws arrangements that result in price-fixing or limiting access to trade or commerce (for example, dividing markets). However, the act is loaded with exclusions and ambiguities. Thus, the Sherman Act only applies to monopolies in trade (commerce), not to monopolies in manufacturing. Moreover, under a series of cases in 1911 involving American Tobacco and Standard Oil, it was ruled that the act applied only to *unreasonable* trade combinations and did not exclude consolidation per se. The definition of a *reasonable* combination, of course, is a matter of judicial opinion. Under the Sherman Act's price-fixing definitions, businesses that are already regulated by the federal government (such as the Civil Aeronautics Board's regulation of the nation's airlines) are excluded from the law. This exclusion also applies to interstate water carriers, railroads, and trucks. Other loopholes are present in the act, as well. While the act specifies that it is illegal to fix the price of a product by agreement, this practice is legal in states that authorize it under so-called fair laws.[81]

In 1914, the Federal Trade Commission Act was passed, making it unlawful to restrict competition and to engage in unfair and deceptive trade practices. However, the power of the FTC is limited to issuing cease-and-desist orders, which it can do only upon securing the permission of a federal court. The FTC can recommend prosecution of criminal cases, but the Justice Department is specifically charged with this task.

In 1936, the Robinson–Patman Act made it illegal to discriminate between various buyers of products by charging different prices to different buyers. But the act has several limitations. First, it applies only to products, not to services, which are supposedly covered by other laws. In addition, the law specifically exempts U.S. companies that have joined together for purposes of export. The antitrust laws also exempt such items as bank mergers, agricultural cooperatives, and insurance companies, which are unregulated by state laws.[82]

During the Reagan–Bush years, the enforcement of antitrust and other laws designed to control corporate crime became a very low priority. So lax was the enforcement that, by 1982, 60 percent of corporations had failed to pay their fines following conviction or court settlement. As a result, $38 billion in fines were outstanding.[83] Moreover, the Reagan administration made clear its dislike of the very structure of antitrust laws. In 1986, it sent to Congress a package designed, in effect, to repeal some key provisions of the Clayton Act, especially those prohibiting mergers that reduce competition and hence create monopoly. It was proposed that the government prove the *significant probability*, not just the *possibility*, of monopoly before antitrust sanctions could be applied. Federal courts would have had to evaluate proposed mergers, considering not simply their effects on U.S. markets but on world markets as well. Most important, the Reagan proposal allowed a five-year exemption from antitrust laws for corporations found to be seriously injured by imports, especially shoes, steel, and textiles.[84]

The Clinton administration showed the same reluctance to enforce the antitrust laws in a meaningful way. Its one great exception concerns its suit against Microsoft, the computer software giant. Microsoft agreed to stop a number of licensing practices, which will give computer manufacturers more freedom in installing programs from other companies. Microsoft used to receive a royalty for each computer sold, even if operating systems made by other manufacturers that had been installed by manufacturers that had a contract with Microsoft for Microsoft's Windows or DOS operating systems. This discouraged the selling of other operating systems, such as Novell's Dr. DOS or IBM's OS-2. The agreement could give Microsoft more competition for dominance over the personal computer (PC) market.[85]

The Higher Immorality and Corporate Crime

If Mills's view of corporate crime is correct, one would expect two effects: (1) widespread violations of antitrust laws and (2) the presence of attitudes condoning such violations. Ample evidence exists to support both propositions. First, two studies have documented the fact that corporate illegalities are widespread.

- **Item:** Edwin Sutherland, who coined the term *white-collar crime*, studied the illegalities of seventy large corporations from 1890 to 1945. He found that there had been 980 decisions against these corporations. Every corporation had at least 1 decision against it, and the average number of decisions was 14.[86] Criminal courts made 159 of the 980 decisions, 45 were made by courts that were under either civil or equity jurisdiction, and 361 were settled by government commission. Of the seventy corporations studied by Sutherland, thirty either were illegitimate in origin or became involved in illegal activities. Eight others, he found, were probably illegal in origin or in beginning policies. The finding of original illegitimacy was made with respect to twenty-one corporations in formal court decisions from other historical evidence in other cases. What Sutherland's study implies is that 60 percent of the corporations, or forty-two in number, with an average of four convictions each, are habitual criminals.[87]

- **Item:** A study of the largest 582 publicly owned corporations indicated that more than 60 percent of such firms had at least one legal action initiated against them during 1975 and 1976. The 300 parent manufacturing firms in the study had an average of 4.8 actions initiated against them by federal agencies. Yet fewer than 10 percent of the violations resulted in any criminal penalties. Moreover, in less than 1 percent of the federal enforcement actions was a corporate officer sent to jail for failing to carry out corporate legal responsibilities.[88] When a jail term was imposed, "sentences almost never exceeded six months."[89]

Corporate executives seem well aware that many businesspeople engage in either criminal or unethical action. A 1961 survey in the *Harvard Business Review* of some 1,700 businesspersons revealed that four out of seven believed that individuals "would violate a code of ethics when asked and 70 percent of 500 believed that price fixing is a common occurrence in their industries."[90]

Corporate executives and small business persons engage in unethical or illegal behaviors for several other reasons, too. One important factor is the capitalist economic system and its dependence on continued profits and economic growth. When antitrust and other business laws are enforced with such laxness and the penalties involved are so minimal, violations of such laws become rational from a profit standpoint. Quite simply, it is much more profitable to violate such laws than to obey them.

Second, most corporate executives who are caught breaking the law often believe that what they have done does not violate the law in any serious sense. Typically, even though found guilty, they believe that they have not harmed anyone.[91]

Third, corporate criminal behavior, like any other type of behavior, is learned. In the case of corporate executives, it is the corporate environment, not the street gang or the college education, that teaches and sometimes demands the learning of such behavior. A 1973 study by the American Management Association concluded that corporate executives and businesspeople must often sacrifice personal morals and ethics in order to remain in business. "About 70 percent...admit they have been expected, frequently or on occasion, to compromise personal principles in order to conform either to organizational standards or to standards established by their corporate superiors."[92]

In one famous case, the convicted executives made it clear that their motives in fixing prices were to increase the profits for the company and further their own careers.

We did feel that this was the only way to reach part of our goals as rangers.... We couldn't accomplish a greater percent of net profit without getting together with competitors. Part of the pressure was the desire to get ahead and the desire to have the goodwill of the man above you. He had only to get the approval of the man above him to replace you, and if you wouldn't cooperate he could find lots of faults to use to get you out.[93]

As Robert Sherrill recently asked,

When is a crime not officially a crime? Simple: When the laws against that activity are not enforced. Antitrust laws—those almost mythical beings so revered by populists—have been on the books for several generations and are supposed to be used to prevent the kind of concentration of market power that leads to price-fixing and the death of competition.... That's why the Federal Trade Commission used the antitrust laws to block Rite Aid's proposed $1.8 billion purchase of Revco, a combination that would have created the nation's largest drugstore chain. Antitrust laws were used...to pry fines from *Reader's Digest* ($40 million) and U.S. Healthcare ($1.2 million). Nowhere was this clearer than in the aerospace and military industry, where, in one of the largest mergers in U.S. history, Boeing bought McDonnell Douglas to become the only—yes, only—manufacturer of commercial jets in the United States, catapulting it ahead of Lockheed Martin, the number-one military contractor, as the world's largest aerospace company. This pairing-off received the same enthusiastic government support that a series of multibillion-dollar military industry mergers have received from the Clinton Administration over the past four years.

Other industries have been promised the same support. Last June the FTC proposed that antitrust enforcers let cost savings justify mergers that would otherwise be considered illegal because they were anticompetitive.

What's more, the commission adopted new rules that would speed mergers and acquisitions by radically shortening the time the FTC takes to consider cases alleging anticompetitive conduct or consumer fraud.[94]

Penalties: The Double Standard

Corporate officials convicted of price-fixing and other corporate crimes invariably receive light sentences (see Chapter 3). McCormick's data (see endnote 89) demonstrate that the heaviest jail sentence imposed in a price-fixing case from 1890 (the year the Sherman Antitrust Act was passed) until 1969 was sixty days. Actually, it was not until the 1961 electrical conspiracy case (discussed at length in Chapter 3) that any businesspersons "were actually imprisoned purely for price-fixing and monopolization. No individuals were sent to jail until twenty years after the passage of the act."[95] In fact, in almost three-fourths of the cases (73.1 percent), convictions were gained not by the government proving any wrongdoing but by pleas of *nolo contendere,* under which defendants merely refuse to acknowledge guilt, instead of admitting guilt, and accept whatever sentence is imposed, thereby avoiding being labeled criminal by the court. Finally, only 45 percent of the cases under the Sherman Act have been criminal in nature; the majority were tried as civil matters, which involved no jail terms. Of those cases in which jail terms were imposed and actually served, only 2 percent were tried under the Sherman Act, and almost all these came under the act's statutes concerning labor unions. (Unions assisting nonunion labor gain control over a labor market is a violation of section 6 of the Sherman Act.)[96]

The laxness with which antitrust laws are enforced is in part attributable to the meager resources devoted to such enforcement. Within the Justice Department, outside Washington, local federal prosecutors (U.S. attorneys) are charged with enforcement of federal laws. In its ninety-four local offices, there are fewer than 2,000 attorneys for the entire nation, only 200 of whom prosecute fraud cases. At the state level, only 30 of 50 state prosecutors had consumer fraud units. While some white-collar prosecutions can cost more than a million dollars, only 40 state prosecutors had budgets that exceeded a million dollars, while 3 had budgets in excess of $500,000. All state prosecutors combined employ fewer than 7,000 attorneys. (The federal government alone employs more than 10,000 lawyers.)[97]

Public Awareness

Corporate crime, as well as other types of white-collar illegalities, is made worse by the ignorance and unwitting cooperation of the public. This is not to suggest that the public is necessarily stupid or gullible. Rather, it is to confirm the fact that, until very recently, consumer education and violations of law by corporations were not part of the public's general knowledge or specific education in the United States. The nature of profitable crime is such that it is invisible. As Thio has stated, "It may be difficult for the victims to know that they are victimized, even if they want to find out the true nature of their victimization. Grocery shoppers, for example, are hard put to detect unlawful substances [such] as residues of hormones, antibiotics, pesticides, and nitrates in the meat they buy."[98]

Even when corporate criminals are caught and convicted, the news media, which are made up of corporations, have not faithfully reported such incidents. Although many criminologists believe that public shame is a key aspect of criminal penalties,[99] the media have failed to do their part. "Even when prosecutions have resulted in conviction, most of the news media—including *Time* and *Newsweek*, the networks, and *The New York Times*—have failed repeatedly to recognize the importance of adequate reporting and have ignored the cases or have treated them trivially."[100]

The mass media, until recently, have very much underreported corporate criminality. Such reporting may be partially responsible for convincing corporate criminals that the illegal acts that they commit are not real crimes.

Coupled with the large majority of antitrust violations that are tried as civil matters, this means that little stigma and little public shame are associated with such crimes. Whether this will change in the face of growing public resentment of big business is yet an open question. At the moment, it is safe to conclude that antitrust and other corporate violations are the most profitable form of crime and carry little risk of detection and genuine punishment.

Organized Crime and the Business Elite

As a formal matter, *organized crime* is defined as "business enterprises organized for the purpose of making economic gain through illegal activities."[101] We are reminded that organized crime, to be defined as such, must display certain features:

> We have defined organized crime as an integral part of the American social system that brings together (1) a public that demands certain goods and services that are defined as illegal, (2) an organization of individuals who produce or supply those goods and services, and (3) corrupt public officials who protect such individuals for their own profit or gain.[102]

However, for most people, organized crime has taken its meaning over the past twenty years from the television series, books, movies, magazine articles, and congressional hearings (televised no less) on the Mafia, or Cosa Nostra.

The image of organized crime, as presented in the mass media, is that of a secret international organization of Italian and Sicilian gangsters who, through corruption and violence, are successful in exerting their will in every task that they undertake. But the media image of organized crime is misleading, especially when the relationships among legitimate businesspeople, politicians, and syndicate criminals are examined.

That is, an element of the higher immorality in the activities of organized crimes is largely unexplored. The higher immorality applies to organized crime insofar as legitimate corporate and political elites utilize the services of the Mafia (or Cosa Nostra) for unethical or illegal purposes. This takes place when organized crime (1) assists economic and political elites in repressing threats to the established order; (2) assists businesses in profit-making ventures; and/or (3) assists federal officials in carrying out U.S. foreign policy objectives.

Organized Crime and Repression

Organized crime has long assisted certain business and political elites in preventing and/or suppressing the powerless in society. Throughout the 1920s, businesspeople entered into union contract negotiations with gangster-dominated unions in order to insure themselves against upsets of any kind (for example, union unrest). Often businesspeople would join with each other by creating trade associations, and the newly formed associations would negotiate with the gangster-dominated unions. Such organizations kept competition from other businesses not belonging to such associations at a minimum. The costs of such protection were usually passed on to consumers. These activities stabilized markets in small, competitive industries, such as trucking, garments, baking, and cleaning and dyeing. When Prohibition ended, gangsters moved into the movie industry using these same tactics.[103]

Mafia figures have been recruited by businesses and politicians to quell labor unrest in a variety of settings.

- **Item:** In the 1940s, Detroit automobile companies used gangsters to suppress efforts to unionize the auto industry. Gangsters such as D'Anna and Adonnis were given a monopoly over the haul-away business at the Ford Motor Company in return for gaining control of the autoworker unions in the city. And even after the American Federation of Labor (AFL) succeeded in unionizing the auto industry, Ford still hired mobsters to act as strike breakers. In 1945 and 1946, there were 41,750 strikes in the United States, more than in the previous ten years combined, so the need for strike breakers was clear. Use of gangsters for this purpose was curtailed in the 1950s as unions supported governmental policies related to the Cold War, and militant unionism, often associated with communism, declined.[104]
- **Item:** During the late 1930s and early 1940s, the International Longshoreman's Association (ILA) was infiltrated by organized criminals in New York Harbor. The docks of New York Harbor are made up of very narrow piers and gridiron street layouts, and congestion is a continual problem. Such congested conditions make it easy to disrupt traffic on the docks. These peculiar physical conditions were part of the reason why gangsters were hired to infiltrate the local ILA. Because of the congestion, drivers did not bring their own loaders to the docks. Rather, loaders were hired at the pier. Loaders could be hired only through loading bosses, who were ILA union members. Bosses charged high prices for using the labor that they controlled, and a syndicate organization, Varick Enterprises, Inc., dominated this trade by charging all truckers a per-ton tax, whether they used the loaders or not. While standardized rates were eventually worked out, the Varick organization, along with the ILA and the local Tammany Hall political machine, kept control of the loading and other rackets along the docks.
- **Item:** In the late 1930s, the West Coast ILA was a so-called clean union headed by a labor radical named Harry Bridges. Bridges had taken his union out of the ranks of the AFL to the Congress of Industrial Organi-

zations (CIO), an act of militant independence. Fearing such independence, as well as the strong socialist sentiment among some New York dock workers, mobster Albert Anastasia murdered Peter Panto, a radical longshoreman leader, who worked on the Brooklyn docks. Militant left-wing union activity continued throughout the 1940s until 1951, when more than a million trade unionists from twelve unions (one-fifth of the CIO membership) were expelled from the CIO in response to the Report of the Investigation of Communism in New York City Distributive Trades.

Other brutal attacks on union dissidents by mobsters occurred throughout the 1940s. This fear concerning socialism within the U.S. labor movement is responsible for the persistence of organized crime's involvement in labor racketeering and violence, at the behest of certain corporate elites. Of course, "both employers and unions have hired gangsters to help them in industrial disputes. It has been employers who have benefited the most. One of the underlying factors was a desire to keep real wages down, and the constant use of terror to destroy rank and file organizations was condoned because of the general American fear of radicalism in the docks, so crucial to the working of the system."[105]

Labor unions are not the only entities that have been repressed by syndicate criminals. Some sociologists feel that organized crime has significantly contributed to the control of U.S. ghettos. Michael Tabor has argued that a conspiracy exists in the U.S. ghetto between organized crime and the police, who are corrupted by organized criminals. Tabor's analysis centers on the role of organized crime in the distribution of heroin in ghetto areas. His contention is that the selling of heroin and the creation of a small army of heroin addicts within the ghetto keep persons who might otherwise challenge the existing social order strung out on dope and in a state of perpetual escapism from inhumane ghetto conditions.[106]

Moreover, Stephen Spitzer has argued that organized crime helps to control problem populations in a number of ways. First, organized crime creates a parallel opportunity structure, a means of employment in illegal activities for persons who might otherwise be unemployed and possibly politically discontent. The goods and services provided by organized crime to the underclasses in society do deflect their energies from the sources of their oppression.[107] In this view, organized crime, insofar as it gains a monopoly over illegal goods and services, actually aids and maintains the public order because monopoly brings with it security that one will make profits and as a result lessens the need for violence.

There is some evidence that the theses of both Tabor and Spitzer are correct. We know that heroin addiction is highly concentrated in the ghetto areas of the United States and that certain illegitimate gambling activities (such as numbers running) not only give poor people a source of hope that they will become wealthy but also provide a source of employment. The *New York Times* has estimated, for example, that the numbers racket employs thousands of people in Harlem alone.[108]

Organized Crime and Profits

Aside from aiding with the control of so-called problem populations, organized crime has increased the profits for certain legitimate businesses. The most obvious source of profit provided by organized crime is as an important customer of corporations. For example, it was estimated that, by 1940, bookies were the fifth-largest customer of AT&T.[109] Moreover, the members of organized crime are themselves consumers of many goods and services. Given the $50 to $80 billion estimates of organized criminal enterprise, the amount of money spent by syndicate members as both capitalists and consumers serves as a rather significant market. As Quinney has stated,

> Organized crime and legitimate businesses may mutually assist one another, as in regulating prices or commodities or enforcing labor contracts. Interdependence between the underworld of crime and the upper world of business ensures that both systems will be maintained. Mutual assistance accompanied by the profit motive provides assured immunity.
>
> Organized crime has grown into a huge business in the United States and is an integral part of the political economy. Enormous amounts of illegitimate money are passed annually into socially acceptable endeavors. An elaborate corporate and financial structure is now tied to organized crime.[110]

The reach of underworld business is extensive, in terms of both economic and social impact. Organized crime remains a billion-dollar-a-year untaxed business in the United States. It includes the traditional Italian–Sicilian Cosa Nostra, as well as numerous motorcycle gangs and drug-profiteering organizations of other origin. Despite 1,200 Mafia convictions made during the 1980s, organized crime remains a powerful force in American life.

The most powerful crime family is the Genovese family of Manhattan. Their profits come through infiltration of labor unions (for example, the Teamsters), waterfront ports, and fish markets (New York's Fulton) through domination of the ILA casinos in Atlantic City and Las Vegas; bid rigging on local construction projects; and selling stolen jewelry ("swag") to Manhattan jewelry exchanges (after which it is resold to the public).[111]

There is also evidence that a number of large corporations (for example, in the 1960s, Pan American Airways and the Howard Hughes Corporation) have entered into partnership with organized crime in a number of gambling casinos and resort ventures in both Las Vegas and the Caribbean.[112] Apparently, certain members of the corporate elite are not above obtaining capital from organized crime for purposes of expanding markets. It is not known how much capital has come from criminal syndicates for ventures of this type, but, as mentioned in Chapter 1, obtaining such capital is now against the law under the Racketeer Influenced and Corrupt Organizations (RICO) Act.

Unquestionably the most important contemporary organized crime phenomenon is global organized crime. [113] The end of the Cold War created new opportunities for transnational organized crime. "Transparent national borders, fewer trade restrictions, and truly global financial and telecommunications systems provide significant opportunities for criminal organizations to expand operations beyond national boundaries."[114] Russian organized crime has formed an unholy alliance with Sicilian, Asian, Mexican, and Colombian syndicates, and the results are devastating:[115]

- In Russia, thousands of poorly guarded nuclear warheads and hundreds of unsafe reactors (20,000 safety violations during 1993 inspections and 78 shutdowns for safety reasons) are rusting away on the Soviet fleet, many with nuclear fuel aboard. The Russian Academy of Sciences estimated in 1995 that the Russian Mafiya now owns 50–80 percent of all voting stock in Russia's legitimate corporations.[116]
- Drug cartels from Colombia, Russia, Italy, Japan, and China instantly transfer huge sums around the world with "wire" (actually satellite) transfers, using offshore banks. The cartels manipulate accounts drawn in the names of "shell" corporations. The economies of a number of tiny sovereign nations, like the Cayman Islands, are completely dependent on laundering transactions.

Organized crime groups from the former Soviet Union, Asia, and Italy are forming partnerships among themselves as well as with the drug barons of Latin America. All syndicates are engaging in corruption on a grand scale.

- In 1995, more than 6,000 Italian bureaucrats, corporate executives, and politicians (among them a staggering 438 deputies and senators) were under investigation or had been indicted on various corruption charges. One estimate is that the Mafia has paid $140 billion in bribes to executives and officials over the past decade. On March 2, 1995, seven-time prime minister Giulio Andreotti was indicted for being a "made member" of the Italian Mafia.[117]
- The Colombian cartels now trade cocaine to the Italian Mafia in exchange for heroin. The Columbian Cali cartel now earns $4 billion annually from cocaine and has invested hundreds of millions in banks in Russia, Europe, and the United States.
- In Mexico,[118] the former Mexican federal deputy attorney general Eduardo Valle Espinosa resigned his official post in frustration in May 1996 and estimated that at least half of Mexico's federal police chiefs and

attorney generals receive illegal payoffs from drug dealers. Some police chief candidates now pay $1 to $2 million just to get hired; from 1988 to 1994, the brother of the former president of Mexico transferred more than $80 million from a Citibank (a U.S. bank) branch in Mexico through Citibank's New York headquarters to a secret Swiss bank account. Mexico's chief drug czar had to resign in 1997 when it was learned that he had ties to Mexico's drug cartel.

- Of the approximately 1.5 million U.S. vehicles stolen each year, several hundred thousand are illegally exported out of the country to Central America and Eastern Europe. One Columbian criminal, Gabriel Taboada, testified at a U.S. Senate committee hearing that he bribed diplomats, who are exempt from paying duty on imported cars, "to import cars in their name."[119] The diplomats were paid $25,000 to $50,000 per car.

Approximately $500 billion in currency is laundered annually utilizing various global financial institutions, making money laundering the third-largest industry in the world. Federal law requires that banks report all cash deposits of $10,000 or more to the IRS. In 1975, only 3,000 such activities were reported. By 1988, 5.5 million were reported annually. It is now estimated that the total amount of drug money laundered each year is an immense $300 billion, about half of all funds connected to the worldwide drug trade. Of this amount, $100 billion is laundered in the United States. Nine-tenths of this amount ends up overseas, often in secret Swiss accounts, from which it can then be freely moved. This outflow of money contributes substantially to the nation's foreign trade deficit.[120]

The largest money-laundering operation ever uncovered took place in 1989. U.S. banks were used to ship $1 billion a year to cocaine traffickers. The drug profits were disguised as stemming from phony front businesses (wholesale gold and jewelry) run largely out of Los Angeles. Another money-laundering investigation in 1990, Operation Polar Cap, resulted in the freezing of hundreds of bank accounts in 173 American banks, more than half of which were in New York and Florida. The accounts contained some $400 million in Colombian drug profits. Other sources of laundered money are storefront check-cashing and money-transmitting services, most of which are unlicensed and run by newly arrived or illegal immigrants. Most of these are in states with only a few regulators, who are thus unable to keep up with the growth of such businesses. This is especially true of Florida, Texas, New York, and California. Each year such operations take billions in cash from drug dealers and send it overseas. These storefront operations also defraud honest customers by failing to send their money to requested addressees. Many customers cannot complain because they are either newly arrived immigrants ignorant of the law or illegals.[121]

A number of major U.S. banks have been more than willing to overlook the IRS reporting requirement, sometimes receiving a 1.5 to 2 percent commission from drug-trafficking depositors for doing so. Other sources of money laundering are investment firms, such as Shearson/American Express and Merrill Lynch, and jewelry wholesalers.

- **Item:** In the 1980s, the famous Pizza Connection case resulted in the conviction of more than 400 Mafia members in Sicily and the United States on numerous charges, including heroin trafficking. The Pizza Connection cons laundered tens of millions of dollars in cash through a number of New York City banks. The banks then electronically wired the millions of dollars into secret accounts in Swiss banks so that they could not be traced. The Pizza Connection traffickers also deposited $5 million in cash with the Merrill Lynch brokerage firm in $5, $10, and $20 bills over a six-week period. Merrill Lynch not only accepted these dubious deposits, but it also provided the couriers transporting the money with extra security. The same couriers also laundered $13.5 million through accounts at the E. F. Hutton & Co. investment firm, which also provided security for them.
- **Item:** The CIA and the Mafia played an important role in establishing the World Finance Corporation. This Florida company laundered drug money and supported terrorist activities in the early 1970s.

Organized crime in the 1990s has become an active force on Wall Street, forming partnerships with investment houses and other financial institutions for illegal purposes. The American Mafia has established a network of stock promoters, securities dealers, and the all-important "boiler rooms" that sell stocks nationwide through hard-sell cold calling.

- Four Mafia families, as well as elements of the Russian Mafia, directly own or control perhaps two dozen brokerage firms that make markets in hundreds of stocks. Other securities dealers and traders are believed to pay extortion money or "tribute" to the Mob as just another cost of doing business on Wall Street.
- Using offshore accounts in the Bahamas and elsewhere, the Mob has engineered lucrative schemes involving low-priced stock under Regulation S of the securities laws. Organized-crime members profit from the run-up in such stocks and also from short-selling the stocks on the way down. They also take advantage of the very wide spreads between the bid and ask prices of the stock issues controlled by their confederates.
- The Mob's activities seem confined almost exclusively to stocks traded in the over-the-counter "bulletin board" and NASDAQ small-cap markets. By contrast, New York Stock Exchange and American Stock Exchange issues and firms apparently have been free of Mob exploitation.

Wall Street has become so lucrative for the Mob that it is allegedly a major source of income for high-level members of organized crime, few of whom have ever been publicly identified as having ties to Wall Street. Don Abramo, who may well be the most active reputed mobster on Wall Street, has remained completely out of the public eye, even staying active on Wall Street after his recent conviction for tax evasion.

All these endeavors require the cooperation and corruption of corporations, government regulators, and banks. These entities are not pawns in the hands of organized criminal syndicates, but part of its fabric.[122] The illegal drug business, both domestically and internationally, cannot exist without the willing participation of money-laundering banks and corrupt public officials, and these legitimate outlets are a major part of America's crime and drug problems.

Organized Crime and the Political Elite

In 1975, revelations by the Senate Intelligence Committee disclosed the hiring of organized crime members by the CIA in the 1960s for the express purpose of assassinating Premier Fidel Castro of Cuba.[123] Thus, organized crime (at certain times, at least) has functioned as an instrument of U.S. foreign policy.

Such activities allegedly began during World War II when the underworld figures in control of the New York docks were contacted by Navy intelligence officials in order to ensure that German submarines or foreign agents did not infiltrate the area. It was thought that waterfront pimps and prostitutes could act as a sort of counterintelligence corps. The man whose aid was sought for this purpose was Lucky Luciano; he was reportedly very successful in preventing sabotage or any other outbreaks of trouble on the New York docks during the war. Following his arrest and conviction for compulsory prostitution in 1936, Luciano was granted parole and given exile for life in 1954 in exchange for the aid he provided during the war.

Mafiosi assistance was also enlisted in other war-related efforts. Some locals were used by the Allies during the invasion of Sicily in 1943. Vito Genovese, a New York gangster, who had earlier escaped to Italy to avoid a murder charge, became an "unofficial advisor to the American military government."[124] After the war, local Mafiosi were installed as mayors in many locations in Sicily because they were antisocialist. And in France in 1950, the CIA recruited a Corsican gangster, Ferri-Pisani, to form an elite terror squad for use on the Marseilles docks. Socialist dock workers had refused to move shipments of U.S. arms bound for use in Vietnam in support of the French military effort there. Corsican gangsters were also used to assault the picket lines of communist unions in France and to harass union officials. The concession granted these international criminals in exchange for such aid was the privilege of using Marseilles as the center for Corsican heroin traffic. In Pearce's words, "The CIA had helped build the French Connection."[125]

In Cuba, it is known that the dictator Fulgencio Batista allowed Mafia financier Meyer Lansky to set up gambling casinos in Havana in 1933. Following Castro's closing of the casinos in the early 1960s, organized crime figures were recruited by the CIA to aid in assassinating Castro. In Vietnam in the 1960s and early 1970s, organized crime figures cooperated with the CIA in setting up Asia's Golden Triangle, Southeast Asia's center for heroin distribution. This triangle stretches for some 150,000 square miles across northeast Burma, northern Thailand, and northern Laos. The CIA's involvement included transporting opium using its own airline, Air America.[126]

Organized crime has long served as a source of campaign funds for political elites on virtually every level of U.S. politics—local, state, and national.[127] At the national level, opposing organized crime factions appear to be linked to opposing political parties. For example, following the presidential election in 1968, the Nixon administration undertook a campaign against organized crime. This campaign was, in fact, directed at those elements of organized crime most closely allied with Nixon's Democratic opponents, especially Meyer Lansky. Under pressure from investigations by the FBI and IRS, Lansky sold his Las Vegas casino interests to Howard Hughes and his Miami-based bank interest to Nixon confidant Bebe Rebozo. In the meantime, Teamsters Union leaders made an arrangement with the Nixon White House that resulted in clemency for jailed Teamsters chief Jimmy Hoffa in return for a campaign contribution. Also, Nixon was promised the availability of Teamsters pension funds should hush money be needed to silence the Watergate burglars.

The final attack on the Lansky faction of organized crime was a result of the Nixon administration's war on drugs. The Republicans tried to close off Lansky's heroin sources by pressuring the Turkish government to enforce laws against growing opium. Between 1969 and 1973, the amount of opium brought from Turkey into the United States fell by 50 percent. Efforts against Lansky's Latin American opium suppliers were also instituted.

By the early 1970s, Southeast Asia's Golden Triangle had become a major new heroin source for the U.S. organized crime syndicate of Santos Trafficante, Jr., a Lansky rival in the heroin trade. Trafficante had ties to both the Nixon White House and the Laotian Chiu Chow syndicate, a major opium source in Southeast Asia and the owner of the Laotian Pepsi Cola Company, whose U.S. counterpart had longtime ties to the Nixon organization.[128]

These illustrations have led some criminologists to conclude that organized crime has served and continues to serve the domestic and foreign political goals of the U.S. political and economic elites. Finally, it is important to understand that, despite recent convictions of aging godfathers in New York and Sicily, organized crime is in key respects stronger than ever. Virtually all the illegal gambling and drug trade remain intact.[129]

There is ample evidence now of links between traditional Italian–Sicilian organized crime and international drug smugglers from Colombia and Mexico, who import cocaine and heroin. Nontraditional organized crime groups in the United States, including the Japanese Yakuza, the Hell's Angels motorcycle gang, Jamaican and Chinese-American vice groups, and many street gangs made up of numerous minority groups, also have ties to the Mafia through illegal drug trade, prostitution, and gambling.[130] (These links are further explored in Chapter 9.)

Certainly, illegal drug trafficking has proved much more intractable than nearly anyone had believed. A chief reason for the tenacity of the drug trade is the corruption of and cooperation with legitimate political and at times economic elites by organized criminal syndicates, which are now an integral portion of the higher immorality.

Conclusion

This chapter has discussed a series of acts that involves the exercise of elite power. C. Wright Mills coined the term *higher immorality* to denote what he felt was systematic corruption among the U.S. economic and political elite. The features of the higher immorality discussed are unique in that most of the acts are not against the law. Indeed, certain types of executive compensation, including expense accounts and stock options, corporate income taxes, and government subsidies to businesses and wealthy individuals, represent special favors that elites have secured for themselves by the passage of special legislation and are therefore perfectly legal.

But what is legal is not necessarily moral or just. Consider the tax situation for a moment. In 1972, Stern estimated that of the $77.3 billion in tax favors granted by the federal government, only $92 million in loopholes went to the nation's 6 million poorest families, while twenty-four times that amount went to 3,000 families with incomes over $1 million.[131] Another study by economist Joseph Peckham concluded that people who earned less than $2,000 per year paid 44 percent of their incomes in state, federal, and local taxes. People earning $2,000 to $15,000 paid about 27 percent of their incomes for these various taxes, and those who earned over $15,000 paid about 38 percent of their incomes for taxes.

Thus, the highest tax rates were paid by the lowest income group, and the second-highest rates were paid by the highest group. This violates the spirit of U.S. tax laws, which are supposedly based on the ability to pay.[132] These examples indicate that individuals of power and wealth are able to influence the law for their personal benefit.[133]

The consequences of tax loopholes are serious. First, such privilege creates cynicism among the majority of taxpayers, who are very much aware that the nation's tax laws favor the rich and powerful. Second, special loopholes for the wealthy create larger government deficits and increase inflation by billions of dollars per year. Third, government subsidies, which go largely to big businesses, violate the basic principles of free enterprise. Why, for example, should Lockheed and Chrysler be allowed loan guarantees to ensure that they will remain in business while only about one in ten of the new businesses begun in this country survives more than five years on average?[134]

We also discussed how political and economic elites attempted to convince the public of the reality of the energy crisis of the 1970s. Yet, when one looks at the facts, as well as at who profited from this so-called crisis, such reality becomes suspect. The energy crisis clearly resulted in huge increases in oil company profits, elimination of competition from independent oil dealers, and fuel bill increases for the billions for consumers serviced by multinational oil companies. Even the government's own studies indicated that the energy crisis of 1973–1974 was due to the oil companies' anticompetitive practices, not to a genuine shortage of crude oil. Such manipulation by elites, involving the creation of favorable media images of their activities and the suppression of important facts, is not illegal unless lied about under oath. Yet how many people consider such activities moral, ethical, or just?

Finally, we described the long history of goods and services provided to political and economic elites by members of organized criminal syndicates. Members of Mafia families have suppressed labor unions, lower-class ghetto dwellers, and anticapitalist political movements; provided capital for certain business ventures; and, on numerous occasions, aided political elites in the execution of U.S. foreign and military policy. In return for such services and capital, certain elites have allowed the activities of organized criminal syndicates to grow and prosper. This, in turn, has contributed to the flourishing of the drug trade in many cities, as well as the corruption of politicians on all levels by organized U.S. crime members (see Chapter 6). The use of capital from illegal businesses is now against the law. And the CIA suffered no little embarrassment when it was revealed that Mafia members had been recruited to assassinate Fidel Castro. Thus, the use of organized criminal syndicates to further the goals of economic and political elites contributes to criminal activity at all levels of U.S. society and occasionally results in scandal for elites. This contributes further to the decline of public confidence in elite rule.

While many of the activities that constitute the higher immorality are not illegal, they are widely regarded as unethical and often possess serious consequences for nonelites. Our discussion tends to confirm Mills's thesis that the higher immorality is an institutionalized feature of the elite power in the United States. Certainly, our discussion of the savings and loan scandal demonstrated that all the behaviors described in this chapter are still central to the deviance of the power elite.

Critical Thinking Exercise 2.1: The Higher Immorality _____

Look up the categories having to do with corporate crime in the latest complete *New York Times Index* or the *Wall Street Journal Index*. These categories include the following:

1. Antitrust violations
2. Pollution law violations

3. False advertising
4. Fraud
5. Sexual harassment

Do you notice any patterns with respect to which industries have the most violations? Many violations take place in the petroleum, automobile, and drug industries. Do these firms serve as models of corporate behavior for others? Were any specific corporations involved in more than one violation?

Endnotes

1. C. Wright Mills, "A Diagnosis of Our Moral Uneasiness," in *Power, Politics, and People,* ed. I. H. Horowitz (New York: Ballantine, 1963), 331.

2. Barry Kreisberg, *Crime and Privilege* (Englewood Cliffs, NJ: Prentice Hall, 1975), 4. For a brief historical view of the higher immorality and corporate crime, see also S. Balkan et al., *Crime and Deviance in America* (Belmont, CA: Wadsworth, 1980), 182–84.

3. C. Wright Mills, "Plain Talk on Fancy Sex," in *Power, Politics, and People,* ed. I. H. Horowitz (New York: Ballantine, 1963), 324–29. For remarks by some expense account girls themselves, see Elizabeth I. Ray, *The Washington Fringe Benefit* (New York: Dell, 1976). The service Ray performed while on the payroll of Congressman Wayne Hayes touched off a scandal in Washington that resulted in Hayes leaving Congress. Ray's story closely parallels Mills's description of the goals and means of the expense account girl. An anonymous article "The Corporation Prostitute," in Judson Landis, *Sociology: Concepts and Characteristics,* 4th ed. (Belmont, CA: Wadsworth, 1980), 354–59, claims that some corporations hire prostitutes on a permanent basis for help in closing a variety of deals, including bidding on factory sites, mergers with other companies, political lobbying, undercutting competitors, gathering stockholder proxy votes, and securing oil leases (ibid., 355).

4. Michael M. Thomas, "The Greatest American Shambles," *New York Review of Books,* January 31, 1991, 30. This article is a first-rate review of seven leading books on the S&L scandal; it is highly recommended as an overview of the crisis.

5. Robert Sherrill, "The Looting Decade: S&Ls, Big Banks, and Other Triumphs of Capitalism," *The Nation,* November 19, 1990, 594.

6. R. Dan Brumbaugh, Jr., *Thrifts under Siege* (Cambridge, MA: Ballinger, 1988), 12.

7. Stephen Pizzo, Mary Fricker, and Paul Muolo, *Inside Job: The Looting of America's Savings and Loans* (New York: McGraw-Hill, 1989), 12.

8. Ibid., 12–13; and Sherrill, 589.

9. Michael Waldman, *Who Robbed America: Citizen's Guide to the Savings and Loan Scandal* (New York: Random House, 1990), 35.

10. *San Diego Union,* April 3, 1991, A-2.

11. The following is taken from Frank Hagan and David Simon, "Elite Deviance in the Bush Era," *Justice Professional,* 1997.

12. Curtis Lang, "Blue Sky and Big Bucks," *Southern Exposure* 1, Spring 1989, 24; Steve Hedges and Gordon Witkin, "The Bulletproof Villains," *U.S. News & World Report,* July 23, 1990, 18; and Rich Thomas, "Feast of the S&L Vultures," *Newsweek,* July 30, 1990, 40.

13. "RTC Target of Stinging Critique," *Seattle Times,* June 11, 1991, B-1, B-8.

14. L. J. Davis, "Chronicle of a Debacle Foretold," *Harper's,* September 1990, 64; and Alan Farnham, "The S&L Felons," *Fortune,* November 5, 1990, 90–108. Farnham notes, for the sake of comparison, that the Credit Mobilier scandal of the Grant era (1870s) cost $243 million in 1990 dollars, the Teapot Dome scandal of the 1920s cost a mere $3 million, and the Billy Sol Estes swindles of the 1950s cost $102 million.

15. See James Glassman, "The Great Bank Robbery: Deconstructing the S&L Crisis," *New Republic,* October 6, 1990, 16–21; "Looking for New S&L Culprits," *Newsweek,* November 26, 1990, 55–56; Steve Weinberg, "The Mob, the CIA, and the S&L Scandal: Does Pete Brewton's Story Check Out?" *Columbia Journalism Review,* November/December 1990, 33; and Steve Pizzo et al., *Inside Job: The Looting of America's Savings and Loans* (New York: HarperCollins), 466–71.

16. Examples in this section are based on Pizzo et al., 466–71.

17. Susan Carland and Mark Lewin, "Centrust, the Saudi, and the Luxembourg Bank," *Business Week,* August 27, 1990, 36–37; Douglas Fritz, "Lax Rules Blamed in Bank Schemes," *Los Angeles Times,* April 28, 1991, A-20, A-22; and James Bates, "BCCI: Behind the Bank Scandal," *Los Angeles Times,* July 30, 1991, D-1.

18. Sara Fritz and Joel Havemann, "Early Signs of BCCI Scandal Were Ignored," *Los Angeles Times,* August 4, 1991, A-1, A-10–11; Jonatha Beaty and S. C. Gwynn, "The Dirtiest Bank of All," *Time,* July 29, 1991, 42–47; and John Greenwald, "Feeling the Heat," *Time,* August 5, 1991, 44–46.

19. Steve Pizzo and Paul Muolo, "Take the Money and Run," *New York Times Magazine,* May 10, 1993, 26.

20. See Frank Hagan and David R. Simon, "Crimes of the Bush Era," presented at the 1993 meeting of the American Society of Criminology, Phoenix, Arizona.

21. See, for example, the evidence assembled in Peter Dale Scott et al. (eds.), *The Assassinations: Dallas and Beyond: A Guide to Cover-ups and Investigations* (New York: Random House, 1976), 353–524; Colonel L. Fletcher Prouty, *The Secret Team: The CIA and Its Allies in Control of the United States and the World* (Englewood Cliffs, NJ: Prentice Hall, 1973); Robert Groden and Harrison Livingston, *High Treason: The Assassination of John F. Kennedy and the New Evidence of Conspiracy* (New York: Berkeley Books, 1990), especially 273–465; and, most recently, Peter Dale Scott, *Deep Politics and the JFK Assassination* (Berkeley: University of California Press, 1993).

22. Mills, "A Diagnosis of Our Moral Uneasiness," 334.

23. S. Lynne Walker, "Pickets Protest GenDyn Bonuses," *San Diego Union,* May 30, December 2, 1991.

24. Peter Phillips and Project Censored, *Censored 2000: The Year's Top 25 Stories* (New York: Seven Stories, 2000), 115.

25. Ellen Schwartz and Suzanne Stoddard, *Taking Back Our Lives in the Age of Corporate Dominance* (San Francisco: Berrett-Koehler, 2000), 18–19.

26. Derek Bok, *The Cost of Talent: How Executives and Professionals Are Paid and How It Affects America* (New York: Free Press, 1993), 96.

27. "The Flap over Executive Pay," *Business Week,* May 6, 1991, 90–96.

28. Bok, 111; and Mein O'Reilley, "CEO Compensation as Tournament and Social Comparison: A Tale of Two Theories," *Administrative Science Quarterly* 330, 257.

29. P. Blumberg, "Another Day, Another $3,000: Executive Rip-off in Corporate America," *Dissent* 2, Spring 1978, 159.

30. "It Ain't Hay, But Is It Clover?" *Forbes,* June 9, 1980, 116–48.

31. Ibid., 164.

32. See, for example, Charles Derber, *Money, Murder, and the American Dream: Winding from Wall Street to Main Street* (Boston: Faber & Faber, 1992), 97–99; Charles Stein, "What Bok Really Thinks," *Boston Globe,* December 14, 1993, 78; and Donald Kanter and Philip Mirvis, *The Cynical Americans* (San Francisco: Jossey-Bass, 1989), 27–40.

33. See, for example, F. Lundberg, *The Rich and the Super-Rich* (New York: Bantam, 1968), 433–35.

34. D. Tussing, "The Dual Welfare System," *Society* 2, January/February 1974, 50–58.

35. Mark Zepezzaur and Arthur Naiman, *Take the Rich Off Welfare* (Tucson, AZ: Odionian, 1996), 6.

36. Ibid., 4–5.

37. *USA Today,* July 2, 1985, 5-B. See also H. Rodgers, "Welfare Policies for the Rich," *Dissent* 2, Spring 1978, 141; Gary Hart, "The Economy Is Decaying: The Free Lunch Is Over," *New York Times,* April 21, 1975; and Jesse Jackson, "Courage of Conviction: The Call of Con-

science," in *Individualism and Commitment in American Life*, ed. Robert Bellah et al. (New York: Harper & Row, 1987), 363.

38. See Donald Bartlett and James Steele, *America: Who Really Pays the Taxes* (New York: Touchstone/Simon & Schuster), 24.

39. Ibid., 144–45.

40. For valuable discussions on these issues, see Philip Stern, *The Rape of the Taxpayer* (New York: Random House, 1973), 214, 232; and Frank Ackerman, *Reaganomics: Rhetoric vs. Reality* (Boston: South End Press, 1982), 50–54.

41. Bartlett and Steele, 140–49.

42. *The Foundation Directory*, 11th ed. (New York: The Foundation Center, 1987), xiv.

43. Lundberg, 292.

44. Examples cited in Ovid Demaris (New York: Harper's Magazine Press, 1974) 303–304.

45. Examples cited in Demaris, 317–18.

46. Michael Parenti, *Democracy for the Few*, 2nd ed. (New York: St. Martin's Press, 1977), 76.

47. Ibid.

48. E. Currie and J. Skolnick, *America's Problems: Social Issues and Public Policy* (Boston: Little, Brown, 1984), 138–39.

49. Cited in Parenti, 77.

50. Ira Katznelson and Mark Kesselman, *The Politics of Power* (New York: Harcourt, Brace, Jovanovich, 1975), 142.

51. Al Gore, *From Red Tape to Results: Creating a Government That Works Better and Costs Less* (Washington, DC: U.S. Government Printing Office), 98.

52. Ibid., 20.

53. Martin L. Gross, *The Government Racket: Washington Waste from A to Z* (New York: Bantam), 179–81.

54. Ibid., 136.

55. Ibid., 206.

56. Ibid.

57. Gore, 105–6.

58. Sidney Lens, "Socialism for the Rich," *The Progressive* 91, September 1975, 14.

59. Cited in Donald McDonald, "Militarism in America," in Robert Perrucci and Mark Pilisuk, *The Triple Revolution Emerging* (Boston: Little, Brown, 1971), 42 (originally appeared in *The Center Magazine* 3, January 1, 1970).

60. Office of Management and Budget, *The United States Budget in Brief* (Washington, DC: U.S. Government Printing Office, 1988), 41.

61. Mills, "A Diagnosis of Our Moral Uneasiness," 338.

62. David Mermelstein, "The 'Energy Crisis,'" in *The Economic Crisis Reader*, ed. D. Mermelstein (New York: Random House, 1975), 268.

63. Cited in Demaris, 228. The oil-depletion allowance was repealed in 1975.

64. Dave Pugh and Mitch Zimmerman, "The 'Energy Crisis' and the Real Crisis Behind It," in *The Economic Crisis Reader*, ed. D. Mermelstein (New York: Random House, 1975), 275–76.

65. See G. David Garson, *Power and Politics in the United States* (Lexington, MA: D.C. Heath, 1977), 251–52. See also Robert Scheer, *America after Nixon: The Age of the Multinationals* (New York: McGraw-Hill, 1974), 143.

66. Michael Tanzer, "The International Oil Crisis: A Tightrope between Depression and War," in *The Economic Crisis Reader*, ed. D. Mermelstein (New York: Random House, 1975), 293–94 (originally appeared in *Social Police* 5, November–December 1974).

67. K. Dolbeare and M. Edelman, *American Politics*, 3rd ed. (Lexington, MA: D.C. Heath, 1977), 5.

68. Pugh and Zimmerman, 257.

69. Demaris, 229. The above examples of oil company profit sources due to the crisis are based on Demaris's discussion, 229–49.

70. S. F. Singer, "The Oil Crisis That Isn't," *New Republic,* February 24, 1979, 13.

71. Cited in Demaris, 228–29.

72. Ibid., 229.

73. See Alexander Cockburn and James Ridgeway, "The Worst Domino," *Village Voice,* February 19, 1979, 1, 7–8.

74. See Singer, 14–15.

75. See, for example, *New York Times,* December 26, 1990, D-127; December 1990, D-2; January 1, 1991, 1–53; January 22, 1991, 111–14; January 29, 1991, D-8; and *Wall Street Journal,* October 3, 1990, C-1; September 7, 1990, A-3; January 16, 1991, C-13.

76. *Wall Street Journal,* October 20, 1988, 1.

77. Thomas Dye, *Who's Running America?* 4th ed. (Englewood Cliffs, NJ: Prentice Hall, 1986), 175–76.

78. *New York Times,* June 14, 1994, A-1, A-8.

79. Mills, "A Diagnosis of Our Moral Uneasiness," 335–36.

80. J. G. Vancise, *The Federal Antitrust Laws,* 3rd rev. ed. (Washington, DC: American Enterprise Institute, 1979), 7.

81. August Bequai, *White Collar Crime: A 20th Century Crisis* (Lexington, MA: D.C. Heath, 1978), 96.

82. Ibid., 100–1.

83. Robert Sherrill, "White-Collar Thuggery," *The Nation,* November 28, 1988, 573.

84. *Newsweek,* January 27, 1986, 46.

85. See *San Francisco Chronicle,* July 17, 1994, C-1, C-4.

86. Quoted in Lundberg, 137.

87. E. Sutherland, "Crime of Corporations," in *White-Collar Crime,* rev. ed., ed. G. Geis and R. F. Meier (New York: Free Press), 73.

88. M. B. Clinard, *Illegal Corporate Behavior* (Washington, DC: Law Enforcement Assistance Administration, 1979), 108.

89. A. E. McCormick, "Rule Enforcement and Moral Indignation: Some Observations on Antitrust Convictions upon the Societal Reaction Process," *Social Problems* 25, October 1977, 34.

90. Bequai, 148–50.

91. National Council on Crime and Delinquency, *Criminal Justice News Letter* 7, March 26, 1979, 2.

92. Cited in A. Rogow, *The Dying of the Light* (New York: Putnam, 1975), 89.

93. M. Green et al., *The Closed Enterprise System* (New York: Grossman, 1972), 149, 150, 472.

94. Sherrill, "White-Collar Thuggery," 573.

95. M. Clinard and R. Quinney, *Criminal Behavior Systems: A Typology,* 2nd ed. (New York: Holt, Rinehart and Winston, 1973).

96. Cited in Rogow, 89.

97. R. Smith, "The Incredible Electrical Conspiracy," in *The Sociology of Crime and Delinquency,* ed. M. Wolfgang et al. (New York: Wiley, 1970), 363.

98. A. Thio, *Deviant Behavior* (Boston: Houghton Mifflin, 1988), 352.

99. G. Geis, "Upper World Crime," in *Current Perspectives on Criminal Behavior,* ed. A. S. Blumberg (New York: Knopf, 1974), 132–33.

100. Ibid., 116.

101. F. A. J. Ianni and F. Ianni (eds.), *The Crime Society: Organized Crime and Corruption in America* (New York: New American Library, 1976), xvi.

102. Clinard and Quinney, 225.

103. See Mary McIntosh, "The Growth of Racketeering," *Economy and Society* 2, 1973, 63, 64.

104. The items in this section are from Frank Pearce, *Crimes of the Powerful* (London: Pluto Press, 1976), 140.

105. McIntosh, 64.

106. See M. Tabor, "The Plague: Capitalism and Dope Genocide," in *The Triple Revolution Emerging,* ed. R. Perrucci and M. Pilisuk (Boston: Little, Brown, 1971), 241–49.

107. Stephen Spitzer, "Toward a Marxian Theory of Deviance," *Social Problems* 22, February 1975, 649.

108. For details, see *New York Times,* January 30, 1975, 1; March 21, 1975, 41; August 7, 1975, 38; and November 4, 1975, 38.

109. R. King, "Gambling and Crime," in *An Economic Analysis of Crime,* ed. L. J. Kaplan and D. Kessler (Springfield, IL: Charles C Thomas, 1975), 40.

110. R. Quinney, *Criminology: Analysis and Critique of Crime in America* (Boston: Little, Brown, 1975), 145.

111. Richard Behar, "The Underworld Is Their Oyster," *Time,* September 3, 1990, 54–57.

112. See E. Reid, *The Grim Reapers* (New York: Bantam, 1969), 138–39; and H. Kohn, "The Nixon–Hughes–Lansky Connection," *Rolling Stone,* May 20, 1976, 41–50, 77–78.

113. See Daniel Brandt, "As Criminal Capitalism Replaces Communism: Organized Crime Threatens the New World Order," *NameBase NewsLine* 8, January–March 1995.

114. Office of International Criminal Justice, *Bulletin,* Winter 1996, 1.

115. Frank Viviano, "The Empire of Crime," *Mother Jones,* June–July 1995, 17ff.

116. Senator John Kerry, *The New War* (New York: Simon & Schuster, 1997), 161.

117. Frank Viviano, "The Empire of Crime," *Mother Jones,* June/July 1995, 17ff.

118. Kerry, 160.

119. Ibid., 73.

120. L. Harris, *The Heroin Epidemic* (New York: Macmillan, 1991), 52–53.

121. Ibid., 61–62.

122. Kappeler et al., *The Mythology of Crime & Criminal Justice,* 2nd ed. (Prospect Heights, IL: Waveland, 1993), 85.

123. See Dolbeare and Edelman, 85–89, for Senate Intelligence Committee Report excerpts on this and other CIA assassination plots.

124. Pearce, 149.

125. Ibid., 150.

126. Ibid., 151.

127. For a detailed account of organized crime as a source of political campaign contributions, see William Chambliss, *On the Take: From Petty Crooks to Presidents* (Bloomington: Indiana University Press, 1978), 150–68.

128. For details, see Chambliss; and Alan Block and William Chambliss, *Organizing Crime* (New York: Elsevier, 1981), 34–37.

129. For confirmation of continuing Mafia strength, see *New York Times,* October 9, 1988, 1; and the TV documentary "Sons of Scarface," which aired August 20, 1987, on the Fox Network.

130. See the *President's Commission on Organized Crime Task Force Report* (Washington, DC: U.S. Government Printing Office, 1987) for a discussion of the new Mafia–drug connection.

131. See Philip Stern, "Uncle Sam's Welfare Program for the Rich," *New York Times Magazine,* April 16, 1972, 26.

132. See this and other studies cited in Richard Parker, *The Myth of the Middle Class* (New York: Liveright, 1972).

133. J. Victor Baldridge, *Sociology: A Critical Approach to Power, Conflict, and Change,* 2nd ed. (New York: Wiley, 1980), 489.

134. See Michael Maccoby and K. A. Terzi, "Character and Work in America," in *Exploring Contradictions: Political Economy in the Corporate State,* ed. Philip Brenner et al. (New York: McKay/Longman, 1974), 128.

3

Corporate Deviance:
Monopoly, Manipulation,
and Fraud

Costs of Corporate Crime

Sociologist Stanton Wheeler, in his presidential address to the 1975 annual meeting of the Society for the Study of Social Problems, chided his colleagues for their neglect of one particular area of criminality: "the patterns of illegal activity that lie at the core of large-scale corporate, industrial society."[1] The magnitude of this omission was revealed in 1978 by the first comprehensive investigation of corporate crime. Sociologist Marshall Clinard and his associates gathered data on the illegal actions of the 582 largest publicly owned corporations in the United States. Among their findings were that, during a twenty-four-month period, (1) 60 percent of these corporations had a legal action instituted against them by a federal agency for criminal activity; (2) of those corporations having had at least one violation, the average number of violations was 4.2, with one corporation being formally accused by the government on 62 occasions; and (3) almost one-half of the violations occurred in the oil refining, automobile, and drug industries (a rate 300 percent greater than their size in the sample indicated).[2]

According to a 1991 estimate, corporate crime, which includes antitrust, advertising law, and pollution law violations, costs American consumers an estimated *$261.06 billion. The amount taken in all bank robberies that year was 6,000 times less.* This figure is 40 times more than estimated losses from street crime.[3] Studies of punishment in corporate crime cases reveal that only about 2 percent of corporate crime cases result in imprisonment.

Penalties for Corporate Crime

Just as the Bank of New York and other multinational banks have been able to escape penalties for money laundering (see Chapter 2), so it is that many large corporations escape punishment for corporate crime on a regular basis. As Mokhiber[4] notes:

> Big companies that are criminally prosecuted represent only the tip of a very large iceberg of corporate wrongdoing. For every company convicted of health care fraud, there are numerous others that get away with ripping off Medicare and Medicaid.... For every company convicted of polluting the nation's waterways, there are many others who are not prosecuted because they do not get caught or because their corporate defense lawyers are able to offer up a low-level employee to go to jail in exchange for a promise from prosecutors not to touch the company or high-level executives.... For every corporation convicted of bribery or of giving money directly to a public official in violation of federal law, there are thousands who give money legally through political action committees to candidates and political parties. They profit from a system that effectively has legalized bribery.

The truth of Mokhiber's words is revealed in a mountain of evidence.

- **Item:** In 1996, only fifteen antitrust cases were brought by the federal government, and only eleven each in 1997 and 1999.[5] Compare this with a 1998 Benchmark survey of 1,694 large and medium-sized American firms that found that 27 percent of the respondents indicated that their organization knowingly broke the law "at least sometimes." Or a 1997 survey by the Human Resource Management/Ethics Resource Center that found that 61 percent of 747 human resource professionals felt that their firms did not provide ethics training and 47 percent felt that there was at least some pressure to compromise the organization's ethics code to achieve business goals.[6]
- **Item:** Small, privately held businesses account for more than 95 percent of all of the corporate convictions each year.[7]
- **Item:** In recent years there has emerged a strange pattern concerning corporate punishment. Corporations now take out numerous insurance policies that cover everything from fraud by rogue traders to the costs of violating environmental laws. The risk of loss due to violating the law has now effectively been shifted to an insurance company, assuming that no prison sentence is handed down when a corporation is caught. Prison sentences are extremely rare in corporate crime cases, and the average prison sentence from 1996 through 1998 has been between 2.4 and 6 months.[8] Indeed, "many judges are reluctant to give harsh sentences to first time offenders and usually levy fines instead."[9]

In 1890 when the Sherman Act was passed, the violation was a misdemeanor subject to up to one year in prison and a $5,000 fine (raised to $50,000 in 1955). In 1974, violation of the Sherman Act became a felony, subject to one to three years imprisonment and a maximum fine of $100,000 for individuals and $1 million for corporations. The sentencing guidelines set sentences at eighteen months in 1977, and the individual fine was increased to $250,000 in 1984. In 1990, the maximum fine became $350,000 for individuals and $10 million for corporations.

In 1999, the Antitrust Division of the U.S. Justice Department proposed that the maximum Sherman Act fine be raised to $350,000 for individuals (or twice the gain from the crime or twice the victim loss), up to three years' imprisonment, and a maximum corporate fine of $100 million. Most global antitrust conspiracies greatly exceed the 1997 $10 million fine amount.[10]

- **Item:** A 1990 study by Amatai Etzioni found that between 1975 and 1984, 62 percent of the Fortune 500 companies were involved in one or more incidents of corrupt behavior (bribery, price-fixing, tax fraud, or violations of environmental regulations).[11]
- **Item:** A *Multinational Monitor* study in 1992 of the twenty-five largest Fortune 500 corporations' activities between 1977 and 1990 found that all the corporations were either found guilty of criminal behavior or fined and required to make payment for civil violations.[12]

The fact that so few studies have been done on corporate crime rates speaks volumes concerning the way powerful corporate interests have been able to define the American crime problems as a "street" (that is, lower-class) problem. The neglected subject of corporate deviance is the focus of this chapter, as well as the next. Specifically, this chapter is devoted to five areas of corporate deviance: the problems generated by (1) monopoly, (2) price-fixing, (3) price gouging, (4) deceptive advertising, and (5) fraud.

Monopolies

As noted in Chapter 1, the United States has moved from competitive capitalism to a stage of monopoly capitalism. Karl Marx, well over 100 years ago, correctly predicted this current stage.[13] Free enterprise, he argued, would result in some firms becoming bigger and bigger as they eliminated their opposition or absorbed smaller competing firms. The ultimate result of this process would be the existence of a monopoly in each of the various sectors of the economy. Monopolies, of course, are antithetical to the free-enterprise system because they determine the price and the quality of products, thus interfering with the balance of supply and demand. This, as we will see, increases the benefits for the few at the expense of the many.

For the most part, U.S. society upholds Marx's prediction. Although a few corporations are virtual monopolies (for example, IBM with mainframe computers), most sectors of the U.S. economy are dominated by shared monopolies. Instead of a single corporation controlling an industry, the situation is one in which a small number of large firms dominate an industry. When four or fewer firms supply 50 percent or more of a particular market, a shared monopoly results, one that performs much as a monopoly or cartel would. Most economists agree that, above this level of concentration (a four-firm ratio of 50 percent), the economic costs of shared monopoly are most manifest.[14]

According to a government report, in 1982, the following industries were dominated by shared monopolies: razors and razor blades (the four largest firms control 99 percent of the market); lightbulbs (91 percent); cigarettes (90 percent); electronic calculators (90 percent); linoleum (90 percent); clocks and watches (84 percent); refrigerators (82 percent); cereals (80 percent); sugar (67 percent); and roasted coffee (66 percent).[15]

Shared monopolies raise the costs of products to consumers. For example, in 1980, the Federal Trade Commission (FTC) released the results of an eight-year study that showed that consumers paid more than $1.2 billion in higher prices for ready-to-eat cereals over a fifteen-year period. The commission alleged that these overcharges of 15 percent were the direct result of the monopoly in the cereal industry held by three companies: Kellogg, General Mills, and General Foods. In just one year, consumers paid $100 million more for cereals than they would have had there been a more competitive market.[16]

The existence of shared monopolies indicates the extent of concentration of U.S. business. The evidence is clear that the assets of U.S. businesses are highly concentrated in the hands of a few giants. The 200 largest, for instance, have increased their share of U.S. industry from 45 percent in 1945 to 61 percent in 1984.[17] Two processes account for the superconcentration of assets among a few corporations: (1) growth through competition, where the fittest survive, and (2) growth through mergers. Of the two, the latter is the more significant.

The Corporate Frankenstein

Corporate mergers have become identified with a new type of Wall Street crime: insider trading. In a recent study Data Resources examined some 130 stocks, 70 percent of which ran up sharply in value just before corporate takeovers, "suggesting that insider trading is rampant" among investors.[18] Moreover, "mergers, acquisitions and spinoffs totaled $659 billion in 1996, up 27 percent from $519 billion in 1995."[19]

Corporate mergers in the 1990s were devastating to American workers. According to the *New York Times,* more than 43 million jobs have been erased in the United States since 1979. Increasingly the jobs that are disappearing are those of higher-paid, white-collar workers, many at large corporations, women as well as men, many at the peak of their careers.

Nearly three-quarters of all households have had a close encounter with layoffs since 1980 according to a new poll by the *New York Times.* In one-third of all households, a family member has lost a job, and nearly 40 percent more know a relative, friend, or neighbor who was laid off.

One in 10 adults or about 19 million people, a number matching the adult population of New York and New Jersey combined, acknowledged that a lost job in their household had precipitated a major crisis in their lives, according to the *New York Times* poll."[20]

The oil industry is a good example of how these mergers can lead to ever greater concentration in an industry. In 1984 alone, Gulf Oil purchased Standard Oil of California for $13.2 billion, Texaco bought Getty Oil for $10.1 billion, and Mobil Oil bought Superior Oil for $4.7 billion.[21]

Why do these biggest of businesses feel the urge to merge? The goal of bigness appears to be control. Eugene Rostow has summarized this phenomenon: "The history of corporations is the best evidence of the motivation for their growth. In instance after instance [it] appears to have been the quest for monopoly power, not the technological advances of scale."[22]

The ever greater concentration of power and resources in a few corporations has important negative consequences for U.S. society, exacerbating many social problems.[23] Foremost is the overpricing that occurs when four or fewer firms control a particular market. A study by the FTC estimated that if the control of the four largest firms in an industry were reduced from 50 to 40 percent of sales, prices would fall by at least 25 percent. When industries are so concentrated that four or fewer firms account for 70 percent of sales, they are found to have profits 50 percent higher than the less concentrated industries.[24]

The existence of monopolies is costly to consumers in other ways because consumers ultimately bear the costs of advertising and product changes. The irony is that consumers, even though squeezed by monopolies, are forced to finance the continuation of monopolies.

Overpricing leads to lost output because of fewer sales and excess capacity. Lost output is detrimental for three reasons. First, it reduces potential economic activity. Second, lower output substantially reduces tax revenues that, if not reduced because of lower output, could either reduce the tax burden for all or be spent to alleviate social problems. Third, another negative consequence of overcharging by monopolies is inequitable transfer cost. Excessive prices bring excessive profits. These profits then redistribute income from purchasers to the stockholders of the corporations, and 47 percent of stocks are owned by the wealthiest 0.5 percent of the population.[25] As a result, a relative handful of stockholders (the already wealthy) reap the dividends. Thus, overcharging redistributes wealth, but in the direction of greater inequalities. As Newfield and Greenfield concluded:

> It is this tiny minority of shareholding Americans that gather in the super-profits generated by the power of big business to stifle competition and manipulate prices without fear of challenge. When we recognize that officers of

these superbusinesses often collect more money from their stock-holdings and stock-option privileges than from their salaries, we can see where much of our money goes: not to the community at large, not to wage earners, not into more efficient products, but into the bank accounts, trust funds, and holdings of the richest 1.6 percent of Americans.[26]

Put in a stronger and even more compelling way, two Stanford economists have argued that if there were no monopolies, (1) 2.4 percent of U.S. families would control not 40 percent of the total wealth but only 16.6 to 27.5 percent, and (2) 93.3 percent of U.S. families would be better off. Only the wealthiest 6.7 percent would be worse off. According to these estimates, without monopoly, the current maldistribution of wealth in the United States would be as much as 50 percent less.[27]

Heavily concentrated industries are also sources of inflation. When consumer demand falls, for example, the prices of products in concentrated industries tend to rise. This occurs in such different industries as automobile manufacturing and professional sports. As evidence, economist John Blair studied sixteen pairs of products, one group from a concentrated industry (that is, where a shared monopoly existed), the other group from a more competitive industry (for example, steel building materials versus lumber; pig iron versus steel scraps). During the two recessions of the 1950s, the price of every unconcentrated product fell, while the price of thirteen of the sixteen concentrated products actually rose.[28]

In other words, when a few corporations are large enough to control an industry, they are immune from the rules of a competitive economy. The immediate consequences for consumers are that they will pay artificially high prices. Shared monopolies also cause inflation because they can automatically pass on increased labor costs or increased taxes to the consumer. In competitive industries, however, a corporation may be forced to reduce its profit if it wants to continue to get a share of the market. Moreover, the tendency toward parallel pricing in concentrated industries means that prices only rise. When an industry leader such as General Motors or U.S. Steel announces a price increase of 7 percent, within a few days, similar increases are announced by their so-called competitors. As Ralph Nader and his associates have noted, "Each firm gladly increases its profit margin by getting the same share of a larger pie. There is no incentive to keep prices down, for then all the other firms will have to come down to that price which means the same share of a smaller pie."[29]

It is impossible to know exactly how much monopolies contribute to inflation. Certainly, the profits generated by lack of competition, rather than efficiency or product superiority, are hidden contributors. The existence of monopolies also has important political consequences. The concentration of economic power undermines the democratic process in two fundamental ways. The first is overt, as the powerful marshall their vast resources to achieve favorable laws, court decisions, and rulings by regulatory agencies.

They have the lobbyists, lawyers, and politicians (as noted in Chapter 1) to work for their interests. Second, more subtly (but real, nonetheless), the powerful get their way because of the bias of the politico-economic system. Such time-honored notions as "our economic interests abroad must be protected" and "tax incentives to business will benefit everyone" and "bigness is goodness" go unchallenged because we have been socialized to accept the current system as proper. Thus, decisions continue to be based on precedent, and the idea that "what is good for General Motors is good for the country" prevails. As long as such notions guide decision making, the interests of the wealthy will be served at the expense of the nonwealthy.[30]

For defenders of a competitive free-enterprise system, the existence of monopolies and shared monopolies should be attacked as un-American because the economy has become neither free nor competitive. Green made the following observation:

> Huey Long once prophesied that fascism would come to the United States first in the form of anti-fascism. So too with corporate socialism. Under the banner of free enterprise, up to two-thirds of American manufacturing has been metamorphosed into a "closed enterprise system." Although businessmen spoke the language of competitive capitalism, each sought refuge for themselves: price-fixing, parallel pricing, mergers, excessive advertising, quotas, subsidies, and tax favoritism. While defenders of the American dream guarded against socialism from the left, it arrived unannounced from the right.[31]

In summary, the negative consequences of shared monopolies are important to our understanding of elite deviance in two ways. First, monopolies are themselves deviant because they disproportionately redistribute wealth and advantage toward the already advantaged. And, second, the existence of monopolies aids in creating an environment in which deviant acts are encouraged. An examination of the automobile industry will illustrate these interrelated phenomena.

Case Study: The Automobile Industry

The automobile industry is the nation's largest. One out of six U.S. businesses is related directly or indirectly to the automobile. Sales data for the 1996 top 500 U.S. corporations listed General Motors as first (with $168.3 billion in sales) and Ford as second (with $146.9 billion). The major oil companies, whose fortunes are directly related to automobile usage, were also ranked near the top: Exxon was third (with $119.4 billion in sales), Mobil was eighth, and Texaco was eleventh. Together, these three oil companies had sales of more than $235 billion.[32]

> The pivotal position of the industry in the U.S. economy is underscored by such considerations as the following: One out of every seven workers in this

country is said to be dependent directly or indirectly on the automobile industry; the industry consumes about one-fifth of the nation's steel production, one out of every fourteen tons of copper, more than two out of every five tons of lead, more than one out of every four tons of zinc, one pound in seven of nickel, one-half of the reclaimed rubber, almost three-fourths of the upholstery leather, and substantial proportions of total national output of glass, machine tools, general industrial equipment, and forgings.[33]

The important point is that the automobile industry is one of the nation's most highly concentrated. In the early 1900s, 181 companies manufactured and sold automobiles. But few were to survive. By 1927, there were 44, by 1935 there were 10, and now there are only 3 domestic manufacturers: General Motors (GM), Ford, and Chrysler. Hence, the automobile industry has become a shared monopoly.

The advantages of being big are illustrated by the two largest U.S. automobile companies, GM and Ford. In 1997, these companies had assets worth more than $200 billion.[34] Such huge sums allow these companies to make big capital outlays, to provide credit to their suppliers, and to pay great sums for advertising. Moreover, they can afford a high degree of product differentiation (that is, a number of different models and options), which further reduces competition. As a result of these barriers, it has been estimated that a new company would need at least $1 billion for manufacturing and another $200 million to set up a dealership network. The result of these high entry barriers is that, since 1923, there has not been a successful new domestic entrant into the U.S. automobile market.[35]

But how does this market control affect the consumer? The answer is simple: the consumer pays dearly. Let's briefly look at some examples.

1. Competition is limited to three companies and, in reality, to one, GM. These companies do not compete in price and quality of product, but they do compete in advertising. This cost is passed on to the consumer.
2. Yearly style changes (planned obsolescence) are the industry's strategy for continued growth in sales and profits. This policy has at least three important negative effects: (a) it increases the waste of resources; (b) it increases the likelihood of unsafe products because of insufficient time for planning and testing; and (c) it increases the huge costs paid by the consumer. "The cost of dynamic obsolescence is passed on to the buyer twice: first, by tacking the cost of style changes onto the price of the car (about 25 percent of the price), and, second, in the car's unnecessarily rapid loss of value."[36]
3. Frequent style changes make it prohibitively expensive for outsiders to make spare parts. As a result, 90 percent of automobile parts are available only from the original manufacturers and at a higher cost than one would pay if prices were competitive.

4. Finally, monopoly control of the automobile industry has meant that prices tend to rise regardless of the demand. During the 1973–1974 recession, the number of cars sold fell by 20 percent, yet the prices of domestic new cars increased 9 percent.[37] Obviously, the law of supply and demand is rescinded in monopoly industries. Monopoly conditions, rather than the market, control prices, as shown in the similar price increases among the automakers. In a typical instance, when one manufacturer announces its price increase, within weeks the others make similar increases. If one is out of line with the others, there is a period of adjustment toward the GM price.[38] The result is higher profits for each of the companies, an average annual return on net worth between 1946 and 1967 of 16.67 percent in the automobile industry, compared to 9.02 percent in other manufacturing corporations. "In sum, the automobile industry imposes classic oligopolistic costs on its consumers."[39]

But the costs to consumers do not end here. There is considerable evidence that automobile manufacturers actually create a deviant market structure. Sociologist Harvey Farberman has suggested that the automakers impose on their new-car dealers a pricing policy that requires high volume and low per-unit profit.[40] The dealer is at the mercy of the manufacturers. If the dealer protests the situation, then he or she might lose the dealership or receive unfavorable treatment (slow delivery or not enough of the most popular models). Thus, when the manufacturers demand high volume and a low profit margin, the dealers are forced to look for profits elsewhere in their operations. These solutions are often deviant.

One way to increase profit is to minimize one's taxes. The so-called short sale allows both buyer and seller to escape taxes. This is a tactic whereby the customer pays part of the car's cost by check and the remainder in cash. The sales manager, in turn, records the sale as the amount paid by check. The customer pays sales tax on that amount only, and the dealer does not pay income tax on the cash received. This excess cash is buried or laundered.

When an automobile agency has an abundance of trade-ins, the best are recycled back to the agency's used-car retail line, while the surplus is sold to used-car wholesalers. The dispersal of cars into the wholesale market often involves the receipt of kickbacks by the used-car manager because independent wholesalers must pay graft for their supply.

Another tactic to increase profits in used-car sales is to provide cosmetic changes rather than improve the mechanical condition of the car. This practice is based on the knowledge that customers are especially impressed by observables, such as the paint job and the interior.

Car dealers also make unusually high profits from their repair shops. These profits are elevated by two practices, flat-rate labor costs and the parts monopoly.[41] Under the industry-wide tactic of the flat rate, labor for repairs is charged according to the standard amount of time a given job is supposed to take, not the time it actually takes. The result is that the customer typically pays for shop and mechanic time that were never used. The other scam is charging for parts at the inflated retail cost. As noted earlier, the monopoly pricing of parts is exorbitant. And still another tactic to increase profits is the unnecessary replacement of parts.[42] The totals are impressive: Nearly 40 percent of all auto repairs are wasted.

In sum, the automobile industry is permeated by a rip-off mentality. Clearly, monopoly has costly consequences for consumers, who are victimized in countless ways. (For additional discussion, see Chapter 4.)[43]

Price-Fixing

The sine qua non of capitalism is competition. We have seen, though, that the tendency toward concentration makes a mockery of the claim that the U.S. version of capitalism is competitive. The existence of shared monopolies allows the few corporations that control an industry to eliminate price wars by parallel pricing and product homogeneity. The parallel-pricing, tacit collusion by supposed competitors achieves a common price, and product homogeneity means that prices will be roughly equal because the competitors produce goods with similar specifications. Both practices are common and have the consequence of equal prices, regardless of whether the leading companies in an industry conspire to do so.

The typical practice among the large corporations that dominate an industry is *parallel pricing.* Currie and Skolnick describe how this works:

> Administering prices doesn't involve actual agreements among the large corporations not to undercut one another's prices; such direct "price fixing" is illegal. Instead, the usual pattern is one of "price leadership," in which there is a tacit understanding that if one company raises its prices, the others will follow. This ensures that competition through prices is diminished in the concentrated industries. The effect on the consumer is that prices in such industries...rarely go down and almost always go up, short of a really dramatic slowdown in the economy. This is one key reason why prices have often continued to rise even during recessions. Some economists estimate that the annual cost to consumers of such "monopoly pricing" may run to about 3 percent of gross national product, about $120 billion in 1985.[44]

Prices are also manipulated to maximize profits through collusive activities of the companies supposedly in competition with each other. This practice is called *price-fixing.* It refers to the explicit agreement among competitors to keep prices artificially high to maximize profits. Price-fixing is illegal, and complaints are monitored and brought to court by the Antitrust Division of the Justice Department. The illegality of price-fixing, however, has not deterred competing companies from conspiring to make abnormal profits through this practice, which costs consumers about $60 billion a year.[45] One review of cases from 1963 to 1972 in which price-fixing was proved revealed that the practice occurred among companies producing and marketing the following: steel wheels, pipe, bedsprings, metal shelving, steel castings, self-locking nuts, liquified petroleum gas delivery, refuse collection, linoleum installation, swimsuits, structural steel, carbon steel, baking flour, fertilizer, railroads, welding electrodes, acoustical ceiling materials, hydraulic hose, beer, gasoline, asphalt, book matches, concrete pipe, drill bushings, linen, school construction, plumbing fixtures, dairy products, fuel oil, auto repair, brass fittings, plumbing contracting, bread, athletic equipment, maple floors, vending machines, ready-mix concrete, industrial chemicals, rendering, shoes, garage doors, automobile glass, and wholesale meat. In addition, review these current examples.

- **Item:** Just one week before its shareholders' meeting, Archer Daniels Midland (ADM) pled guilty to price-fixing of several commodities commonly used in processed foods (for example, corn syrup, citric acid, and lysine) and paid a $100 million criminal fine—the largest criminal antitrust fine ever—for its role in conspiracies to fix prices to eliminate competition. The two-count felony charges filed against ADM alleged that the company conspired with other producers (including previously charged Ajinomoto Co., Inc.; Kyowa Hakko Kogyo Co. Ltd.; and Sewon America, Inc.) in the lysine and citric markets to set prices and allocate sales from 1992 to 1995.

Under the plea agreement, all executives and employees of ADM, except for two, were protected from prosecution if they cooperated with the government. Moreover, ADM's stock went up after the announcement of the plea.

"There are a whole number of ADM executives who committed these crimes," said the cofounder of the ADM Shareholders Watch Committee of Hallandale, Florida, who argued that the executives responsible for the crimes should have been indicted first. ADM's political campaign contributions to both political parties insulated ADM and its executives from a just result.

Moreover, there is no disclosure in the plea agreement about the specifics of this crime. The government provided little information on who was involved. One estimate is that the citric acid price-fixing cost clients $400 million, while the lysine price-fixing cost $100 million. Under federal sentencing law, the $500 million total loss could be doubled, thus putting ADM's potential criminal exposure at $1 billion. But the Department of Justice defended the $100 million fine, saying no one at ADM got off the hook.

Federal officials noted that because of ADM's crimes seed companies, large poultry and swine producers, and ultimately farmers paid millions more to buy lysine, an amino acid used by farmers as a feed additive to ensure the proper growth of livestock. Lysine is a $600 million a year industry worldwide. In addition, manufacturers of soft drinks, processed foods, detergents, and other products paid millions more to buy the citric acid additive, which ultimately caused consumers to pay more for these products. Citric acid is a flavor additive and preservative and is used in soft drinks, processed food, detergents, pharmaceuticals, and cosmetic products. Citric acid is a $1.2 billion a year industry worldwide.[46]

Examining a number of price-fixing cases, several researchers have tried to determine if a pattern can be found. They concluded that "conspiracy among competitors may arise in any number of situations but it is most likely to occur and endure when numbers are small [few companies involved], concentration is high (when four or fewer firms control fifty percent or more of the market), and the product is homogeneous."[47] Of the top 100 corporate crime cases of the 1990s, 20 of them involved antitrust matters like price-fixing and another 20 involved fraud. The single largest corporate crime of the last decade was a worldwide scheme to fix the price of certain vitamins and ended when Hoffman–La Roche was assessed a $500 million fine, the largest criminal fine ever levied. [48]

We should not forget, however, that collusive arrangements to keep prices or fees artificially high are not limited to industrial sales. Price-fixing, in one form or another, often occurs in real estate fees, doctors' fees, lawyers' fees, and tax accountants' fees, to name a few. Although the government continues to prosecute price-fixing cases, the problem continues. Apparently, the potential for increased profits is too tempting. Moreover, when individuals have been found guilty, the punishment has been more symbolic than real. Thus, the incentives remain. Once again, profit is the primary source of motivation and the customer be damned.

The extra profits garnered through price-fixing arrangements have an obvious impact on customers, who pay higher prices for goods and services. But they also have negative indirect effects. Two of these subtle consequences are especially noteworthy. First, larger than necessary expenditures fuel inflation. And, second, extra profits exacerbate the gap between the haves and the have-nots.

For an illustration of price-fixing, let's examine the most blatant incident in modern U.S. history.

Case Study: The Electrical Conspiracy

From the mid-1940s through the 1950s, virtually all electrical manufacturing firms were actively involved in collusive activities to keep prices high.[49] Twenty-nine companies, but principally General Electric (GE) and Westinghouse, eventually were found guilty of conspiring to fix prices, rig bids, and divide markets on electrical equipment valued at $1.75 billion annually. The amount of profit generated from price-fixing in the electrical industry was considerable. "The result of these machinations was grossly inflated prices. Generator prices rose 50 percent from 1951 to 1959, while wholesale prices on all commodities rose only 5 percent. The Senate Small Business Committee later asserted that Westinghouse had bilked the Navy by a 500 percent overcharge on certain gear assemblies, and GE had charged 446 percent too much on another contract."[50]

An example of how the prices were fixed occurred in so-called competitive bidding for new business. Public agencies (for example, utilities, school districts, and the government) required companies to make sealed bids for the cost of their products. The conspiring companies used this seemingly competitive practice to ensure high prices by rotating business on a fixed-percentage basis. That is, each company was allowed the proportion of the sales equal to the proportion of the market that they had controlled prior to the conspiracy. For sealed bids on circuit breakers, for example, the four participating companies divided the sales so that GE received 45 percent, Westinghouse 35 percent, Allis-Chalmers 10 percent, and Federal Pacific 10 percent.

Every ten days to two weeks, working-level meetings were called in order to decide whose turn was next. Turns were determined by the ledger list, a table of who had received what in recent weeks. After that, the only thing left to decide was the price that the company picked to win would submit as the lowest bid.[51]

Four grand juries investigated price-fixing allegations in the electrical industry and handed down twenty indictments involving forty-five individuals and twenty-nine corporations. At the sentencing hearing in 1961, Judge Ganey levied fines totaling $1,787,000 on the corporations and $137,000 on different individuals. The highest corporate fines were against GE ($437,500) and Westinghouse ($372,500). Seven individuals were given jail sentences of thirty days (later reduced to twenty-five for good behavior), and twenty others received suspended sentences. In addition, the individuals were assessed fines ranging from $1,000 to $12,500. The corporations also faced settlements to injured parties. By 1964, for example, some 90 percent of the 1,800 claims against GE had been settled for a total of $160 million.

Several significant conclusions can be drawn from this electrical conspiracy case. First and most obvious, this antitrust conspiracy illustrates the willful and blatant violation of the law by some of the leading corporations in the United States. Second, the highest officials in the guilty corporations escaped without fines and jail sentences. Those found guilty were vice-presidents, division managers, and sales managers, not presidents and chief executive officers. Moreover, the sentences were mild, considering the huge amounts of money involved. The government even ruled that the companies' payments of fines and settlements could be considered a business expense and therefore tax deductible.[52]

This type of crime is underplayed by the media. For example, on the day that the defendants pleaded guilty or nolo contendere (no contest), only four of the largest twenty-two newspapers made the story front-page news, and four well-known papers, the *Boston Globe, New York Daily News, Christian Science Monitor,* and *Kansas City Times,* completely omitted the story. Five days later, when the sentencing occurred, 45 percent of the twenty newspapers with one-fifth of all the newspaper circulation in the United States did not consider the story front-page news.[53]

The parties convicted did not consider their acts immoral. Two quotes illustrate this point. First, the president of Allen–Bradley, Fred L. Loock, said "It is the only way a business can be run. It is free enterprise." Second, a GE official said, "Sure, collusion was illegal, but it wasn't unethical."[54]

The punishment for those judged guilty was incredibly light, given the magnitude of the case—a maximum of $12,500 and thirty days in jail. But more important is the discrepancy found when the sentences for these types of crimes are compared to those given to individuals guilty of street crimes. Some extreme examples are provided by Nader and Green:

> A year after seven electrical manufacturers were sent to jail for 30 days apiece, a man in Asbury Park, New Jersey, stole a $2.98 pair of sunglasses and a $1 box of soap and was sent to jail for four months. A George Jackson was sent to prison for ten years to life for stealing $70 from a gas station, his third minor offense; and in Dallas one Joseph Sills received a 1,000-year sentence for stealing $73.10. Many states send young students who are marijuana first offenders to jail for five to ten years' sentence. But the total amount of time spent in jail by all businessmen who have ever violated antitrust laws is a little under two years.[55]

In all probability, antitrust cases like the electrical conspiracy represent only a small portion of the actual amount of price-fixing in U.S. industry.[56] The potential profits are too tempting for many business executives, and the chances of getting caught are slim. The likelihood of escaping conviction, if caught, is great because of two factors: (1) the deals are made in secret and masked by apparently legal activity (for example, sealed bids), and (2) the government's antitrust budget is very small.

Price Gouging

Because many private corporations are entirely profit oriented, they take whatever advantage they can to sell their products or services at the highest possible prices. Shared monopolies, as we have seen, use their control of the market to increase prices an average of 25 percent. Price-fixing, of course, is another tactic to maximize profits. In this section, we discuss yet another manifestation of profit-maximizing behavior: price gouging, or taking extraordinary advantage of consumers because of the bias of the law, monopoly of the market, manipulation of the market, or contrived or real shortages.

Whatever the means used, price gouging is a form of deviancy. Let's examine the procedures used in three areas: (1) selling to the disadvantaged, (2) taking advantage of events, and (3) making extraordinary profits through convenient laws and manipulation.

Taking Advantage of the Disadvantaged

Low-income consumers are the victims of price gouging from a variety of merchants, banks and finance companies, landlords, and the like. The poor pay more due to several factors, including higher rates of street crimes in their neighborhoods, which raise the cost of doing business, and the economic marginality of the poor, making their credit especially risky. But even when these rationales are accounted for, the poor are the victims of unusually high prices, which of course tends to perpetuate their poverty. Many food chains find that it costs 2 or 3 percent more to operate in poor neighborhoods, yet low-income consumers pay between 5 and 10 percent more for their groceries than those living in middle-income areas. Perhaps the best example of price gouging by ghetto stores is that they tend to raise prices on the first and the fifteenth of each month because these are the days when welfare checks are received. Similarly, there is evidence that grocers in the Mississippi Delta raised prices when food stamps were introduced.[57]

Banks and other financial organizations also take advantage of the poor. Because they are not affluent and therefore have inadequate collateral or credit standing, the poor must pay higher interest rates or may be forced to deal with loan sharks because they are denied resources through legitimate financial outlets.

The greater risk of lending to the poor is used to justify extremely high prices in poor neighborhoods. In the jewelry business, for example, the normal markup is 100 percent, but for jewelry sold in poor neighborhoods, the markup often is 300 percent or higher. A ring selling wholesale for $50 will sell for up to $300 in the poverty market. To protect themselves from default, credit jewelers in such a situation will try to get the maximum down payment, say, $60. If so, the dealer has already made a $10 profit, and the future payments mean even more profit.[58]

The merchants in poor areas engage in such price gouging for several reasons: (1) the stores are essentially monopolies (no competition present); (2) the stores can argue legitimately that their costs are higher than in middle-class areas (although their prices, as we have seen, tend to exceed their increased risks by a wide margin); (3) the poor are unorganized and have no access to the powerful in society; (4) the poor are often unaware of the available avenues through which to complain of abusive practices; and (5) the poor tend to be apathetic because of the hopelessness of trying to change the practices of powerful banks, supermarket chains, finance companies, and other seemingly monolithic organizations.

Cross has summarized the economic plight of the poor: "Caught in a vicious cycle of poverty, the poor and the stores which serve them are trapped by the worst aspects of the free enterprise system. And it is likely that the poor are also at the receiving end of a greater amount of deliberate fraud and price discrimination than the suburban middle class."[59]

Taking Advantage of Unusual Events

The sharp entrepreneur is always looking for special events that might lead to spectacular profits. For example, when California passed Proposition 13 in 1978, local property taxes were dramatically reduced by $7 billion. This event was used by some to increase profits substantially. For example, land-lords did not reduce rents accordingly but tended to pocket the difference. And California-based corporations made an instant additional profit of $2 billion yet did not lower prices on their products.

In the mid-1970s, a worldwide shortage caused the price of sugar to in-crease rapidly for U.S. consumers, bringing a concomitant rise in a number of products containing sugar. The cost of candy bars increased while their size dwindled (the price tripled while the bar shrank to one-third its former size). The cost of soda also increased markedly during this period. Canned soda from vending machines went from 15 to 25 cents a can. Interestingly (and re-vealing of the tendency of corporations to gouge whenever possible), the cost of diet soda (which, of course, contains no sugar) went up in price to 25 cents as well. When the sugar shortage subsided, the cost of soda stayed at the shortage-created level and continued to increase. Also, all major soda compa-nies had the same pricing strategy, a form of parallel pricing or price-fixing.

But the best example of using a crisis to one's economic advantage and the one that has had the greatest impact on the U.S. consumer is price gouging by the oil companies ever since the oil boycott of the Organization of Petro-leum Exporting Countries (OPEC) in 1973–1974 and the shortages caused by the upheavals in Iran in 1979 (which were discussed in detail in Chapter 2).

As a final example of corporations taking advantage of unusual events, some companies have practiced price gouging during the acquired immune deficiency syndrome (AIDS) crisis. In 1983, the Food and Drug Administra-tion (FDA) granted Lypho Med, Inc., seven years of exclusive U.S. rights for the antibiotic pentamidine, which is used to treat pneumocystis carinii pneu-monia, the first sign of AIDS in about three-fifths of all patients. Over the next three years, the company raised its price for a typical three-week course (using one vial a day) from about $500 to more than $2,000. The chief AIDS physician at the University of California Medical Center in San Francisco said, "Without reservation this is needless and shameless price-gouging."[60] Also, a study in New York City found that pharmacies charged between $900 and $3,384 for a month's supply of AZT (the only FDA-approved drug for treating AIDS), while the wholesale cost was $752.55.[61]

Making Extraordinary Profits through Deception

Although there are many examples of price gouging because of deception, we will focus on this phenomenon in one industry: the pharmaceutical industry. The sale of prescription and nonprescription drugs is a large industry, representing 10 percent of all medical costs in the United States.

- Mary Nathan suffers from a rare condition called Gaucher's disease, which is potentially fatal. The drugs she takes for it cost $270,000 per year. She worries about what will happen when she reaches the maximum amount that her insurance will pay. Her experience with drug costs is representative of the problems that stem from this $77 billion per year industry.
- When drug prices in the United States increased 81 percent between 1980 and 1985, the Drug Manufacturers Association told Congress that the increases were merely temporary, but during the following six years (1986–1992) drug prices increased another 66 percent. In 1993, the average prescription drug cost $22.50 (versus $6.62 in 1980). In the 1990s, prescription prices increased almost 9 percent per year, far exceeding inflation in other costs.[62]

Why are Americans charged so much for prescriptions? The drug companies claim that it costs $231 million on average to bring a new drug to market, and they are merely recuperating their investment costs. Yet, consider the case of premarin, a hormone found in horses' urine. The drug has been used for more than fifty years, and all research and development costs on the drug were recovered long ago. Since 1985, however, the cost of the drug has increased 75 percent (from 20 to 35 cents for a daily dose). The real reason for this great price increase is profit margins.

Sidney Wolfe of the Public Interest Research Group claims that 104 of the 287 most frequently prescribed drugs are too dangerous to use. Their side effects can cause death in some cases.

The pharmaceutical firms spend thousands of dollars for each of the nation's doctors in order to convince them to prescribe their drugs. Also, a great deal of misleading and fraudulent advertising is associated with the drug industry. In 1992, 150 health professionals examined 109 full-page ads for drugs in medical journals. The group found that more than 90 percent of the ads violated the FDA's standards in some way.[63]

In 1988, sixteen drug companies sponsored some 34,000 symposia for doctors at a cost of $89.5 million. These events are held in expensive locations and are little more than long commercials designed to get doctors to prescribe various drugs. The meetings often contain misleading claims about various drugs and are not subject to oversight by the FDA due to their private nature.[64]

The American pharmaceutical industry made $10 billion in profits on $76 billion in sales in 1992, a 13 percent profit margin. This is the highest profit margin of any industry in the country. The top executives of large drug firms earn from $1.9 million to $13 million per year, and the nation is poorer and less healthy for the actions of this industry. About half of all prescription drugs come in two forms: under a brand name or under the generic name. Although the drugs are identical chemically, the brand-name form is very much more expensive and therefore profitable.

The situation in drug sales is very different from that of the typical purchaser–seller relationship. The choice of prescription drugs is not made by the consumer but by the physician, whose decision is not based on price but on knowledge. Doctors prescribe drugs they know about, and most of their information is supplied by large pharmaceutical firms, which spend from $3,000 to $5,000 per doctor per year promoting their own brand-name drugs.

Drug manufacturers also benefit by the proliferation of drugs, which leaves physicians inundated with a virtual sea of drugs and drug names. For example, sixty-one firms offered their own version of one chemical compound, PETN. Busy physicians will opt, in most cases, for the drugs with which they are most familiar, and drug firms do all they can to familiarize doctors with their branded (and expensive) products. But drug companies have done more than just advertise their products to physicians. According to Ben Gordon, a drug consultant to the U.S. Senate for twenty years, "The larger drug manufacturers have been misleading and lying to the American public, to the medical profession, and to the Congress about the quality of their drugs, as against that of the generic drugs."[65] They have used several scare tactics, such as films in which generic drugs were compared to defective cars and warnings to pharmacists that the increased use of generic drugs would cause the druggists' insurance rates to increase.[66]

Another tactic used by drug firms has been to lobby for laws prohibiting generics to be substituted for the branded drugs prescribed by physicians. At one time, all fifty states had such laws, but in recent years, many have been changed. In late 1978, forty states and the District of Columbia allowed pharmacists to substitute generic drugs for brand-name prescription drugs. Also, in 1984, Congress finally passed a law that eliminated the costly and time-consuming delays facing companies seeking government approval to market generic drugs.

This shift in the laws and greater consumer familiarity with generic drugs have brought about a shift in policy by the large drug firms. They are fighting generics with what they call branded generics, which are prescription drugs that carry different names and are priced midway between the brand-name drugs and the products that come from the generic drug houses. Although the chemicals used are identical, the large drug firms argue that the higher prices of the branded generics are justified. According to Joseph Stetler, president of the Pharmaceutical Manufacturers Association, "Those larger companies have heavy investments in quality control research, which is relatively incidental, but they have a backup capability that is of value to a consumer. So there's a justification for a price differential."[67]

Such reasoning sounds good, but in many cases the large companies do not manufacture their highly advertised products. In 1978, "20/20," the ABC newsmagazine program, visited the Mylan Pharmaceutical Company and found one machine producing erythromycin tablets. Some of the tablets were then dyed pink, others yellow, and still others orange. The only difference among the three sets of tablets was the color, yet the three would be priced very differently. The pink pills were the generic and would sell for $6.20; the yellow pills were marketed by Smith–Kline and would sell for $9.20; and the orange ones were called Bristamycin and marketed for $14.00. Similarly, at the Phillips–Roxanne Laboratories, 60-milligram cidamenphene-todene tablets were placed in a Smith–Kline bottle to be sold wholesale for $13.20 a hundred, but when they were put in a Phillips–Roxanne package, they sold for $10.80. Again, the products were identical and even manufactured at the same place.[68] The only differences were color, packaging, price, and "man in the plant," as explained by Jack Anderson:

> Many large drug companies actually don't manufacture some of their highly advertised products. Usually, officials from a big drug company will hire a smaller firm to manufacture a product for them. Then the big firm will stamp its brand name on the product, jack up the price and sell the drug as its own. The big name firm is required only to send someone to the factory to watch over the manufacturing process. The ruse is known as "man in the plant." Thus, the industry giants are able to charge consumers millions of dollars more than generic firms' products that are essentially the same.[69]

In 1999, protests erupted in Atlanta when the city's only public hospital substantially raised the price of prescription drugs necessary to the health of some 26,000 patients, some 6,500 of whom would be adversely affected by the price increase within thirty to sixty days. The episode is symbolic of a much more widespread condition. The United States is the only industrialized nation that does not place a ceiling on prescription drug prices, and, for thousands of Americans, the cost of these drugs has become an intolerable burden. Hundreds of people all over the nation suffer or die every year because they cannot afford to pay for medicines they need.[70]

Deceptive Advertising

One tenet of capitalism is expansion. Every corporation wishes to produce an increasing amount so that profits likewise will inflate. The problem, of course, is that the public must be convinced to consume this ever larger surplus.[71] One way to create demand is through advertising.

In 1973, advertising expenditures amounted to $25 billion, and by 1993, they had increased to more than $110 billion. A strong argument could be made that advertising expenditures are wasteful in three ways: (1) they create a demand to consume that increases the waste of natural resources; (2) they increase the cost of products because consumers pay all the advertising costs; and (3) the money spent serves no useful purpose (other than profits).

But advertising is a problem to the public in another way: It is sometimes designed to be deceptive. In a fundamental way, all advertising is deceptive because it is designed to manipulate. Symbols are used to make the observer concerned with his or her status, beauty, or age or to associate sex appeal with a certain look. Advertising is deceptive because it creates a desire to consume new products. But the deception we want to consider goes beyond this type of illusion. We are concerned with a more willful form of deception, where the goal is to sell, even through lies.[72]

A retired advertising executive discussed the cardinal principle in U.S. advertising.

> Don't worry whether it's true or not. Will it sell?...The American people ...are now being had from every bewildering direction. All the way from trying to persuade us to put dubious drug products and questionable foods into our stomachs to urging young men to lay down their lives in Indochina, the key will-it-sell principle and the employed techniques are the same. Caveat emptor has never had more profound significance than today, whether someone is trying to sell us war, God, anti-Communism or a new improved deodorant. Deceit is the accepted order of the hour.[73]

The tendency toward deception in advertising takes two forms, blatantly false advertising and puffery. Let's examine these in turn. Several examples will show how advertising can be outright false.

- **Item:** In 1994, Unocal oil company agreed to stop advertising claims concerning the performance of its high-octane gasoline. Several studies have found that American motorists waste billions of dollars per year on higher-octane fuels, which add nothing to a vehicle's performance.[74]
- **Item:** Other recent advertising fraud cases have centered around two American obsessions, eating and weight loss:

> Coors Light beer had to stop advertising "a taste of the Rockies," as long as its water came from Virginia.[75]

> General Nutrition Centers paid a $2.4 million fine for unsubstantiated health claims involving more than 40 of its products.[76]

> Eggland's Best had to stop advertising their egg substitute as "better than real eggs."[77]

In 1997, numerous home exercise equipment makers were forced to stop advertising that their products would automatically cause weight loss and abdominal size decreases when used only a few minutes three times per week.

Diet Centers, Nutri/System, and Physicians Weight Loss Centers were forced to stop advertising their claims concerning losing weight and keeping it off. Studies demonstrate that more than 90 percent of dieters gain back the weight that they lose.[78]

- **Item:** Companies commonly use bait-and-switch advertising, although it is a clear violation of FTC rules. The bait involves advertising a product at an extremely low price. The switch is made when customers arrive to buy it; none is available, so the salespersons pressure people to buy other, more expensive articles.
- **Item:** In 1996, the FTC signed agreements with five major auto manufacturers to resolve false-claim advertisements for car leases. General Motors Corporation; Mitsubishi Motor Sales of America, Inc.; American Honda Motor Co., Inc.; American Isuzu Motors, Inc.; and Mazda Motor of America, Inc., are now prohibited from featuring low monthly payments or low down payments in large, bold print while hiding additional costs and sometimes contradictory information in tiny print. The FTC states that nearly one-third of all automobile retail transactions are now leases. Deceptive leasing practices include the following:

    Not crediting consumers with part or all of the trade-in allowances or rebates that they were promised

    Misrepresenting the costs or terms of lease transactions

    Failing to disclose that a contract is a lease, not a regular purchase agreement

    Charging exorbitant or unjustified lease-end fees for excessive mileage or vehicle damage[79]

- **Item:** Products are advertised at exaggerated sizes. Lumber is uniformly shorter than advertised; a 12-inch board really is $11\frac{1}{4}$ inches wide. The quarter-pounder advertised by McDonald's is really $3\frac{7}{8}$ ounces. Nine-inch pies are in truth $7\frac{3}{4}$ inches in diameter because the pie industry includes the rim of the pan in determining the stated size.[80]
- **Item:** When Libby Owens–Ford Glass Company wanted to demonstrate the superiority of its automobile safety glass, it smeared a competing brand with streaks of Vaseline to create distortion and then photographed it at oblique camera angles to enhance the effect. The distortion-free marvels of the company's own glass were shown by taking photographs of a car with the windows rolled down.[81]

- **Item:** Nutritional labeling is currently a major issue. The FDA is cracking down on companies advertising and labeling products as "cholesterol free" that are nevertheless made with highly saturated fats. Many other examples of misleading labeling have yet to come to the FDA's attention. For instance, many products advertised as "sugar free," including Equal and Sweet 'n Low, contain dextrin (or corn syrup), which is made of calorie-containing carbohydrates, very similar to sugar in chemical makeup. These products are not safe for diabetics and/or mold allergy sufferers.[82]
- **Item:** Montgomery Ward paid a fine for false advertising in 1993. It claimed it was selling items at sale prices when it was really selling them at everyday prices.[83]

A more subtle form of deceptive advertising is called *puffery*. This term refers to the practice of making exaggerated claims for a product. Although advertisers routinely make such false claims and the result is deception, the law considers such practices to be legal.[84] Some examples follow:

"Blatz is Milwaukee's finest beer"
"Nestles makes the very best chocolate"
"Ford gives you better ideas"
"GM always a step ahead"
"Zenith Chromacolor is the biggest breakthrough in color TV"
"Wheaties, Breakfast of Champions"
"You can be sure if it's Westinghouse"
"Barnum and Bailey, The greatest show on earth"
"Every kid in America loves Jello brand gelatin"
"Coke is it"
"Seagram's, America's Number One Gin"
"Winston, America's Best"

Such claims are false or unsubstantiated. Even though they are considered legal, their intent is to mislead. The goal, as is always the case with advertising, is to use whatever means will sell the product. If that includes trifling with the truth, then so be it.

Even though knowledge concerning puffery in advertising is far from complete, some important facts have emerged from research on this topic:

- People perceive more content in ads than the ads actually contain. Additional values are perceived by consumers and attached to products. For example, one study of sweaters concluded that when sweaters were shown with belts and captions were read by someone with a Scottish accent, consumers were twice as likely to perceive that the sweaters were imported.[85]

- Implied deceptions (puffery claims) are believed more than outright lies. In one study of seventeen puff claims, 70 percent of respondents felt that the claims were either wholly or partially true.[86]
- Puffery claims are often indistinguishable from factual claims. In another study, a sample of 100 people were placed in a room and presented with both real and puff claims. The researchers found that "many of the puff claims were believed by a large proportion of the respondents.... The subjects could not tell that these puffs might not be literally true." Researchers found that the factual claims were believed just as often as the puff claims used in their survey.[87]
- Puffery "has the potential to deceive consumers and, as well, injure the credibility of advertising."[88] In sum, research indicates that a "large proportion of the sample interpret the [puff] claim to suggest superiority."[89] Consumers fed a constant diet of puffery ads may confuse fact and fiction. Moreover, they may actually come to distrust advertising, on the one hand, yet unconsciously be manipulated by it, on the other.[90]

Fraud

Fraud is committed when one is induced to part with money or valuables through deceit, lies, or misrepresentation. Although the law recognizes fraud as a crime, it has traditionally assumed that fraud directed against a private individual is not a crime because of the principle of caveat emptor. Preston has summarized this principle:[91]

This principle of the marketplace is an open invitation for fraud. Some criminologists have contended that fraud is probably "the most prevalent crime in America."[92] The types of frauds perpetrated on victims involve numerous schemes applied to a wide variety of economic activities, as seen in the following cases.

- **Item:** Toshihide Iguchi of the American branch of Japan's Daiwa Bank was the head of U.S. government bond trading. According to charges brought by the U.S. Attorney General's office in 1995, Iguchi made an astronomical 30,000 unauthorized transactions while trying to cover up losses totaling $1.1 billion. Whenever he lost money as a government-bond trader, Iguchi sold bonds from Daiwa's own accounts or those of its customers and then forged documents making the trades look like authorized transactions. Likewise, Nicholas Leeson, a Singapore-based derivatives trader, racked up $1.4 billion in hidden losses that broke Britain's Barings Bank when they came to light in February 1995.[93]

- **Item:** In 1995, three former executives of C.R. Bard, Inc., were convicted of conspiring to defraud the FDA. Bard, a leading health care product company, pleaded guilty to 391 counts of fraud and was fined $61 million in criminal and civil fines, the largest FDA fine ever. Unsuspecting patients, many of whom were elderly and infirm, were used as human guinea pigs in a deadly experiment in which Bard concealed malfunctions, including balloon rupture, deflation problems, and tip breakages that caused heart injuries requiring emergency coronary bypass surgery to remove the tips.[94]
- **Item:** In 1993, Prudential Securities paid a $371 million fine to settle charges that fraud permeated the sale of its limited partnerships and its retail branch agents' commissions. Many of its agents were not licensed to sell securities but did so anyway. Securities brokers and agents illegally split commissions using computer programs that also involved senior Prudential executives.[95]
- **Item:** Beech-Nut Nutrition Corporation, the nation's second-largest babyfood maker, admitted to 215 counts of shipping mislabeled products purporting to be apple juice with the intent to defraud and mislead the public. The bogus product, misrepresented as pure apple juice with no sugar added, was actually a concoction of beet sugar, cane sugar syrup, corn syrup, water, flavoring, and coloring. It contained little or no apple juice. The intended consumers were babies.[96]
- **Item:** In 1996, the General Accounting Office estimated Medicaid fraud at $100 billion a year. Currently, there are 1,000 investigations into health care fraud. Some recent examples include some of the largest corporations in the nation:

> Smith Kline Beecham's clinical laboratory unit agreed to pay more than $300 million to the government to settle charges that it had defrauded Medicare for unneeded blood tests.
>
> In July 1999, Olsten Corporation and a subsidiary of Kimberly Home Health Care agreed to pay $61 million to settle allegations that both firms had defrauded Medicare. Kimberly also pled guilty to three separate felony charges involving conspiracy, mail fraud, and violating the Medicare Anti-Kickback statute and agreed to pay an additional $10.8 million for defrauding Medicaid. Olsten agreed to pay $51 million for its role in the scheme.[97]

- **Item:** In 1999, the Sears Recovery Management Services pled guilty to one count of bankruptcy fraud involving fraudulent reaffirmation practices that had been ongoing since 1985. The $60 million fine levied was the largest ever in a bankruptcy fraud case and came on top of $180 million in restitution to about 188,000 debtors and $40 million in civil fines.[98]

Many fraudulent schemes are based on the classic pyramid system perfected by Bostonian Charles Ponzi in the 1920s whereby early investors are paid off handsomely with proceeds from sales to later participants. The result is often a rush of new investors, greedy for easy profits. An example of the Ponzi scam was the HomeStake swindle perpetrated by Robert Trippet, which consisted of selling participation rights in the drilling of sometimes hypothetical oil wells. The beauty of this plan was that since oil exploration was involved, it provided a tax shelter for the investors. Thus, the plan especially appealed to the wealthy. As a result, many important persons, including the chair of Citibank, the head of United States Trust, the former chair of Morgan Guarantee Trust, the former chair of General Electric, and entertainers such as Jack Benny, Candice Bergen, Faye Dunaway, Bob Dylan, and Liza Minnelli were swindled of a good deal of money. John Kenneth Galbraith, the noted economist, in reviewing a book about the HomeStake swindle, said that it should have been titled *How the Rich Swindled Each Other and Themselves.*[99]

- **Item:** In 1993, the U.S. Postal Service discovered that numerous businesses had learned to rig the postage meters, cheating the government out of more than $100 million in postage fees annually. The Postal Service offered a $50,000 reward for information leading to the arrest and conviction of anyone altering one of the 1.4 million postage meters currently used by U.S. businesses. [100]

Conclusion

Two issues that have historically concerned Americans are street crime and inflation. Our discussion in this chapter should provide new insight into both of these problems. Street crime, for example, is miniscule in terms of economic costs when compared to the illegal activities by corporations. To cite just one example, the $2 billion to $3 billion lost in the Equity Funding fraud involved more money "than the total losses of all street crimes in the United States for one year."[101]

The primary source of inflation, many argue, is huge governmental expenditures. Of course, these expenditures do affect the inflationary spiral, but the blame lies elsewhere, as well. Ignored by most critics are the sources of inflation found in our corporate economy. In 1982, U.S. consumers spent $1.08 trillion on retail items. Much of that money purchased nothing of value. We have seen that the existence of shared monopolies increases prices by 25 percent. We have seen that consumers pay all the costs of advertising, which amounted to $66.5 billion in 1982.[102] We have seen that consumers pay inflated prices brought about by price-fixing and other collusive arrangements by so-called competitors. Finally, we have seen that consumers spend billions on products sold under false pretenses, products that do not perform as claimed, products identical to cheaper ones but unavailable or unknown, and the like.

The point is clear: These extra costs to consumers do not bring anything of value back to them. What could be more inflationary than that? Put another way, the corporate economy diverts scarce resources to uses that have little human benefit.

To conclude, Edwin Sutherland, the sociologist who first examined white-collar crime extensively, made several observations relevant to the understanding of such corporate deviant behavior as price-fixing, misleading advertising, and fraud.[103]

1. The criminality of corporations tends to be persistent. Recidivism (repeat offenses) is the norm.
2. The level of illegal behavior is much more extensive than the prosecutions and complaints indicate.
3. Businesspeople who violate the laws designed to regulate business do not typically lose status among their associates. In other words, the business code does not coincide with the legal code. Thus, even when they violate the law, they do not perceive themselves as criminals.

Critical Thinking Exercise 3.1: The Dehumanization of Women and Crime

Two excellent videos concerning the dehumanization of women in ads are *Killing Us Softly* and *Still Killing Us Softly.* These are available in most college video collections and are also owned by a number of public libraries. Each is about thirty minutes long. Write a brief paper (two to four pages) concerning your reactions to these videos.

You may wish to focus your paper on the following issues:

1. What is the relationship suggested by the video between how women are presented in ads and the victimization of women in crimes such as rape and murder?
2. What messages does advertising send women regarding their independence, beauty, and ability to love their families?
3. What messages does advertising send to men concerning what women want from them?
4. How are men depicted in ads, and what messages do you think men are given by such images?

Endnotes

1. Stanton Wheeler, "Trends and Problems in the Sociological Study of Crime," *Social Problems*, June 23, 1976, 525. This criticism has been made by others, as well. See especially Alexander Liazos, "The Poverty of the Sociology of Deviance: Nuts, Sluts, and Preverts," *Social Problems* 20, Summer 1972, 10–20.

2. Marshall B. Clinard, *Illegal Corporate Behavior* (Washington, DC: U.S. Department of Justice, Law Enforcement Assistance Administration, 1979). See also Marshall B. Clinard and Peter C. Yeager, "Corporate Crime: Issues in Research," *Criminology* 16, August 1978, 255–72.

3. See Robert Sherrill, "A Year in Corporate Crime," *The Nation*, April 7, 1997.

4. Russell Mokhiber, "Crime Wave!: The Top 100 Corporate Criminals of the 1990s," *Multinational Monitor*, July/August 1999, 9.

5. Wendy Enloe, *Effective Deterrence for White-collar Crime: Perceptions of Attorneys Specializing in Antitrust* (masters thesis) (San Jose State Univerity, 2000), 7.

6. William S. Laufer, "Corporate Liability, Risk Shifting, and the Paradox of Compliance," *Vanderbilt Law Review* 52, October 1999, 1409.

7. Ibid., 1344.

8. Ibid., 15. During these years, 1996–1998, between 23 and 44 percent of antitrust offenders received prison sentences.

9. Enloe, 12–13.

10. Ibid., 13.

11. J. Donahue, "The Missing Corporate Rap Sheet: Missing Government Records of Corporate Abuses," *Multinational Monitor*, December 1992, 14–16.

12. Ibid., 19.

13. Karl Marx, *Capital: A Critique of Political Economy* (New York: International Publishers, 1967). Originally published in 1866.

14. From Mark J. Green, Beverly C. Moore, Jr., and Bruce Wasserstein, *The Closed Enterprise System*, 7. Copyright © 1972 by The Center for Study of Responsive Law. Reprinted by permission of Viking Penguin, Inc.

15. U.S. Bureau of the Census 1982, *Census of Manufacturers: Concentration Ratios in Manufacturing* (Washington, DC: Government Printing Office, 1986), 524.

16. Associated Press, October 3, 1980. Some of the material in this section is adapted from D. Stanley Eitzen and Maxine Baca Zinn, *Social Problems*, 4th ed. (Boston: Allyn & Bacon, 1989).

17. *Statistical Abstract of the United States, 1986* (Washington, DC: U.S. Government Printing Office, 1986), 524.

18. Amati Etzioni, "Is Corporate Crime Worth the Time?" *Business and Society Review* 36, Winter 1990, 33.

19. Sherrill.

20. *New York Times*, March 3, 1996, A-1.

21. Eddie Correia, "The Reagan Assault on Antitrust," *Multinational Monitor* 7, February 15, 1986, 3–7. Some of the material in this section is adapted from Eitzen and Zinn, *Social Problems*, 4th ed.

22. Quoted in Green, Moore, and Wasserstein, 13–14.

23. This section on the consequences of shared monopolies is taken primarily from Green, Moore, and Wasserstein, 14–26; and Jack Newfield and Jeff Greenfield, *A Populist Manifesto* (New York: Warner Paperback Library, 1972), 48–56.

24. Green, Moore, and Wasserstein, 14.

25. Richard B. DuBoff, "Wealth Distribution Study Causes Tinge of Discomfort," *In These Times*, December 1984, 17.

26. Newfield and Greenfield, 51.

27. William Conner and Robert Smiley, quoted in Ralph Nader, Mark Green, and Joel Seligman, *Taming the Giant Corporation* (New York: W.W. Norton, 1976), 216.

28. Green, Moore, and Wasserstein, 15. See also "The Monopoly Inflation Game," *Dollars and Sense,* January 23, 1977, 12–13.

29. Nader, Green, and Seligman, 213.

30. For comparison, see Michael Parenti, *Power and the Powerless* (New York: St. Martin's Press, 1978).

31. Mark J. Green, "The High Cost of Monopoly," *The Progressive* 36, March 1972, 4; and "The Forbes Sales 500," *Forbes,* April 25, 1988, 136–37.

32. *Fortune,* May, 6 1997.

33. Ibid.

34. Green, Moore, and Wasserstein, 244.

35. David Hapgood, *The Screwing of the Average Man: How the Rich Get Richer and You Get Poorer* (New York: Bantam, 1975), 152.

36. "The Monopoly Inflation Game," 12.

37. Robert F. Lanzillotti, "The Automobile Industry," in *The Structure of American Industry,* (New York: Macmillan), 282.

38. Green, Moore, and Wasserstein, 246.

39. The following is taken primarily from Harvey A. Farberman, "A Criminogenic Market Structure: The Automobile Industry," *Sociological Quarterly* 16, Autumn 1975, 438–57. See also W. N. Leonard and N. G. Weber, "Automakers and Dealers: A Study of Criminogenic Market Forces," *Law and Society* 4, February 1970, 407–24.

40. For comparison, see Hapgood, 164–67.

41. For comparison, see Gerald F. Seib, "Dallas Ordinance against Car Repair Frauds," in *Crime at the Top: Deviance in Business and the Professions,* ed. John M. Johnson and Jack D. Douglas (Philadelphia: J.B. Lippincott, 1978), 319–22.

42. For a description of these techniques, see Roger Rapoport, "How I Made $193.85 Selling Cars," in *The Marketplace: Consumerism in America,* edited by the editors of Ramparts with Frank Browning (San Francisco: Canfield, 1972), 39–47.

43. Green, Moore, and Wasserstein, 155.

44. Elliott Currie and Jerome H. Skolnick, *America's Problems,* 2nd ed. (Glenview, IL: Scott, Foresman, 1988), 86.

45. George A. Hay and Daniel Kelley, "An Empirical Survey of Price Fixing Conspiracies," *Journal of Law and Economics* 17, April 1974, 13–38.

46. "The Ten Worst Corporations," *Mother Jones,* January 1997, 30ff.

47. Hay and Kelley, 26–27.

48. Mokhiber, 11.

49. The following account is taken primarily from three sources: Gilbert Geis, "White Collar Crime: The Heavy Electrical Equipment Cases of 1961," in *Corporate and Governmental Deviance,* ed. M. David Erman and Richard J. Lundman (New York: Oxford University Press, 1978), 59–79; Richard A. Smith, "The Incredible Electrical Conspiracy," *Fortune,* Part I, April 1961, 132–37, 170–80; Part II, May 1961, 161–64, 210–24; and Green, Moore, and Wasserstein, 154–57.

50. Smith, Part I, 137.

51. For comparison, see *Wall Street Journal,* July 27, 1964, 22. For the account of more recent cases of corporations and their executives receiving little if any punishment for their crimes, see Robert Stuart Nathan, "Coddled Criminals," *Harper's,* January 1980, 30–35; "Crime in the Suites: On the Rise," *Newsweek,* December 3, 1979, 114–20; and Russell Mokhiber, *Corporate Crime and Violence* (San Francisco: Sierra Club Books, 1988).

52. Green, Moore, and Wasserstein, 152; and *New Republic,* February 20, 1961, 7.

53. Quoted in Smith, Part I, 133.

54. Ibid., 135.

55. Ralph Nader and Mark Green, "Crime in the Suites," *New Republic,* April 29, 1972, 20–21.

56. For a late 1970s example of a price-fixing violation in the forest products industry, see Jean A. Briggs, "For Whom Does the Bell Toll?" *Forbes,* June 25, 1979, 33–36.

57. For comparison, see Jennifer Cross, *The Supermarket Trap,* rev. ed. (Bloomington: Indiana University Press, 1976), 119, 124; and Eric Schnapper, "Consumer Legislation and the Poor," in *Consumerism,* 2nd ed., ed. David A. Aaker and George S. Day (New York: Free Press, 1974), 87.

58. Paul Jacobs, "Keeping the Poor Poor," in *Crisis in American Institutions,* 4th ed., ed. Jerome H. Skolnick and Elliott Currie (Boston: Little, Brown, 1979), 96.

59. Cross, 122.

60. "Price of Antibiotic Used by Victims of AIDS Quadrupled in 3 Years," *Denver Post,* October 31, 1987, 4-A. See also Kathryn Phillips, "Making a Killing from AIDS Drugs," *In These Times,* November 11–17, 1987, 6, 10.

61. Tim Kingston, "The Unhealthy Profits of AZT," *The Nation,* October 17, 1987, 408–9.

62. D. Drake and M. Uhlman, *Making Drugs Making Money* (Kansas City, MO: Andrews & McMeel, 1993), 3, 8, 21–22.

63. M. Konner, *Dear America* (Reading, MA: Addison-Wesley, 1993), 54.

64. Ibid., 54–55.

65. "20/20."

66. Ibid., 19–20 (transcript).

67. Ibid., 21.

68. Ibid., 21–23.

69. Jack Anderson, "Secret Documents That Unveil the Drug Industry's Deception," *Rocky Mountain News,* September 28, 1978, 65.

70. Peter Phillips and Project Censored, *The Top 25 Censored Newstories of 1997* (New York: Seven Locks, 1998), 114.

71. Harold Freeman, "On Consuming the Surplus," *The Progressive* 41, February 1977, 20–21.

72. For an elaboration of the role of television in the manipulation of people, see Rose K. Goldsen, *The Show and Tell Machine: How Television Works and Works You Over* (New York: Dial Press, 1975).

73. John Philip Cohane, "The American Predicament: Truth No Longer Counts," in *Criminology: Crime and Criminality,* 2nd ed., ed. Martin R. Haskell and Lewis Yablonsky (Chicago: Rand McNally, 1978), 172 (originally appeared in *Los Angeles Times,* October 1, 1972).

74. See *New York Times,* January 1, 1994, A-27.

75. *Los Angeles Times,* August 20, 1992, D-2.

76. *New York Times,* April 29, 1994, C-2.

77. *Wall Street Journal,* February 11, 1994, B-6.

78. *Washington Post,* September 30, 1993, D-11.

79. *National Fraud Information Center Newsletter,* January 1997, 1.

80. Ivan L. Preston, *The Great American Blow-up: Puffery in Advertising and Selling* (Madison: University of Wisconsin Press, 1975), 220, 229–31.

81. Ibid., 235.

82. See, for example, Harold Takooshain and Richard Tashjian, "The Unnatural Use of Natural Advertising," *Business and Society Review* 76, Winter 1991, 41–47; and Doug Podolsky et al., "Hype-Free Food Labels," *U.S. News & World Report,* June 3, 1991, 67–70.

83. *Washington Post,* December 23, 1993, D-10.

84. Preston, 18–20; and H. J. Rotfeld and L. Preston, "The Potential Impact of Research on Advertising Law," *Journal of Advertising Research* 21, 1981, 9–16.

85. Rotfeld and Preston.

86. H. J. Rotfeld and K. B. Rotzall, "Is Advertising Puffery Believed?" *Journal of Advertising Research* 9, 1980, 16–20.

87. R. G. Wyckham, "Implied Superiority Claims," *Journal of Advertising Research* 27, February/March 1987, 54–63.

88. Ibid., 55.

89. Hal Hemmelstein, *Understanding Television* (New York: Praeger, 1984), 68, 271.

90. Rotfeld and Preston, 10.

91. Preston, 32–33.

92. Edwin H. Sutherland and Donald R. Cressey, *Criminology,* 9th ed. (Philadelphia: J.B. Lippincott, 1974), 42.

93. John Greenwald, "A Blown Billion: Daiwa Bank's Rogue Employee Allegedly Made 30,000 Illicit Trades. Why Didn't Anybody Notice?" *Time,* October 9, 1995.

94. *Multinational Monitor,* October 1995.

95. See *New York Times,* November 11, 1993, C-1.

96. Leonard Buder, "Jail Terms for Two in Beech-Nut Case, *New York Times,* June 17, 1988, 29, 31; and James Traub, "Into the Mouths of Babes," *New York Times Magazine,* July 24, 1988, 18–20, 51.

97. Mokhiber, 19.

98. Ibid., 14.

99. John Kenneth Galbraith, "Crime and No Punishment," *Esquire,* December 1977, 102–6. See also David McClintick, "The Biggest Ponzi Scheme: A Reporter's Journal," in *Swindled,* ed. Donald Moffett (New York: DowJones Books, 1976), 9–126.

100. See *San Francisco Chronicle,* September 29, 1993, A-7.

101. Johnson and Douglas, 151.

102. Bureau of the Census, *Statistical Abstract of the United States, 1984* (Washington, DC: U.S. Government Printing Office, 1983), xxvi, 567.

103. The following is taken from Edwin H. Sutherland, *White Collar Crime* (New York: Holt, Rinehart and Winston, 1961), 21–33.

4

Corporate Deviance:
Human Jeopardy

This chapter addresses the corporate disregard for the welfare of people, which involves the abuse of consumers, workers, and society itself. Our thesis is that the profit-maximizing behaviors practiced by corporations under monopoly capitalism are hazardous to our individual and collective health and therefore constitute another manifestation of elite deviance. The first part of this chapter examines four manifestations of corporate deviance that jeopardize individual health: unsafe products, food pollution, tobacco products and dangerous working conditions. The second part focuses on two problems that society faces from various corporate activities: the waste of natural resources and pollution of the environment.

Individual Jeopardy

Unsafe Products

Commonly, the concern over violence in society is directed toward murder, rape, child abuse, and riots. We do not include in the context of violence the harm inflicted on people by unsafe products. The National Commission on Product Safety has revealed that 20 million Americans are injured in the home as a result of incidents connected with consumer products. "Of the total, 110,000 are permanently disabled and 30,000 are killed. A significant number could have been spared if more attention had been paid to hazard reduction."[1] The commission also made two additional points:

> Manufacturers have it in their power to design, build, and market products in ways that will reduce if not eliminate most unreasonable and unnecessary hazards. Manufacturers are best able to take the longest strides to safety in

the least time….[However,] competitive forces may require management to subordinate safety factors to cost considerations, styling, and other marketing imperatives.[2]

Considerable evidence points to numerous unsafe products, from clothing to toys to tires, but nowhere has the poor corporate safety record been more visible than in the auto industry. The indictment against this industry involves two basic charges: (1) faulty design and (2) working against governmental and consumer efforts to add safety devices as basic equipment.

The Auto Industry.   In 1929, the president of Du Pont tried to induce the president of General Motors (GM) to use safety glass in Chevrolets, as Ford was already doing. The president of GM felt that this addition was too costly and would therefore hinder sales. In his reply to Du Pont, he said, "I would very much rather spend the same amount of money in improving our car in other ways because I think, from the standpoint of selfish business, it would be a very much better investment. You can say, perhaps, that I am selfish, but business is selfish. We are not a charitable institution; we are trying to make a profit for our stockholders."[3]

This example shows how the profit motive superseded the possibility of preventing deaths and serious injuries. Unfortunately, this is not an isolated instance in the auto industry. We will review two representative cases, one involving GM and the other, Ford.

Ralph Nader attacked GM's Corvair in *Unsafe at Any Speed* (1972), showing how that car had many dangerous defects, including a heater that gave off carbon monoxide and an instability that increased its likelihood of overturning.[4] GM's response to this indictment was to attack his credibility and hide evidence supporting his allegations.[5]

Throughout much of the 1970s, the fastest-selling domestic subcompact was Ford's Pinto. From the very beginning, however, the Pinto was flawed by a fuel system that ruptured easily in rear-end collisions.[6] Preproduction crash tests established this problem, but since the assembly-line machinery had already been tooled, Ford decided to manufacture the car as it was, despite the fact that it could produce a much safer gas tank. This decision was made partly because the Pinto was on a tight production schedule; Ford was trying to enter the lucrative subcompact market dominated by Volkswagen as quickly as possible. The time span from the conception of the Pinto to production was targeted at twenty-five months, when the normal time for a new car was forty-three months. Also involved in the decision to go with the original gas tank were styling considerations and the effort to maximize trunk space. The profits over human considerations was clearly evident in Ford's reluctance to change the design of the Pinto as fatalities and injuries occurred because of the faulty gas tank. Although the company calculated that it would cost only $11 to make each car safe, it decided that this was too costly. Ford reasoned that 180 burn deaths, 180 serious burn injuries, and 2,100 burned vehicles would cost $49.5 million (each death was figured at $200,000). But doing a recall of all Pintos and making each $11 repair would amount to $137 million (see Table 4.1).

In addition to the decision to leave the Pinto alone, Ford lobbied in Washington to convince government regulatory agencies and Congress that auto accidents are caused not by cars but by (1) people and (2) highway conditions. This philosophy is rather like blaming a robbery on the victim. Well, what did you expect? You were carrying money, weren't you? It is an extraordinary experience to hear automotive "safety engineers" talk for hours without ever mentioning cars. They will advocate spending billions educating youngsters, punishing drunks, and redesigning street signs. Listening to them, you can momentarily begin to think that it is easier to control 100 million drivers than a handful of manufacturers. They show movies about guardrail design and advocate the clear-cutting of trees 100 feet back from every highway in the nation. If a car is unsafe, they argue, it is because its owner doesn't properly drive it. Or, perhaps, maintain it.[7]

Meanwhile, fiery crashes involving Pintos occurred with some regularity. Liability suits against Ford increased, with judgments routinely found against the company. In 1978, a jury in California awarded $127.8 million, including $125 million in punitive damages, to a teenager badly burned when

TABLE 4.1 *$11 vs. a Burn Death: Benefits and Costs Relating to Fuel Leakage Associated with the Static Rollover Test Portion of FMVSS 208*

Benefits		*Costs*	
Savings:	180 burn deaths 180 serious burn injuries 2,100 burned vehicles	Sales:	11 million cars 1.5 million light trucks
Unit Cost:	$200,000 per death $67,000 per injury $700 per vehicle	Unit Cost:	$11 per car $11 per truck
Total Benefit:	180 × ($200,000) + 180 × ($67,000) + 2,100 × ($700) = $49.5 million	Total Cost:	11,000,000 × ($11) + 1,500,000 × ($11) = $137 million

Source: Ford Motor Company internal memorandum, "Fatalities Associated with Crash-Induced Fuel Leakage and Fires," cited in Mark Dowie, "Pinto Madness," *Mother Jones* 2 (September/ October 1977), 24. © Mother Jones. Used with permission.

his 1972 Pinto burst into flames after being hit in the rear by a car traveling at thirty-five miles per hour.[8]

In that same year, ten years after the government had begun investigating the Pinto problem, the Department of Transportation finally announced that its tests showed conclusively that the Pinto was unsafe and ordered a recall of all 1971 to 1976 Pintos. One critic of Ford's defiance of human considerations made this telling observation: "One wonders how long Ford Motor Company would continue to market lethal cars were Henry Ford II and Lee Iacocca [the top Ford officials at the time] serving twenty-year terms in Leavenworth for consumer homicide."[9]

In a similar but less celebrated case, GM executives were repeatedly warned by test drivers and internal company documents of serious braking problems in 1980 X-body automobiles before production. The Justice Department charged that GM failed to act on the braking problem and later withheld information from federal officials regarding these cars (the 1980 Chevrolet Citation, Pontiac Phoenix, Oldsmobile Omega, and Buick Skylark). By August 1983, the government had received more than 1,700 complaints about brakes locking in the X-body cars, including accidents involving 15 deaths when the cars went into spins.[10]

An important element in automobile safety is tire safety. Here, too, there have been instances of corporate wrongdoing. Beginning in 1972, Firestone was aware of extensive failure problems with its 500-type belted radial tires. In 1975, company tests revealed a serious problem with tire separation. In 1976, the Center for Auto Safety noted the high incidence of Firestone 500 blowouts and reported the data to the National Highway Traffic Safety Administration (NHTSA). Meanwhile, Firestone continued to manufacture, advertise (spending $28 million annually), and sell the defective tires, a total of 23.5 million by 1978.

The government wanted Firestone to recall the 11 million tires in use voluntarily, but Firestone refused. Firestone also argued in court that NHTSA should not make public a survey it took of consumers, that was particularly critical of the 500s. When this effort failed and the survey results were publicized, Firestone's response was to dump its remaining 500s onto the market at clearance prices. The director of the Center for Auto Safety called this sale "a callous display of corporate disregard for human life."[11] In sum, a House of Representatives committee reported that Firestone 500 separations "had caused thousands of accidents, hundreds of injuries, and 34 known fatalities."[12] In 1980, Firestone was fined a token $50,000 for selling a defective product.

Resistance to Consumer and Governmental Pressures to Provide Safety Devices. The automobile industry has traditionally resisted new safety devices because the added cost might hurt sales.[13] Following tests conducted by the government and the insurance industry in the late 1950s, the government ruled that lap belts must be installed in all new cars built after January 1, 1965. The auto industry resisted (as it has since resisted other requirements such as lap-and-shoulder belts, ignition interlocks, and buzzers), despite clear evidence that these devices would be effective in saving lives: "between 1968 and 1977, the stock of cars on the road grew from 83 million to 112 million, an increase of 35 percent. Over the same period traffic fatalities declined 6 percent."[14]

Since lap belts are effective only when used and relatively few were being used at the time, the government reasoned that safety could be improved significantly if a passive restraint such as the air bag were included as standard equipment. A study by Allstate Insurance concluded that air bags would reduce occupant crash deaths by 65 percent. Had all cars been so equipped in 1975, 9,500 fewer persons would have died in car crashes in that year instead of the 27,200 who did. Additionally, 104,000 serious injuries could have been prevented each year.[15]

Recent research indicates that General Motors, Standard Oil (now Exxon), and Du Pont colluded for decades to make and market lead-containing gasoline, a deadly poison, despite the existence of safe alternatives. Abetted by the U.S. government, these corporations suppressed the scientific knowledge that lead kills. Today lead-containing gasoline is still sold in poor nations all over the world.[16]

Health Products.   Corporations have marketed numerous products to promote health that are known to be dangerous. What follows is a representative sample of such cases.

- **Item:** In 1995, three Luv'N'Care baby pacifier marketing firms pled guilty to fourteen violations of federal law and Consumer Product Safety Commission (CPSC) regulations. Under the August 1995 plea agreement, the companies will pay a $140,000 criminal penalty for marketing pacifiers that put defenseless children at risk of suffocating or choking to death. The CPSC claimed it had received dozens of complaints between 1990 and 1994 about the pacifiers.[17]
- **Item:** Eli Lilly and Company pleaded guilty in 1985 to federal charges that it had failed to report to the government deaths and toxic reactions associated with its arthritic drug Oraflex.[18] Lilly had also marketed DES (diethylstilbestrol), which had been found to cause reproductive problems in the children of mothers who used it in the 1950s. The Lilly product Darvon has been associated with 11,000 deaths and 79,000 emergency room visits.[19]

Food Pollution

The food industry is obviously big business. In this section, we examine how the food industry, in its search for more profits, often disregards the health of consumers, which constitutes deviance. We explore four areas in which human considerations are often secondary to profit: (1) the sale of adulterated products, (2) the extensive use of chemical additives, (3) the increased use of sugar and fats, and (4) the sale of products known to be harmful.

Adulterated Products.   We will use the meat industry as our illustration of blatant disregard for the health of consumers. Upton Sinclair's exposé of the Chicago stockyards and meatpacking houses around 1900 showed how spoiled meat was sold, how dangerous ingredients (such as rats and dung) were included in sausage, and how rats overran piles of meat stored under leaking roofs.[20] President Theodore Roosevelt commissioned an investigation of Chicago meatpackers, and, as a result, the Meat Inspection Act of 1906 required that meat sold in interstate commerce had to be inspected according to federal standards. However, meat processed and sold within a state was not subject to the law, thus omitting as late as 1967 nearly 15 percent of the meat slaughtered and 25 percent of all meat processed in the United States. As a result,

> Surveys of packing houses in Delaware, Virginia, and North Carolina found the following tidbits in the meat: animal hair, sawdust, flies, abscessed pork livers, and snuff spit out by the meat workers. To add even further flavoring, packing houses whose meat did not cross state lines could use 4-D meat (dead, dying, diseased, and disabled) and chemical additives that would not pass federal inspection. Such plants were not all minor operations; some were run by the giants Armour, Swift, and Wilson.[21]

In 1967, the Wholesome Meat Act was passed, specifying that state inspection standards must at least match federal standards. This was accomplished in 1971, but there have been continuing violations. One problem is meat that is returned by a retailer to a packer as unsatisfactory and is then resold as number 2 meat to another customer if it meets standards of wholesomeness. As an example of how this can be abused, consider the following occurrence in a Los Angeles Hormel plant.

> When the original customers returned the meat to Hormel, they used the following terms to describe it: "moldy liverloaf, sour party hams, leaking bologna, discolored bacon, off-condition hams, and slick and slimy spareribs." Hormel renewed these products with cosmetic measures (reconditioning, trimming, and washing). Spareribs returned for sliminess, discoloration, and stickiness were rejuvenated through curing and smoking, renamed Windsor Loins, and sold in ghetto stores for more than fresh pork chops.[22]

This Hormel abuse occurred because the U.S. Department of Agriculture inspector, who was paid $6,000 annually by Hormel for overtime, looked the other way.[23]

Meatpackers are also deceptive about what is included in their products. The labels on packages are not always complete. Consider, for instance, the ingredients of the hot dog.

The hot dog…by law can contain 69 percent water, salt, spices, corn syrup and cereal and 15 percent chicken; that still leaves a little room for goat meat, pigs' ears, eyes, stomachs, snouts, udders, bladders and esophagus—all legally okay. There is no more all-American way to take a break at the old ball game than to have water and pigs' snouts on a bun, but you might prefer to go heavier on the mustard from now on.[24]

Upton Sinclair's lurid description of the 1900s-era Chicago slaughterhouses fits some situations even today. In 1984, Nebraska Beef Processors and its Colorado subsidiary, Cattle King Packing Company, the largest supplier of ground meat to school lunch programs and also a major supplier of meat to the Department of Defense, supermarkets, and fast-food chains, was found guilty of (1) regularly bringing dead animals into its slaughterhouses and mixing rotten meat into its hamburgers, (2) labeling old meat with phony dates, and (3) deceiving U.S. Department of Agriculture inspectors by matching diseased carcasses with the healthy heads from larger cows.[25]

The Nebraska Beef–Cattle King scandal was not an isolated case. Two additional examples make this point. In 1979, a New Jersey firm was convicted of making pork sausage with an unauthorized chemical that masks discoloration of spoiled meat. And in 1982 a California company used walkie-talkies to avoid inspectors while doctoring rotten sausage.[26]

Extensive Use of Chemical Additives.   The profits from the food industry come mainly from processing farm goods by fortifying, enriching, and reformulating them to produce goods that look appealing, have the right taste and aroma, and will not spoil. More than 1,500 food additives have approved use as flavors, colors, thickeners, preservatives, and other agents for controlling the properties of food. Let's briefly look at some of these additives.[27]

- Sodium nitrates and nitrites are added to keep meat products appearing blood red. Nitrates are also used to preserve smoked fish.
- A variety of preservatives is used to prevent the spoilage of bread, cereals, margarine, fish, confections, jellies, and soft drinks. The most commonly used are BHT, BHA, sodium benzoate, and benzoic acid.
- About 95 percent of the color in the food we eat is the result of added synthetic colors. The use of red dye No. 2 was prohibited by the government when it was found to cause cancer in mice, although it is still allowed in maraschino cherries because it is assumed that no one will eat more than one or two at a time.
- Flour, that all-purpose staple, is bleached and conditioned by a number of potent poisons: hydrogen acetone, benzyl peroxide, chlorine dioxide, nitrogen oxide, and nitrosyl chloride. Also added to flour are such strengtheners as potassium bromate and ammonium presulfate.

An indirect additive that affects the health of consumers is one that is fed to animals. DES, an artificial female sex hormone, fattens about 75 percent of the beef cattle in the United States. This hormone is added because it causes dramatic weight gain on less feed. It has been outlawed for use with poultry, although hens are fed arsenic because it makes them lay more eggs.

Sugar substitutes are another type of food additive that has questionable health consequences. Cyclamates were banned in 1970 after tests linked them to various types of cancer. And saccharin, another additive, has been shown to be dangerous but has not been banned; Congress has only decreed that food containing saccharin must carry warning labels. The latest sugar substitute, aspartame (or Nutrasweet), is also believed by some scientists to pose a health danger to some 50 million regular users. However, no ban or warning has been issued for products containing Nutrasweet. The per-capita consumption of the various noncaloric sweeteners has increased from the sugar-sweetness equivalent of 2.2 pounds in 1960 to 20.0 pounds in 1988.[28]

According to a growing number of scientists, aspartame is the most dangerous substance added to foods. Aspartame currently accounts for more than 75 percent of the adverse reactions to food additives reported to the U.S. Food and Drug Administration. Many of these reactions are very serious.[29] A few of the ninety different documented symptoms listed in a 1994 Heath and Human Services report as being caused by aspartame include the following:[30]

Headaches and migraines	Dizziness
Seizures resulting in death	Nausea
Numbness	Muscle spasms
Weight gain	Rashes
Depression	Fatigue
Irritability	Tachycardia
Insomnia	Vision problems
Hearing loss	Heart palpitations
Breathing difficulties	Anxiety attacks
Slurred speech	Loss of taste
Tinnitus	Vertigo
Memory loss	Joint pain
Brain tumors	Multiple sclerosis
Epilepsy	Chronic fatigue syndrome
Parkinson's disease	Alzheimer's
Mental retardation	Lymphoma
Birth defects	Fibromyalgia
Diabetes	

Aspartame is 10 percent methanol, a form of alcohol that can be a deadly poison. Symptoms from methanol poisoning include headaches, ear ringing, dizziness, nausea, gastrointestinal disturbances, weakness, chills, memory lapses, numbness and extremity pains, behavioral disturbances, and neuritis. The most well known problems from methanol poisoning are vision problems, which can range from blurred vision to blindness.

Even the Air Force and Navy magazines, such as *Flying Safety* and *Navy Physiology*, have warned in articles about the hazards of aspartame's cumulative deleterious effects, which include the greater likelihood of birth defects and the danger to pilots of seizures and vertigo.[31]

There is a great deal of controversy among scientists about the effects of additives in our diet. "Altogether, laboratory tests have produced evidence that some 1,400 substances, drugs, food additives, pesticides, industrial chemicals, cosmetics, might cause cancer. But there are only a few chemicals which all the experts see as linked to human cancer."[32] Typically, government scientists disagree with the scientists hired by industry.[33] Several considerations, though, should make us cautious about what we eat.

First, many of the additives are poisons. The quantities in food may be minute, but just what are the tolerance levels? Is any poison, in any amount, appropriate in food? Is there the possibility of residue buildup in vital organs?

Second, what happens to laboratory animals fed relatively large quantities of these additives? They are poisoned, get cancer, and suffer from other maladies induced by the additives.

Finally, what happens with the interaction of these additives on humans? Scientists may be able to test the effects of a few chemicals, but what about the hundreds of thousands of possible combinations? In a slice of bread, for example, there can be as many as ninety-three possible different additives. The danger is that it takes years, maybe twenty or thirty, of eating a particular diet for an individual to develop cancer. Since most of the additives are relatively new, we do not know what they may eventually cause. We do know that the average American has increased his or her yearly intake of food additives from 3 pounds in 1965 to about 5 pounds in 1977.[34] And cancer rates continue to rise.

Why, then, do companies insist on adding these potentially harmful chemicals to our food? One possibility is that consumers demand more variety and convenience. But, more importantly, the food industry has found that processing synthetic foods is very profitable. As one food marketer remarked, "The profit margin on food additives is fantastically good, much better than the profit margins on basic, traditional foods."[35] Hightower has shown how this works:

> It gets down to this: Processing and packaging of food are becoming more important pricing factors than the food itself. Why would food corporations rather sell highly processed and packaged food than the much simpler matter of selling basics? Because processing and packaging spell profits.
>
> First, the more you do to a product, the more chances there are to build in profit margins—Heinz can sell tomatoes for a profit, or it can bottle the tomatoes for a bigger profit, or it can process the tomatoes into ketchup for still

more profit, or it can add spices to the ketchup and sell it as barbeque sauce for a fat profit, or it can add flavors and meat tenderizer to the barbeque sauce for the fattest profit of all.

Second, processing and packaging allow artificial differentiation of one company's product from that of another—in other words, selling on the basis of brand names. Potatoes can be sold in bulk, or they can be put in a sack and labeled Sun Giant, which will bring a higher price and more profit.

Third, processing and packaging allow the use of additives to keep the same item on the shelf much longer and they allow for shipment over long distances, thus expanding the geographic reach of a corporation.

Fourth, processing and packaging separate consumers from the price of raw food, allowing oligopolistic middlemen to hold up the consumer price of their products even when the farm price falls. When the spinach crop is so abundant that spinach prices tumble at the farm level, the supermarket price of Stouffer's frozen spinach souffle does not go down.[36]

What's more, American corporations, in their quest for profits, have knowingly marketed defective medical devices, lethal drugs, carcinogens, toxic pesticides, and other harmful products overseas when they have been banned for sale in the United States. (A more detailed discussion of such practices is found in Chapter 5.)

Sugar and Fat Consumption.   Consumers have begun to question the types of food provided by the food industry and the advertising efforts to push certain questionable items. In particular, we will address how the food industry has promoted the consumption of sugar and fats. In the previous section, we noted the problem with chemical additives. However, we did not discuss the foremost food additive—sugar. The introduction of processed foods has increased the annual amount of sweeteners consumed (refined sugar, corn sweeteners, and noncaloric sweeteners) from 116.2 pounds per capita in 1960 to 179.6 pounds in 1988.[37]

A 1991 study by the Center for Science in the Public Interest concluded that Saturday morning children's television programs were loaded with commercials for foods high in sugar and fat, including drinks, chips, salty canned pastas, and fast food. The number of commercials promoting high-sugar cereals has increased 25 percent since 1977.[38]

The use of sugars presents four health dangers. First, dental disease, such as cavities and gum problems, is clearly exacerbated by sugar. Another problem is that refined sugar, although an energy source, offers little nutritional value. Not only does it deprive the body of essential nutrients found in complex carbohydrates, but it actually increases the body's need for certain vitamins. Third, there appears to be a relationship between the proportion of refined sugar calories in the diet and the incidence of diabetes. Finally, there is the problem of obesity.

Another trend in the U.S. diet is the increased consumption of fats. From 1960 to 1989, the average annual amount of fat consumed per person rose from 45.1 pounds to 60.7 pounds.[39] One source of this fat for modern Americans is the potato chip. Potato chips are 40 percent fat compared to 0.1 percent fat in baked potatoes.[40] Food processors push us to eat potato chips rather than fresh potatoes because the profit is 1,100 percent more.[41] In 1977, the Senate Select Committee on Nutrition recommended that Americans reduce their consumption of fats by 40 percent because fat consumption leads to problems of obesity, cancer (breast and colon), and heart disease.[42]

Enticing Children.   The increased consumption of additives, sugar, and fats in food by children is a special health concern. Children are an important market, and food producers have spent multimillions of dollars in advertising aimed at them. Obviously, these corporations believe that their advertising influences the interests, needs, and demands of children. This belief is backed by research findings that show that children are susceptible to this influence. One study of youngsters in grades 1 to 5 found that 75 percent had asked their mothers to purchase the cereals that they had seen on television. In another study, 80 percent of the mothers of children aged two to six expressed the conviction that television ads caused their children to ask for certain products.[43]

The nutritional problem emanating from the television advertising blitz aimed at children is that the most advertised food products are sugar-coated cereals, candies, and other sweet snack foods. One study, for example, found that 96 percent of all food advertising on Saturday and Sunday children's TV programs was for sweets.[44] This report by the Federal Trade Commission (FTC) shows that these advertisements are effective, for several reasons:

> (a) [C]hildren's requests for specific, brand-name cereals and snackfoods are frequently, if not usually, honored by their parents; (b) very high proportions of children are able to name specific (heavily advertised) brands as their favorites; (c) when asked to list acceptable snacks, high proportions of children mention cookies, candy, cake, and ice cream, including specific (heavily advertised) products; (d) U.S. consumption of snack desserts has increased markedly since 1962, and significant proportions of the purchases are made by children.[45]

The television advertising directed at children is effective because the advertisers have done their research. Social science techniques have been used by motivation researchers in laboratory situations to determine how children of various ages react to different visual and auditory stimuli. Children are watched through two-way mirrors, their behavior is photographed, and their autonomic responses (for example, eye pupil dilation) are recorded to see what sustains their interest, their subconscious involvement, and the degree of pleasure that they experience.[46] Thus, advertisers have found that if one can associate fun, power, or a fascinating animated character with a product, children will want that product.

The staff of the FTC has argued that all television commercials aimed at children are inherently unfair and deceptive. The young, they contend, are unable to be rational consumers. Therefore, in 1978, the commission proposed that (1) there be a ban on all ads for children under age eight, (2) a ban on all ads for highly sugared foods for those under eleven be enforced, and (3) there be a requirement for nutritional counter-ads to be paid for by industry.

This stance has been met with derision from the advertising and corporate industries. In hearings conducted by the FTC, advertisers and manufacturers argued against the evils of government regulation. The attorney for Mattel, a major manufacturer of children's toys, testified, "Our position, simply stated, is that the proposed ban is unconstitutional, economically injurious and unnecessary."[47] A spokesman for the National Association of Broadcasters also argued that self-regulation by the industry has worked: "Industry self-regulation has in fact been successful and now provides the mechanisms for effective regulation of advertising to children."[48] Also at the hearings, the counsel for the Kellogg Company said that, "in an American democratic capitalistic society we must all learn, top to bottom, to care for ourselves. And the last thing we need in the next twenty years is a national nanny."[49]

These arguments have been countered by others. A child psychologist agreed with the FTC ban, saying, "I'm angry. In fact, I'm mad as hell. I'm furious that the most powerful communications system and the most powerfully and persuasive educational device that has ever existed in human history is being used systematically to mislead and lie to children." Friedlander added that children under the ages of six to eight "are absolutely unable to understand and defend themselves against the ulterior motives of our business system."[50]

Syndicated columnist Ellen Goodman has said,

> Personally, I can't imagine why we should allow advertisers into our homes when they behave like decadent tooth fairies offering our gullible children candy bars and Frankenberrys in return for their molars. But the thing that continues to evade my understanding is how business people have the nerve to bellow against government when they won't address their own faults and hazards. They are the ones, after all, making us choose between nutrition and regulation.[51]

Bill Moyers, after confessing a bias for the necessity of advertising in general, ended his television program with these words:

> It's astonishing to me that advertising to young children is even a matter of debate; that high-powered people with enormous skills and resources

should have unbridled access to the minds of young children is no less absurd because those who profit from it consider it a sacrosanct right. If the government wanted to shower 20,000 propaganda messages a year on our children [the average number of advertisements seen annually by a child in the United States], we would take to the barricades and throw the scoundrels out. Yet the words of an advertising executive are treated as constitutional writ when he tells the FTC: "Children, like everyone else, must learn the marketplace. Even if a child is deceived by an ad at age four, what harm is done? Even if a child perceives children in advertisements as friends and not actors, selling them something, where's the harm?…" In the end, this debate is between two views of human nature. One treats young children as feeling, wondering, and wondrous beings to be handled with care because they're fragile; the other treats them as members of a vast collective to be hustled. We shall know a great deal about our society when we know, in this battle, which view prevails.[52]

The Tobacco Industry

Although a number of industries have been guilty of manufacturing, advertising, and selling harmful products, we will consider only the tobacco industry. In 1979, fifteen years after the surgeon general's first warning that smoking is linked to lung cancer and other ills, the secretary of health, education, and welfare issued the new surgeon general's report on the health hazards of smoking cigarettes. The report summarized 30,000 previously published scientific studies and provided strong evidence for the following:

1. Smoking is a leading cause of lung cancer and a major factor in heart disease, bronchitis, and emphysema.
2. The babies of mothers who smoke while pregnant are born lighter and display slower rates of physical and mental growth than babies born to nonsmokers.
3. Two-pack-a-day smokers have a 100 percent greater risk of dying in any given year than nonsmokers.
4. Smoking is especially hazardous to workers in certain occupations (asbestos, rubber, textile, uranium, and chemical industries).
5. Smoking kills 400,000 Americans and costs taxpayers $18 billion annually, and passive smoke kills an additional 50,000 Americans.[53]

No medical group or scientific group in the world has disputed the conclusion that smoking is very injurious to health, yet the tobacco industry continues to push its products (buttressed, we might add, by government subsidies). In 1988, the tobacco industry spent an estimated $2.5 billion promoting its products, much of it aimed at portraying smoking as a youthful and attractive habit. In this regard, the FTC has characterized cigarette advertising as follows: "Cigarette ads associate smoking with good health,

youthful vigor, social and professional success and other attractive ideas...
that are both worthy of emulation and distant from concerns relating to
health.... Thus the cigarette is portrayed as an integral part of youth, happiness, attractiveness, personal success, and an active, vigorous life style."[54]

In addition to regular advertising, the tobacco industry has countered
the antismoking campaign in several ways, each of which indicates disregard for the health of consumers. First, the industry has refused to accept the
evidence against smoking, especially passive smoking. It argues that the
links between smoking and various diseases are merely inferences from statistics. As Bill Dwyer of the Tobacco Institute has said, "Statistics are like a
bikini bathing suit: what they reveal is interesting; what they conceal is vital."[55] Representatives of the industry argue in the media and in speeches
before civic groups that they don't encourage anyone to smoke.

A second tactic used by the tobacco industry has been to shore up its
power in Washington through extensive lobbying efforts and contributions
to the political campaigns of key decision makers.

A more subtle strategy is giving and withholding advertising money to
publications, depending on their editorial treatment of the tobacco issue.[56]
Although several publications (for example, *Reader's Digest, Good Housekeeping,* and *The New Yorker*) do not accept cigarette advertising based on principle, most do. As a result, many publications depend on these revenues and
thus do not wish to anger their sponsors by running articles critical of tobacco. *Time* and *Newsweek,* for example, have published supplements on
health topics in cooperation with prestigious medical organizations such as
the American Medical Association; however, most of the physician-prepared
materials on smoking were edited out.[57] Tobacco companies have targeted
women in particular as potential smokers and stepped up advertising in
women's magazines. In response, these magazines have shown near silence
on the dangers of cigarettes. A study by the American Council on Science
and Health found the following with respect to women's magazines:

> *Cosmopolitan,* which receives $5.5 million a year in cigarette advertising
> (nearly ten percent of its total revenue), devoted only 2.3 percent of its total
> health coverage to smoking ("although smoking was noted as a risk factor in
> heart disease, it was never mentioned in private or in reference to lung cancer"). *Mademoiselle,* which receives $1 million in cigarette advertising (seven
> percent of its total revenue), devoted less than two percent of its health coverage to smoking ("unreliable source of information about the hazards of
> smoking. Used editorial ploys to deemphasize smoking, gave misinformation, and excluded smoking from mention on relevant health topics altogether. One of the worst")....*Redbook,* which receives $7.5 million in cigarette
> advertising (sixteen percent of its total revenue), ran eighty health-related articles, but not one of them on smoking.[58]

These magazines seem to shy away from articles against tobacco use
because they are afraid of losing advertising revenues from tobacco compa-

nies. Actually, these publications are afraid of more that just lost revenues. The tobacco companies are parts of huge conglomerates, and if all the companies in the conglomerates withheld their advertising dollars, the magazines and newspapers would be in serious financial trouble. Economic power clearly explains why a society permits and even encourages the production, distribution, and sale of a dangerous drug.

Another strategy used by tobacco companies to increase sales in the face of antismoking pressures is to target marketing toward those categories of people most likely to smoke—the young, women in their early twenties, blue-collar men, and racial and ethnic minorities. African Americans and Hispanics, for example, have been the special targets of cigarette promotion.

- **Item:** Cigarettes are heavily advertised in black-oriented magazines such as *Ebony, Jet,* and *Essence.* Billboards advertising cigarettes are used in black communities four to five times more often than in white communities. Smoking rates among African Americans increased from 26 to 29 percent in the 1990s, but smoking rates among whites stayed constant at 25.5 percent.
- **Item:** African American men are 30 percent more likely than white males to die from smoking-related diseases, and blacks who give up smoking are more likely than whites to start smoking again.[59]
- **Item:** Of the top ten companies advertising in Hispanic markets, two are cigarette companies (Philip Morris was number 1, and R. J. Reynolds was number 10).
- **Item:** In 1989, the Canadian government charged that Imperial Tobacco Ltd. (which owns Brown and Williamson in the United States) and RJR–MacDonald (owned by U.S. conglomerate RJR Nabisco) deliberately attempted to hook children ages eighteen and under through their advertising. Evidence was produced documenting tobacco firms' marketing plans for young smokers, which attempted to change youths' attitudes on smoking and health. Documents also made clear attempts at convincing French-speaking Canadian youths ages twelve to seventeen to begin smoking filtered and so-called light cigarettes.
- **Item:** It has been estimated by the United Nations that 500 million people in Third World nations will die within the next decade from smoking-related illnesses. Cigarettes are very heavily advertised in Asia, Africa, and Latin America due to a lack of the legal restrictions faced by tobacco producers in other parts of the world, such as North America and Europe (for example, warning labels).[60] Tobacco companies hope to expand their market overseas, particularly in developing countries, which present a growing market. Philip Morris, for example, sells more than 175 brands in 160 countries, and its foreign sales have grown rapidly.[61] The foreign market also provides companies with a market for the high-tar brands that are losing sales in the United States.

The problem with all this, of course, is that the tobacco firms are promoting the use of a known health hazard for their own profit.

Finally, in 1997, a federal judge ruled that the FDA has some authority to regulate sales and labeling on cigarettes but cannot regulate the promotion and advertising of tobacco products.[62] Moreover, in a separate agreement between the Liggett Company and a number of state attorneys general around the nation, the tobacco company agreed to the following:

To admit that smoking is addictive and that the tobacco industry withheld such information from the public

To admit that cigarettes cause lung cancer and heart problems

To admit that cigarette advertising has targeted children

To pay 25 percent of its profits for the next twenty-five years ($750 million in total) to combat the medical and other costs of smoking

To agree to put on its packages that nicotine is addictive and can cause lung cancer[63]

Unfortunately, this settlement will do very little to punish the tobacco companies in any way. The profit forfeiture will be paid for by smokers, who will pay fifty cents more per pack to slowly kill themselves and those around them. Moreover, tobacco advertising is still largely protected by the First Amendment right to free speech.

Dangerous Working Conditions

In a capitalist economy, workers represent a cost to profit-seeking corporations. The lower that management can keep labor costs, the greater its profits. Historically, this has meant that workers labored for low wages, for inferior or nonexistent fringe benefits such as health care, and in unhealthy environments. The labor movement early in this century gathered momentum because of the abuse experienced by workers.

After a long and sometimes violent struggle, unions were successful in raising wages, adding fringe benefits, and making conditions safer. But owners were slow to change, and worker safety was (and continues to be) one of the most difficult issues. Many owners of mills, mines, and factories continue to consider the safety of their workers a low-priority item, presumably because of the high cost.

The mining industry provides an excellent example of this neglect. In numerous instances, mining disasters have occurred after repeated government warnings. In 1981, for example, an explosion in a Colorado mine killed fifteen workers. Since 1978, the mine had received 1,133 citations and 57 orders for immediate correction of known dangers from federal inspectors, but the owners did nothing.[64] Similarly, the Utah Power and Light Company was cited for 34 safety violations in one of its coal mines. The mine was the site of an underground fire in 1984 that killed twenty-seven miners; 9 of the violations were linked directly to the ignition and spread of the fire.[65]

In addition to mining disasters, coal miners face the long-term consequences of breathing coal dust. The United Mine Workers has estimated that 11 coal miners die every day from miner's asthma, silicosis, and "black lung," an incurable respiratory disease that has killed at least 100,000 American coal miners. The typical corporate response to black lung is to blame the victim, arguing that respiratory problems are a consequence of the miner's lifestyle or genetics and not the condition of the mine (which would make mining corporations liable).

The coal companies have sometimes used two other tactics: (1) when required to provide the government with dust samples, they have submitted fraudulent samples; and (2) they have ignored the federally permissible coal dust concentration limits. In the latter instance, companies pay slap-on-the-wrist fines; in 1983, the average fine for this offense was $117 per company. In the end, paying the fines is cheaper than providing workers with a relatively safe working environment.

The mining industry illustrates the two major dangers of the workplace: injuries from on-the-job accidents and exposure to toxic chemicals at work that have long-term negative effects. On-the-job accidents annually cause 3.3 million injuries requiring hospital treatment. Exposure to toxic chemicals causes at least 100,000 worker deaths each year and 390,000 new cases of occupational diseases.[66] We will focus on this latter type of workplace hazard.

The dangers today are invisible contaminants such as nuclear radiation, chemical compounds, dust, and asbestos fibers in the air. Because of increased production and use of synthetic chemicals in industry over recent decades, the level of danger from these contaminants is increasing. Just in the microelectronics industry, for example, 5,000 chemicals (solvents, acids, and gases) are used, and, of these, about 500 are rated as dangerous.[67]

- **Item:** Freeport McMoRan, a large multinational mining company, operates a virtual colony in Irian Jaya, Indonesia, where it maintains exploration rights to about 7 million acres of copper, gold, and other minerals. Freeport has dumped mine tailings from its open-pit copper mine into rivers for sixteen years. In April 1995, the Australian Council for Overseas Aid (ACFOA) reported that thirty-seven Irianese civilians had been killed by Indonesian military personnel operating in an area of a Freeport mine and alleged that Freeport security personnel "engaged in acts of intimidation, extracted forced confessions, shot three civilians, disappeared five Dani villagers and arrested and tortured 13 people."[68] In August 1995, Bishop Munninghoff of the Roman Catholic Church of

Jayapura published a detailed report that reaffirmed many of the ACFOA allegations. In April 1996, the Amungme people of Irian Jaya filed a $6 billion class-action lawsuit against Freeport in U.S. federal court in New Orleans. The lawsuit alleges human rights violations and environmental damages caused by Freeport's Indonesian operations. [69]

- **Item:** In San Carlos, Ecuador, from 1972 to 1992, Texaco discharged an estimated 4.3 million gallons of highly toxic "produced water" per day. The water leached into the region's local streams and rivers. The massive pollution caused by the runoff is now the subject of a class-action lawsuit on the part of the indigenous tribes of the region.[70]

Of the 38 million workers in manufacturing industries, 1.7 million are exposed to a potential carcinogen each year. Workplace carcinogens are believed to cause an estimated 23 to 38 percent of all deaths resulting from cancer each year.[71]

Moreover, exposure to certain chemicals has negative consequences for reproduction.

The government estimates that 15 million to 20 million jobs in the United States expose workers to chemicals that might cause reproductive injury. According to the National Institute for Occupational Safety and Health (NIOSH), 9 million workers are exposed to radio frequency/microwave radiation, which causes embryonic death and impaired fertility in animals; at least 500,000 workers are exposed to glycol ethers, known to cause testicular atrophy and birth defects in animals; and some 200,000 hospital and industrial employees work with anesthetic gases and ethylene oxide, both linked to miscarriage in humans.[72]

Consider the following examples of the specific risks of continued exposure in certain industries.

- **Item:** Workers in the dyestuffs industry (working with aromatic hydrocarbons) have about thirty times the risk of the general population of dying from bladder cancer.[73]
- **Item:** The wives of men who work with vinyl chloride are twice as likely as other women to have miscarriages or stillbirths.[74]
- **Item:** In 1978, Occidental Chemical Company workers handling the pesticide DBCP were found to be sterile as a result of the exposure, substantiating a 1961 study by Dow Chemical that indicated that DBCP caused sterility in rats.[75]
- **Item:** A 1976 government study determined that if 129,000 workers were exposed to the current legal level of cotton-dust exposure, over a period of time, 23,497 would likely become byssinotics (victims of "brown lung").[76]

- **Item:** Starting with 632 asbestos workers in 1943, one researcher determined each of their fates after twenty years of employment. By 1973, 444 were dead, a rate 50 percent greater than for the average white male. The rate for lung cancer was 700 percent greater than expected, and the rate for all types of cancers was four times as great.[77]

The case of Karen Silkwood is a well-known illustration of industry's disregard for the safety of its employees. Silkwood, a plutonium plant worker, charged that the Kerr–McGee plant in which she worked was unsafe and that she was contaminated by plutonium radiation exposure. After her death in a somewhat questionable car accident, Silkwood's family sued Kerr–McGee. During the trial, Kerr–McGee employees testified that they were provided little or no training on the health hazards involved in handling plutonium. They were never told that radiation exposure could induce cancer. Attorneys for Kerr–McGee argued in court, however, that there had been no documented case of plutonium cancer in humans. This was countered by the testimony of John Gofman, one of the first physicists to isolate plutonium, who said that Silkwood had an instant "guarantee of cancer based on her exposure."[78]

Industry has historically ignored data or stalled through court actions rather than make its plants safer. Two examples forcefully make its point.

In 1970, an Italian toxicologist reported that long-term intermittent exposure of rats to vinyl chloride in air resulted in several types of cancer.[79] This was the first test on possible carcinogenicity in the plastics industry. In 1972, these earlier findings were confirmed by a major study supported by British, Belgian, and French firms. Cancer was found at the lowest level tested, 50 parts per million (ppm). (At that time, the permissible exposure level for U.S. workers was 500 ppm.) Representatives of U.S. industry were given the full details of these studies in January 1973 but entered into an agreement with the European consortium not to disclose the information without prior consent. The U.S. organization involved in this agreement, the Manufacturing Chemists Association, failed to disclose the dangers of vinyl chloride, despite a request from a government agency for all available data on the toxic effects of vinyl chloride. The data were finally revealed to the government fifteen months later, after three workers exposed to vinyl chloride at a B.F. Goodrich plant died of angiosarcoma of the liver. According to a special committee report of the American Association for the Advancement of Science, the Manufacturing Chemists Association had deliberately deceived the government and "because of the suppression of these data, tens of thousands of workers were exposed without warning, for perhaps some two years, to toxic concentrations of vinyl chloride." [80]

Unlike vinyl chloride, the health dangers of asbestos have long been known. The link with asbestosis, a crippling lung disease, was established in 1900, and the relationship between asbestos and lung cancer was first noted in 1935. Studies of asbestos insulation workers in subsequent years have revealed a death rate from lung cancer seven times above normal and a death rate from all causes three times that of the general population.[81]

Despite these facts, asbestos workers have been consistently uninformed about the serious health hazards associated with working in that industry. In a Johns–Manville plant, for example, company doctors diagnosed lung disease in workers yet never told them that their lung problems were related to asbestos.

Plants have also been lax about meeting government standards for exposure. The maximum exposure level set by the government was twelve fibers per cubic meter for plants that had government contracts. An inspection of an asbestos plant in Tyler, Texas, revealed, for instance, that 117 of 138 samples in the plant exceeded the limit. The government fined the owner of the plant, Pittsburgh Corning, a total of $210 for these violations.

When the hazards of working with asbestos became more generally known, the industry reacted by sponsoring research to disprove the dangers of asbestos. One such industry study was faulty on at least two counts. First, it used researchers who had long been consultants to industry and therefore might be suspect for their lack of objectivity. Second, the study examined workers who had worked a relatively short time. Since lung cancer has a latency period of twenty years or so, the use of short-term workers in the study had the effect of whitewashing the real situation.[82]

The lack of concern for the safety of workers in the plastics and asbestos industries is typical of other industries, as well. Safety regulations for cotton dust have been opposed by the textile industry. As usual, industry argued that it would cost billions to clean up the mills, jobs would be lost, and prices to consumers would rise dramatically. Similarly, copper refiners have resisted rigorous safety regulations. For example, a study of mortality among Tacoma, Washington, smelter workers found the death rate from lung cancer to be between three and four times as high as normal and ten times as high for workers exposed to the highest toxic concentrations. Moreover, a study found that children within a half-mile of the smelter had absorbed as much arsenic as the workers themselves.[83] Despite these findings, the owner of the smelter in Tacoma, ASARCO, led an industry-wide campaign against the government's new standards. Again, the company offered the familiar argument that the costs of compliance would be $100 million, adding 15 cents to the now 72 cents needed to produce a pound of copper.

This raises the critical question: At what point are profits more important than human lives? Speaking of the cotton industry, which is representative of other major industries, one observer has argued as follows:

> In a society in which profits did not take precedence over people,...the finer points of byssinosis [brown lung disease] would have been considered tangential long ago and the road to its prevention would now be clear: Better air

filtration systems would have been installed and other capital expenditures made. But in the United States, where society is tuned to a different chord, the present delay over preventive measures, like the oblivion which preceded it, is rooted not in science and technology but in economics and politics—in the callous traditions of the cotton industry and in government's compromising ways.[84]

Finally, we should ask: What is a crime? Is it not when a victim is hurt (physically, emotionally, or financially) by the willful act of another? When 100,000 Americans die annually from occupationally related diseases, is that a crime?

Officially, these deaths and the human suffering induced by willful neglect for worker safety are not considered crimes. (See Chapter 1 for a discussion of criminal versus noncriminal deviance.) One observer, Joel Swartz, has argued that these deaths should be considered criminal—as murders.

> By any legitimate criteria corporate executives who willfully make a decision to expose workers to a dangerous substance which eventually causes the death of some of the workers should be considered murderers. Yet no executive has ever served even a day in jail for such a practice, and most probably are well rewarded for having saved the company money. The regulatory apparatus that is complicit with such practices should of course be considered an accomplice.[85]

But the guilt does not stop with corporate executives, as Swartz goes on to argue.

> In the long run it is not the outright deception, dishonesty and cunning of corporate executives, doctors and bureaucrats which is responsible for the problem. Rather, the general functioning of the system is at the heart of the problem.... The tremendous toll in occupational illnesses results from the oppression of one class by another. The people who own corporations try to exact as much wealth as they can from the workers. Improvements in working conditions to eliminate health hazards would eat into the profits that could be exacted.... In particular the asbestos industry would rather spend millions of dollars trying to prove that asbestos is safe, than spend the money necessary to eliminate exposures. In oil refineries many of the exposures to chemicals result from inadequate maintenance of plant equipment. Maintenance costs come to 15 percent of total refinery costs, but these costs are considered controllable. In other words, skipping on maintenance is a good way to cut costs. Only the worker suffers.
>
> Another reason that the system causes occupational illnesses is the pressure it applies for expansion, especially in certain industries such as chemicals and plastics. The chemical industry, especially, is able to reap high profits by rapidly introducing new chemicals.... Thus demands that chemicals be adequately tested before use, and the possibilities that new chemicals

found to be dangerous might be banned, constitute a tremendous threat to the industry.... The ultimate reason for the problem is the drive of corporations to extract as much profit as possible from the workers. But to continue to function this system requires constant efforts by people from corporate executives to scientists to bureaucrats. These efforts result in a staggering toll in death and disease which should qualify the perpetrators as criminals by any reasonable human standards. But the system, functioning the way it is, rewards certain criminals very handsomely. The ultimate success in the battle to improve health and safety conditions will require getting rid of these criminals and the system which enables them to operate.[86]

Collective Jeopardy

The first part of this chapter focused on the hazards that individuals face at work or from the products that they purchase. In this section, we broaden our scope somewhat. Here the victims of corporate deviance are not individuals per se but the collectivities of people who comprise individual communities, U.S. society, and even the world. The discussion will center on two broad areas of this collective jeopardy—wasting natural resources and polluting the environment.[87]

Wasting Resources

Since earth's creation billions of years ago, the ecosystem has worked intradependently, relatively undisturbed by the impact of human beings. But recent developments have begun to disturb the delicate balance of nature. Explosive population growth, modern technology, and high rates of consumption have combined to pollute the environment and deplete resources. We will focus on the waste of resources.

A most pressing concern for humanity is the accelerated rate of the consumption of nonrenewable resources. Obviously, the amounts of metals and fuels (except for wood and sun) available are finite. And the greater the number of people, the faster these resources will be consumed. If technology is added to the equation, the result is a further increase in the ratio of resource depletion.

Mineral resources have remained relatively untouched until the last 100 years or so. Total mineral production during the last 30 years was greater than that from the beginning of the Bronze Age until World War II. In 1976, the U.S. Bureau of Mines estimated that world consumption of aluminum will be twice today's level in 9 years, that use of iron will double in a decade and a half, and that demand for zinc will double in 17 years.[88]

The problem is exacerbated when these resources are not evenly distributed. The indigenous reserves of minerals and fuel of those countries that industrialized first are being exhausted. And these are the very nations in which the demand is greatest. Western Europe must now import nearly all the copper, phosphate, tin, nickel, manganese ore, and chrome ore that it uses. In 1950, the United States depended on foreign sources for 50 percent or more of four of the thirteen basic minerals; by the year 2000, it relied on imports for at least 50 percent of twelve of these thirteen minerals.

Except for coal, the major deposits of raw materials are found in the poor and developing nations of the world, yet because of high technology, most of these resources are consumed by only about one-fourth the world's population. Because these resources are rapidly diminishing (except for coal), severe shortages and dislocations will occur. The well-endowed countries will raise prices and be able to trade their surpluses for other needed resources. The high-technology countries (and therefore those with the greatest appetite for natural resources) will not be hurt in the short run because they will be able to purchase necessary resources.

In the long term, however, the technological societies will suffer for at least three reasons. First, as resources are exhausted (and if not replaced by adequate synthetics or renewable fuels such as the sun, wind, and tides), these societies will be forced to reduce their productivity, resulting in economic dislocations and dissatisfactions. Second, discontentment will also be found in resource-rich nations. Although they will benefit monetarily, they will no doubt feel exploited eventually as their resources are dissipated. Certainly, these countries will insist on even higher prices for their resources as they near depletion, which will increase the probability of hostile acts by wealthy nations against resource-rich nations.

A third source of international unrest brought about by the disproportionate use of limited resources by the wealthy nations will be from the have-not nations. The gap between the haves and the have-nots will continue to widen as the rich get the benefit of more resources and whatever gains are accomplished by the have-nots are canceled by rapid population growth. The result from such a situation is the heightened likelihood of hostile outbreaks between the rich and poor nations as the latter become more and more desperate in their need for resources.

The United States is the world's largest per-capita consumer of the world's resources. One example makes the point: The United States, with only 5 percent of the world's population, consumes 30 percent of the world's energy resources. The enormous U.S. consumption of energy and raw materials is a huge drain on U.S. and world storehouses.

Why do we consume so much? Although there are many reasons, we will focus on the major one: the American economic system, a system based on profits, the quest for which is never satiated. Companies must grow. More sales mean more profits. Sales are increased through advertising, product differentiation, new products, and creative packaging. Advertising creates previously nonexistent demand for products. The introduction of new products makes the old ones obsolete. Product differentiation (many models with different features) is redundant and wasteful, but it increases sales. The automobile industry is an excellent illustration of both product differentiation and planned obsolescence. Minor styling changes for each model year, with massive accompanying advertising campaigns, have the effect of making all older cars obsolete, at least in the minds of consumers.

Writing in 1960, Vance Packard warned of the waste demanded by our economic system.[89] Progress through growth in profits is maximized by consumers who purchase products because they feel the need to replace old ones when they are used up or outmoded. This supposed need is promoted by manufacturers who produce goods that do not last long or who alter styles so that consumers actually discard usable items. These two marketing strategies—creating obsolescence through poor quality and through desirability—produce growing profits. But both strategies are fundamentally based on waste, a societal problem that cannot continue indefinitely.

One type of obsolescence is positive: the introduction of a new product that outperforms its predecessor. However, even this type can be orchestrated to increase waste and profit. The technology may exist for a major breakthrough, but the manufacturer or industry may choose to bring out a series of modifications that eventually lead to the state of the art. The rationale for this procedure is to saturate the potential market with the stepped-up technology, move to the next stage of development, and so on until the major breakthrough is attained. In this way, the consumer purchases a number of products rather than immediately purchasing the ultimate. The history of high-fidelity sound equipment provides a good illustration of this marketing principle.[90]

The waste of our throwaway age is easy to see. Beverages are packaged in convenient disposable cans. Meat can be purchased in disposable aluminum frying pans, to be thrown away after one use. TV dinners are warmed and eaten in the same containers. We can purchase disposable cigarette lighters and cameras and plastic razors with built-in blades. What's more, we junk 7 million cars annually, as well as 10 million tons of iron and steel. These are but a small sample of the products that are quickly used and destroyed.

To maximize profits, one must minimize costs. Among other things, this search for profits results in abusing the environment. Consider the role of the profit motive in raping the land, which is the ultimate waste of resources.

It is cheaper to extract minerals from the earth by strip mining than to remove them carefully and restore the land to its original state. Because the costs of restoration are subtracted from profits, mining companies have vigorously resisted governmental efforts to curb the environmental abuses of strip mining. The following is a description of the waste that occurs in the strip-mining process.

In the flat country of western Kentucky, where thousands of acres had already been devastated by strip mining, the coal seams lie only thirty to sixty feet beneath the surface. The overburden is scraped off and the coal is scooped out. Inevitably such topsoil as the land affords is buried under the towering heaps of subsoil. When the strippers move on, once-level meadows and cornfields have been converted to jumbled heaps of hardpan, barren clay from deep in the earth. This hellish landscape is slow to support vegetation and years elapse before the yellow waste turns green again. In the meantime, immense quantities of dirt have crept into the sluggish streams, have choked them, and brackish ponds have formed to breed millions of mosquitoes.

The evil effects of open-cut mining are fantastically magnified when practiced in the mountains. Masses of shattered stone, shale, slate, and dirt are cast pellmell down the hillside. The first to go are the thin layer of fertile topsoil and such trees as still find sustenance in it. The uprooted trees are down the slopes by the first cut. Then follows the sterile subsoil, shattered stone, and slate. As the cut extends deeper into the hillside, the process is repeated again and again. Sometimes the "highwall," the perpendicular bank resulting from the cut, rises ninety feet; but a height of forty to sixty feet is more often found. In a single mile, hundreds of tons are displaced.

Each mountain is laced with coal seams. Sometimes a single ridge contains three to five veins varying in thickness from two-and-a-half to fourteen feet. Since each seam can be stripped, a sloping surface can be converted to a steplike one.

After the coal has been carried away, vast quantities of the shattered mineral are left uncovered. Many seams contain substantial quantities of sulfur, which when wet produces toxic sulphuric acid. This poison bleeds into the creeks, killing minute vegetation and destroying fish, frogs, and other stream dwellers.[91]

This devastation of the land and its inhabitants is perpetrated by the owners of coal companies for two reasons. Foremost, this type of operation is very profitable. For example, in 1962, a small crew with an auger and a fleet of trucks made a profit of $15 a minute working a 4- to 6-foot seam.[92] Second, until recently, laws have allowed companies complete authority over the land that they controlled. The historical bias of the courts toward the coal companies is seen in some of their decisions.

- **Item:** The courts ruled that the rights to mine included the authority to cut down surface trees without compensating the owners of the land.
- **Item:** The courts ruled that the companies had the right to divert and pollute water in or on the lands over which they had mineral rights.
- **Item:** The courts ruled that the companies could build roads wherever they desired.
- **Item:** When a gob dam (created by dumping refuse from mining into streams) broke during a 1945 storm, causing a flood and tremendous damage in Pike County, Kentucky, the court ruled that the Russell Fork Coal Company was innocent of wrongdoing and negligence because the rain was an act of God.[93]

Summarizing the situation, Caudill stated, "The companies, which had bought their coal rights at prices ranging from fifty cents to a few dollars an acre, were, in effect, left free to do as they saw fit, restrained only by the shallow consciences of their officials."[94]

Polluting the Environment

The assault on the environment is the result of an ever larger population, higher rates of consumption, and an increasing reliance on technology. These are worldwide trends. "Not only are more societies acquiring more efficient tools wherewith to exploit the earth; nearly everywhere, there are increasing numbers to do the exploiting, and befoul the air, water, and land in the process."[95] As an example, let's look at one major consequence of the increased use of technology: heat pollution.

Thermal pollution takes two basic forms: waste heat from the generation of electric power that (1) raises the temperature of the water (affecting fish and plant life in waters) and (2) increases heat in the atmosphere. Obviously, a rapidly expanding population increases the demands for more electricity and more industrial output, thereby adding to the creation of heat. Moreover, the addition of 70 to 80 million people each year (the current world rate) adds heat to the atmosphere just by the metabolism of these bodies.

Another source of heat is the greenhouse effect, caused by the existence of more carbon dioxide than nature's mechanisms can recycle. Modern technology, through its reliance on the burning of fossil fuels, is the source of great quantities of carbon dioxide. Just like the glass roof of a greenhouse, the molecules of carbon dioxide allow sunlight to reach earth's surface but block the escape of heat radiating off the ground. According to the theory, earth's heat level will rise 5 degrees Fahrenheit over the next 30 to 100 years because of this greenhouse effect. Obviously, earth's climate will be changed unless the world's usage of fossil fuels (oil, oil shale, tar sands, and coal) is reduced dramatically in the near future.

There is a countervailing force, however, that is believed to have a cooling effect. It, too, comes from pollution: airborne dust, which has increased in every daily activity from suburban driving to farming the soil.

> Periods of global cooling have been recorded over the past two centuries after major volcanic eruptions spewed tons of dust particles into the air. Meteorologist Helmut Landsberg estimates that, along with world population, the amount of dust in the atmosphere has doubled since the 1930s, despite the absence of major volcanic eruptions. Some scientists fear that increased amounts of atmospheric dust may act as insulation, reflecting the sun's rays away from the earth and lowering temperatures.[96]

So, technology creates in its wake two forces, one that screens the sun out and another that traps the heat in. Although both effects are negative for human life as we know it, the exact impact of these forces is not fully understood. Clearly, climate will be affected, but we are unsure of exactly how. What is known is that when modern technology tampers with the climate, it produces negative consequences.

Heat pollution, however, is only one form of pollution. In the short term, it is the least hazardous. Pollution comes in many forms, and we are all guilty. Each of us pollutes as we use fossil fuel transportation, burn wood in our fireplaces, use aerosol sprays, kill weeds with pesticides, and throw away junk. Indirectly, we pollute when we use electricity, heat our homes with natural gas, and use the thousands of products created by industry.

Wildlife.   In 1993, *National Wildlife* magazine published the twenty-fifth in its series of annual reports on the environment. According to the report, conflict continued to increase in 1992 over whether economic or ecological concerns should be of primary importance in the allocation of America's natural resources. The continued sluggishness of the U.S. economy rendered this debate increasingly political as the environment once again became a theme in the presidential election.

The Endangered Species Act expired in 1992, and while it would continue to be enforced, the controversy surrounding reauthorizing the law centered on a few publicized conflicts between economic development and species survival. One example was provided by a controversy in the Southeast over the use of turtle excluder devices (TEDs), which allow endangered sea turtles to escape from shrimping nets. In December, the National Marine Fisheries Service extended mandatory use of TEDs to year-round, despite industry fears that the devices might reduce catches. Meanwhile, the decline in duck populations, a traditional indicator of the health of North America's ecosystems, was the worst recorded since the 1930s. This decline prompted calls for increased protection, that is, decreased development, of wetlands, which play roles in the life cycles of ducks and many other endangered and threatened animals.

- **Item:** "An EPA study reported that U.S. water pollution had decreased in the two decades since the law's original passage. The study noted that two-thirds of surface water meet water-quality standards, despite continued problems with contaminated runoff from farms, streets, and lawns. Agricultural runoff figured prominently in an EPA analysis that found nearly half of more than 500,000 miles of rivers tested to be too polluted for their intended uses. There was also bad news concerning U.S. coastal waters, where pollution had closed a third of all shellfish fisheries, and where there were more than 2,000 beach closings because of sewage contamination in 1991. The beach closings were spread among 14 states; another 10 coastal states did not regularly test for contamination."[97]

- **Item:** "In mid-1992, a change in the regulations of the Clean Air Act was made that allowed large companies to increase pollutant emissions by up to 245 tons a year.... The Clean Air Act also authorized the trading of pollution credits and debits, in an attempt to use market incentives to lower pollution. The first sales of credits were made by Wisconsin Power and Light in 1992. The purchaser, the Tennessee Valley Authority, paid $2.5–4 million for the credits, which would allow it to discharge as many as 25,000 tons of sulfur dioxide."

But what influences our consumer choices? Do we have a choice to travel by mass transit? Do we have a choice to buy products transported by truck or rail (railroads are much less polluting because they are more efficient)? Do we have a choice to use soap instead of detergent? The role of the corporations in limiting our consumer choices is an especially instructive way to understand how a laissez-faire economic system works to the ultimate detriment of people and society.

In a capitalist system, private businesses make decisions based on making profit. This places the environment in jeopardy. Best and Connolly have shown how corporate decision makers choose alternatives that have negative impacts on the ecology.[98] They describe the logic of capitalism in the following:

> Under such circumstances [capitalism] it is quite irrational for any individual producer or consumer to accept the higher costs involved in curtailing various assaults on the environment. Thus a company that purified the water used in production before disposing it into streams would add to its own costs, fail to benefit from the purified water flowing downstream, and weaken its competitive market position with respect to those companies unwilling to institute purified procedures. Since it is reasonable to assume that other companies in a market system will not voluntarily weaken their position in this way, it is irrational for any single company to choose to do so.... Thus a range of practices which [is] desirable from the vantage point of the public [is] irrational from the vantage point of any particular consumer or producer. And a range of policies which [is] rational from the vantage point of individual consumers and producers [is] destructive of the collective interest in preserving nonrenewable productive resources and in maintaining the environment's capacity to assimilate wastes.[99]

Why, for example, does the United States depend on an irrational transportation system? If mass transit for commuting replaced the automobile in our urban centers, 50 percent of the fuel now consumed by cars would be saved. Best and Connolly argue that the automobile industry has intervened to suppress a viable mass transit alternative. In the mid-1920s, GM, sometimes with Standard Oil and Firestone, purchased control of electric trolley and transit systems in forty-four urban areas. After purchase, the electric rail systems were dismantled and replaced by diesel-powered bus systems supplied by GM. When the systems were subsequently sold, part of the contract stated that no new equipment could be purchased that used a fuel other than gas. GM favored the diesel bus because its life was 28 percent shorter than its electric counterpart, resulting in more profit for the company. Standard Oil and Firestone obviously benefited from such an arrangement.[100] The results are well known: We are dependent on gasoline for transportation, and our cities are smothered in toxic emissions of carbon monoxide, lead, and other deadly chemical combinations from internal-combustion engines.

Other examples come from the substitution of synthetic for organic materials. Industry decided to displace soap with synthetic detergents because the profit margin increased from 30 percent of sales to 52 percent.[101] The decision was not made by consumers but by management. These decisions and others (for example, the change from wool and cotton to synthetic fibers; plastics substituted for leather, rubber, and wood; and synthetic fertilizers replacing organic fertilizers) have often been incompatible with good ecology because the new chemicals are sometimes toxic and/or nonbiodegradable.

Remember, citizens, as voters and consumers, were not involved in these decisions to shift from organic to synthetic products. Rather, the decisions were made for them and, it turns out, against their long-term interests by companies searching for more lucrative profits. Barry Commoner has claimed that these new technologies have invariably been more polluting but were introduced nonetheless because they yielded higher profits than the older, less polluting displaced technologies. Moreover, the costs to the consumers are borne in the increased health hazards and in the cost for cleaning up the environment.

> Environmental pollution is connected to the economics of the private enterprise system in two ways. First, pollution tends to become intensified by the displacement of older productive techniques by new ecologically faulty, but more profitable technologies. Thus, in these cases, pollution is an unintended concomitant of the natural drive of the economic system to introduce new technologies that increase productivity. Second, the costs of environmental degradation are chiefly borne not by the producer, but by society as a whole, in the form of "externalities." A business enterprise that pollutes the environment is therefore being subsidized by society; to this extent, the enterprise, though free, is not wholly private.[102]

Pollution, as we have seen, is a direct consequence of an economic system in which the profit motive supersedes the concern for the environment. This is clearly seen when corporations are unwilling to comply with government regulations and to pay damages for ecological disasters such as oil spills. In 1999, Russell Mokhiber published an article about the 100 most serious corporate crime cases of the 1990s. The environmental crime cases are especially instructive. Of the 100 cases discussed, 38 were environmental, the most of any category. When a corporation such as Royal Caribbean was charged with dumping oil and other hazardous wastes (some mixed with ordinary garbage) into U.S. harbors and coastal areas, the firm hired a former U.S. attorney general and two former members of the U.S. Department of Justice's Environmental Crimes Section to defend itself. Nevertheless, in the end, Royal Caribbean lost and was fined $18 million, the largest fine ever levied against a cruise line in connection with polluting American waters.[103]

- **Item:** In 1991, Exxon pled guilty to spilling 11 million gallons of crude oil in Prince William Sound, Alaska, fouling 700 miles of Alaska shoreline. The corporation paid a $125 million fine.
- **Item:** In 1996, the Summerville Mining Company was fined $20 million on forty counts of violating the Clean Water Act and other federal statutes in connection with spraying cyanide into ponds as part of a process used in mining gold.
- **Item:** In 1998, the Louisiana–Pacific Corporation was fined $37 million and convicted of eighteen felony counts, including conspiring to violate the Clean Air Act, lying to the Colorado Department of Public Health, and submitting nonrepresentative samples to the American Plywood Association.
- **Item:** In 1996, the Iroquois Pipeline Operating Company was fined $15 million for violations of the Clean Water Act. The case stemmed from the construction of a 370-mile pipeline from Canada through upstate New York and Connecticut to Long Island. Damage was done to more than 200 streams and was not cleaned up.
- **Item:** In 1999, the Colonial Pipeline Company was fined $7 million after pleading guilty to spilling 1 million gallons of oil into the Reedy River in South Carolina, killing approximately 35,000 fish.
- **Item:** In 1996, Rockwell International Corporation paid a $6.5 million fine in connection with charges following a 1994 explosion at its Santa Susana Field Laboratory in Simi Hills, California. The explosion was the result of illegally stored and disposed-of hazardous waste and killed two scientists.
- **Item:** In 1991, the Aluminum Company of America paid a $3.75 million fine and $7.5 million in other damages for hazardous waste violation, at the time the largest fine ever assessed for hazardous waste violation.
- **Item:** In 1992, Bristol–Myers Squibb, one of the world's largest pharmaceutical companies, paid $3 million for discharging pollutants into area waters around Syracuse, New York. The company also agreed to build a pretreatment plant that will cost $10 million.
- **Item:** In 1997, another major drug firm, Warner–Lambert, paid a $3 million fine for falsifying reports on the level of pollutants it was releasing into a drainage channel that feeds the Cibuco River in Puerto Rico. The

firm paid an additional $670,000 in civil penalties for routinely releasing excessive pollutants.

- **Item:** In 1996, International Paper's subsidiary Arizona Chemical paid $2.5 million and $1.5 million in restitution fines for violations of the Clean Water Act. The violations occurred when the firm manipulated the waste treatment system's sampling procedure so that more favorable results could be reported.
- **Item:** In 1995, the Conrail Corporation pled guilty to six felony counts of violating federal environmental laws by knowingly discharging harmful quantities of grease and oil into New England's Charles River. Conrail paid a $2.5 million fine for causing an oil slick hundreds of yards long.
- **Item:** In 1998, HAL Beheer BV, owner of the Holland America cruise line, was fined $2 million and placed on five years' probation for dumping untreated bilge water into coastal waters within three miles of U.S. shores. The firm also pled guilty to failing to keep proper records of oily mixture discharge.
- **Item:** In 1998, Browning–Ferris, Inc., paid a $1.5 million fine for discharging contaminated wastewater from its medical waste facility in Washington, D.C., in violation of the Clean Water Act.
- **Item:** In 1994, the United Oil of California (UNOCAL) Corporation, a major oil company, pled no contest to three pollution charges and paid a $1.5 million fine for leaking petroleum thinner into the ocean groundwater at a southern California oil field.
- **Item:** In 1990, Eastman Kodak, a leading photo corporation, pled guilty to state charges of unlawful dealing in hazardous waste and paid a $1 million fine. The company spilled some 5,100 gallons of methylene chloride and failed to notify government officials of the spill. Neighborhood groups fighting Eastman were disappointed with the fine, claiming that it was the equivalent of an individual getting a ticket for jaywalking.[104]

The environmental crime patterns of the 1990s reveal that most of these offenses were not accidents; they were deliberate. In a number of cases, conspiracies were engaged in to cover up what took place. Second, for the most part, the fines imposed were meager compared to the multibillion-dollar resources of the corporations involved. Third, in none of the cases discussed did anyone go to prison. Probation was the most serious punishment levied, besides a fine. Finally, serious damage to the local environments was done in many cases, especially concerning the pollution of lakes, rivers, and oceans.

The government thus has enacted laws to curb pollution, but they are very mild. Turner has listed the defects in these conservation laws.

1. The laws are often phrased in ambiguous language, making prosecution difficult.

2. The laws typically mandate weak civil penalties and hardly ever carry criminal penalties.
3. The vast majority of the laws do not attack the sources of pollutants but rather require treatment of pollutants after they have been created.
4. Many state antipollution laws are enacted with "grandfather clauses" that allow established companies to continue their harmful activities.[105]

The mildness of the pollution laws and their enforcement indicates the power of the powerful to continue their disregard for people and nature in their search for profits. The government could take a much firmer stance if it chose to do so. Suppose, for example, that the situation were reversed: "Can you possibly reverse this situation and imagine the poor polluting the streams used by the rich, and then not only getting away with it and avoiding arrest, but also being paid by the rich through the government to clean up their own pollution?"[106]

In such a case, how would the poor be treated? The answer is obvious: The powerful would punish them severely and immediately curb their illegal behaviors. The implication is that whoever has the power can use it to his or her own benefit, disregarding the masses and nature.

Conclusion

This chapter has shown conclusively the fundamental flaw of capitalism. Corporations are formed to seek and maximize profits. All too often, the result is a blatant disregard for human and humane considerations. It is too simplistic to say that corporations are solely responsible for these dangers to individuals and society. In many cases, consumers insist on convenience rather than safety. They would rather smoke or drink diet cola with saccharin than have the government demand that they quit. Moreover, consumers typically would rather take an unknown risk than pay higher prices for products, which would pay for the cost of cleaning up the pollution. So, too, workers would rather work in an unsafe plant than be unemployed. But, for the most part, these attitudes are shaped by corporate advertising and corporate extortion (threatened higher prices and unemployment if changes are enforced). Also, corporations are guilty of efforts to persuade us that the dangers are nonexistent or minimal when the scientific evidence is irrefutable. They also do everything possible to block efforts by the government and consumer groups to thwart their corporate policies. For example, despite evidence that many forms of cancer are environmentally related, corporations have refused to alter their behavior. Instead, they counterattack in two characteristic ways.

> Monsanto Chemical Co…has embarked on a costly advertising campaign to persuade us that chemical products are essential to our way of life. More

than 100 industrial corporations have banded together to form the American Industrial Health Council, a lobby that is spending more than $1 million a year to combat the stricter carcinogen controls proposed by the Occupational Safety and Health Administration (OSHA).[107]

The probusiness approach argues that risks are inherent in living. But the consumer is the ultimate arbiter. He or she may choose. If the consumer does not buy dangerous or wasteful products, then industry will provide alternative products to suit his or her wishes.[108] Likewise, the worker in an asbestos plant or a cotton mill can change jobs if he or she feels that the current job is unsafe. Companies continue to argue that what goes on in the marketplace is not within the domain of government. We argue, to the contrary, that the government must serve a watchdog function. We also argue that individuals do not have the simple options that the corporations suggest. We buy the products that are available. Our attitudes are shaped by advertising. Employees cannot shift from one job to another in the hopes of finding safer conditions when most of the plants in the industry for which they are trained have similar problems and when the unemployment rate is high.

The dangers pointed out in this chapter direct attention to the fundamental irrationality of our economic system. When the pursuit of profits supersedes the health of workers and consumers, when corporate decisions encourage enormous waste and pollution, then the economic system is wrong and will ultimately fail.

Critical Thinking Exercise 4.1: Business Crime and Punishment in America

The *Wall Street Journal* calls itself "the daily diary of the American Dream." As argued in Chapter 2, the values connected with the American dream, as well as a lack of opportunity, encourage a great deal of criminal behavior, including crimes among corporations. Using recent issues of the *Wall Street Journal,* do a content analysis of the amount of corporate and employee crime. In your analysis, answer the following questions:

1. What is the most common crime committed by corporations?
2. What percentage of the articles mention prison as part of the sentence imposed on convicted executives and employees?
3. What is the average fine imposed on corporations? On employees?
4. Who are the most frequent victims of corporate criminals? The public? The government? Women? Children? Minorities?

What do the results of your study indicate about the way corporate and white-collar employees are treated by the criminal justice system?

Endnotes

1. National Commission on Product Safety, "Perspectives on Product Safety" in *Consumerism: Search for the Consumer Interest,* ed. David A. Aaker and George S. Day (New York: Free Press, 1974), 321–22. See also Amitai Etzioni, "Mindless Capitalism, an Unyielding Elite," *Human Behavior* 4, November 1975, 10–12; and Ralph Nader (ed.), *The Consumer and Corporate Accountability* (New York: Harcourt Brace Jovanovich, 1973), 51.

2. National Commission on Product Safety, 322, 325.

3. Quoted in Morton Mintz and Jerry S. Cohen, "Crime in the Suites," in Nader (ed.) 79.

4. Ralph Nader, *Unsafe at Any Speed: The Designed-in Dangers of the American Automobile* (New York: Bantam, 1972).

5. Morton Mintz, "Confessions of a GM Engineer," in Nader (ed.), 301–9. For a similar situation among tire manufacturers, see "Forewarnings of Fatal Laws," *Time,* June 25, 1979, 5–61.

6. The following is taken from Mark Dowie, "Pinto Madness," in *Crisis in American Institutions,* 4th ed., ed. Jerome Skolnick and Elliott Currie (Boston: Little, Brown), 23–40 (originally appeared in *Mother Jones* 2, September/October 1977, 24–25).

7. Ibid., 30. This is the argument made in Walter Guzzardi, Jr., "The Mindless Pursuit of Safety," *Fortune,* April 1979, 54–64.

8. Francis T. Cullen, William J. Maakestad, and Gray Cavender, *Corporate Crime under Attack: The Ford Pinto Case and Beyond* (Cincinnati, OH: Anderson, 1987). See also Russell Mokhiber, *Corporate Crime and Violence* (San Francisco: Sierra Club Books, 1988), 373–82.

9. Dowie, 39.

10. H. Joseph Hebert, "Files Show GM Knew X-Car Brakes Locked," *Denver Post,* October 21, 1983, 1-A, 12-A.

11. Cited in Mokhiber, 202–4.

12. Ibid., 203.

13. The following is taken from Fred R. Harris, "The Politics of Corporate Power," in *Corporate Power in America,* ed. Ralph Nader and Mark J. Green (New York: Grossman, 1973), 27–29; and "Detroit Fights Airbags," *Dollars and Sense,* July/August 1978, 6–7.

14. "Detroit Fights Airbags," 6.

15. "Detroit Fights Airbags," 7.

16. James L. Kitman, "The Secret History of Lead," *The Nation,* March 20, 2000, 270, 11–44.

17. *Multinational Monitor,* October 1995.

18. John Summa, "Eli Lilly," *Multinational Monitor,* June 9, 1988, 20–22.

19. Mokhiber, 334, 340.

20. Upton Sinclair, *The Jungle* (first published in 1905 reprint: New York: New American Library, 1960).

21. Charles H. McCaghy, *Deviant Behavior: Crime, Conflict, and Interest Groups* (New York: Macmillan, 1976), 215.

22. Harrison Wellford, *Sowing and Wind: A Report from Ralph Nader's Center for Study of Responsive Law on Food Safety and the Chemical Harvest* (New York: Grossman, 1972), 69.

23. McCaghy, 216.

24. Robert Sherrill, cited in McCaghy, 216 (originally appeared in *New York Times Book Review,* March 4, 1973, 3). See also Gene Marine and Judith Van Allen, *Food Pollution: The Violation of Our Inner Ecology* (New York: Holt, Rinehart and Winston, 1972), Chapter 2; and Jennifer Cross, *The Supermarket Trap: The Consumer and the Food Industry,* rev. ed. (Bloomington: Indiana University Press, 1976), Chapter 9.

25. Neal Karlen, "A 'Mystery Meat' Scandal," *Newsweek,* September 24, 1984, 29; and Mark Thomas, "Ex-Cattle King Worker Acknowledges Fraud," *Denver Post,* January 31, 1984, 1, 11.

26. Norm Brewer, "Bad School Meat Spurs Crackdown in Inspecting," *USA Today,* December 21, 1983, 8-A.

27. The following discussion of additives is taken primarily from Daniel Zwerdling, "Food Pollution," in *The Capitalist System,* 2nd ed., ed. Richard C. Edwards, Michael Reich,

and Thomas E. Weisskopf (Englewood Cliffs, NJ: Prentice Hall, 1978), 19–24. See also Jacqueline Verrett and Jean Carper, *Eating May Be Hazardous to Your Health* (Garden City, NY: Doubleday, 1975).

28. *Statistical Abstract of the United States, 1987* (Washington, DC: U.S. Government Printing Office, 1986), 110.

29. Department of Health and Human Services, "Report on All Adverse Reactions in the Adverse Reaction Monitoring System," February 25 and 28, 1994.

30. "Safety of Amino Acids," Life Sciences Research Office, FASEB, FDA Contract No. 223–88–2124, Task Order No. 8; and Hearing Before the Committee on Labor and Human Resources, United States Senate, First Session on Examining the Health and Safety Concerns of Nutrasweet (Aspartame), November 3, 1987.

31. U.S. Air Force, "Aspartame Alert," *Flying Safety* 48(5), 1992, 20–21. See also Aspartame (NutraSweet) Toxicity Home Page: http://www.tiac. net/users/mgold/aspartame/aspartame. html for full discussion and documentation.

32. Julie Miller, "Testing for Seeds of Destruction," *The Progressive* 39, December 1975, 37–40. See also Richard F. Spark, "Legislating against Cancer," *New Republic,* June 3, 1978, 16–19.

33. It is even possible that financial ties to huge food corporations may shade the so-called expert testimony of nutritionsists, as argued by Benjamin Rosenthal, Michael Jacobson, and Marcy Bohm, "Professors on the Take," *The Progressive* 40, November 1976, 42–47.

34. 1965 data are from Marine and Van Allen, 38; 1977 data are from Hugh Drummond, "Add Poison for Flavor and Freshness," *Mother Jones* 2, April 1977, 13.

35. Quoted in Zwerdling, 20.

36. From Jim Hightower, *Eat Your Heart Out: Food Profiteering in America.* Copyright 1975 by Jim Hightower. Reprinted by permission of Crown Publishers, Inc.

37. *Statistical Abstract of the United States, 1987,* 110.

38. *Detroit Free Press,* June 7, 1991, 1-F, 6-F.

39. *Dietary Goals for the United States,* 2nd ed. (Washington, DC: U.S. Government Printing Office, 1977), 35, 39.

40. U.S. Senate, Select Committee on Nutrition and Human Needs, 35, 19.

41. Hightower, 631.

42. U.S. Senate, Select Committee on Nutrition and Human Needs, 35–48.

43. Marilyn Elias, "How to Win Friends and Influence Kids on Television (and Incidently Sell a Few Toys and Munchies at the Same Time)," *Human Behavior* 4 (April 1974), 20. For an extensive review of research, see National Science Foundation, *The Effects of Television* (Washington, DC: U.S. Government Printing Office, 1976).

44. Federal Trade Commission, *Staff Report on Television Advertising to Children* (Washington, DC: U.S. Government Printing Office, 1978), 57.

45. Summarized in U.S. Commission on Civil Rights, *Window Dressing on the Set: An Update* (Washington, DC: U.S. Government Printing Office, 1979), 49.

46. Elias, 16–23.

47. Michael Weinstock, quoted in *Broadcasting* 96, January 22, 1979, 25.

48. John Summers, quoted in *Broadcasting* 96, March 26, 1979, 84.

49. Frederick Furth, quoted in "Keep Out of the Reach of Children: Bill Moyers' Journal," April 30, 1979 (p. 3 of transcript).

50. Bernard Friedlander, quoted in *Broadcasting* 96, April 2, 1979, 64.

51. Ellen Goodman, "Why Allow Decadent Tooth Fairies to Invade Our Homes?" *Rocky Mountain News,* December 5, 1978, 61. For an opposite opinion, see Christopher De Muth, "Hands Off Children's TV," *Rocky Mountain News,* April 15, 1979, 55.

52. "Bill Moyers' Journal," 11.

53. See "Slow Motion Suicide," *Newsweek,* January 22, 1979, 83–84; United Press International, January 12, 1979; and Associated Press, January 12, 1979.

54. Cited in Ruth Darmstadter, "Snuff and Chaw: The Tobacco Industry Plugs Nicotine by Osmosis," *Business and Society Review* 47, Fall 1983. Copyright © 1983, Warren Gorham & Lamont, 210 South Street, Boston, MA 02111. All rights reserved.

55. Gwenda Blair, "Why Dick Can't Stop Smoking: The Politics behind Our National Addiction," *Mother Jones* 4, January 1979, 36.

56. The following is adapted from D. Stanley Eitzen and Maxine Baca Zinn, *Social Problems*, 4th ed. (Boston: Allyn & Bacon, 1989), 588–89.

57. Michael Schudson, "The Smoking Gun: A Nation at Risk," *In These Times* 9, December 15, 1987, 18.

58. Peter Taylor, *The Smoke Ring: Tobacco and Multinational Politics* (New York: New American Library, 1985), 57–58.

59. Darmstadter, 24.

60. Darmstadter, 24–25.

61. These examples are taken from Larry C. White, *Merchants of Death: The American Tobacco Industry* (New York: William Morrow, 1988), 129–31. See also Morton Mintz, "Marketing Tobacco to Children," *The Progressive* 5, May 1991, 24–29.

62. Eric Eckholm, "Four Trillion Cigarettes," *The Progressive* 42, July 1978, 26; White, 199–200.

63. Reuters, March 29 & April 25, 1997

64. G. M. Seigel, "Safety Citations at Dutch Creek Called Average," *Rocky Mountain News,* April 22, 1981, 24.

65. Ben A. Franklin, "Violations Cited in Utah Mine Fire That Killed 29," *New York Times,* March 25, 1987, 24. The following information on black lung is based on Mokhiber, 97–106.

66. Joan Claybrook, *Retreat from Safety: Reagan's Attack on America's Health* (New York: Pantheon, 1984), 78.

67. "High Tech and Health," in *Diagnosis: Capitalism, by Dollars & Sense* (Somerville, MA: Economic Affairs Bureau, 1985), 15.

68. "The Ten Worst Corporations, 1995," *Multinational Monitor,* Oct.

69. Ibid.

70. Mokhiber, 16–17.

71. Carolyn Marshall, "An Excuse for Workplace Hazards," *The Nation,* April 25, 1987, 532.

72. Philip Cole and Marlene B. Goldman, "Occupation," in *Persons at High Risk of Cancer,* ed. Joseph F. Fraumeni, Jr. (New York: Academic Press, 1975), 171.

73. Eyal Press, "Texaco on Trial," *The Nation,* May 31, 1999, 11–12, 16.

74. Dorothy McGhee, "Workplace Hazards: No Women Need Apply," *The Progressive* 41, October 1977, 25.

75. Daniel Ben-Horin, "The Sterility Scandal," *Mother Jones* 4, May 1979, 51–63.

76. Jeanne Schinto, "The Breathless Cotton Workers," *The Progressive* 41, August 1977, 29.

77. Reported in Samuel S. Epstein, *The Politics of Cancer* (San Francisco: Sierra Club Books, 1978), 84–86. See also Lea Zeldin, "The Asbestos Menace," *The Progressive* 42, October 1978, 12.

78. Reported in "Silkwood Vindicated," *Newsweek,* May 28, 1979, 40, 102–6.

79. Epstein, 10–12.

80. J. T. Edsall, "Report of the AAAS Committee on Scientific Freedom and Responsibility," *Science* 188, 1975, 687–93 (reported in Epstein, 103–4).

81. See Richard Doll, *British Journal of Industrial Medicine* 12, 1955, 81.

82. The following account is taken primarily from Joel Swartz, "Silent Killers at Work," *Crime and Social Justice,* P.O. Box 4373, Berkeley, CA, 94704.

83. Roger M. Williams, "Arsenic and Old Factories," *Saturday Review,* January 20, 1979, 26.

84. Schinto, 28. For a description of how the government has waffled in this area, see "Brown Lung Compromise," *The Progressive* 42, August 1978, 13.

85. Swartz, 18.

86. Swartz, 19–20.

87. Portions of this section are based on D. Stanley Eitzen, *Social Problems* (Boston: Allyn & Bacon, 1980), Chapters 3 and 11.

88. Lester R. Brown, Patricia L. McGrath, and Bruce Stokes, *Twenty Two Dimensions of the Population Problem,* Worldwatch Paper 5 (Washington, DC: Worldwatch Institute, 1976), 58.

89. Vance Packard, *The Waste Makers* (New York: David McKay, 1960).

90. Ibid., 55–56.

91. From Harry M. Caudill, *Night Comes to the Cumberlands* (Boston: Little, Brown, an Atlantic Monthly Press Book, 1963), 311–12; used with permission. See also Harry M. Caudill, *Theirs Be the Power: The Moguls of Eastern Kentucky* (Urbana: University of Illinois Press, 1983); and John Egerton, "Appalachia's Absentee Landlords," *The Progressive* 45, June 1981, 42–45.

92. Caudill, 314.

93. Ibid., 306–24.

94. Ibid., 307.

95. Harold Sprout and Margaret Sprout, *The Context of Environmental Politics* (Lexington: University Press of Kentucky, 1978), 17.

96. Brown, McGrath, and Stokes, 35–36.

97. The following is based primarily on Michael H. Best and William E. Connolly, "Nature and Its Largest Parasite," in *The Capitalist System*, 2nd ed., ed. Richard C. Edwards, Michael Reich, and Thomas E. Weisskopf (Englewood Cliffs, NJ: Prentice Hall, 1978), 418–25, excerpted from their book *The Politicized Economy* (Lexington, MA: D.C. Heath, 1976).

98. Best and Connolly, 419.

99. Best and Connolly, 420–21. See also Mokhiber, 221–28.

100. Barry Commoner, "The Economic Meaning of Ecology," in *Crisis in American Institutions*, 4th ed., ed. Jerome H. Skolnick and Elliott Currie (Boston: Little, Brown), 285, excerpted from *The Closing Circle* (New York: Knopf, 1971).

101. Commoner, 291.

102. See Barry Weisbert, "The Politics of Ecology," *Liberation*, January 1970, 20–25.

103. The above examples are taken from two speeches by Ralph Nader at Colorado State University, May 1970 and November 1977.

104. Mokhiber, 248–57.

105. Jonathan H. Turner, *Social Problems in America* (New York: Harper & Row, 1977), 419–20.

106. James M. Henslin and Larry T. Reynolds, *Social Problems in American Society*, 2nd ed. (Boston: Holbrook, 1976), 220–21. See also Michael Parenti, *Power and the Powerless* (New York: St. Martin's Press, 1978), 19–20.

107. "The Politics of Cancer," *The Progressive* 43, May 1979, 9.

108. See Guzzardi, 54–64; and "Diseased Regulation," *Forbes*, February 19, 1979, 34.

5

National Defense, Multinational Corporations, and Human Rights

This chapter focuses on the international dimensions of deviance by economic and political elites. We examine three types of acts: (1) unethical or illegal practices relating to U.S. defense policy, (2) the conduct of multinational corporations (MNCs) abroad, and (3) violations of human rights by nations supported by the United States.

We begin with a discussion of the military–industrial complex. Consider the following recent examples:

- **Item:** "In possibly the largest spy scandal since World War II, the Pentagon has admitted the existence of a spy network, jointly operated by the U.S., the UK, Canada, Australia and New Zealand, capable of tapping every telephone, fax and e-mail communication in the world. Britain's *Sunday Telegraph* reported (February, 2000) that the communication was passed on to U.S. firms to secure contracts against competition from French, Japanese and other firms of the non-English speaking world. The information was allegedly used even against Airbus to favour Boeing though the UK has a share in Airbus. The project, called Echelon, has been in operation since 1947 and operates from the highly secretive U.S. National Security Agency's (NSA) Meredith Hill listening station in north Yorkshire. The U.S. and the UK were the only two original members of the group which was later expanded."[1]
- **Item:** In 1994, Teledyne, a major defense contractor, was ordered to pay $112 million in two whistle-blower suits. The payments were made to

settle charges that Teledyne sold the Pentagon millions of improperly tested electronic relays.[2]

Another whistle-blower was awarded $22.5 million from United Technologies Corporation (UTC). UTC's chief financial officer Douglas D. Keeth exposed the corporation's fraudulent billing practice to the Defense Department.[3] Rohr is said to agree to plead guilty in $7 million settlement of U.S. charges. Rohr falsified C-5 transport aircraft engine pylon tests.[4]

- **Item:** According to a U.S. Senate hearing, between 1985 and 1995, $13 billion paid to weapons contractors by the Pentagon was simply "lost," and another $15 billion remains unaccounted for due to "financial management troubles."[5] The most recent estimate is that military waste and fraud cost the American taxpayer $172 billion per year.[6]
- **Item:** According to a 1996 report by the Council for a Livable World, an arms-control advocacy group that has sought reductions in defense spending, there are at least $29 billion in wasteful programs. Titled "The Pentagon Follies," the report details such things as the following:

> A third golf course at Andrews Air Force Base in Maryland was constructed.

> The Naval Academy keeps a herd of 319 cows at an annual cost of $1.2 million. The academy says it is now trying to sell the cows.

> Funds from the Pentagon's Morale, Welfare, and Recreation program are used to lease part of a 287-room hotel at Disney World. The hotel loses $27.2 million, which is compensated for by a federal subsidy.

> A door hinge for the C-17 aircraft cost $2,187 after a subcontractor failed to provide the part. The part regularly costs $31.[7]

- **Item:** Large shipments of illegal arms are moving undetected across U.S. borders.[8] Fewer than 500 of the Customs Service's 18,000 employees watch arms exports along U.S. borders. Each year more than 75,000 license exports applications for weapons are granted by the U.S. State and Commerce departments. While the process is supposed to prevent violations of the Export Administration Act, which prohibits arms sales to terrorist nations, and the Arms Export Control Act, which controls arms exports in general, procedures are relatively ineffectual. Each year between $2 billion and $10 billion in illegal arms are traded, often to terrorists or oppositional groups seeking to overthrow legitimate governments, such as the Provisional Irish Republican Army, factions attempting to overthrow the government of Trinidad, and Iraqi interests seeking assault rifles. Only twenty-one cases for Arms Export Control violations were brought by the U.S. Department of Justice in 1992, representing less than 10 percent of the illegal weapons that are either exported from or imported to the United States.

Many readers may be asking why a discussion of deviance within the military establishment remains necessary. The Cold War clearly ended about 1990, more than 130 closures of domestic military bases were announced in 1993, and hundreds of thousands of defense-related jobs have been lost in the last few years (500,000 in California alone since 1991). However, as the examples demonstrate, the deviance (fraud) that made defense contracting so infamous is still occurring at a brisk pace.

Moreover, although some sectors of the military budget have been reduced, the reductions are much less than most people believe. The United States still spends about twice as much on defense as all its major allies combined. The Pentagon requested an additional $1.3 trillion be spent on defense by 1998. This will keep military spending at Cold War levels, around $230 billion per year. Likewise, the United States still maintains some 561 global military bases, 375 commissaries (doing $48 million a month in sales), and 149 hospitals. The military is supported by 20 defense industry PACs, which contributed $5 million to congressional candidates in 1992.[9]

Second, the United States sells 70 percent of all arms sold in the international arms trade, including $38 billion in armaments to nations of the Middle East since Saddam Hussein's Kuwaiti invasion.[10]

Clearly the influence of the U.S. military establishment and the deviance in which it engages remain serious social problems. The above examples, however, are merely the tip of a monstrous iceberg about which President Eisenhower warned the nation nearly forty years ago.

The Military–Industrial Complex

The Defense Establishment and Its Origins

In 1945, the United States emerged victorious from World War II, its economy and military forces intact. There was, at that time, a crucial need to help rebuild the war-torn economies of Western Europe. In addition, the communist revolution in China (1949) pointed out the necessity of preventing newly independent Third World nations from entering the communist orbit. Thus, from 1945 to 1975, $170 billion in loans and grants were made by the United States to friendly nations all over the world.[11] In return for such aid, recipients agreed to adopt the dollar as the standard currency of exchange and to give U.S. firms certain advantageous trade and investment opportunities.

Those nations agreeing to accept U.S. aid were to be protected by a worldwide U.S. military network. As of 1988, the United States possessed some 360 military bases in 40 countries, with more than one-third of U.S. military personnel stationed overseas.[12] Since World War II, U.S. troops and naval forces have been involved in 215 so-called shows of force and have intervened militarily in Korea, Lebanon, the Dominican Republic, Vietnam, and most recently Grenada, Nicaragua (through employment of mercenary Contras), the Persian Gulf, and Bosnia.[13] Militarily, the United States has provided what the Douglas Aircraft Company, in a report for the Army Research Office, called the "Pax Americana" (the American peace).[14]

These strategies have resulted in an unprecedented situation: Between 1945 and 1977, the United States spent an astounding $1,500 billion on defense.[15] During the Reagan years alone (1981–1989), an additional $1 trillion was spent on defense. The defense budget for fiscal 1996 was $265 billion, $7 billion more than the Pentagon had requested. This is 37 percent of the world's entire defense budget. Actually, if one includes the hidden military expenses in other departmental budgets, such as the Energy Department's fuel for nuclear weapons, the military portion of the NASA budget, and the interest for past military budgets, total expenditures are closer to $494 billion ($1.3 billion a day).[16] These expenditures, together with the nearly worldwide deployment of U.S. military forces, have created a huge permanent military establishment.

In fact, on January 13, 1961, outgoing President Eisenhower warned of the consequences of the military–industrial complex in his farewell address:

> In the councils of government, we must guard against the acquisition of unwarranted influence, whether sought or unsought, by the military-industrial complex.... We must never let the weight of this combination endanger our liberties or democratic processes. We should take nothing for granted. Only an alert and knowledgeable citizenry can compel the proper meshing of the huge industrial and military machinery of defense with our peaceful methods and goals, so that security and liberty can prosper together.[17]

Despite Eisenhower's warning, the military–industrial complex has continued to increase in both size and influence. Moreover, the nature of the complex is poorly understood by the public. It is not a malevolent conspiracy, as some believe, but an interrelated "community of interests."[18] It is really a MITLAMP (military–industrial–technological–labor–academic–managerial–political) complex:

1. The military sector consists of some 1.5 million active-duty military personnel; their current pay and allowances comprise about 30 percent of the defense budget.[19] In addition, in 1992, military retirees and veterans received payment of approximately $16,145, 203,000. Finally, in 1992, more than $34 billion was budgeted for the Veterans Administration (VA), which wields considerable political pressure.[20]

2. The industrial segment consists of more than 100 defense contractors whose economic base consists of the weapons portion of the defense budget. In 1973, 3,233 retired officers worked for such companies. And

between 1979 and 1983, 1,455 additional officers above the rank of colonel accepted positions with defense contractors (along with 335 civilian Pentagon employees with equivalent rank and 31 National Aeronautics and Space Administration [NASA] employees).[21]

3. The labor component of the complex consists of part of the Pentagon workforce, 5 percent of whom are directly involved and 16 percent of whom are indirectly involved in military matters.

4. The academic division of the MITLAMP complex consists of university departments involved in Pentagon-funded research on various U.S. campuses. In 1992, twelve universities received more than $10 million each in grants from the Department of Defense. Two universities, Johns Hopkins and the Massachusetts Institute of Technology (MIT), received more than $406 and $389 million, respectively.[22]

5. The managerial component consists of the 7.8 percent of U.S. managers who are directly involved in administering the intellectual, scientific, technological, and workforce requirements essential to MITLAMP goals. Another 9 percent of the managerial contingent is indirectly employed in such administration.

6. Finally, the political component of the MITLAMP complex consists of Congress members whose districts contain military facilities and/or employers receiving defense contracts. Such members often sit on congressional committees (such as the Senate and House Armed Services committees) that oversee the Pentagon budget.

At the apex of the military–industrial complex stand the National Security Managers, a group of politicians, civil servants, and businesspersons who tend to rotate among various posts in the Pentagon, Department of State, Atomic Energy Commission, Federal Bureau of Investigation, and the Central Intelligence Agency (CIA), the agencies that administer foreign aid and certain national and international police training programs, the White House, and big business. Such people (as was mentioned in Chapter 1) sit on the boards of trustees of the universities that receive the bulk of defense-related research funds and compose the directors of leading foundations that fund the think tanks and elite associations that regularly make policy recommendations to the executive branch of the federal government, as discussed in Chapter 1. Not surprisingly, the corporations that receive the most financial benefit from defense contracting are the same multinational corporations whose overseas holdings are protected by the military-counterinsurgency umbrella provided by the U.S. worldwide military establishment.

Another way to view the military–industrial complex is as a triangle. One leg of the structure is the military itself, consisting of 1 million civilian and 2 million military employees. A second leg consists of major corporations involved in defense contracting. Out of 30,000 firms engaged in prime contracting, the top 25 are awarded more than 50 percent of all defense weapons business. The third leg of the triangle consists of the politicians and their constituencies (districts) that are economically dependent on military bases and/or defense contractors. Here, ten states receive almost two-thirds of the prime contracts awarded for weapons procurement, with California receiving between one-fifth and one-quarter of all Pentagon money each year throughout the 1980s. Moreover, ten states receive more than half of all funds spent on military bases and personnel. Finally, almost 3 million private-sector employees work in defense industries, making politicians representing such districts extremely sensitive to the tax bases and local incomes involved.[23]

Among the firms garnering the lion's share of defense contracts are corporate giants like General Dynamics, McDonnell–Douglas, Lockheed, Rockwell, General Electric, Boeing, United Technologies, Raytheon, Westinghouse, IBM, RCA, Ford, General Motors, and Exxon. Eight of the top ten contractors in 1963 were still among the top ten in 1992, and two others were still in the top fifteen. Among the top fifty contractors were oil companies (Shell and Exxon), telephone firms (AT&T and ITT), universities (MIT and Johns Hopkins), and a health care firm (Foundation Health). Thus many firms not usually thought of as weapons makers have a large stake in defense contracting. [24]

The weapons industry is notoriously noncompetitive; inefficiency, cost overruns, waste, and corruption are rampant. Purchases of $7,000 coffee pots, $900 Allen wrenches, $700 toilet seats, and $400 hammers have been well documented. In addition, as of 1994, government investigations of contract abuse were initiated against 70 percent of the Pentagon's top 100 contractors, and fines for that year totaled a record $1.2 billion.[25]

Perhaps most disturbing is the quality of what is produced: "During the 1980s, nearly every major weapons system [was] plagued with performance shortcomings and cost overruns—including the Bradley fighting vehicle, the DIVAD gun, the Viper missile, the F-18 fighter and attack submarines, and the B-1B, Stealth, and F-15 aircraft."[26]

In fact, the government's own investigations have revealed surprising patterns of unethical practices. In 1965, the comptroller general described the following aspects of the military contract system to a House committee:

1. Excessive prices in relation to available pricing information
2. Acceptance and payment by the government for defective equipment
3. Charges to the government for costs applicable to contractors' commercial work
4. Contractors' use of government-owned facilities for commercial work for extended periods without payment of rent to the government
5. Duplicate billings to the government.
6. Unreasonable or excessive costs
7. Excessive progress payments held by contracts without payment of interest thereon[27]

Defense Contract Practices

- **Item:** According to a 1996 General Accounting Office report, 80 percent of the Navy's purchase orders are inaccurate. Moreover, an Air Force purchase order of $888,000 worth of ammunition was listed as $333 million, 37,500 percent overpriced. In 1992 alone, the Army Corps of Engineers misplaced $1.3 billion of its own equipment.[28]

One of the most notorious defense contract practices is known as *buying in.* Using this device, contractors set very low bids on the costs of weapons systems, but should the costs rise (and they inevitably do), the government agrees to pay for such increases under a contract change notice. Here, changes are made by either the Pentagon or the contractors. And in a complex weapons system, the number of such notices runs at times into thousands of dollars.[29] The practice has resulted in two negative consequences: (1) the cost overrun, by which the original price of an item easily multiplies; and (2) the Department of Defense's receipt of weapons of very questionable quality. (In some cases, no weapons at all are received.)

- **Item:** In 1993, the C-17 transport plane's production was so plagued by fraud and mismanagement that its price rose to $35 billion, nearly double the originally contracted price. In 1984, the military falsified tests for the Star Wars weapon system, resulting in increased funding for a project that never worked and is now unneeded. In 1993, the Clinton administration declared that the "Star Wars era is over" and then asked for $3.8 billion to continue developing the system under a different name![30]
- **Item:** J. P. Grace, head of a commission appointed by President Reagan to improve management and reduce costs within the federal government, estimated that fourteen weapons systems begun in 1983–1984 would end up costing 2.3 times as much as the amount of funds likely to be available for their production. According to Grace, as much as $100 billion in defense spending could have been saved over a three-year period by adopting such practices as competitive bidding.

Defense contractors also practice *pyramiding profits:* Prime contractors purchase components for systems from subcontractors, who in turn purchase other components from other subcontractors. Each company involved bills the company to whom it sells costs plus profits, which is perfectly legal; but taken to an extreme, this system breeds gigantic amounts of profit taking.

One example of pyramiding occurred in the 1950s, when Western Electric was given the contract for the Nike missile and subsequently the launcher for the missile. Western Electric subcontracted the launcher project to Douglas Aircraft, which subcontracted the project to a subsidiary of U.S.

Steel. The U.S. Steel affiliate's bill for the transaction, including its profit, was $13.5 million. The Douglas company manufactured the covers that fit over the missile and earned more than $1.2 million on the transaction, a return of more than 36,000 percent on its original investment. Western Electric based its bill to the government on Douglas's reported costs and profit, $14.7 million. Western Electric's total investment was $14,293, charged for inspecting equipment on various Army bases. Its profit on the transaction amounted to almost $1 million, a return on investment of more than 6,000 percent. The pyramiding arrangement clearly allows the prime contractor and each subcontractor to add on tremendous profits at each level.

The costs to the government in some defense contracts have reached unbelievable proportions at times. Several years ago, the Boeing Aircraft Corporation delivered eighty-two beds to the Air Force at a cost of $1,080 per bed. Standard Air Force beds were usually purchased for around $38 each.

J. P. Grace has also estimated that about two-thirds of all congressional districts contain or are near military installations. However, only 312 of these 4,000 defense installations are necessary and significant to U.S. defense. Most installations represent storage and support facilities and employ fewer than 150 people. Yet Congress requested $6 billion more than did the Department of Defense for the fiscal year 1985 defense budget. Why? Because such money will funnel into congressional districts, creating a few jobs and giving congressional members reelection themes.

In addition to buying-in and cost-plus contracting, several other wasteful and inefficient practices are commonplace in the defense industry:

1. *Goldplating* is the tendency to build into new systems needless levels of technological sophistication. The purchase of exotic features is encouraged by competition between the military services and among the corporations and is relatively uncontrolled because of military self-regulation in the definition of tactical needs.
2. *Managers without power* cannot effectively supervise contracts. Weapons programs tend to be overseen by middle-ranking military officers who must carry every decision to superiors and who are prevented from developing expertise by frequent job rotation.
3. *Concurrency* is the practice of beginning weapons production before development is complete, to speed deployment and cut lead time. Problems discovered later must be corrected on already produced units, driving up costs.

Defense contracting seems to invite incidents of fraud. For example, in the early 1970s, the B. F. Goodrich Company was granted a contract to develop the brake assemblies on the Air Force's A7D fighter aircraft. When the models developed by Goodrich consistently failed to pass their own laboratory tests, Goodrich engineers began falsifying test data and changing testing methods so that the brakes would meet Air Force specifications. Upon being tested on the actual aircraft, the brakes malfunctioned, causing a number of near crashes. Because of the nature of the doctored test data, Goodrich employee Kermet Vandivier (who later appeared as the government's witness) resigned. In his letter of resignation, Vandivier described a falsified report that was sent to the Air Force: "As you are aware, this report contained numerous deliberate and willful misrepresentations which, according to legal counsel, constitute fraud and expose...myself [to] charges of conspiracy to defraud." In the end, no charges of fraud were brought against either Goodrich or any of its officials. Goodrich merely announced that it would replace its original brake system with a new and better one.

Other examples of illegal or unethical practices with the Department of Defense have included outright bribery. From 1980 to 1988, the United States spent $2.2 trillion on defense, authorizing more than fifty new weapons systems and spending more than $300,000 per minute on procurement. Contractors have only forty-five to sixty days to submit proposals for weapons systems following their announcement. Consultants can earn up to $1,000 per day for gaining access to Department of Defense procurement officers and at times privileged information through bribery. The result is that there is now more bribery, graft, payoffs, and document smuggling by career personnel in responsible positions than ever before. In the end, the total waste amounted to hundreds of billions of dollars during the 1980s.

The scandal that shook the Pentagon in the summer of 1988 was about U.S. Navy Undersecretary Paisley passing classified information to McDonnell-Douglas in return for bribes. The scandal spread to include fifteen defense contractors in twelve states. In addition to Paisley, other procurement officials in the Navy and Air Force leaked insider information in return for payoffs.

Between 1988 and 1990, the investigation into the scandal, code named Operation Ill Wind, resulted in almost thirty-six guilty pleas. Eleven Unisys officials pleaded guilty to a variety of crimes, from tax evasion to bribery. Three United Technologies officials were convicted of fraud. Nine other defense contractors also pleaded guilty to defense contracting fraud and received fines of $1 million to $5.8 million (see Table 5.1 for details).

There is also a continuing pattern of fraud and other crimes among defense contractors.

- **Item:** In March 1991, a Unisys official pleaded guilty to conspiracy after attempting to obtain a $100 million Marine Corps communications contract. The official, Robert Elfering, also paid Pentagon consultants for insider information regarding the status of a radar command and control contract and then tried to hide this illicit activity. The issue of whether other high-ranking Unisys officials knew of these activities is also under investigation.

- **Item:** A McDonnell–Douglas subsidiary received a $7.5 million civil fine for charging the government greatly inflated costs on a 1983 contract for the M242 gun, used on the Bradley fighting vehicle. Douglas settled the case without having to admit falsifying any data but received the largest fine in the history of defense fraud cases since the March 1989 Rockwell case (see below).[31]
- **Item:** In March 1989, an ex-Singer employee joined in a lawsuit brought by the Navy accusing Singer of fraud by overcharging the Pentagon $77 million for flight simulators sold between 1980 and 1988. The government was seeking $231 million, plus civil damages of $5,000 to $10,000 for each of six counts involving false claims, fraud, breach of contract, and unjust enrichment.[32]
- **Item:** Also in March 1989, Rockwell was fined $5.5 million for double-billing the Air Force on the NAVSTAR satellite program. This was the largest fine ever in a defense fraud case. The company was also placed on five years' probation. Rockwell pleaded guilty to one fraud count and one criminal contempt of count.

TABLE 5.1   *Defense Fraud Convictions in Operation Ill Wind, 1988–1990*

Company	Pleaded Guilty To	Penalty Paid (millions of dollars)
Hazeltine	Conspiracy, making false statements	$2.0
Teledyne	Conspiracy, making false statements	4.3
Whittaker	Conspiracy, bribery of a public official, making false claims	3.5
Boeing	Illegally obtaining and distributing Defense Department documents	5.2
Loral	Conspiracy, receiving secret U.S. information, false certification	5.8
RCA	Illegally obtaining and distributing secret Pentagon plans	2.5
Hughes Aircraft	Unauthorized acquisition of Pentagon documents	3.7
Grumman	Illegal acquisition of Defense Department documents	2.5
Raytheon	Illegally obtaining and passing on a secret Air Force planning document	1.0

Source: Reprinted from April 16, 1990, issue of *Business Week* by special permission, copyright © 1990 by McGraw-Hill, Inc.

Moreover, as the following case study explores, revelations of deviance within the military–industrial complex continue to reach surprising heights.

Case Study: The Pentagon's Black Budget. On the campaign trail in 1979, President Reagan dismissed notions of a military–industrial complex as paranoid and fictitious. But, in fact, not only is there a military–industrial complex, but there is also a good deal of secretive deviance institutionalized within it. Much but by no means all of this behavior stems from the fact that a good deal of what happens within military and intelligence agencies is labeled secret and thus sealed from both congressional and public views.

Perhaps the clearest example of the deviance stemming from excessive secrecy has been uncorked by Pulitzer prize–winning journalist Tim Weiner. In his recent book, *Blank Check,* he describes a "black" or secret budget. So-called black funds originated in World War II with the Manhattan Project, which created the atomic bomb used on Japan in 1945. After the war came the creation of the national security state, the CIA, the National Security Council (NSC), and numerous other intelligence organizations within the armed services. These agencies justified continuation of the secret budget by lying to Congress about the level of Soviet military spending. The net result was to hide control over the nation's nuclear strategy from Congress and the American people. The budget is controlled by only three people: the president, the secretary of defense, and the director of the CIA. Items can be hidden from public view under titles like Special Programs and Selected Activities.

Since its beginnings, the black budget has continually been expanded; in 1990, it was estimated at $36 billion. Hidden within it is money for numerous questionable weapons projects, as well as money for the cover-up of a variety of covert, sometimes criminal operations. Weiner has chronicled a number of examples.

- **Item:** MILSTAR, a proposed $20 billion top-secret satellite project, was designed to coordinate a six-month nuclear war with the Soviet Union. Given that the Cold War has been declared "won" by the first Bush administration and that the U.S.S.R. has been dissolved, justification for this proposed overpriced system is puzzling. Now that Congress has finally learned of the MILSTAR plans, perhaps some hard questions can be asked.
- **Item:** The B-2 Stealth bomber has become the costliest airplane in U.S. history. The Stealth's initial cost was estimated at $22 billion in 1981 and was finally pegged at more than $68 billion ($820 million per plane) in 1991. The B-2's development is laced with incidents of crime.

  1. In 1985, the Stealth's manufacturer, Northrop, hired William Reinke as chief engineer. Reinke promptly set up his own firm, RE Engineering, and awarded it $600,000 in subcontracts from Northrop. Before being sentenced to five years in prison for

fraud, Reinke sold Northrop $20 Radio Shack headphones for $90 and $1.24 cables for $4.50.

2. Ron Brousseau, Northrop's buyer of Stealth parts, was concerned about his retirement fund. He demanded and received a 5 percent kickback from subcontractors, a practice so common in the defense industry that it has been nicknamed the "nickel job." Brousseau also assisted subcontractors in a "courtesy-bidding" (price-fixing) scheme, wherein different firms take turns being low bidders on contracts, creating the illusion of competition. Brousseau was sentenced to a three-year prison term for fraud.

- **Item:** The Northrop corporation itself was involved in numerous illegalities regarding the Stealth and other projects.

    1. Northrop overcharged the government $400 million for the Stealth and was indicted for fraud and conspiracy. Northrop's chairman, William Jones, resigned in disgrace.
    2. In May 1991, Northrop agreed to a unique $18 million settlement with its shareholders. The payments were made in response to a suit by shareholders challenging the conduct of corporate officials who had become enmeshed in wrongdoing or controversy. Among the breaches of duties cited were the following:

        The Cruise missile scandal, in which Northrop pleaded guilty to criminal fraud for falsifying missile test results (funds for the Cruise were a black item in the Pentagon budget)

        The MX missile guidance system, the subject of a Department of Justice civil suit brought in 1990

        The Tacit Rainbow missile project, terminated by the Air Force following years of problems

        The Harrier jet stabilizer, the subject of a heated congressional hearing in 1990

- **Item:** Voishan, the company that provided fasteners for the Stealth, defrauded the government by providing defective parts "approved" by a fictitious inspector.

Aside from questionable and sometimes illegal projects, the black aspect of the Pentagon budget has also involved covert operations, knowledge of which was unconstitutionally hidden from congressional oversight.

- **Item:** After the failed hostage rescue in Iran in 1981, a secret operations unit continued activities, funded by a secret budget funneled from other projects approved by Congress. Funds totaling $320 million were utilized for these operations, code-named Yellow Fruit, but a great deal of the money was illegally misspent on activities including vacations, prostitutes' services, drugs, clothing, and high-tech equipment. As a result of the fraud connected with Operation Yellow Fruit, only 10 to 20 percent of the $320 million was actually spent on covert operations. Three U.S. Army officers responsible for the funds were sentenced to prison terms ranging from eighteen months to ten years and fined $5,000 to $50,000 in the first secret court martial held by the U.S. Army since the Vietnam era.[33]

- **Item:** In another black operation between 1986 and 1991, the CIA secretly aided Afghan rebels who were fighting Soviet troops. The CIA also prompted China, Saudi Arabia, and Iran to provide aid. Some of the arms provided to the Afghans were sold to Pakistan in acts of self-enrichment, and some of the funds earmarked for the Afghans were diverted to the Contras in violation of the Boland Amendment.

- **Item:** In 1984, the CIA received Palestinian arms captured by Israel and provided them illegally to the Nicaraguan Contras. In one of the CIA deals, Israel received CIA weapons credits for sending captured arms to the Contras. Israel would then sell a like amount of arms to China, which would promptly export an equal sum of weapons to a CIA dummy corporation. In turn, the CIA would funnel the secret arsenal to Iran and/or the Contras. Other weapons were stockpiled for Afghan use, not in fighting the Soviets but in the bloody civil war that followed the Soviet withdrawal in 1990.

Consequences of Defense Policies

By the mid-1970s, many economists and social analysts had escalated their criticisms of the social costs of defense. First, there was the Vietnam War, with its $150 billion price tag and loss of 55,000 American lives. The social costs of Vietnam are something from which American society has yet to recover.

Although unethical and illegal defense contracting practices have been supported by American beliefs in free enterprise and the need for a strong national defense, ironically, neither has been provided by the system.

Despite these criticisms, defense spending continues to absorb more than half the money in the federal budget that is not a fixed cost and one-half of the federal research and development funds. By 1986, military spending accounted for 83 percent of the value of everything human made in the United States. A mere 7 percent of the defense spending from 1981 to 1986 could have completely rehabilitated U.S. Steel Corporation's outdated plants and equipment, and the cost of a single F18 aircraft could modernize the machine-tool stock of the entire U.S. economy.

The continued growth of military spending contributed for decades to international tension between the United States and the Soviet Union, which were locked in an international arms race. More arms made it less likely that either country would survive a full-scale war and thus created more insecurities. The only alternative was to enter into treaties that limited the production of weapons, which would of course diminish the profits that accrue from military spending. In the meantime, by mid-1983, the United States had produced 30,000 deliverable nuclear warheads, 12,000 of which could be used against the Soviet Union. The United States possessed enough nuclear weaponry to destroy the 218 Soviet cities with a population of 100,000 or more more than 230 times. Should a nuclear war have erupted, it is estimated that both the United States and the Soviet Union would have lost 95 million to 120 million citizens, and three-fourths of their respective economies would have been destroyed.

Despite these catastrophic potentials, the military–industrial complex continued to spend billions of dollars each year to convince itself and the American public of the dangers of Soviet aggression and of the inferior U.S. position in the arms race. General David Shoup, former commandant of the Marine Corps and head of the Joint Chiefs of Staff, noted that all service associations (e.g., the Association of the U.S. Army, the Navy League, and the Air Force Association) published journals that reflected the "party line" within the various services. Defense industries supported these journals with expensive ads that also lent credence to the anti-Soviet viewpoint. Such rhetoric develops an attitude among active-duty and retired personnel that allows them to believe their own propaganda, contributing to the creation of what General Shoup termed a *militaristic culture,* where force of arms is viewed as an acceptable solution to international problems.

Another factor in the overestimation of Soviet military strength was that largely unreliable data were used. For example, the CIA determined how much the Soviets spent on equipment and labor by estimating how much such items would cost in the United States. This was hardly a valid comparison, considering the small labor costs in the Soviet Union. Moreover, the CIA assumed that Soviet draftees received the same pay as U.S. soldiers. According to this logic, each time U.S. service members received a pay raise, so did the Soviets. Thus, for every $1 million U.S. pay increase, the CIA estimated a $2 million increase in the Soviet military budget! This estimation was also unrealistic because military pay in the Soviet Union was much lower than that in the United States. A Soviet recruit earned about $8 a month, whereas a U.S. recruit earned about $500. Moreover, U.S. estimates of its own military strength rarely compared spending by NATO nations with those of the Warsaw Pact, which are lower on average.

Finally, estimates of national military strength are by nature quantitative. They say little concerning the quality of weapons. In general, U.S. weapons are thought to be more lightweight, more accurate, and more efficient than their Soviet counterparts. This is especially true of missiles, combat aircraft, and radar sensors.

Documents declassified in 1993 demonstrate that the military–industrial complex "systematically and repeatedly lied to Congress and the public to frighten them into an ever-larger military.... The military has sucked away public investment, both dollars and talent, from many of the areas now so deeply in need—education, health care, public infrastructure, social services and research and development for civilian economic enterprise."

Meanwhile, the waste, fraud, and abuse inherent in the militarized economy continue apace.

- There is now $90 billion in surplus equipment in Pentagon warehouses, about $30 billion in excess of what would be needed if World War III broke out.
- The Air Force had $5 million in unneeded engine blades, and an Air Force computer routinely misclassifies one-time orders as needed recurrently, causing repeated reorders of items needed one time. Three hundred aircraft engines had to be scrapped because of improper storage. The Army spent $35.9 million for replacement of equipment that was repairable.
- Even the Pentagon admits that the Sea Wolf submarine ($2.8 billion) and a new aircraft carrier ($4.5 billion) are unneeded. The systems are being built just to keep defense workers employed.[34]

- The number of veterans in the United States fell from 28 million in 1980 to 23 million in 1995. So VA facilities, especially hospitals, are now underutilized. However, this has not stopped the VA's waste. Currently, it spends $560 a year on new hospital beds, including $104 million for a new 105-bed hospital wing in Hawaii, despite the fact that 63 beds in the facility were eliminated due to underuse. Moreover, a recent audit of one VA hospital in Southern California noted that the thirteen surgeons on staff (whose average salaries were $135,000 per year) had performed *no surgery whatsoever* during the preceding three months. Nationally, the VA has 500 more surgeons than it needs, with annual salaries of $67 million.[35]

The New Global Economy

- **Item:** The Indonesian government diverted millions of dollars in World Bank aid money to finance the establishment of the militia groups that laid waste East Timor in 1999, Australian television claims. At least $59 million of World Bank aid money was used to fund militia activities in East Timor.[36]
- **Item:** Art dealers were furious when rumors appeared that incriminating evidence of collusion existed between two of the world's leading multinational auction houses, Christie's and Sotheby's.[37] In January

2000, Christie's admitted handing over evidence to the antitrust division of the U.S. Justice Department of possible collusion between the two rivals.

- **Item:** "Swiss authorities investigating a Russian money-laundering affair have issued an international arrest warrant for former top Kremlin official Pavel Borodin, who was a key aide to Boris Yeltsin before the former Russian president resigned unexpectedly." The charges are part of an investigation into alleged payoffs to Russian government officials by Swiss-based construction firm Mabetex.[38]

- **Item:** British American Tobacco (BAT), the world's second-largest cigarette company, established a black market in its own products in China and across Asia, according to company documents. One set of papers, released by British health campaigners, showed how in 1993 the firm, alarmed by advances made by its competitor Philip Morris, actively planned to circumvent the China state tobacco monopoly, stating that "alternative routes of distribution of unofficial imports need to be examined, evaluated and, if appropriate, maximised."[39] In another document of about the same time, the firm's American subsidiary, Brown and Williamson, told its U.K. headquarters that the best growth prospects in China were in the black market. BAT managed and supplied smugglers with its cigarettes and condoned their activities. Likewise, in February 2000, a group of class-action lawyers announced in New York that they planned to file an antitrust lawsuit accusing cigarette makers of illegally fixing prices since the 1980s and of meeting secretly to make illegal agreements on wholesale prices. One of the companies named is BAT's American subsidiary, Brown and Williamson Tobacco Corporation.

- **Item:** U.S. defense contractor Lockheed Martin announced in 1999 that it would give South Korea aircraft parts, military software, and instrumentation equipment worth about $25 million as compensation for overcharging the South Korean government on purchases of eight P-3C antisubmarine aircraft. Daewoo, a large Korean corporation, blew the whistle on Lockheed because Lockheed failed to share the profits as promised.[40]

Moreover, the collapse of the former Soviet Union has resulted in the first truly global capitalist economic system. Among the characteristics of this new global economy are the following:

1. The internationalization of business, by which anything can be made anywhere on earth and sold everywhere. The result is that MNCs and finance capital now know no boundaries.
2. A great shift from manufacturing industries to service industries, such as computers, management, and finance.

3. A dramatic population shift in which tens of millions of people from the poor Third World nations of Asia, Africa, and Latin America migrate to prosperous First World nations of North America and Europe.
4. Growing economic inequality both within and between nations. Per capita incomes in Third World nations now range from $500 to $2,000 per year, while those of First World nations typically average around $23,000.[41] This means, among other things, that labor costs in poor nations are a mere fraction of what they are in rich nations.[42]

The new global economy has also created new opportunities for deviant behavior on a massive scale.

Deviance and Multinational Corporations

The U.S. economy, with its needs for investment outlets, cheap labor, and access to scarce raw materials, has created an environment in which certain types of deviance tend to occur. In Haiti, for example, it is common for workers to earn 67 cents to $1.67 per day working in multinational clothing factories.

- **Item:** "At Quality Garments S.A., a clothing contractor in the SONAPI Industrial Park, the factory is hot, dimly lit, crowded.... There is no ventilation.... For their labor, the workers are in many cases paid as little as 15 gourdes per day, or 12 cents per hour, well below the legal minimum wage of 30 cents per hour."[43] The same exploitive conditions prevail at other factories:

  > Seamfast Manufacturing, which produces dresses for Ventura Ltd. under the Ventura label, sold at Kmart and J.C. Penney, and Universal Manufacturing; and at Chancerelles S.A., a subsidiary of Fine Form USA, which produces bras and underpants for Elsie Undergarments of Hialeah, Florida. The garments are sold under the Shuly's and Elsie labels at J.C. Penney and smaller retailers.

  > National Sewing Contractors, which produces Disney pajamas, which are sold under the Sister Sister label at Wal-Mart, Kmart, J.C. Penney, and Kids 'R' Us.

  > Excel Apparel Exports, which produces women's underwear for the Hanes division of Sara Lee Corporation, under the Hanes Her Way label sold at Wal-Mart. The plant also produces women's slips sold at Dillard Department Stores and nightwear for Movie Star, to be sold at Sears and Bradlees.

- **Item:** Alpha Sewing, which produces industrial gloves for Ansell Edmont of Coshocton, Ohio, claims that it is the world's largest manufacturer of safety gloves and protective clothing, but the workers at Alpha Sewing lack the most basic safety protection. They produce Ansell Edmont's Vinyl-Impregnated Super-Flexible STD gloves with bare hands while working polyvinylchloride (PVC), which removes layers of skin.

- **Item:** At Classic Apparel, which produces sports team merchandise for H. H. Cutler, workers attach Made in USA labels to clothes made in a Haitian factory and sold as American goods in Wal-Mart. Wal-Mart has a policy of selling goods made in America. But a 1992 "Dateline NBC" investigation found that goods sewn by children in Bangladesh for Wal-Mart were labeled Made in USA. Walmart promised to investigate the situation. Over half of the nearly fifty assembly plants producing in Haiti for the U.S. market are paying less than the legal minimum wage, and while the U.S. Agency for International Development (AID) gave $215 million in 1995 for economic development to Haiti, the United States has opposed raising the Haitian minimum wage to $2.40 a day.

In recent decades, deviance by MNCs has included illegal payments to foreign governments and the exporting of hazardous goods. By the late 1970s, a practice known as *corporate dumping* had aroused a good deal of concern among public-interest groups and government agencies. The practice involves exporting goods that have been either banned or not approved for sale in the United States.

Most often, the greatest market for such unsafe products is among the poor of the Third World. Hazardous products are often legal in such countries. And because many of the poor in these nations are illiterate, they are often unaware of the hazards involved with the use of these products.

Examples of the products involved in corporate dumping are growing at a rapid pace.

An undisclosed number of farmers and over 1,000 water buffaloes died suddenly in Egypt after being exposed to leptophos, a chemical pesticide, which was never registered for domestic use by the Environmental Protection Agency (EPA), but was exported to at least 30 countries.

After the Dalkon Shield intrauterine device killed at least 17 women in the United States, the manufacturer withdrew it from the domestic market. It was sold overseas after the American recall and is still in common use in some countries.

No one knows how many children may develop cancer since several million children's garments treated with a carcinogenic fire retardant called Tris were shipped overseas after being forced off the domestic market by the Consumer Product Safety Commission (CPSC).

Lomotil, an effective antidiarrhea medicine sold only by prescription in the U.S. because it is fatal in amounts just slightly over the recommended doses, was sold over the counter in Sudan, in packages proclaiming it was used by astronauts during Gemini and Apollo space flights and [was] recommended for use by children as young as 12 months.

Winstrol, a synthetic male hormone, which was found to stunt the growth of American children, is freely available in Brazil, where it is recommended as an appetite stimulant for children.

Depo-Provera, an injectable contraceptive banned for such use in the United States because it caused malignant tumors in beagles and monkeys, is sold by the Upjohn Co. in 70 other countries, where it is widely used in U.S.-sponsored population control programs.

450,000 baby pacifiers of the type that has caused choking deaths have been exported by at least five manufacturers since a ban was proposed by the CPSC. 120,000 teething rings that did not meet recently established CPSC standards were declared for export and are on sale right now in Australia.[44]

Another example of corporate dumping involves the pesticide DCBP, which has been blamed for the sterilization of some 800 plantation workers in Latin America. A suspected carcinogen, DCBP has been banned for sale in the United States, yet U.S. law permits export of this product. Some 150 million pounds of this and other blacklisted products worth up to $800 million are exported overseas each year, which represents about one-quarter of U.S. pesticide production.[45] In 1990, Congress voted to outlaw export of DCBP, but lobbying by pesticide interests, including companies like Shell Oil, Occidental Petroleum, and Dow Chemical, left the measure hung up in a conference committee.

The fact remains that DCBP causes 20,000 deaths per year among Latin American plantation workers who cannot read warning labels; other effects include sterility, breathing problems, convulsions, nerve damage, and blindness. American workers sued Occidental in 1977, claiming that DCBP had made them sterile and won a $2.3 million settlement. While DCBP is no longer manufactured in the United States, other dangerous pesticides, such as chlordane (a potent carcinogen) and heptachlor (a suspected carcinogen), both manufactured by Velsicol, continue to be exported. In fact, 1.5 to 2 million pounds are exported per year, despite a ban on these products by forty-eight nations.[46]

Government Policy

In some cases, corporate dumping has been aided by government policy. In one instance, the population office of AID purchased hundreds of shoe-box-sized cartons of unsterilized Dalkon Shields for distribution in the Third World. The birth control device, which causes uterine infections, blood poisoning, spontaneous abortion in pregnant women, and perforation of the uterus, was sold to AID at a 48 percent discount because of its unsterile condition.[47] The device was distributed in forty-two nations, largely in the Third

World. Moreover, insufficient information concerning the use and hazards of the shield accompanied the shipment.

Some companies dump workplace hazards as well as hazardous products in poor nations. One example is the case of asbestos, a cancer-causing agent. Thanks to the Occupational Carcinogens Control Act of 1976, fines of $1,000 for violations and $5,000 for repeat violations are provided for U.S. manufacturers that expose workers to carcinogenic agents. However, no such regulations protect foreign workers from contracting cancer from asbestos fibers. On the contrary, Mexican law merely provides a light fine ($45 to $90) for failure to warn workers that they are working around a health hazard. As a result, U.S. asbestos makers increasingly locate plants in Mexico and other Third World nations with lax workplace hazard laws (e.g., Brazil) and are now producing quantities of asbestos there.[48]

Corporate dumping is undesirable for two main reasons. First, it poses serious health hazards to the poor and uninformed consumers of the Third World. In the long run, this contributes to the anti-Americanism of many nonaligned nations. Second, many types of corporate dumping produce a boomerang effect. That is, some of the hazardous products sold abroad by U.S. companies are often used in the manufacture of goods that are exported to the United States and other developed nations.

> The "vast majority" of the nearly one billion pounds of pesticides used each year in the Third World is applied to crops that are then exported back to the U.S. and other rich countries.... This fact undercuts the industry's main argument defending pesticide dumping. "We see nothing wrong with helping the hungry world eat," is the way a Velsicol Chemical Company executive puts it. Yet, the entire dumping process bypasses the local population's need for food. The example in which DCBP manufactured by Amvac is imported into Central America by Castle Cooke to grow fruit destined for U.S. dinner tables is a case in point.[49]

The boomerang effect of corporate dumping may represent the breeding ground of yet another major scandal regarding the practices of MNCs and certain U.S. governments agencies in the Third World.

Dumping Toxic Waste

Many Third World nations, especially Turkey, Haiti, the Philippines, Nigeria, and Guinea-Bissau, are now routinely approached by advanced nations to become sites for the dumping of toxic waste. A virtual armada of ships circles the globe in search of cheap storage facilities to dump waste that can cause cancer and birth defects. Some of the waste has even been found radioactive. International toxic dumping is currently a $10 billion a year business, and much corruption accompanies it.[50]

The advanced nations of the world generate about 400 million tons of toxic waste annually; 60 percent comes from the United States. The Environmental Protection Agency (EPA) requires U.S. companies to provide on-site disposal facilities for toxic waste that cost upward of $30 million and take years to build. However, such waste can be dumped in Third World nations for a fraction of this cost, even providing handsome financial rewards to the recipient nations. For example, Guinea-Bissau, which has a gross national product of $150 million, will make $150 to $600 million over a five-year period in a deal to accept toxic waste from three European nations.[51]

Third World participation in the waste dumping of advanced nations has generated a host of scandals.

- **Item:** In April 1988, five top government officials in Congo were indicted after they concluded a deal to import 1 million tons of chemical waste and pesticide residue, receiving $4 million in "commissions" from a firm specializing in hazardous waste disposal. The total contract was worth $84 million.
- **Item:** After dumping toxic waste in Nigeria and Lebanon in 1988, Italy agreed to take back some 6,400 tons. Nigeria recalled its Italian ambassador and arrested twenty-five people when it discovered that some of the waste was radioactive. To complicate matters, Italian dock workers in ten port cities have refused to handle the waste. Italy has pledged to ban further toxic exports to the developing world and plans to spend $7 billion a year to clean up its own toxic dumps at home. The Italian government has also sued twenty-two waste-producing firms to force them to turn over $75 million to pay for transporting and treating incoming waste.[52]
- **Item:** In 1987, Weber Ltd., a West German waste transporter, found a Turkish cement plant willing to accept 1,500 tons of toxic-waste-laden sawdust for about $70 a ton. Instead of being burned, the sawdust waste sat in the open air for nearly sixteen months, slowly leaking poison into the ground. A newspaper reported that the sawdust contained lethal PCBs and a scandal ensued. Under pressure from the governments of Turkey and West Germany, Weber finally agreed to transport the waste back to West Germany. Normally, Weber charges its customers $450 to $510 a ton to dispose of waste in Germany. With Third World costs of $110 per ton, the amount of profit involved is substantial.
- **Item:** In late 1991, three South Carolina metal smelting firms contracted with waste disposal firms to send waste containing life-threatening levels of cadmium and lead to Bangladesh. Once in that country, the waste was used to make fertilizer and used by Bangladeshi farmers.

Ironically, the greatest problem with toxic dumping in Third World nations is that much of the time it is perfectly legal. About all that concerned citizens in developing nations can do is publicize the dangers involved. What environmental disasters may befall such nations in the future is anyone's guess.

Third World dumping involves a series of related implications. For instance, some suggest that deliberate racist and genocidal policies are being practiced by certain corporations and government agencies. We suggest that corporate dumping may well have such effects on the nonwhite people of the world. The same may be said concerning support by corporations and governments for regimes that violate human rights.

Human Rights, Multinationals, and U.S. Foreign Policy

Under Presidents Ford and Carter, the United States went on record as supporting the cause of human rights around the world. In a United Nations speech of March 17, 1977, President Carter pledged to "work with potential adversaries as well as...close friends to advance the cause of human rights."

The United States is also a party to the International Bill of Rights. Passed by the U.N. General Assembly in 1948, this document supports a variety of civil and economic rights and specifically pledges member nations not to subject anyone to "torture or to cruel, inhuman or degrading treatment, or punishment" or to "arbitrary arrest, detention, or exile."

Finally, the United States is also a signatory to the famous Helsinki Agreement of 1975, which contains a detailed human rights clause, specifically stating that participating nations will "respect human rights and fundamental freedoms, including freedom of thought, conscience, religion, or belief, all without distinctions as to race, sex, language, or religion." Thus, by pronouncement and by legal agreement, the United States has firmly committed itself to the cause of human rights.

Unfortunately, a mounting body of evidence indicates that U.S. policy makers have, on many occasions, either placed in power and/or aided in retaining power some of the world's most repressive dictatorships. The chief characteristic of such regimes is that they are right-wing, military dictatorships and hence friendly to the goals of multinational capitalism. With U.S. support (ranging from foreign aid to military protection), many Third World regimes have done away with democratic practices and instituted brutally repressive measures, including arbitrary imprisonment, torture, death squads, and kidnapping.

In fact, a pattern has been established showing that U.S. economic and military aid (and aid from U.S.-dominated lending agencies) has been "positively related to investment climate (for U.S. multinationals) and inversely (negatively) related to the maintenance of the democratic order and human rights." This relationship is described in Table 5.2. Moreover, the decline in aid for South Korea and Chile is somewhat misleading. In South Korea, the decline was caused by the end of expenditures for the Vietnam War, in which South Korea participated. And the decline in aid for Chile was, in fact, due to a successful right-wing coup (supported by the CIA) in 1973; high levels of aid had been given before that date.

Between 1973 and 1978, the United States continued its aid to many of the regimes cited by Chomsky and Herman, as well as to others cited by organizations like Amnesty International, the U.N. Commission on Human Rights, and the International Commission on Human Rights for persistent "torture, assassination, and arbitrary arrest."

Moreover, the Foreign Assistance Act of 1974 provides that the president "shall substantially reduce or terminate security assistance to any government which engages in gross violations of human rights." Under this act, it became illegal (as of July 1, 1975) to provide aid to any law enforcement organization (e.g., police prisons) of any foreign government. However, under the International Narcotics Control Act, both training and weapons have been given to police departments in many foreign countries, including those listed in Table 5.2.

In the cases of Guatemala (1953), Iran (1953), the Dominican Republic (1965), and South Vietnam (1963), either U.S. troops and/or the CIA played an active role in actually installing such regimes, through either aid or armed forces or both. Aside from bringing advantages to multinationals, these regimes have done little to improve the lot of the people over whom they rule. This is especially the case in Third World nations in Asia, Africa, and Latin America.

- **Item:** In 1996, Nigerian troops executed nine environmentalists, including a former Nobel prize winner. The activists were involved in protests against Shell Oil's parent company, which had destroyed large tracts of farmland in their quest for Nigerian oil. Shell refines and imports into the United States almost 50 percent of Nigeria's entire oil production. Evidence uncovered by the *Village Voice* in 1995 indicates that Shell Oil had been paying the Nigerian military to take action against environmental protesters and that Shell had offered bribes to witnesses in trials of murdered protesters.[53]
- **Item:** In 1996, released manuals from the CIA-run School of the Americans (SOA) indicate that the training advocated such tactics as murder, extortion, physical abuse, and bounty for enemy dead. Other tactics advocated included the use of blackmail, false arrest, imprisonment of parents, and execution of all other members of the "enemy's" local cell. Such tactics are illegal for U.S. intelligence agents, in part because they violate the human rights treaties to which the United States is a signatory. The SOA has trained members of death squads throughout Latin

TABLE 5.2 Relationship between U.S. Aid, Investment Climate, and Human Rights in Ten Countries

Country	Strategic Political Dates (1)	Positive (+) or Negative (−) Effects on Democracy (2)	Means an Increased Use of Torture or Death Squads (−) (3)	Means an Increase in Number of Political Prisoners (−) (4)	Improvement in Investment Climate: Tax Laws Eased (+) (5a)	Improvement in Investment Climate: Labor Repressed (+) (5b)	Economic Aid (% Change) (6)	Military Aid (% Change) (7)	(6) + (7) (% Change) (8)	U.S. and Multinational Credits (% Change) (9)	Total Aid (8) + (9) (% Change) (10)
Brazil	1964	−	−	−	+	+	+ 14	−40	− 7	+ 180	112
Chile	1973	−	−	NA	+	+	+588	− 8	+259	+1,079	+ 770
Dominican Republic	1965	−	−	NA	+	+	+ 57	+10	+ 52	+ 305	+ 133
Guatemala	1954	−	−	−	+	NA	NA	NA	NA	NA	+5,300
Indonesia	1965	−	−	−	+	+	− 81	−79	− 81	+ 653	+ 62
Iran	1953	−	−	−	+	+	NA	NA	NA	NA	+ 900
Philippines	1972	−	−	−	+	+	+204	+67	+143	+ 171	+ 161
South Korea	1972	−	−	−	+	+	− 52	−56	− 55	+ 183	+ 9
Thailand	1973	+	+	NA	−	−	− 63	−64	− 64	+ 218	+ 5
Uruguay	1973	−	−	+	+	−	11	+ 9	− 2	+ 32	+ 21

Source: N. Chomsky and E. S. Herman, "U.S. vs. Human Right in the Third World," *Monthly Review* 29 (July/August 1977), 30–31. Reprinted by permission.

America. The squads are responsible for the deaths of thousands of innocent civilians in Latin America since 1954.

Examples of human rights abuses in Latin America and elsewhere by regimes supported by U.S. military aid and having death squads or police units trained by the CIA are legion.

- **Item:** Currently, Colombia has the highest recorded homicide rate in the world, averaging about 35,000 murders per year (ten times higher than the United States). Many people assume that the high homicide rate is due to drug cartels, but only 2 percent of such killings are drug related. Over 70 percent of Colombia's homicides are due to the activities of the Colombian army, police, and paramilitary killer squad organizations, originally trained by the CIA. Among the frequent targets of government murderers are farming coop members, who have protested for higher wages, and protesters fearing that Colombia's state-owned oil company will soon be privatized. Government groups received $1.6 billion in military aid from the United States between 1986 and 1996, with about $1 billion more scheduled for release in 2001.[54]
- **Item:** In Turkey, an automobile accident in 1997 killed Abdullah Calti, a convicted drug trafficker and murderer, and his girlfriend, Conca Us, a Mafia hitwoman and former beauty queen. Evidence found at the crash scene indicated that Turkish officials had given special diplomatic credentials and various weapons permits to Calti. A subsequent investigation demonstrated the following:

  > Calti had ties to the Turkish Secret Police and he belonged to a neofacist terrorist group called the Grey Wolves. The Wolves were responsible for bombing attacks that killed thousands of Turkish civilians in the 1960s and 1970s and were responsible for the 1981 shooting of Pope John II (which the CIA tried to blame on the Russians).[55]

  > Calti also possessed close ties to the Turkish crime syndicate, which smuggles arms and heroin across Eastern Europe to various nations in the Middle East. The same smuggling mechanism was also used by the CIA in the 1980s to get weapons to the Nicaraguan Contras. The Grey Wolves also received funds and training from U.S. advisors and were affiliated with the CIA in the 1970s. In 1980, the violence committed by the Wolves led to a CIA-backed military coup in Turkey. Following the collapse of the USSR in 1991, extremist Grey Wolf members infiltrated many of the former Soviet provinces (now independent nations) and became

active in the politics of a number of Central Asian nations. Meanwhile, the Turkish government continues to use the Wolves to repress Turkish minorities, especially the Kurds.

Iran

In 1953, the CIA was responsible for placing the Shah's family in power when it assisted in overthrowing leftist Prime Minister Mohammad Mossadegh in a violent coup. From 1953 until the 1979 Khomeini revolution, Congress, the U.S. military, the CIA, and private corporate interests all supported the Shah's army and secret police with various types of aid. Under the U.S. Office of Public Safety program, between 1961 and 1973, Iran received $1.7 billion. This money was used to purchase police hardware (e.g., guns, teargas grenades, computers, and patrol cars) and to train 179 Iranian police officials at the International Police Academy in Washington, D.C. (and other special U.S. police schools). From 1946 to 1976, Iran received $1.6 billion under a variety of U.S. military assistance programs: outright grants of arms, equipment, and services; credit for purchasing U.S. arms; training Iranian military personnel; and subsidies awarded under an act designed to aid threatened pro-U.S. regimes. Between 1950 and 1976, 11,025 Iranian military officers received training under these programs.

Iran also purchased arms from private concerns. For example, the Bell Helicopter Company helped Iran develop a Sky Cavalry Brigade, operating from helicopters, which was modeled after similar U.S. units that fought in Vietnam.[56] Finally, between 1971 and 1978, the United States sold Iran $15 billion in military supplies.[57] Moreover, at the moment of the revolution, some 40,000 military advisors,[58] along with an unknown number of CIA agents, were stationed in Iran. In short, the United States had a long history of assistance to the Shah's regime.

While the Shah was in power, almost 1,500 people were arrested every month. In one day alone (June 5, 1963), the SAVAK (Iran's secret police) and the Shah's army killed 6,000 Iranian citizens. Amnesty International's report for 1975 indicated that Iranian authorities had arrested and imprisoned between 25,000 and 100,000 political prisoners.[59] The Iranian press was strictly controlled by the police under the Shah's direct orders. Minorities were not allowed to learn their native languages, and poverty was widespread. Iran was a nation in which political stability was maintained by repression—a nation on the brink of massive political turmoil.

Since 1973, Iran has been one of a number of nations cited for constant abuses of human rights by organizations such as Amnesty International, the International Commission of Jurists, and the U.N. Commission on Human Rights.[60] Thus, while U.S. officials and the press knew full well what was taking place in Iran, the government continued to support the Shah with various types of military aid, and the press remained nearly silent on the Shah's abuses.

By mid-1980, the United States had paid a tragic price for its rather blind support of the Shah's regime: In 1979, an anti-American revolution led by Moslem holy man Ayatollah Ruhollah Khomeini, exiled from Iran by the government in 1963, overthrew the Shah's rule. U.S. support for the Shah may also have been partially responsible for the catastrophic increases in oil prices since 1973 (see Chapter 2). A number of sources, including Jack Anderson and CBS's "60 Minutes," reported that the Shah:

Was installed in power in the 1950s when the Rockefellers helped arrange the CIA coup that overthrew Mossadegh.

Demonstrated his gratitude to the Rockefellers by making heavy deposits of his personal funds in the Rockefeller-owned Chase Manhattan Bank.

Raised Iranian oil prices in 1973–1974 by 470 percent, with the approval of then Secretary of State Henry Kissinger, a Rockefeller associate. (This cost the oil-consuming nations of the West an estimated $95 billion in inflated oil prices.)[61] The price hike was requested by the Shah in part to purchase American-made arms.

Was admitted into the United States for medical care in 1979 as a result of pressure by Chase Manhattan president David Rockefeller and Henry Kissinger.[62] As a result, in November 1979, militants overran the U.S. embassy in Tehran, capturing sixty-one U.S. employees. An aborted effort to rescue the hostages in early May 1980 resulted in the deaths of eight U.S. servicemen.

Speculation still persists whether a secret deal was made by the Reagan campaign regarding the release of the hostages in exchange for weapons (see Chapter 9). A congressional investigation into this matter is underway.

The Khomeini regime spread anti-American fever throughout the Middle East. In October 1983, a truck driven by members of a Khomeini-supported regime smashed into a Beirut, Lebanon, building housing U.S. Marines, killing 241 servicemen.[63] Such terrorism and instability have seriously weakened perception of the strength and consistency of U.S. foreign policy.

U.S. support for the Shah was quite profitable for Chase Manhattan, which continued to be the repository for the Shah's sizable fortune, and Exxon Oil, which is controlled through Rockefeller trust funds and private holdings.[64] Yet these events have never been investigated by Congress. The consequences suffered in return for U.S. support for the Shah are also indicative of other consequences of supporting regimes that violate human rights.

Latin America

In Latin America, another trouble spot, U.S. support for authoritarian dictatorships contributes to suffering and political instability throughout the region.

- **Item:** From 1976 to 1983, some 15,000 to 20,000 residents of Argentina simply disappeared. Many were tortured to death and then buried in secret locations in unmarked graves by Argentina's military dictatorship. In 1982, the U.S.-backed government declared amnesty for those responsible for the disappearances of these 20,000 suspected subversives, which primarily benefited those guilty of torture and murder. However, in December 1983, Argentina elected a democratic government under Raul Alfonsin, and judicial action began against many of the military officers responsible for the crimes.[65]
- **Item:** In El Salvador, a poor Central American nation, 2 percent of all families own 60 percent of the nation's most fertile land. And between 1961 and 1975, the number of families owning no land at all grew from 30,000 to 167,000. Between 1979 and 1983, some 40,000 civilians were killed largely by government-supported, right-wing death squads, and 20 percent of the Salvadoran population (800,000 people) became refugees. U.S. aid to El Salvador between 1979 and 1984 was $100 million, six times that provided in the previous twenty-nine years, despite the fact that the government's death squads brutally raped, tortured, and murdered four U.S. nuns in 1980. Amnesty International declared that the Salvadoran death squads were a gross violation of human rights. Nonetheless, aid continued, as the Reagan administration continued to argue that the situation was constantly improving. Meanwhile, investments in El Salvador by U.S.-based MNCs, such as Chevron, Texaco, and Kimberly-Clark, total $100 million.[66]
- **Item:** In 1994, a declassified cable sent by special envoy General Vernon Walters confirmed U.S. knowledge of Salvadoran leader Roberto d'Aubuisson's plan to murder U.S. Ambassador Thomas Pickering in 1984. Other cables demonstrated that the United States suspected d'Aubuisson of death squad activity as early as 1978 but feared alienating him. The CIA was aware of the death squad's plan to murder Archbishop Oscar Romero, which it did. D'Aubuisson also had a close relationship with North Carolina's senator Jesse Helms throughout the 1980s. D'Aubuisson's death squads murdered several thousand leftists and suspected leftists in the 1970s and 1980s at the behest of wealthy landowners. D'Aubuisson died of throat cancer in 1992.[67]
- **Item:** In March 1993, the U.N. commission on the truth on crimes committed against civilians in El Salvador's twelve-year civil war released its official report. Among its conclusions was that the majority of the political murders in that nation's civil war occurred at the very least

with the reluctant agreement and financial support of the Reagan and Bush administrations. More than 80,000 people, 1 in 70 Salvadorans and mostly unarmed civilians, were murdered in the war. The CIA in its own report described one leader, Roberto d'Aubuisson, as a drug trafficker, arms smuggler, and plotter in the assassination of Archbishop Oscar Romero.[68]

- **Item:** In another poor Central American nation, Guatemala, the United States sponsored a CIA-directed coup in 1954 when it was learned that Guatemala's president, Jacobo Guzman, planned to redistribute 387,000 of the 500,000 acres of Guatemalan land owned by a U.S.-based company, United Fruit. Secretary of State John Foster Dulles, whose law firm had represented United Fruit in the 1930s, and CIA Director Allan Dulles (J.F. Dulles's brother and former president of United Fruit) launched a massive public relations campaign, accusing Guzman's government of being communist. The CIA coup that overthrew the Guatemalan president replaced him with a U.S.-trained army officer, Castillo Armas. Under Armas, political parties and trade unions were abolished, and U.S. aid totaling $6 million was used to thwart guerrilla resistance in the 1960s in which 10,000 people were killed and 100,000 people were left refugees. Even the U.S. Department of State criticized the operation.

Since 1954, 80,000 Guatemalan civilians, mostly peasants, have been murdered, many women and children. Eyewitness accounts report children being hacked to death with machetes and their heads smashed against walls, while infants have been thrown into the air and bayoneted. In 1982 alone, 80,000 peasants fled Guatemala, and Amnesty International estimates another 10,000 were killed. Yet the Reagan administration insisted that criticism of Guatemala was a "bum rap."[69]

Since July 1982, the Guatemalan government has been involved in the attempted genocide of ethnic groups living on its northern border, violating a 1948 U.N. convention against genocide (to which Guatemala was a signatory). In August 1983, General Montt was overthrown in a barracks coup and replaced by another military leader, General Victories. At the time of the coup, unemployment was 40 percent and business was angered over Montt's policies restricting oil investment.

Following the coup, the Reagan administration quickly approved an aid package totaling $10.25 million in military aid and $66.5 million in development aid.

- **Item:** In Guatemala in 1982–1983, 1 million Indians were "internally displaced" in a counterinsurgency campaign by the government. Between 1978 and 1984, 75,000 Guatemalans were killed and another 200,000 fled across the Mexican border. By 1988, another 60,000 to

70,000 Indians were forcibly relocated by the government. Moreover, 10,000 homeless children now roam the capital city.[70]

- **Item:** Between 1929 and 1979, the U.S.-backed Samosa family ruled Nicaragua with a dictatorial hand. Ousted by a popular revolution in 1979, Samosa's former supporters are now being armed and trained by the CIA in Central America and Miami. Although the revolutionary Sandinista government has reduced illiteracy in Nicaragua from 50 to 12 percent, redistributed land, and achieved self-sufficiency in food production, its regime was forced to turn to the Soviet Union for aid when the Reagan administration cut off $30 million in funds approved under the Carter presidency. Since 1980, the United States has engaged in a covert war against Nicaragua, training counterrevolutionaries in more than a dozen Latin American nations, giving $3.1 million in military aid to the Honduran military, and arming 4,000 to 10,000 men in Nicaragua itself. The United States also illegally mined harbors in Nicaragua and refused to accept judgment against this action by the World Court. The CIA also used the Salvadoran Air Force to fly sorties over Nicaragua.[71]

- **Item:** Another case concerns the activities of General Roberto Viola. Invited to the White House in 1981 by newly elected President Reagan, the meeting marked the beginning of U.S. recruitment of right-wing regimes in its attempted overthrow of Nicaragua's Sandinista government. Aid to Viola's regime had been suspended during the Carter administration, when it was learned that the military junta engaged in human rights abuses against its own people. Viola was eventually sentenced to seventeen years in prison for murder, kidnapping, and torture and for commanding death squads that killed 9,000 Nicaraguans. Nevertheless, the Reagan administration gave substantial covert military aid to the Nicaragua junta and entered into covert actions against the Sandinistas with Viola's regime.[72]

Chile

Perhaps the most repressive noncommunist nation in the world was General Pinochet's Chile. By 1975, two years after Pinochet's CIA-assisted bloody coup, 1 in every 125 Chileans had been detained for more than a day. By 1988, 1 in every 55 Chileans had become a political exile. People were routinely held up to twenty days without government acknowledgment of their arrest. A wide range of torture methods was reported, including the use of electrodes on the genitals and knees, mock executions, sleep deprivation, constant loud music, sexual abuse, and submersion in water. Live rats are sometimes shoved into victims' mouths. One captive described his experience:

> I shouted and screamed from the intensity of the pain, and the method used: It was as if pincers were being applied to my testicles.... Scabs formed on my

mouth. I couldn't speak.... My penis, testicles, and glands were torn open and all bloody. Later they told me they had run over my younger son, who is six, and that he was dead.... They told me they were going to torture my daughter also, that they would open her up and leave her menstruating for the rest of her life.[73]

Commonly, police and military troops searched entire poor neighborhoods in the early morning and pulled all adult males from the houses. The men were then transported to sports complexes, where their identifications were checked against computerized lists. This done, they were either released or taken into custody for several days.[74]

In short, this regime that the United States helped to install tortured hundreds of thousands of its own people. The economy was in a shambles, with unemployment in poor areas around 60 percent and those employed at the minimum wage unable to afford less than half their essential food costs. Social programs for the poor were either drastically cut or completely eliminated. And the work of artists, poets, novelists, and writers was suppressed. In the meantime, the Pinochets lived in a 15,000-square-foot house, built at a cost of between $10 and $13 million, with eighty guards and an infrared security system. In late 1988, Pinochet lost a plebiscite (vote of public confidence) on his regime,[75] and a new president was elected. Pinochet fled in 1999 to England, which has refused to extridite him for trial.

Assessing U.S. Support

Amnesty International has declared that more than one-third of the world's governments use some form of torture. The choice faced by the United States is one between supporting a butchering regime that faces opposition from a revolutionary movement or supporting a resistance willing to accept aid from wherever it can get it. The result is often a completely unstable situation.[76]

The assessment of U.S. support for regimes that violate human rights may be made by viewing (1) conditions of people who live under them and (2) the effect of such support on U.S. foreign policy. It must be stressed that the inhabitants of the Third World often live under conditions that violate elementary human rights. Thus, throughout Asia, Africa, and Latin America:

- An estimated 1.5 billion people are without effective medical care. There is an average of 4,000 people per doctor; in some areas, the ratio goes above 50,000 per doctor.
- Half the school-age children are not yet in schools.
- Twenty thousand persons per day die from starvation, 12,000 of them in Africa alone. Another 1.5 billion suffer from malnutrition.
- Unemployment is now 30 percent in most countries.

- Per capita income ranges from less than $250 per year (e.g., Ethiopia, India, Kenya, and Pakistan) to less than $1,600 per year (e.g., Turkey, Mexico, and Chile).
- More than 700 million adults are unable to read and write.[77]

To the extent that U.S. support for such regimes is based on arms rather than development, U.S. policy becomes a factor in exacerbating these wretched conditions. By 1993, yearly U.S. weapons sales to foreign nations had reached $33 billion. In 1983, the United States was the major supplier to at least twenty of the world's nations engaged in war at the time.[78] Moreover, in 1982–1983, the United States signed another $24 billion in arms export agreements.[79] By 1984, the United States was the supplier of half the arms bought by Third World nations.

Although it is true that not all Third World peoples live under repressive dictatorships, the majority of Third World governments are repressive. Such sales of weapons help to maintain repressive regimes and fuel wars in the Third World. They do not foster peaceful economic development.

In the India–Pakistan War of 1965, for example, "the Sherman tanks of the Indian Army battled the Patton tanks of the Pakistani Army."[80] These weapons were sold to the two nations with the promise that they would be used defensively to resist communist aggression, yet they helped to support a war between the two noncommunist nations. Such incidents have also taken place between Israel and her Arab neighbors. Certainly, U.S. arms sales to nations in conflict are not the sole cause of such wars. But the presence of arms may contribute to the heightening of tensions. In any case, it is unfortunate that a world that spends billions of dollars a year on arms cannot (or will not) spend funds for projects so desperately needed in the Third World.

U.S. support for dictatorships in underdeveloped countries helps to create a favorable business climate for multinational firms. However, the economic activity of multinationals is often a hindrance to the development of these countries. Consider, for example, the effects of repatriation (return of profits made overseas to the corporation's home base): "From 1950 to 1970…U.S. firms added $1.7 billion to their holdings in four…countries—Chile, Peru, Bolivia, and Venezuela—primarily to increase production of such export commodities as copper, tin, and oil. But in the same period, these multi-nationals repatriated $44.2 billion to the United States, leaving a net loss to those countries of $9.5 billion."[81]

This net loss often translates into massive indebtedness, with such debts usually owed to multinational banks, governments, and other lending institutions made up largely of members from advanced industrial countries. The results have been very favorable for multinational banks but devastating to Third World nations. From 1965 to 1972, overseas assets of U.S.

banks grew from $9 billion to $90 billion. By 1976, U.S. banks held $181 billion in overseas assets, a 100 percent increase over four years.[82]

A great share of such assets was actually loans to Third World governments. By the late 1970s, this indebtedness reached about $200 billion, a 300 percent increase.[83] By 1982, Third World governments owed $640 billion, an increase of nearly 1,200 percent over just ten years.[84] This means that certain MNCs have an immense stake in preserving certain Third World governments so that they may collect on their loans. Such stakes have sometimes required multinationals to favor foreign policy measures that are bitterly opposed by the U.S. public. The Panama Canal treaties are a case in point. Thirty-nine percent of the national budget of Panama is spent just to pay the interest on that nation's national debt of $1.8 billion, 77 percent of which is owed to multinational banks. Ronald Steel claims that it was for this and other reasons favorable to business interests that MNCs lobbied hard for the passage of the canal treaties, which assured Panama of an income from the canal, plus various foreign aid payments, which in turn assured Panama's creditors that repayment would continue.[85] The passage of the treaties also meant continued military assistance to the repressive regime of General Omar Torrijos. This, despite polls showing a majority of Americans opposed the treaties!

Not only does support for repressive regimes inhibit economic development and foster unpopular foreign policy measures; such support often has a detrimental effect on U.S. foreign policy, as well. That is, repressive regimes and U.S. support of them are often very unpopular with Third World peoples. As seen in Iran, such support has touched off revolutions in nations that are anti-American and often anticapitalist, as well. U.S. support for regimes that violate human rights sometimes has the effect of driving poor nations into the hands of the communists. This has been the case with Cuba and certain African nations and may yet be the case with Nicaragua, the Philippines, and dozens of others. Thus, the policy designed to prevent communist influence in developing nations often has precisely the opposite effect.

Conclusion

In this chapter, we have examined those U.S. defense and foreign policy areas in which deviance abounds: questionable defense contracting practices, bribery, the sale of hazardous goods by multinational firms, and U.S. support for repressive Third World regimes. A closer look at these types of deviance indicates that they are interrelated. That is, many of the corporations involved in defense contracting with the federal government have also been found guilty of bribery overseas (e.g., Lockheed and Northrop). And many of these same firms are enriched by U.S. arms sales to repressive regimes. Likewise, the needs of the U.S. economic system for cheap labor, raw materials, and investment outlets have contributed immensely to the world-wide deployment of U.S. military forces and U.S. support for dictatorships that are ostensibly anticommunist.

These policies prove profitable for major corporations in the short term but may be devastating to the nation and much of the world in the long term. Waste, inefficiency, and cost overruns within the Department of Defense threaten to create domestic inflation and a weakened U.S. military capability. And bribery, the sale of hazardous products, and support for repressive regimes often foster resentment toward the United States, further weakening its strength at home and abroad. Such practices also hinder the economic development of the world's poorest and most desperate citizens. In short, nothing less than the future well-being of the United States and much of the world is now at stake, in part because of such deviance.

Critical Thinking Exercise 5.1: The Pentagon Follies _____

Use the Infotrack II database, Internet libraries, or a database chosen by your instructor to locate examples of fraud, waste, and abuse in Pentagon weapons contracting since the publication of the current edition of this book. List the number and types of problems in a table. Do you think that such deviance has become more or less serious in recent years? Write a brief (one- to two-page) paper to explain your answer.

Endnotes _____

1. Reuters, February 14, 2000.
2. *Los Angeles Times*, April 22, 1994, A-1.
3. *New York Times*, April 1, 1994, C-1.
4. *Wall Street Journal*, January 5, 1994, A2.
5. M. Zepezzauer and A. Naiman, *Take the Rich off Welfare* (Tuscon, AZ: Odonian, 1996), 15.
6. Ibid., 13.
7. Council for a Livable World, *Pentagon Follies* (Washington, DC: Council for a Livable World, 1996).
8. The following is based on Deborah Lutterbeck, "License to Deal: How Uncle Sam Helps Weapons Merchants Arm the World," *Common Cause,* June 1994, 9.
9. Robert Borosage, "All Dollars and No Sense," *Mother Jones,* September–October, 1993, 41–44.
10. David Evans, "We Arm the World," *In These Times,* November 15, 1993, 14; and Jennifer Washburn, "Twisting Arms," *The Progressive,* May, 1997, 26.
11. S. Lens, "Thirty Years of Escalation," *The Nation* 27, May 1978, 624.
12. Tom Riddell, "The Political Economy of Military Spending," in *The Imperiled Economy,* vol. 2, ed. Robert Cherry et al. (New York: Union for Radical Political Economics, 1988), 229.
13. Lens, 624.

14. M. T. Klare, *War without End: American Planning for the Next Vietnams* (New York: Knopf, 1972), 25.

15. R. L. Sivard, "Arms or Alms," *National Catholic Reporter* 24, April 8, 1977, 8.

16. Zepezzauer and Naiman, 15.

17. Dwight D. Eisenhower, "Farewell Address," in *The Military–Industrial Complex*, ed. C. W. Pursell, Jr. (New York: Harper & Row, 1972), 206–7.

18. Senator William Proxmire, *Report from Wasteland: America's Military–Industrial Complex* (New York: Praeger, 1970), 162.

19. Center for Defense Information, *The Defense Monitor*, February 1996, 3.

20. Reprinted from A. Sanseri, "The Military–Industrial Complex in Iowa," in *War, Business, and American Society: Historical Perspectives on the Military–Industrial Complex*, ed. B. F. Cooling (Port Washington, NY: Kennikat Press, 1977), 158–59; and Funk & Wagnalls, *World Almanac and Book of Facts, 1994* (Mahwah, NJ: Funk & Wagnalls, 1993), 705.

21. James Fallows, *National Defense* (New York: Random House, 1981), 65.

22. *World Almanac and Book of Facts, 1994*, 704.

23. Data in this section come from Riddell, 229.

24. Richard Stubbing and Richard Mendel, "How to Save $50 Billion a Year," *Atlantic Monthly*, June 1989, 55.

25. Zepezzauer and Naiman, 15.

26. Stubbing and Mendel, 55.

27. D. McDonald, "Militarism in America," in *The Triple Revolution Emerging*, ed. R. Perrucci and M. Pilisuk (Boston: Little, Brown, 1971), 36 (originally appeared in *The Center Magazine* 3, January 1970).

28. Zepezzauer and Naiman, 16.

29. McDonald, 42.

30. See Colleen O'Conner, "The Waste Goes On—& On & On," *The Nation*, October 4, 1993, 350.

31. *Wall Street Journal*, March 1, 1991, A-12.

32. *Aviation Week & Space Technology* 130, March 20, 1989, 263.

33. Tim Weiner, *Blank Check: The Pentagon's Black Budget* (New York: Simon & Schuster, 1990) 187–88.

34. O'Conner, 350–51.

35. Zepezzauer and Naiman, 17–18.

36. *South China Morning Post*, February 27, 2000.

37. *London Daily Telegraph*, February 27, 2000.

38. *Reuters*, January 2000.

39. "Tobacco Giant 'Condoned Smuggling into Mainland,'" *South China Morning Post*, February 2, 2000.

40. *South Korean Times*, December 31, 1999.

41. See David R. Simon, with J. Henderson, *Private Troubles and Public Issues: Social Problems in the Postmodern Era* (Ft. Worth, TX: Harcourt Brace, 1997), 304–7.

42. See Lester Thurow, *The Future of Capitalism* (New York: Penguin, 1996), Chapter 1ff, for an elaboration of these and other global economic themes.

43. Eric Verhoogen, "The U.S.–Haiti Connection, Rich Companies, Poor Workers," *Multinational Monitor*, April 1996, 5.

44. Mark Dowie, "The Corporate Crime of the Century," *Mother Jones*, November 9, 1979, 24–25. © *Mother Jones Magazine*. Used with permission.

45. Michael Satchell, "A Vicious Circle of Poison," *U.S. News & World Report*, June 10, 1991, 31–32.

46. Ibid., 32.

47. Barbara Ehrenreich et al., "The Charge: Genocide; U.S. Government," *Mother Jones* 9, November 1979, 28.

48. B. Castleman, "Industries Export Hazards," *Multinational Monitor 1,* Winter 1978/1979, 14.

49. David Weir et al., "Me Boomerang Crime," *Mother Jones 9,* November 1979, 43.

50. "The Global Poison Trade," *Newsweek,* November 7, 1988, 66–68.

51. Franz Schurman, "Opinion," *National College Newspaper,* October 1988, 9; and *Multinational Monitor,* June 1988, 4.

52. James Brooks, "Waste Dumpers Turning to West Africa," *New York Times 17,* July 1988, 1.

53. Peter Phillips and Project Censored, *The 25 Most Censored News Stories of 1996* (New York: Seven Locks, 1997), 31–32.

54. M. Conklin, "Terror Stalks a Columbian Town," *The Progressive,* February 1997, 23.

55. See Martin Lee, "The Cop, the Gangster and the Beauty Queen," *In These Times,* April 28, 1997, 18–20.

56. For several interesting assessments, consult the following articles: Richard Falk, "Iran's Home-Grown Revolution," *The Nation,* February 10, 1979, 135–37; A. Cockburn and J. Ridgeway, "The Worst Domino," *Village Voice,* February 19, 1979, 1, 11–12; W. Laqueur, "Trouble for the Shah," *New Republic,* September 23, 1978, 18–21; M. Kondracke, "Who Lost Iran," *New Republic,* November 18, 1978, 9–12; and F. Halliday, "Shah's Dreams of Economic Growth & Income Nightmares," *In These Times,* December 26–28, 1978, 9.

57. Klare, 20, 33, 36, 41, 45.

58. Kondracke, 12.

59. R. Baraheni, "Terror in Iran," *New York Review of Books,* October 28, 1976, 21.

60. Amnesty International, *Report on Torture* (New York: Farrar, Straus, and Giroux, 1975), 227–29.

61. J. Anderson, "Kissinger Cleared Iran's Oil Gouge," *Washington Post 5,* December 1979, 13–17.

62. J. Anderson, "Rockefeller–Shah–Kissinger Connection," *Washington Post,* December 26, 1979, D-12; and "60 Minutes," May 4, 1980.

63. "Octoberfuss," *The New Republic,* May 13, 1991, 7–8.

64. J. Anderson, "Kissinger Cast in a Questionable Light," *Washington Post,* December 10 1979, C-27.

65. R. A. White, *The Morass* (New York: Harper & Row, 1984), 29–30.

66. H. Caldicott, *Missile Envy* (New York: Morrow, 1984), 160; and J. Kwitney, *Endless Enemies* (New York: Cogdon/Weed, 1984), 10–11.

67. *The San Francisco Chronicle,* January 4, 1994.

68. See Frank Hagan and David Simon, "Elite Deviance in the Bush Era," *The Justice Professional,* 1997.

69. Caldicott, 98; and R. A. White, *The Morass* (New York: Harper & Row, 1984), 97.

70. Penny Lernoux, "Guatemala's New Military Order," *The Nation,* November 28, 29, 30, 1988, 556–58; and A. Neir, "Repression in Central America Since the Arias Plan," *New York Review of Books,* March 17, 1988, 22 ff.

71. Caldicott, 100.

72. Weiner, 203–4.

73. Jocobo Timerman and Robert Cox, "Reflections: Under the Dictatorship," *New Yorker,* November 2, 1987, 74.

74. A. Neier and C. Brown, "Pinochet's Way" *New York Review of Books,* June 25, 1987, 17–20; and Amado Padilla and Lillian Gomez-Diaz, "A State of Fear," *Psychology Today,* November 1986, 60.

75. Timerman and Cox, 130ff; Neier and Brown, 20.

76. See James David Barber, "Rationalizing Torture: The Dance of Intellectual Apologists," *Washington Monthly 17,* December 1985, 17.

77. Sivard, 9; Scheer, 163–64; and Tiranti, 61.

78. Evans, 16.

79. Sherrill, 128; and *The Defense Monitor,* June 6, 1984, 6–7.

80. Freeman, 46.

81. *Daily World in U.N. Action Pact for World Development* (New York: United National Information Division, n.d.), 1.

82. S. Lens, "The Sinking Dollar and the Gathering Storm," *The Progressive* 5, May 1978, 23.

83. Ibid., 23.

84. "The IMF," 1.

85. Ronald Steel, "Beneath the Panama Canal," *New York Review of Books,* March 23, 1978, 12.

6

Political Corruption: Continuity and Change

Political corruption is an integral part of U.S. politics.[1] Political corruption is defined as "any illegal or unethical use of governmental authority for personal or political gain."[2] Corruption occurs, then, to accomplish one of two broad goals, material gain or power. Material gain can involve personal enrichment or illicit contributions to election campaigns. Abuses of power involve illegal acts of electioneering, violations of civil and human rights, and, more recently, sexual harassment by the powerful (usually men) of the less powerful (usually women).

This chapter is divided into two sections, one discussing each goal. In each case, the discussion will illustrate political corruption at one or more of the various levels of government: community, state, and national. We should note at the outset, however, that the examples used are just a small sample of the political crimes, known and unknown, that have occurred throughout U.S. history.[3]

Money and Politics

Money and politics have always been closely intertwined. Since political campaigns are costly, candidates must either be relatively affluent or accept money from the wealthy or special interests. We have discussed some aspects of the money–politics relationship already, but our concern in this section is with another facet, graft.

Political graft is the illegal act of taking advantage of one's political position to gain money or property. Graft can take several forms. First is the outright bribe, through which an individual, group, or corporation offers money to a public official for a favor. Or the government official may demand money in return for a favor, which is political extortion. Second is a subtle form of bribery: the public figure accepts exorbitant lecture fees from organizations or accepts retainers at his or her law office.

A third type occurs when a public figure is offered the opportunity to buy securities at a low price; then, when the price goes up, the briber purchases the securities back, at a great profit to the person bribed. Finally, a fourth variant is the kickback: contractors, engineering and architectural firms, and others pay back a percentage of a contract to the official responsible for granting the lucrative government contract.

The government, city, state, and national, is involved in a number of activities, including law enforcement, the granting of contracts, the use of public funds, the hiring and firing of employees, tax assessment, and land use. Quite certainly, all these activities are prone to corruption.

As this is being written (summer 2000), Yung Soo Yoo is scheduled to go on trial on charges of campaign corruption and obstruction of justice. The case involves the parents of three violent felons. In exchange for $36,000 in campaign donations in the mid-1990s, allegedly brokered by Yoo and a top campaign aide to New York governor George Pataki, came the promise of a parole. Yoo has implied that the governor knew exactly what was going on. The governor has denied all such allegations. Yoo has been raising money for Republican causes since 1988.[4]

Purchasing Goods and Services

The federal government spends billions of dollars on an array of goods and services from U.S. businesses, including military hardware, space systems, research projects, musical instruments, desks, clothing, and brooms. Suppliers and repair contractors have been guilty of graft by billing the government for undelivered materials and work never performed. Also, store managers have accepted money and other gifts from firms that sell to the government; in return, the companies were allowed to charge in excess for their merchandise. What's more, Government Services Administration (GSA) officials have deliberately purchased inferior goods at premium prices for their personal gain, with both the companies and the GSA officials sharing in the bounty.

Bidding for contracts is a process that is very susceptible to bribery, especially when the bidding is not competitive. Approximately 90 percent of all contracts for new weapons systems are exempt from competitive bidding so that the Department of Defense may select the superior system rather than just the most economical one. Unfortunately, this process is especially open to graft.

What does it take to win a defense contract? The answer is not easy, for there are many possibilities, including superior design, more efficient programs, performance on schedule, and better quality control. Perhaps most important is influencing a few key personnel in the Pentagon, as noted in Chapter 5. A good deal of time and money are spent on this cause, including the hiring of former military officers by industry. Jack Anderson describes this practice:

> The giant contractors, such as Northrop Corporation and Rockwell International, court Pentagon officials assiduously. The way to many a defense contract has been greased by a mixture of booze, blondes, and brass. The brass hats and the industrialists shoot together in duck blinds. They ski together on the Colorado slopes. They drink together and play poker together. And invariably, the tab is picked up by some smiling corporate executive. The relationship is so cozy that many Pentagon officials, upon retirement, go to work for the companies that had come to them for contracts.... It's a rare contractor that doesn't employ a few retired generals and admirals who are on a first-name basis with the Pentagon's big brass.[5]

At the local level, competitive bidding is avoided in several ways. So-called emergencies are exempt. So it was that James Marcus, New York City's water commissioner under Mayor John Lindsay, gave an $840,000 contract without bidding to a firm that had agreed to pay a kickback for cleaning a reservoir in the Bronx.[6] Purchases below a specified amount are also not subject to competitive bidding. One creative way to stay below the cutoff in such a situation is to split the contract into smaller parts so that each part can be awarded without bidding.

A common exception to competitive bidding is the purchase of professional services by engineers, architects, auditors, and others. While the rationale for this exception is logical, that is, the need for a specialist may mean that there is no competition, the negotiation process is vulnerable to graft. The most celebrated case involving this type of corruption caused Spiro Agnew to resign as vice-president of the United States. Let's briefly look at this interesting and common type of graft.[7]

During the 1960s, suburban Baltimore County was growing rapidly. This growth required the creation of new streets, sewers, and bridges, as well as numerous rezoning decisions. Great sums of money were made by those fortunate to receive favorable zoning or contracts from the county. A government investigation revealed that those favorably treated (including contractors, architectural firms, and engineering firms) often kicked back 5 percent to those responsible for the decision. This practice of kickbacks was not new. In fact, it was a time-honored Maryland custom.

Included among those regularly receiving kickbacks was Spiro Agnew. The payoffs began in 1962 when Agnew became a Baltimore County executive and continued when he became governor in 1967; even as late as 1971, when Agnew was vice president, he received a payment in the basement of the White House. Agnew received these payments for all the design jobs in the county, and later, as governor, he received a percentage of the highway contracts and other engineering work. While serving as vice president, the payments continued, amounting to $80,000 during those few years.

During the dark days of the Watergate investigation, the inquiry into Agnew's possible criminal activities became public. The evidence against him was irrefutable, and he was forced to plea-bargain to reduce the penalty. Agnew resigned, pleaded no contest to one charge of income tax evasion, and was given a sentence of three years of unsupervised probation and a fine of $10,000.

Public Funds

The use of public money is a ready source of corruption by those in political power. In fact, the first corruption scandal in American history involved a sort of "insider trading" arrangement whereby public funds were used to enrich those close to the office of the U.S. treasury secretary. Forty of the fifty-five delegates to the Constitutional Convention of 1787 held debt certificates issued by the federal and state governments during and after the Revolutionary War (1776–1783) with Great Britain. These certificates were worth $5,000 or more when issued, but their value had steadily declined as the new nation became embroiled in financial chaos under the Articles of Confederation. Another twenty-four delegates to the Constitutional Convention had other money on loan, and fourteen were land speculators.

The delegates had some important decisions to make about land, especially about where to locate the new national capitol after the Constitution's adoption. Benjamin Franklin, who had loaned the national government $3,000 at 6 percent interest, noted that such loan certificates had fallen drastically in value and hoped and believed that their value would "mend when our new Constitution was adopted."[8]

The nation's first treasury secretary, Alexander Hamilton, had to decide what to do about the $80 million owed by national and state governments. He decided that the government would honor what had become worthless paper. Word of this policy was leaked to Hamilton's friends and in-laws, all of whom began buying up certificates at a record pace. The policy was officially announced on January 14, 1790, at which time the certificates were almost totally owned by speculators. Hamilton agreed to pay in full people owning the certificates at the time of redemption, not necessarily the original owners.

Hamilton's assistant, William Duer, ignored all charges of conflict of interest and engaged in numerous shady schemes. Besides benefiting from insider information about the debt certificates (he bought as many as he could with borrowed money), Duer demanded kickbacks on government contracts. An outraged public finally forced Hamilton to request Duer's resignation. But Hamilton's relatives and associates were guilty of some of the same conflicts of interest, and their punishment was merely to have their fortunes greatly increased.

Public Property

Another potential area for corruption is the misuse of public property. Government officials have discretionary powers over public lands. They decide, for example, which ranchers will have grazing rights, which lumber companies will have rights to timberlands, and what policies will control the extraction of minerals and petroleum from lands owned by the government. Fortunes can be made or lost, depending on favorable access to these lands. Of course, such a situation is susceptible to bribery and extortion.

Early in U.S. history, there were several instances of the improper use of political influence in the disposition of public lands. One example involved a large area of virgin land west of South Carolina known as the Yazoo Territory (much of which is now Alabama and Mississippi), which was claimed by the federal government, Georgia, and numerous Indian tribes. In 1794, the Georgia legislature sold its land (30 million acres) to four companies for 1.5 cents per acre. "The haste of the legislature in concluding such an unprofitable sale was apparently the result of the attentions paid them by the companies which had peddled shares at very low prices to nearly all the legislators."[9]

This congressional largesse to help business for mutual gain was typical after the Civil War. "Congressmen gave huge grants, subsidies, and loans to railroad promoters, and bought their stocks at preferred prices or accepted gifts outright.... In 1876 they repealed all restrictions on the sale of public federal land in the South, ordering it sold to private interests as soon as possible—and got huge shares of it as the silent partners of the timber speculators who bought it."[10]

The most infamous case involving the fraudulent use of public lands was the Teapot Dome scandal. During the administration of Warren Harding (which, along with that of Ulysses S. Grant, is considered among the most corrupt in U.S. history), a scandal broke concerning the leasing of oil lands. In 1921, Secretary of the Interior Albert Fall persuaded President Harding and the Navy secretary to transfer naval oil reserves from the Navy to his jurisdiction in the Department of the Interior. When this was accomplished, Fall then transferred the oil reserves at Teapot Dome, Wyoming, and Elk Hills, California, to two private oil producers, Henry Sinclair and E. L. Doheny, for their use. The leases were signed secretly and without competitive bidding. In return, Fall collected $100,000 from Doheny for Elk Hills and $300,000 from Sinclair for Teapot Dome. When the scandal broke, the government canceled the leases. Fall was sent to prison for a year (the first cabinet officer in U.S. history to be put in prison), but no penalties were given to the two guilty oil companies or their officers.

Tax Assessment and Collection

The taxation function of government is one that has enormous potential for graft. Tax assessors have great latitude because many of their decisions are subjective. They are obvious targets for bribes to reduce assessments. In the 1920s, Chicago had a particularly corrupt tax system. Individual members of the board of review could raise, lower, or eliminate assessments made by the tax assessors. Workers in Chicago's political machine "were rewarded by ridiculously low assessments, a precinct captain's house being assessed at one-fifteenth the value of a similar house next door."[11] The situation in Cook County (where Chicago is located) was remarkably similar some fifty years later. In 1972, the county assessor was investigated by the state for assessing certain properties on a system subject to manipulation and preference. Upon learning of the pending investigation, the assessor, P. H. Cullerton, reassessed nine high-rise properties in Chicago, adding $34 million to the city's tax base.[12]

Officials at the federal level are also susceptible to bribes involving taxation. Internal Revenue Service (IRS) personnel investigating income tax evasion can be bribed to look the other way. So, too, can customs officials. An additional example of an abusive practice involving taxes is illustrated by the 1875 Whiskey Ring scandal, which broke during the Grant administration. More than 350 distillers and government officials were indicted for defrauding the government of tax revenues. This was accomplished when distillers falsified reports on the amount produced and bribed government inspectors to verify the fraudulent reports.[13]

Regulation of Commercial Activities

Government officials are required by law to inspect foods (such as grain and meat) to ensure that they are not contaminated and to grade them according to quality. Again, we know of numerous instances when agents have received bribes to allow questionable items to pass inspection. Abuses also abound in government efforts to control certain business activities, such as gambling and the sale of alcohol. Because these activities are generally restricted by law, the granting of licenses is a lucrative plum for which people are willing to pay extra. They are also willing to pay for favorable legislation. In a celebrated 1960 case, Governor Otto Kerner of Illinois was bribed by certain racetrack interests for political favors. The bribe was subtle because it was in the form of stock. Kerner was offered racetrack stock for a fraction of its value. He paid $15,079 for stock, which he later sold for $159,800 (a profit of 1,050 percent). This was a disguised bribe in return for Kerner's help in securing legislation favorable to the racetrack owned by the donor of the securities.[14] Not so incidentally, the donor, Marjorie Everett, also contributed $45,000 to Kerner's 1960 campaign and another $40,000 in 1964. These moneys, plus the sweet stock deal, seem related to some of Governor Kerner's decisions concerning racing.

1. Kerner directed the chair of the Harness Commission to cancel racing dates awarded a competitor of Everett and to divide them among two other tracks, one owned by Everett. (When the chairman resisted, he was forced to resign.)
2. Kerner was instrumental in getting parimutual taxes on a graduated basis rather than a fixed percentage, saving Everett and her co-owners of Washington Park $3 million between 1966 and 1968.
3. Kerner signed a bill abolishing the troublesome Harness Commission, giving its duties to the Racing Board, whose membership was expanded with Kerner appointments. Kerner was found guilty in federal court of bribery and conflict of interest in 1973.[15]

Zoning and Land Use

The areas of zoning, planning, and building codes are highly subject to graft because the decisions can provide or eliminate great financial advantage. Decisions in these areas can establish which individuals or organizations will have a monopoly. Overnight, such decisions can make cheap land valuable or priceless land ordinary. And the decisions can force all construction to be done by certified employees, and so on. Again, we can see that the government's discretionary powers, while necessary, can be abused by government officials and businesspeople. The problem, of course, is that the decisions are not always made in the public interest.

The examples of graft in zoning decisions are plentiful, but we will only present two illustrative cases.[16] The first example occurred in a small borough in southern New Jersey called Lindenwold. From 1950 to 1970, it had undergone rapid population growth, tripling in size. In this setting, a group of speculators was able to make a 2,400 percent gross profit on a tract of sixty-nine acres because of favorable zoning decisions greased by bribes. They purchased the land at public sale for $40,000. At that time, the land was relatively cheap because of strict zoning and a clause that demanded that the land be developed within a specified time or revert back to the municipality. The investors then used $30,000 for payoffs to the borough tax assessor and the secretary of the county tax board, who allowed the investors to exceed the deadline without any construction. Another $90,000, given to the mayor, the tax assessor, and at least one councilman, got the land rezoned for townhouses, making it much more salable than when it was zoned for industry. The land was then sold for $1 million, which meant a gross profit of $960,000 or a net profit of $840,000 when the expenses for bribes were deducted. Once again, the political decisions, orchestrated with money, were lucrative to all parties, except the public.

The second example involves attempts by contractors to receive favorable zoning decisions in New York City from 1980 to 1989. Zoning decisions are made by the mayor, the borough presidents, and the city council president. These elected officials receive generous contributions for their political campaigns, which might be interpreted as using money for influence. Donald Trump, for example, in the 1985 election, contributed more than $350,000 to the zoning commissioners (the board of estimate), including $50,000 just to Manhattan Borough President Andrew Stein. Trump evaded state election laws that limit corporate contributions to $5,000 per candidate by giving $5,000 through each of eighteen subsidiary companies.

In total, more than $4 million was contributed to board of estimate members in the 1985 election, most of which came from the same people who come before the board for approval of projects. For example, developer Ian Bruce Eichner needed a zoning variance to build a luxury tower in Manhattan. Soon after this project was proposed, Eichner gave Mayor Edward Koch a $10,000 contribution and another $7,500 to the Brooklyn borough president. Eichner's lawyer contributed another $10,000 to the mayor, $12,500 to the Manhattan borough president, and another $1,000 to the Brooklyn borough president. The board of estimate later approved the zoning variance for Eichner's project, which was worth an estimated $46 million.[17]

The Legislative Process

What effect does receiving campaign contributions and other favors have on a legislator? Will his or her actions be biased? Clearly, it is difficult to affirm that a legislator acted because of money, as Amick has argued.

> When people are exercising legislative roles, they have to be given wide latitude. The law can and does forbid them to sell their votes, but it cannot force them to cast those votes in an objective way, or an intelligent way, or a well-informed way. And there is no test that can be designed that will automatically disclose whether a given vote is corrupt; the necessary freedom given to legislators to make honest decisions also makes it easier for them to get away with making dishonest ones.[18]

The relationship between giving money to and receiving favorable decisions from legislators is not always a subtle one, however. A few examples make this point, beginning with the Credit Mobilier scandal.[19] In the late 1860s, some of the major stockholders of the Union Pacific Railroad concocted a scheme whereby they would get their company, the railroad, to contract with their construction company, Credit Mobilier. This cozy arrangement allowed the conspirators to charge Union Pacific exorbitant costs. In effect, then, the money that Union Pacific raised through the sale of stocks went to the construction company, which made enormous profits. Concerned over a possible congressional investigation, one member of the conspiracy, who was also a U.S. representative from Massachusetts, Oakes Ames, gave away or sold Credit Mobilier stocks at very low cost to selected members of Congress. In 1872, the bribes were exposed, which led to the expulsion of Ames and another congressman, James Brooks. Also implicated were the outgoing vice-president of the United States and a future president, James A. Garfield.

Another instance of an outright bribe occurred in 1910, when the American Bridge Company bribed New York legislators to defeat a bill that would have improved the procedure for constructing bridges by requiring a referendum and approval by the state engineer.[20]

More recently, we have seen the efforts of Tongsun Park to purchase favorable legislation. Park, a Korean businessman, gave thirty-one congressional members $850,000 in cash from 1968 to 1975 (in addition to throwing lavish parties and giving expensive gifts). Park testified, under immunity, that he bribed Louisiana Congressman Otto Passman, who served as chair of the Foreign Relations Committee, to get South Korea to appoint Park as its sole rice agent. The bribe was successful; Park became that agent and made $9 million in commissions during a four-year period.[21]

From 1971 to 1983, thirty-two current or former members of the House of Representatives went to prison, faced criminal charges, or were disciplined by their colleagues.[22] The list of charges included mail fraud, salary kickbacks from aides, accepting bribes, election law violations, defrauding the government, making false statements to the government, tax evasion, and perjury.

The largest congressional scandal in recent years was the FBI sting operation known as ABSCAM. This operation set up a fictional Arab sheik, Kambir Abdul Rahman, who offered financial inducements to legislators for their favors. Meetings between the sheik and legislators were secretly videotaped. Seven legislators (six representatives and one senator) were indicted and convicted of accepting cash or stock as bribes for their favorable influence. Most noteworthy, only one legislator, Senator Larry Presler of South Dakota, was offered the rich inducement but refused the bribe.[23]

The Housing and Urban Development (HUD) scandal is somewhat typical of the influence-peddling scandals that have taken place in recent years.[24] Waste, fraud, and abuse from the scandal will cost taxpayers $4 to $8 billion. From 1984 to 1988, HUD, under Secretary Samuel Pierce, became an agency wherein political insiders and well-connected developers received hundreds of millions of dollars in contracts by paying Republican consultants thousands to make a few visits or phone calls. In this respect, the scandal mirrors insider-trading episodes in the Pentagon or on Wall Street, with dozens of former officials earning millions in consulting fees in return for their efforts at winning HUD grants and subsidies for clients.

- **Item:** Former Interior Secretary James Watt, who knows nothing about public housing, received $300,000 for making eight phone calls and attending a thirty-minute meeting with Secretary Pierce to obtain a $25 million rent subsidy contract. All tolled, Watt earned fees of $420,000.
- **Item:** A number of high-ranking government officials, none of whom had anything to do with HUD, found ways to get HUD money: John Mitchell, Nixon's attorney general during the Watergate scandal, received $75,000 for his services; Richard Shelby, a former Reagan White House personnel officer, received $445,000 for himself and his consulting firm; Gerald Carman, a former Reagan GSA appointee, and his partner made $2.3 million by selling tax credits for a HUD-subsidized project; former Ford and Reagan appointee Carla Hills obtained $138,000 for HUD contracts that resulted in subsidies for two housing projects; and finally, former Reagan aide Paul Manafort gained $348,000 for helping a client to obtain HUD housing project subsidies.[25]
- **Item:** More than 700 cases of HUD fraud are being investigated by the Justice Department, with the costs of fraudulent practices at the local level estimated in the billions. Gross mismanagement and other abuses are also present. In one instance, eleven out of twenty-five low-income housing projects failed HUD requirements but were still awarded $36 million in grants. In Biloxi, Mississippi, investigators uncovered expenses of $1.9 million for ineligible costs, $2.1 million in undocumented funds, and $2 million worth of land with unclear title. Elsewhere, $937 million (80 percent) of HUD-backed loans are in default. The Federal Housing Authority (FHA), a HUD agency, is also in trouble. It has $296 billion in outstanding loans, but no auditor has been willing to sign its operating statement in ten years.
- **Item:** Many "revolving-door" examples are present, whereby individuals hired from the private sector are appointed to public office and then use their connections to obtain lucrative positions upon leaving government. At least fourteen politically appointed HUD officials used revolving-door strategies to obtain such positions. Lance Wilson, former HUD executive assistant, actually received a one-third interest in a $92 million HUD contract upon leaving office.

Other various patterns of corruption found in the HUD scandal include the following:

- *Equity skimming:* Real estate agents falsely procure an FHA loan, rent property without making mortgage payments, and eventually go into default, sticking HUD with a bad loan. Such losses amounted to $240 million in 1989.
- *Defaults on coinsurance:* Private lenders inflate real estate appraisals to collect higher fees, with HUD picking up the tab if default occurs. Some $937 million is currently in default.

- *Ginnie Mae bailout:* Ginnie Maes are government-backed bonds that guarantee Veterans Administration (VA) loans. Such defaults have cost the FHA $700 million.
- *"Robin Hud":* Marilyn Harrell, known as "Robin HUD," embezzled $5.5 million. Although she claimed to have given the money to the poor, she was nevertheless convicted of embezzlement.

The Reagan administration used tens of millions in HUD and Environmental Protection Agency (EPA) funds to buy support for GOP (Republican) congressional candidates. EPA head Rita Lavelle was convicted of perjury and conflict of interest in using EPA funds to elect Republican candidates. HUD official Deborah Dean acted as White House liaison to elect GOP candidates by attempting to give grant money in areas that voted Republican. Dean's previous work experience had been as a bartender in Georgetown, but her family's important GOP connections, especially through John Mitchell, landed her a high-ranking HUD post, one which Dean claimed was designed to be political. As such, Dean solicited donations, sponsored receptions, and intervened on behalf of many influential former officials who profited from HUD projects.

It is a felony to use federal grant money for political purposes. Despite this, while campaigning for New Jersey Republican Milicent Fenwick, President Reagan told a gathering that he would award HUD grants to New Jersey but that they would be withdrawn if Fenwick did not win.

For reasons considered in Chapter 8, padding one's own pocket remains the most widespread form of elite deviance. One of the long-cherished functions of members of Congress is to secure government facilities and contracts for their districts. The study of which districts are the recipients of government largesse is a reliable guide to who is in power in Washington.

The current champion in the U.S. Senate in securing government facilities is Senator Robert Byrd of West Virginia, former majority leader and current chair of the Senate Appropriations Committee. West Virginia is among the nation's poorest states, and in need of all the money and jobs it can import. However, some of Senator Byrd's acquisitions of government funds make little sense. Some examples follow:

A $4.5 million federal project to renovate a downtown movie theater in Huntington, West Virginia.

The entire U.S. Coast Guard Computer Operation Center was relocated to Martinsburg, West Virginia, a landlocked city, and a NASA research center was relocated to Wheeling, West Virginia.

The FBI Identification Unit, home of 190 million fingerprints, was located in Clarksberg, West Virginia (population 18,000), in a new $185 million building that will house 2,800 employees.

Senator Byrd has won his battle to relocate up to 3,000 CIA agents to Charles Town, a rural West Virginia village, at a cost of $1.4 billion.[26]

- **Item:** A recent California scandal points out the cooperation that takes place between government and big business in modern corruption. In 2000, California's insurance commissioner Chuck Quackenbush resigned after it was learned that he used millions of dollars in official settlements with insurers to boost his own political career. The deals Quackenbush concluded with insurance companies in 1999 allowed insurance companies to escape $3.3 billion in fines stemming from underpaid claims in exchange for donations of some $12 million to the California Research and Development Foundation, a nonprofit organization set up by Quackenbush to further his future political ambitions. His insurance department lawyer Robert Hagedorn testified that department chief counsel Brian Soublet told him in March 2000 that the commissioner had demanded $4 million from the title company fund for a "media buy" to finance commercials that ended up featuring the commissioner.
- **Item:** Of the top 100 corporate crimes of the 1990s, 7 involved campaign finance matters and 1 involved public corruption. Some examples follow:

> In 1997, Tyson Foods, a major contributor to the Clinton campaign, paid a $4 million criminal fine and pled guilty to giving former Agriculture Secretary Mike Espy more than $12,000 in gratuities in 1993 and 1994 while Tyson had a number of matters pending before Espy's department.

> In 1997, the Crop Growers Corporation, the second-largest private seller of crop insurance, pled no contest to conspiring to defraud the Federal Election Commission by concealing $46,000 in contributions to the Henry Espy for Congress campaign in 1993 and 1994 and was fined $2 million.

> In 1998, Sun-Land Products of California paid a $400,000 fine for making illegal "conduit" contributions to the 1992 Bush–Quayle campaign.

> In 1995, Korean Airlines paid a $250,000 fine for contributing to the Jay Kim for Congress Campaign Committee. This was a violation of federal election law under which it is illegal for foreign corporations and foreign nationals to contribute to candidates.

Law Enforcement

Formal law enforcement policy begins with the police, who decide if a law has been broken. They must interpret and judge: What behavior is *disorderly?* How much noise is a *public nuisance?* When does a quarrel become a *criminal assault?* When does protest become *riotous?* What constitutes *public drunkenness?*

These questions reveal that the police have great decisional latitude. Unlike other aspects of the criminal justice process, the police often deal with their clients in isolation, their decisions not subject to review by higher authorities. According to Skolnick, "Police work constitutes the most secluded part of an already secluded system and therefore offers the greatest opportunity for arbitrary behavior."[27]

The police, then, have the power to continue or terminate the criminal-processing procedure. Accordingly, the position of the police personnel exposes them to extraordinary pressures. The President's Commission on Law Enforcement and the Administration of Justice noted:

> The violations in which police are involved vary widely in character. The most common are improper political influence; acceptance of gratuities or bribes in exchange for nonenforcement of laws, particularly those relating to gambling, prostitution, and liquor offenses, which are often extensively interconnected with organized crime; the "fixing" of traffic tickets; minor thefts; and occasional burglaries.... Government corruption in the United States has troubled historians, political reformers, and the general public since the middle of the 19th century. Metropolitan police forces—most of which developed during the late 1800s when government corruption was most prevalent, have often been deeply involved in corruption. The police are particularly susceptible to the forms of corruption that have attracted widest attention, those that involve tolerance or support of organized crime activities. But the police, as one of the largest and most strategic groups in metropolitan government, [were] also likely targets for political patronage, favoritism, and other kinds of influence that have pervaded local governments dominated by political machines.[28]

Police corruption is most likely with the enforcement of laws against victimless crimes, especially involving narcotics and other drugs. Legislatures have typically enacted laws to enforce the morality of the majority, making criminal certain offensive acts that may harm the individual who performs them but not others. Laws prohibiting gambling, sex between consenting adults, pornography, liquor, and drug use create such victimless crimes. More than 80 percent of the police work in the United States has to do with the regulation of private morals. While many police officers are unwilling to accept bribes from murderers and thieves, they may accept them from the perpetrators of victimless crimes for several reasons: (1) they believe these crimes are harmless and impossible to control anyway, (2) they may feel strong community pressures against enforcement of such laws, and (3) they face organized crime, with its threats and enticements, which encourages cooperation.

There is a long history of police corruption in the United States, so long that every source investigating the problems since the 1890s has consistently discovered substantial forms of police bribery. About 100 drug-related bribery cases involving police at all levels of the criminal justice system now come before American courts each year. A partial list of recent cases reveals the presence of organized crime and illegal drugs in American society. Consider the following cases:

- **Item:** In 1987, Mike "Mad Dog" Roark (so named for his fierce pursuit of drug dealers while outfitted in combat fatigues and packing a pistol), prosecutor and mayor of Charleston, West Virginia, pleaded guilty to six counts of cocaine possession.[29]
- **Item:** In 1988, nine police officers pleaded guilty and twenty more were suspended from the force for stealing three or four boatloads of cocaine.[30]
- **Item:** In 1989, Edward O'Brien, a Drug Enforcement Agency (DEA) agent, was arrested at Logan Airport in Boston, Massachusetts, with 62 pounds of cocaine in his suitcase. Agent O'Brien was a "high ranking and decorated" agent. John and Paul O'Brien, Edward's brothers, were also arrested on the same charge. This was the fourth DEA agent arrested on drug charges in 1989.[31]
- **Item:** In 1990:

> The FBI produced a forty-two-count indictment of Kentucky law officers for conspiracy to extort and protect illegal drug traffickers. Arrested were John Mann, sheriff of Lee County, allegedly the mastermind; Lester Dickerson, sheriff of Wolfe County; Billy MacIntosh, sheriff of Owsley County; Dean Spencer, sheriff of Breathitt County; Wilson Stone, deputy sheriff of Wolfe County; and Omer Noe, police chief of Beattyville.

> In the Los Angeles County Sheriff's Department, $1.4 million was skimmed by the departmental drug squad. Approximately thirty indictments were rendered. This source of revenue spread from the Los Angeles Police Department to the Feds.

> DEA agents Daniel Garcia, Wayne Countryman, and John Jackson "liberated" 150 kilograms of heroin and sent it to New York by Federal Express for sale. The two pleaded guilty.

> In Sea Girt, New Jersey, population 2,500, 20 local people were arrested in a drug-dealing ring. School officials don't know how to explain to the children how some of the cops indicted could give antidrug speeches in schools while dealing at the same time.[32]

- **Item:** In 1991, Detroit Police Chief William Hart was accused of embezzlement and tax fraud for diverting $2.5 million from the police department undercover narcotics fund to his own private businesses.
- **Item:** In 1992 a number of Florida sheriffs were arrested for shaking down people for multimillions of dollars under the guise of drug for-

feiture. The people were never charged, but they never complained either. The rat got out of the bag when a woman was relieved of her federal hurricane relief check.

- **Item:** Circuit Court Judge Thomas Brothers was indicted in Nashville, Tennessee, for his part in laundering $1.3 million in cocaine profits into several corporations. Also indicted were Russell Brothers, nephew of the judge, and G. Thomas Newell, their attorney.

- **Item:** In 1992, New York City police officer Michael Dowd was indicted for cocaine trafficking. Dowd reportedly received $5,000 to $8,000 per week in payments from drug gangs. Four other officers were also arrested. Reportedly, the U.S. attorney had obtained evidence necessary for indictment in 1988 but delayed the arrest for four years for unexplained reasons.[33] In 1993, thirty-five New York City police officers were arrested for preying on drug dealers. The officers had robbed the drug dealers of cocaine, guns, and money. Judge Milton Mullins's commission released a preliminary report on New York City police corruption, drug trafficking, police brutality, and so on, decrying the "blue wall of silence" in trying to investigate police corruption.

- **Item:** In Dorchester, Massachusetts, in 1994, Hazaline Williams, a seventy-five-year-old retired minister, died when thirteen narcotics agents mistakenly raided his home, handcuffed him, and threw him to the floor. After ransacking his apartment and finding no drugs, it was noticed that the minister died choking on his own vomit. Williams's crime was to have his address confused with that of a drug dealer fingered by a confidential informant. The police apologized to his widow but maintain that because their informant was right twice before, they were within their rights.

- **Item:** In 1995:

> In Philadelphia, six cops pleaded guilty to charges such as setting up innocent victims, selling drugs, and beating and threatening people, primarily poor blacks in the 39th District. As a result, forty-six criminal convictions were overturned, with many more still to come. The shakedowns began in the 1980s when more than thirty Philadelphia cops were convicted for shaking down drug dealers.
>
> In Los Angeles, a commission formed to identify problem areas in policing identified forty-four problem officers. The officers had histories of excessive force, forging evidence, and murder. In late 1999, another scandal rocked the Los Angeles Police Department. The department has for decades prided itself on its clean image of hero cops battling the underworld's forces of evil. It has cooperated in the making of numerous television shows and movies designed to reinforce this image in the minds of the public.

Underneath, however, looms a long history of racism, brutality, and bribery. In September 1999, a scandal broke in Los Angeles that the press dubbed the "L.A. Confidential for Real" (*Time*, 1999: 44). The scandal was the worst since the 1930s. In the 1930s, officers accepted bribes from whorehouse madams, gamblers, and bootleggers in return for letting these vice rackets flourish. In 1999, it was revealed that a judge sent Javier Ovando, a Hispanic male, to prison in 1997 for twenty-three years after two antigang squad officers, who had shot Ovando multiple times, claimed that he had threatened the officers with a gun. The shooting left Ovando paralyzed for life. In 1999, one of the officers involved admitted that they had framed Ovando. Not only was he un-armed, but also the officers planted a gun on him after shooting him. The two officers in question are currently under investigation for stealing from drug dealers. Meanwhile, the case against Ovando has been dismissed, and because he admitted framing Ovando, the officer in question, Rafael Perez, will have his sentence reduced for stealing cocaine. In addition, more than a dozen other officers have been relieved of duty and are being investigated for selling drugs, use of excessive force, and/or covering up the scandal within the antigang division. Other officers may soon be indicted over a 1996 shootout with gang members that resulted in the death of one gang member and the shooting of two others. Cops may have planted guns on the members involved. Federal authorities have joined the investigation and are now looking into incidents as far away as Las Vegas. It seems some of the Los Angeles officers partied in Las Vegss with a fellow officer after he committed a bank robbery.[34]

In New Orleans, forty officers were arrested on charges including bank robbery, auto theft, narcotics, rape, and aggravated assault between 1993 and 1995. The local U.S. attorney, Eddie Jordan, and several watchdog groups estimate that between 10 percent and 15 percent of the 1,500-officer police department is corrupt. One of the officers caught in the drug sting, Len Davis, allegedly arranged the murder of a woman who had filed a police-brutality complaint against him.[35]

- **Item:** By 1994, New York City police officials had conducted 68 internal sting operations involving 82 officers. By 1995, the number rose to 564 stings involving 1,222 officers.[36]
- **Item:** In 1995 an investigation by author Anthony Summers concluded that former FBI Director J. Edgar Hoover protected organized crime for years because the Mafia knew about Hoover's homosexuality, includ-

ing his cross-dressing in miniskirted drag and engaging in orgies. Mafia bosses Frank Costello and Meyer Lansky obtained photographs of the FBI director having sex with aide and lover, Clyde Tolson. The ability to corrupt politicians, policemen, and judges is key to organized crime activities. Hoover's activity was compounded by his involvement in Plaza Hotel orgies with attorney Roy Cohn and Lewis S. Rosensteil, of Schenley Liquors. Rosensteil had ties to both Lansky and Costello. Young boys would sometimes join the orgies and have sex with Hoover and his cronies. Hoover once had a boy read from the Bible while another boy played with him. Hoover also benefited from fixed Mafia-controlled horse races. In exchange for Hoover agreeing to have the FBI leave the Mafia alone, Hoover was flown to racetracks around the country (at government expense), where Mafia bosses would fix races so that he would win.[37]

- **Item:** A growing number of American cities and counties are suing gun manufacturers for negligence, irresponsibility, and the distribution of dangerous products. However, some of these same counties and cities, including Boston, New Orleans, Detroit, and Alameda County, California, have engaged in tacit deals with these same gun makers to exchange old police weapons for new and, at times, have even traded confiscated criminal weapons for newly manufactured guns for their officers.[38]

The Organization of Power

So far, we have focused on public officials who have taken bribes or demanded them from moneyed interests. More important than these random and sometimes patterned actions are the organizational forms that promote a climate where corruption flourishes. We will examine briefly three of these organizational forms: organized crime, the political machine, and the invisible government.

Organized Crime and Corruption.   Organized crime involves businesses seeking profit by supplying illegal goods and services, especially drugs, prostitution, pornography, gambling, and loan sharking (see Chapter 3). The profits from organized crime are enormous. Of course, we cannot know the exact figures, but it is estimated that the *gross income* of organized crime is twice that of all other kinds of illegal activity and the *net income* is higher than that of any single legitimate industry.

Several characteristics of organized crime help to perpetuate it. First, organized crime supplies illegal goods and services that are in great demand. In other words, one reason for the continued existence of organized crime is that it fills a need. If victimless crimes were decriminalized, organized crime would be left with products and services that could be easily and cheaply supplied from legitimate sources, thereby possibly destroying organized crime's profits and existence.

A second characteristic of organized crime is that it depends on the corruption of police and government officials for survival and continued profitability. Bribery, campaign contributions, delivery of votes, and other favors are used to influence police personnel, government attorneys, judges, media personnel, city council members, and legislators. Each of the major crime families has at least one position in their organization entitled *corrupter*.

> The person occupying this position bribes, buys, intimidates, threatens, negotiates, and sweet-talks himself into a relationship with police, public officials, and anyone else who might help "family" members maintain immunity from arrest, prosecution, and punishment.... More commonly, one corrupter takes care of one subdivision of government, such as the police or city hall, while another will be assigned a different subdivision, such as the state alcoholic beverage commission. A third corrupter might handle the court system by fixing a judge, a clerk of court, a prosecutor, an assistant prosecutor, a probation officer.[39]

The role of organized crime is a very important source of political corruption at all levels, not just at the level of the police. William Chambliss discusses this in the introduction to his book on corruption in Seattle, Washington.

> Money is the oil of our present-day machinery, and elected public officials are the pistons that keep the machine operating. Those who come up with the oil, whatever its source, are in a position to make the machinery run the way they want it to. Crime is an excellent producer of capitalism's oil. Those who want to affect the direction of the machine's output find that the money produced by crime is as effective in helping them get where they want to go as is the money produced in any other way. Those who produce the money from crime thus become the people most likely to control the machine. Crime is not a byproduct of an otherwise effectively working political economy: It is a main product of that political economy. Crime is in fact a cornerstone on which the political and economic relations of democratic-capitalist societies are constructed.
>
> In every city of the United States, and in many other countries as well, criminal organizations sell sex and drugs, provide an opportunity to gamble, to watch pornographic films, or to obtain a loan, an abortion, or a special favor. Their profits are a mainstay of the electoral process of America and their business is an important (if unrecorded) part of the gross national product. The business of organized crime in the United States may gross as much as one hundred billion dollars annually, or as little as forty billion—either way the profits are immense, and the proportion of the gross national product represented by money flowing from crime cannot be gainsaid. Few nations in the world have economies that compare with the economic output of criminal activities in the United States.[40]

The Political Machine.   The political machine became the dominant pattern of government for U.S. cities in the last part of the nineteenth century. This type of government is formed when a clique gets elected to all the major posts in a city. Once in, the leaders use their appointing power to fill the municipal boards, thus controlling the decision-making apparatus. To stay in power, the political organization actively seeks votes. One technique to get votes is to appoint key persons from various factions in the community who deliver the votes of their followers. The other method is to gain the allegiance of voters by providing them with governmental services or public works projects that appeal to large voting blocs. The city is also organized so that each precinct or ward has a machine representative who uses patronage, bribes, favors, and other techniques to keep voters in his or her district loyal to the machine. Political machines have been almost universally corrupt. The pattern of corruption is not limited to the city, however; usually, there are links to the state and national levels.

The corruption of U.S. cities was typical around the turn of the century.

> The persuasiveness of machine politics and of the accompanying corruption in nineteenth-century America is astounding. In his *American Commonwealth* James Bryce estimated that the government of every American city with more than 200,000 inhabitants was corrupt during this last quarter-century. Many cities of 50,000 to 200,000 were corrupt, and even several cities smaller than 50,000 were riddled with corruption, although on a less grandiose scale than, say, New York or San Francisco. The findings of the municipal historian Ernest S. Griffith are also grim. He noted that from 1870 to 1900 Newark was the only large city to remain reasonably honest. The New England towns of Cambridge, Worcester, and Springfield were the only medium-sized cities he discovered that were consistently uncorrupted. Every city he examined in the middle states and all the Southern cities except Atlanta, Charleston, and possibly Richmond and Memphis were persistently or intermittently corrupt. In the West only Oakland and in the mid-West only Milwaukee seem to have avoided the corruption tendency of politics in this era.[41]

For an example of graft rampant in one political machine, let's briefly examine the situation in New York City under the nefarious Boss Tweed, where the Tweed Ring robbed the city of somewhere between $30 and $200 million from 1866 to the mid-1870s.[42]

William March Tweed and two associates gained control of Tammany Hall, New York City's Democratic party organization, in 1863. Under Tweed, the organization gained popular support in the city by providing public works and by actively courting the foreign born, about one-half the city's population in 1870. Ward leaders helped their constituents by finding jobs, fixing minor problems with the law, and remembering families on special occasions. As a result, the ward captains could deliver votes and power.

Tweed used this power to become wealthy as he and his associates orchestrated the city government to extract money.

The most accessible and secure source of income was from graft on municipal contracts. Before 1869, city contractors expected to pay 10 percent in graft to the machine. Under Tweed this rapidly rose to 65 percent, of which 25 percent went to Tweed, while the remaining 40 percent was distributed among lesser accomplices. The history of the New York Court House is the most familiar and notorious example of the ring's method of operation. Planned in 1868 at a cost not to exceed $250,000, the Court House under Tweed management eventually absorbed over $8 million of city revenue. Many of the contracts were lent to friends of the ring or to companies owned by the ring's members at inflated prices. The ring collected its 65 percent from the contract on top of the inflated prices. All the costs were passed along to the taxpayers.[43]

As a result of these frauds and others, Boss Tweed and his associates plundered the city. "Of every tax dollar, only fifteen cents went for legitimate uses. The rest went into the pockets of the ring, the overpaid builders, or bribe-welcoming officials."[44]

The Invisible Government and Legal Graft.   Who really rules a city, a state, or the nation? The obvious answer is that elected officials do because they make the laws and enforce them. But a strong case can be made that, at each level of government, there is a permanent alliance of special interests that is more powerful than the elected government.

We live in a nation where private profit is officially perceived as the maximum good—the engine of all progress. The permanent government...at the national level [is the level at which] giant oil companies, defense contractors, and multinational corporations have effectively defined the nation's priorities and allocated its resources through a long series of administrations that have unswervingly agreed with Calvin Coolidge's observation that "the business of America is business." In the early 1960s, John Kennedy quickly learned that a president, no matter how popular, who confronts the combined interests of corporate America is walking into a meat grinder. Faced with the choice between massive public works and social spending, or the "trickle-down" economics of business to cure the Eisenhower recession, he found it expedient, in the face of a carefully orchestrated corporate propaganda campaign, to opt for investment credits for industry and tax cuts that aided the wealthiest segment of society. In dealing with the nation's balance-of-payments problems, he encountered the same wall of opposition and finally observed: "It's a ridiculous situation for us to be squeezing down essential public activities in order not to touch private investment and tourist spending, but apparently that's life."

"Life" hasn't changed much in Washington, New York, or hundreds of other cities across the land as we begin the nation's third century. *Corporate power still dominates public need* (emphasis added).[45]

   Chapter 7 will focus on this phenomenon at the national level. In this chapter, we will examine how it works at the municipal level, using New York City as the case study. Newfield and DuBrul argue forcefully that a permanent, invisible, and unelected government holds ultimate power over public policy in New York City.[46] It is a government of bankers, brokers, developers, landlords, union leaders, and lawyers. The power of this loose confederation of elites is in their control of institutions, money, property, and even the lawmaking process. It gets its way no matter who the voters elect as mayor or council members. "Whenever an assemblyman casts a vote, or when a public-works project is begun, or when a developer gets a zoning variance to build a high-rise, or when federal funds come into a district, or when a decision is made to raise the interest rates that the banks charge the city, in all these situations, the real decision-makers are usually off stage, and unknown to the public."[47]

   This permanent government makes enormous sums of money through what Newfield and DuBrul call *legal graft*. The money they receive is not under the table; instead, it is paid in the form of finders' fees, title insurance, city contracts, interest-free deposits of the city's funds, zoning variances, insurance premiums, bond-sale commissions, public relations retainers, real estate leases, mortgage closings, and legal fees. For example, over fifteen years, from 1954 to 1969, Robert Moses, head of the New York Port Authority, spent more than $4.5 billion on public works, much of it for legal graft. For instance, three Democratic politicians shared the insurance business from the Triborough Bridge and Tunnel Authority, worth $100,000 annually in commissions. All the insurance for the 1964 World's Fair was funneled to one insurance agency, providing it with $3 million in commissions. All the legal fees for the Fair Corporation were given to the law firm of a former city administrator, who had helped to draft the legislation exempting the Fair Corporation from the city's code of ethics.[48]

   When Yankee Stadium was refurbished, Mayor John Lindsay used urban-renewal funds, saying that it would cost $24 million, including $2 million to rehabilitate the streets and shops around the stadium. The stadium was eventually completed at a cost of $101 million, and the $2 million for the community was never spent. As expected, some contractors did very well. One outfit, Kinney Systems, was awarded a contract without competitive bidding to build two parking garages and remodel another. They were paid $22 million, a management fee from the city, most of the parking fees collected, and a $2 million tax exemption. The city counsel who negotiated the contract in 1972 was, by 1976, working for Kinney Systems as a lawyer.

   Legal graft occurs in every conceivable area of city activities, resulting in money, patronage, and other perquisites. In the case of New York City, citizens pay multimillions annually for which they receive nothing. Ironically, though, New York's severe fiscal problems are typically blamed on a variety of sources other than the graft perpetuated by the invisible government.

Corruption and Power

This section discusses the illegal and unethical means used by various people and organizations to gain, retain, or enlarge political power. We will focus on four problem areas: the powerful controlling the powerless; the administration of elections; the conduct of campaigns; and the influence of money in elections. In conclusion, we will elaborate on the various forms of political corruption manifested in the Watergate-related crimes.

The Powerful Controlling the Powerless

The hallmark of representative democracy is that all people have the fundamental right to vote for those who will make and administer the laws. Those in power have often defied this principle of democracy, however, as they have minimized, neutralized, or even negated the voting privileges of the lower classes, minorities, third parties, and the opposition.

The writers of the Constitution, who represented wealth and property, were concerned about the potential power of the masses.[49] Thus, they objected to democracy as we know it today. Their attitude was well stated by Alexander Hamilton.

> All communities divide themselves into the few and the many. The first are the rich and the well born, the other the mass of the people. The voice of the people has been said to be the voice of God; and however generally this maxim has been quoted and believed, it is not true in fact. The people are turbulent and changing; they seldom judge or determine right. Give therefore to the first class a distinct, permanent share in the government. They will check the unsteadiness of the second and as they cannot receive any advantage by a change, they therefore will ever maintain good government.[50]

Even more blatant was the statement by Gouverneur Morris at the Constitutional Convention.

> The time is not distant when this Country will abound with mechanics and manufacturers [industrial workers] who will receive their bread from their employers. Will such men be the secure and faithful Guardians of liberty? ...Children do not vote. Why? Because they want prudence, because they have no will of their own. The ignorant and the dependent can be as little trusted with the public interest.[51]

As a result of this type of thinking (which, by the way, was characteristic of the complaints by intellectuals throughout history until the last 100 years or so),[52] the Constitution was designed to retain power for the propertied few while utilizing seemingly democratic principles. The appearance of democracy actually had the effect of fragmenting the power of the masses.

> By separating the executive, legislative and judiciary functions and then providing a system of checks and balances among the various branches, including staggered elections, executive veto, Senate confirmation of appointments and ratification of treaties, and a two-house legislature, they [the Founding Fathers] hoped to dilute the impact of popular sentiments. To the extent that it existed at all, the majoritarian principle was tightly locked into a system of minority vetoes, making swift and sweeping popular actions nearly impossible.[53]

The blatant disregard for the masses, as determined by the Constitution, is seen in the following provisions.

- **Item:** The senators from each state were to be elected by their respective state legislatures. The Seventeenth Amendment, adopted in 1913, finally provided for the direct election of senators.
- **Item:** The election of the president was, on the surface, to be decided by the voters, but in reality, the president was to be selected by an electoral college composed of political leaders. This procedure allowed the upper classes to control the presidential vote, regardless of the popular vote. Each state had as many electors as it had senators and representatives. Each political party would select a slate of electors, who would vote for president if their party's candidate carried the state. Interestingly, and indicative of the contempt for the masses, some states allowed their electors to vote for anyone, not necessarily the presidential candidate of their party. (Five states still retain that right.)[54]

The 1876 election illustrates how the electoral college can run counter to the popular will: The winner, Republican Rutherford B. Hayes, received some 250,000 fewer votes than his Democratic opponent, Samuel J. Tilden. Two sets of returns arrived from three southern states, each having one set that showed a Republican plurality and another with a Democratic one. The issue was resolved by a special commission of Congress, which gave all the disputed nineteen electoral votes to Hayes, making him the winner by one electoral vote. A deal was made whereby the southern Democrats aligned with northern Republicans because Hayes promised that (1) all remaining federal troops in the three states would be removed, (2) the federal government would subsidize a southern transcontinental railroad, and (3) a southerner would be appointed to the cabinet.[55]

- **Item:** Supreme Court justices were to be nonelected. They were to be appointed to life tenure by the president and confirmed by the Senate.

- **Item:** The matter of who was allowed to vote was left to the individual states, which meant, in effect, the disenfranchisement of many voters. All the states disallowed women from voting (changed in 1919 by the passage of the Nineteenth Amendment). All the states denied voting to those held in bondage (changed following the Civil War by the passage of the Fourteenth Amendment). And in various states, it was common to require that voters own certain amounts and kinds of property.

Other nondemocratic practices occurred throughout the states early in U.S. history, some continuing into the present. Most significant was the requirement that political candidates be wealthy candidates who had to pass steep property qualifications for holding office. This meant that most voters could not qualify as candidates. "The result was that the gentry, merchants, and professionals monopolized the important offices."[56]

An important historical example of this relationship between the wealthy and political leaders is the robber barons of the late nineteenth century. These so-called captains of industry, including Jay Gould, Andrew Carnegie, Pierpont Morgan, John D. Rockefeller, and Cornelius Vanderbilt, made fabulous fortunes, often with the aid of favorable government actions, but most notably through chicanery, ruthless plundering, and conspiracy. They were successful clearly because of a cozy relationship with the government, involving several tactics. For instance, at the formal level, some robber barons ruled in the highest councils of government as senators and cabinet members. Moreover, their lawyers and other employees were sometimes appointed to government office. Robber barons made large contributions to the political campaigns of candidates from both parties, and they freely used bribes when necessary. Summarizing the robber-baron philosophy, Frederich Townsend Martin said,

> It matters not one iota what political party is in power, or what President holds the reins of office. We are not politicians or public thinkers; we are the rich; we own America; we got it, God knows how; but we intend to keep it if we can by throwing all the tremendous weight of our support, our influence, our money, our political connection, our purchased senators, our hungry congressmen, our public-speaking demagogues into the scale against any legislation, any political platform, any Presidential campaign, that threatens the integrity of our estates.[57]

Throughout U.S. history, it has been common practice for the majority in legislatures (at all levels) to revise political boundaries for their advantage. This tactic, known as *gerrymandering*, occurs when the party in power designs the political boundaries to negate the power of the opposition. Assume, for instance, that the Democrats control the state legislature. The boundary lines can be redrawn in order to take Republican strongholds from problematic districts, placing them in nearby strong Democratic districts. The Democratic district is strong enough to absorb the Republicans without losing their advantage, and in the Republican district the Democrats have a better chance of gaining control.

Although the Fourteenth Amendment to the Constitution gave African Americans the right to vote following the Civil War, the white majority in the southern states used a variety of tactics to keep blacks from voting. Most effective was the strategy of intimidation. African Americans who tried to assert their right to vote were often subject to beatings, destruction of property, or even lynching. A more subtle approach, however, was quite effective in eliminating the black vote in the southern states. Through legal means, laws were passed to achieve illegal discrimination. One tactic was the white primary, which excluded blacks from participating in the party primary. The Constitution prohibited the states from denying the vote on the basis of race. A political party, however, since it was a private association, could discriminate. The Democratic party throughout most of the South chose the option of limiting the primary to whites. African Americans could legally vote in the general election, but only for candidates already selected by whites. And since the Democratic party in the South was supreme, the candidate selected in the primary would be the victor in the general election. This practice was nullified by the Supreme Court in 1944.

Other legal obstacles for African Americans in the South were the literacy test and the poll tax, which were eventually ruled illegal by the Supreme Court, but only after many decades of denying blacks the right to vote. Both obstacles were designed as two southern suffrage requirements to admit whites to the electorate and exclude blacks, without mentioning race. The literacy test and its related requirements were blatantly racist.[58] The object of the test was to allow all adult white males to vote while excluding all blacks. The problem with this test was that many whites would be excluded because they were also illiterate. In response, legislators in various southern states contributed alternatives to the literacy requirements that would allow the illiterate whites to vote. One loophole was the "grandfather clause, which, using Louisiana law as the example, exempted persons from the literacy test who were registered voters in any state on January 1, 1867, or prior thereto, the sons and grandsons of such persons, and male persons of foreign birth naturalized before January 1, 1898."[59] Another alternative designed to allow illiterate whites to vote was the understanding clause, which allowed a person who could not read any section of the Constitution to qualify as an elector if he could understand and give a reasonable interpretation of what was read to him. This procedure gave registrars great latitude to decide who could vote. Thus, they had the ability to discriminate, which they did uniformly. A similar law in some states authorized registration of illiterates if they were of good character and could "understand the duties and obligations of citizenship under a republican form of government."

Unfortunately, efforts by whites to limit the power of African Americans are not just a historical anomaly. A number of racist strategies are still employed. Howard Ball, head of the political science department at Mississippi State University, has noted a number of "voting wrongs" still used by the white power structure in Mississippi to keep whites in power, even though blacks hold a numerical majority.

1. Holding at-large elections in multimember legislative districts gives whites the advantage even when outnumbered because more than twice as many whites as blacks are registered voters.
2. Counties have been gerrymandered to dilute African American voting strength. As a result, blacks, who represent 35 percent of Mississippi's population, hold only 7 percent of the county supervisor positions.
3. Once African Americans have been successful in winning elections, elective offices have been changed to appointive ones.
4. White subdivisions have been annexed to produce municipalities, thus diluting the black vote.
5. Polling places have been switched literally the night before an election.[60]

Election Fraud

Certainly, more than one election has been won through illegal activities. Violence and intimidation have been used by the supporters of certain candidates to control the vote. Various forms of harassment were used especially prior to 1850, when voting was done orally. This practice allowed bystanders to know how votes were cast and thus intimidate or punish persons who voted contrary to their wishes. In the twentieth century, violence was aimed at southern African Americans to keep them from registering, thus ensuring white supremacy.

Most election frauds involving illegal voting, false registration, and bribery have occurred in areas of one-party dominance, especially in cities controlled by a political machine. This has kept the machine in power at the local level and has delivered votes in state and federal elections to one party, thus increasing the scope of the machine's power.

> In the heyday of machine politics, the use of repeaters and personators—to "vote early and often"—was widespread, from the North Side in Kansas City to the South Side in Chicago, from the Strip in Pittsburgh to South of the Slot in San Francisco. No less important, and generally used in conjunction with these, was the practice of wholesale manipulation of registration lists. The names of aliens (sometimes as the result of illegal naturalization), minors, and nonresidents were added to the registration list, along with fictitious

names and the names of reliable nonvoters. In combination, such illegal techniques could yield large numbers of fraudulent votes. In the 1869 election in New York, for example, between 25,000 and 30,000 votes were attributed to repeating, false registration, and illegal naturalization.[61]

These tactics have been used throughout history to influence elections in the United States. For example, Harry Truman would not have been elected senator from Missouri without the help of 50,000 fraudulent votes from the Pendergast machine in Kansas City.[62] So, too, have more recent Democratic victories been predicated on the massive help from Mayor Richard Daley's delivery of the votes in Cook County, Illinois.

Votes have also been purchased and continue to be today, especially in poor areas, through bribes of money and liquor. The *Los Angeles Times* alleged, for example, that $5,000 was channeled through four African American ministers for street money to recruit votes during the Carter campaign in the 1976 California primary.[63]

Another form of election fraud is to bypass manipulation of the voters in favor of forgery and false accounting by election officials. Corrupt election officials can (1) complete ballots when the voter has failed to vote for a particular office, (2) declare ballots for the opposition invalid by deliberately defacing them or marking two preferences for a single office, (3) destroy ballots for the opposition, (4) add premarked ballots to the total, and (5) simply miscount.

One of the most famous instances of election fraud involved the election of Lyndon Johnson to the Senate.[64] In 1948, Johnson ran for the Democratic nomination (which meant certain election in Democratic Texas) against Governor Coke Stevenson. Stevenson won the primary by 71,000 votes but lacked a majority in the crowded field. A runoff was then held for the two top vote-getters, Stevenson and Johnson. Stevenson again won, or so everyone thought. Days after the polls had closed, a questionable correction of the vote from Duval County gave Johnson 202 more votes than the original count, enough to give him the Democratic nomination by 87 votes. The new vote was orchestrated by George B. Parr, the Democratic county boss. It was alleged that the new votes came from the graveyard and Mexico; some Chicanos testified that Parr had voted their names without their knowledge. When the defeated candidate charged fraud, the Senate voted to investigate. Senate investigators found, however, that the ballots had mysteriously been destroyed. The investigation ended and Johnson became a senator, taking a big step in his political career, which later included terms as the powerful majority leader of the Senate and finally as president of the United States.

Unfair Campaign Conduct

Political campaigns often involve illegal or at least immoral behavior by the candidates and their supporters to achieve the advantage over one another. Behavior such as espionage, bribery, sabotage, crowd agitation, lying, and innuendo occur regularly. The primary goal of these tactics is to negate the opponent's strengths by spreading rumors about his or her character, especially regarding his or her sex life and association with unsavory individuals, such as communists and criminals. For example, in 1983, Bill Allain was elected governor of Mississippi, despite a very rough campaign. Allain's opponent, Leon Bramlett, accused him of having sexual relations with three black transvestites. Allain denied this involvement and was able to win the election. Afterward, the three transvestites repudiated their allegations, claiming that they had been paid to lie.[65]

Another tactic has been to place hecklers in an opponent's rally, which the Mondale–Ferraro campaign accused the Reagan campaign of doing in the 1984 presidential race. Or opponents can steal campaign information, as occurred when Reagan forces secured secret information from the Carter campaign prior to the crucial television debates in the 1980 election. In other instances, billboards have been defaced, public address systems and lights for rallies have been sabotaged, and African Americans have been hired to pose as workers for the opposition, going door-to-door in so-called redneck precincts.

Political dynamiting, another common tactic, gives the voters misinformation about the opposition.[66] This may be accomplished by designing, printing, and distributing pamphlets and brochures that blacken the candidate's reputation; when they are distributed at the end of the campaign, the victim has no time to respond to the charges. The techniques here may be blatant, such as those used by Richard Nixon in his early campaigns for office. He defeated Jerry Voorhis for a House seat in 1946 by stating that Voorhis had been formally endorsed by a labor group (political action committee or PAC) tainted with known communists. (Voorhis, in fact, was a vigorous anticommunist during his four terms in the House and was never endorsed by the PAC.) A newspaper ad placed by Nixon in that campaign proclaimed, "A vote for Nixon is a vote against the Communist-dominated PAC with its gigantic slush fund."[67] Another alleged violation in this campaign was the hiring of workers by Republican headquarters to work at a phone bank, asking people at random, "Did you know Jerry Voorhis was a communist?"

In 1950, Nixon was elected to the Senate after a race characterized by unethical attacks on his opponent, Helen Gahagan Douglas, a liberal, three-term congresswoman. According to the campaign rhetoric, Douglas was "soft on communism." Moreover, "on 353 times the actress candidate voted exactly the same as Vito Marcantino, the notorious Communist party-line Congressman from New York." She was called the "pink lady" and described, along with Marcantino, as a hero of the communist movement. A pamphlet, colored pink, was distributed to thousands of voters. "On September 9, in San Diego, Nixon stated that 'if she [Douglas] had her way, the Communist conspiracy would never have been exposed, and Alger Hiss would still be influencing the foreign policy of the United States.'… On

November 1, Nixon repeated an earlier charge…that Douglas 'gave comfort to Soviet tyranny.'"[68]

The Nixon campaign was aided by favorable treatment in many of California's newspapers. A cartoon that appeared in two Hearst papers, the *San Francisco Examiner* and the *Los Angeles Examiner,* is illustrative of this political help:

> The cartoon, entitled "Rough on Rats," shows Nixon resolutely standing guard with a shotgun in front of a walled farm. His sleeves are rolled up, and in addition to the shotgun, he carries a net labeled "Communist Control." Uncle Sam is farming contentedly behind the wall, while rats (labeled variously, "Appeaser," "Professional Pacifist," "Conspirator," "Spy," "Soviet Sympathizer," and "Propagandist") run about. Hearst cartoons and editorials in those days left very little to the imagination. The editorial under this cartoon, for example, accuses Douglas of offering "reckless government spending" and "giving away atomic bomb secrets" and of opposing military assistance programs, Selective Service, the Communist Control Act…and "weeding out poor security risks."[69]

The Nixon–Douglas campaign rhetoric was based on falsehood and smears. Douglas was not a communist sympathizer. She did vote on the same side as Marcantino 354 times, but so did Nixon, 112 times, the gap being primarily the difference between Republican and Democratic votes on various issues. But, in this case, slander was a successful tactic, and Nixon won 56 percent of the vote.

Tactics need not be as blatant as Nixon's but can be more subtle, like Johnson's famous anti-Goldwater television advertisement in 1964: It never mentioned Goldwater or his "hawk" position; instead, it showed a child amid nature with an atomic mushroom cloud exploding in the distance.

Other times, unfair conduct can border on the criminal. During the presidential reelection campaign of 1992 (more specifically September 30 and October 1), for example, rival Democratic candidate Bill Clinton's passport files were searched in an attempt by Republicans to attack his anti–Vietnam War activities while a student at Oxford University in England. Also searched were his mother's records and those of Independent candidate Ross Perot. Before leaving office, Bush dismissed Assistant Secretary Elizabeth Tamposi, who was the most apparent official responsible for the search. A special prosecutor was appointed by Attorney General Barr in part to investigate whether the Bush White House instigated the illegal search.

The impact of television in campaigns has been significant in developing and manipulating opinion. In this case, the tactic is not directed at smearing an opponent but at building a particular image of the candidate of choice. Scenes showing one's war exploits or role as a devoted parent, dedicated humanitarian, lover of nature, or whatever are displayed without reference to the candidate's positions on the issues. The intent of these brief ads (generally thirty or sixty seconds long) is strictly to manipulate the viewers to think positively of the candidate. There is a debate as to whether this technique is moral or not.

This very issue was raised in the 1984 presidential election, as the Reagan campaign employed a strong image-building technique. Reagan's strategy was to act and appear presidential, evoking confidence and determination and speaking in platitudes about American strength and patriotism. Lost in this carefully prepared rhetoric were clear-cut, definitive positions on the political issues at hand. Nonetheless, Reagan won the election by a landslide.

Another borderline technique that has emerged with the growth of the computer is the use of form letters. Millions of letters can be mailed in a political campaign that give personalized messages referring to the recipient's race, ethnicity, religion, children (by name), and issues that they favor or oppose (e.g., abortion, busing). Again, the effort is the manipulation of voters by making it appear as if the candidate is taking a personal interest in their concerns. The Nixon campaign of 1972, for example, could employ 35,000 different combinations in a single letter. This tactic, although legal, subverts the intent of democracy.

Money in Elections

Democracy is a system of government that expresses the will of the people. In theory, since all persons and groups have a right to contribute to the candidate or party of their choice, all interests and points of view will be represented. In practice, however, wealthy individuals and large organizations provide the most money and have the greatest influence on the political process, as we have discussed earlier.

Money intrudes in a variety of ways to thwart democracy, not just through the voluntary contributions to the few. One problem is that political leaders may extort money, producing two sets of victims. One set is the businesses and individuals dependent on the government for contracts, favorable laws, and sympathetic regulations. When confronted with the charge that he had authorized an illegal political contribution of company funds, the chairman of the board of a large corporation replied, "A large part of the money raised from the business community for political purposes is given in fear of what would happen if it were not given."[70] Maurice Stans, Nixon's chief fund-raiser in the 1972 campaign, who gathered some $60 million, was especially adept at this form of extortion.

> Stans would approach potential donors threatening that if they did not contribute the desired sum, he would initiate unfavorable pollution action against their corporations. He would take this action, he said, through the Pollution Council he helped establish at the Commerce Department. The

scope of Stans' fundraising operations while he was still Nixon's Secretary of Commerce was revealed recently by two oil company executives. They told the Senate Watergate committee that a hundred-thousand-dollar contribution was expected from all large corporations.[71]

The other set of victims of political extortion is government employees who are forced to make campaign contributions. Although such contributions were made illegal by federal law in 1967, they continue to be required, although perhaps less frequently. The practice has most commonly occurred at state and local levels and has been connected to the patronage system. Around 1900, the rate varied from 10 percent of one's salary (in Louisiana) to a sliding scale of from 3 to 12 percent. In 1972, state employees in Indiana paid 2 percent of their salaries to the party in power.[72]

Closely related to political extortion is the sale of jobs for contributions. This used to be a common practice for postmasterships and other federal positions. Apparently, it is still possible for the most prestigious jobs.

It is clear that the sale of embassies flourished extensively under Richard Nixon, his 1972 campaign reaping $1,324,442 merely from the eight individuals who headed embassies in Western Europe at the time. After this reelection, Nixon made ambassadors of a further eight individuals, each of whom had given no less than $25,000 to the campaign, and in aggregate $706,000. In February 1974, Herbert Kalmbach [sic], Richard Nixon's personal attorney, pleaded guilty to a charge of promising J. Fife Symington, the ambassador to Trinidad and Tobago during 1969–71, a more prestigious European ambassadorship in return for a $100,000 contribution to be divided between Republican senatorial campaigns and the Committee to Re-elect the President.[73]

Pervasive throughout the money–politics connection is routine circumvention of the law.[74] Candidates and donors commonly exploit loopholes. They give less than the amount that the law requires must be reported, but they give in multiples to a number of committees, each of which supports the same candidate. Another ruse is to give money to others, who then make donations in their name. Corporations evade restrictions on giving by laundering money through other sources or by contributing to trade associations such as the National Association of Manufacturers, which in turn pass the money on to the candidates of the original donor. They may also give bonuses to their employees, which are then given as individual contributions. Unions may assess their members a fee, which is then given to the unions' candidates. As noted earlier, some of the largest corporations have given money under the table in a variety of ways to finance candidates. Indeed, a good share of talent in our largest organizations and political organizations is devoted to finding ever more creative ways to outwit the letter and the intent of the law for their political and monetary advantage.[75]

Watergate

The Watergate-related crimes committed by government officials represent the acts of official secrecy and deception taken to the extreme.[76] They demonstrate forcefully and fearfully just how far away from the Democratic ideal the U.S. political system had moved at the time and how close it was to approaching totalitarianism. In the words of David Wise,

> Watergate revealed that under President Nixon a kind of totalitarianism had already come to America, creeping in, not like Carl Sandburg's fog, on little cat feet, but in button-down shirts, worn by handsome young advertising and public relations men carrying neat attache cases crammed with $100 bills. Men willing to perjure themselves to stay on the team, to serve their leader. It came in the guise of "national security," a blanket term used to justify the most appalling criminal acts by men determined to preserve their own political power at any cost. It came in the form of the ladder against the bedroom window, miniature transmitters in the ceiling, wiretaps, burglaries, enemies lists, tax audits, and psychiatric profiles. It is not easy to write the word totalitarian when reporting about America, but if the word jars, or seems overstated, consider the dictionary definition: "Of or pertaining to a centralized government in which those in control grant neither recognition nor tolerance to parties of differing opinion."
>
> And that is very close to what happened, for, as we learned from the Watergate investigation, the enormous power of the government of the United States, including the police power and the secret intelligence apparatus, had been turned loose against the people of the United States, at least against those who held differing opinions, against the opposition political party, and the press.[77]

The Watergate investigation revealed a number of criminal and undemocratic actions by President Nixon and his closest advisors.[78]

- **Item:** Burglars, financed by funds from the Committee to Re-elect the President, broke into and bugged the headquarters of the Democratic party in the Watergate apartment complex. These individuals were paid hush money and promised executive clemency to protect the president and his advisors.
- **Item:** Burglars also broke into the office of the psychiatrist of Daniel Ellsberg, the person who leaked the Pentagon Papers to the press. These papers, of course, were instrumental in showing the public how it had been systematically deceived by a series of presidents during the long Vietnam War. While the trial was in session, the White House offered the judge in the Ellsberg case the possibility of his being named director of the FBI.
- **Item:** President Nixon's personal attorney solicited money for an illegally formed campaign committee and offered an ambassadorship in return for a campaign contribution. Money gathered from contribu-

tions, some illegally, was systematically laundered to conceal the donors. Much of this money was kept in cash so when payoffs occurred,
the money could not be traced.

- **Item:** President Nixon ordered secret wiretapping of his own aides,
  several journalists, and even his brother. Additionally, he had secret
  microphones planted in his offices to record clandestinely every
  conversation.
- **Item:** John Mitchell, attorney general of the United States, participated
  in preliminary discussions about bugging the Democratic headquarters. He even suggested that one means of gaining information about
  the Democrats was to establish a floating bordello at the Miami
  convention.
- **Item:** The president's men participated in a campaign of dirty tricks to
  discredit various potential Democratic nominees for president, including the publication and distribution of letters, purporting to come from
  Senator Muskie, claiming that Senator Jackson was a homosexual. The
  White House also requested tax audits of administration opponents.
- **Item:** The White House used the Central Intelligence Agency (CIA) in
  an effort to halt the FBI investigation of Watergate. The director of the
  FBI even destroyed vital legal evidence at the suggestion of the president's aides.
- **Item:** President Nixon offered aides H. R. Haldeman and John Erlichman as much as $300,000 from a secret slush fund for their legal fees
  after they were forced to resign.
- **Item:** The president and his advisors, using the cloak of national security, strongly resisted attempts by the special prosecutor, the courts,
  and Congress to get the facts in the case. Various administration officials were found guilty of perjury and withholding information.
- **Item:** When the president, under duress, did provide transcripts of the
  tapes or other materials, they had been edited.
- **Item:** The president, on television and in press releases, lied to the U.S.
  public, over and over again.

This infamous list of discretions comprises a tangled web of activities
that posed a significant threat to the U.S. democratic political system. All the
efforts were directed at subverting the political process so that the administration in power would stay in power, regardless of the means. There was a
systematic effort to discredit enemies of the administration, to weaken the
two-party system, and to control the flow of information to citizens.

Although the Nixon administration was guilty of these heinous acts, we
should not assume that Nixon was the first U.S. president to be involved in
such chicanery. Watergate was no aberration. Rather, it was a startling illustration of government practices that have been significant throughout U.S. history.

Moreover, there is ample evidence of various linkages between the Watergate scandal and other major American scandals since 1963, including the

Iran–Contra affair.[79] These interrelationships demonstrate a pattern of involvement by the CIA, members of organized criminal syndicates, and certain military officials. They are explored in depth in Chapters 8 and 9.

Conclusion

This chapter has focused on the dark side of politics. Hopefully, politics is not completely corrupt, as one may be tempted to conclude from our discussion.

We have looked at two types of political deviance: the use of political clout for material gain and the unfair means used to gain, maintain, or increase political power. In both cases, the deviance can be achieved by corrupt individuals or by a corrupt system. But even when accomplished by individuals, the important sociological point is that the deviance is only possible because the elite occupy positions of power. Because of the duties and powers inherent in their political positions, they are susceptible to the appeals of the moneyed interests who want to use them or they are persuaded by the appeal of greater power.

Although political corruption is found in all types of societies and in all types of political and economic systems, the amount of political corruption found in the United States is astounding. Benson, after carefully studying the phenomenon, offers this conclusion:

> Today it is probably fair to say that America has as much corruption, both absolutely and proportionately, as any other modern constitutional democracy. There are no international indices of corruption, but the available data indicate that corruption here is at least as severe and extensive as in other modern democracies. American idealism does not appear to be reflected in our political ethos.[80]

Why is the United States plagued by this high rate of political corruption? The answer is complex and requires an understanding of the historical factors, character, values, and political–economic systems that characterize the United States. The rip-off mentality that pervades the economic system is found throughout the social structure, as this chapter has amply demonstrated. The goal of individual or corporate success supersedes group concerns; therefore, any means are used to achieve the goal. The following chapter should provide further insight into this complex societal problem.

Critical Thinking Exercise 6.1: Subsidies without Reason _____

Senator William Proxmire used to present an annual "Golden Fleece" award for the most ridiculous expenditures by the federal government. One of his awards included things like funding research to discover why monkeys fall in love. As you can tell from our discussion of subsidies, the federal government continues to spend money on wasteful projects. Do a search of databases like Infotrac, Proquest, or the Reader's Guide for the past three years. Make a list of what newspapers and magazines consider the most questionable expenditures. On what basis are most of these grants and subsidies questioned? Who are the recipients of most such programs?

Endnotes

1. The organization and many of the examples used in this chapter are from two sources: George Amick, *The American Way of Graft* (Princeton, NJ: The Center for Analysis of Public Issues, 1976); and reprinted by permission of the publisher, from *Political Corruption in America* by George C. S. Benson (Lexington, MA: Lexington Books, D.C. Heath and Company, 1978).

2. Benson, xi.

3. In addition to Amick and Benson, the following source provides an excellent review of the magnitude of political crime in the United States: Carl J. Friedrich, *The Pathology of Politics* (New York: Harper & Row, 1972).

4. Tom Hays, "GOP Fund Raiser Faces Trial on Campaign Corruption Charges," *Asian Week*, July 13, 2000, 8.

5. Benson, 49.

6. Amick, 40–41.

7. The Agnew case is taken primarily from Amick, 42–50; and J. Anthony Lukas, *Nightmare: The Underside of the Nixon Years* (New York: Viking, 1976), Chapter 12.

8. This section is based on the discussion in Nathan Miller's *Stealing from America* (New York: Paragon House, 1992), p. 88 ff.

9. Frank Browning and John Gerassi, *The American Way of Crime* (New York: G. P. Putnam's Sons, 1980), 214.

10. Ibid.

11. Benson, 12.

12. Amick, 98–99.

13. Benson, 81–82.

14. Amick, 146–49.

15. Ibid., 109–14.

16. Ibid., 76–94.

17. Doug Turetsky, "New York City: Where Money Talks and Ethics Walks," *In These Times*, April 1988, 5.

18. Amick, 77.

19. Ibid., 146–49.

20. Benson, 13.

21. Mark Green, *Who Runs Congress?* 4th ed. (New York: Dell, 1984), 255–58.

22. Ibid., 235–39.

23. Ibid., 258–62.

24. The following discussion is based on April Hejka-Ekins, "The HUD Scandal: Lessons from the Firing Line," paper presented at the meeting of the American Society for Public Administration, April 10, 1990, Los Angeles, California.

25. This section and the next are based on Haynes Johnson, *Sleep Walking through History: America in the Reagan Years* (New York: W. W. Norton, 1991), 180–83; and Sara Fritz, "Sununu Apologizes for Breaking Travel Rules," *Los Angeles Times*, June 22, 1991, A-1, A-22.

26. Martin L. Gross, *The Government Racket: Washington Waste from A to Z* (New York: Bantam, 1992), 183–85.

27. Jerome H. Skolnick, *Justice without Trial: Law Enforcement in Democratic Society* (New York: John Wiley, 1966), 14.

28. President's Commission on Law Enforcement and the Administration of Justice, "The Challenge of Crime in a Free Society," in *Official Deviance*, ed. Jack D. Douglas and John M. Johnson (Philadelphia: Lippincott, 1977), 254–55.

29. *Time*, November 30, 1987, 29.

30. Associated Press, January 6, 1988.

31. Associated Press, August 15, 1989.

32. PBS Frontline, "When Cops Go Bad," November 18, 1990.

33. *New York Times*, July 31, 1992, B-1.

34. *Time*, September 27, 1999, 44.

35. *Time*, September 11, 1995, 11.

36. *Detroit News*, May 3, 1996.

37. See Anthony Summers, *Official and Confidential: The Secret Life of J. Edgar Hoover* (New York: Putnam, 1995).

38. Peter Phillips and Project Censored, *Censored 2000: The Year's Top 25 Stories* (New York: Seven Stories, 2000), 117–18.

39. Donald R. Cressey, *Theft of the Nation: The Structure and Operation of Organized Crime in America* (New York: Harper & Row, 1969), 250–51.

40. Reprinted from William J. Chambliss, *On the Take: From Petty Crooks to Presidents*, 1–2. © 1978 by William J. Chambliss. Reprinted by permission of Indiana University Press.

41. Benson, 33.

42. This account of the Tweed Ring is based on three sources: Benson, 37–43; Allen Weinstein and R. Jackson Wilson, *Freedom and Crisis* (New York: Random House, 1974), 530; and Gustavus Myers, *The History of Tammany Hall*, rev. ed. (New York: Burt Franklin, 1917), Chapter 13.

43. Benson, 39.

44. Weinstein and Wilson, 530.

45. From Jack Newfield and Paul DuBrul, *The Abuse of Power* (pp. 84–85). Copyright 1977 by Jack Newfield and Paul DuBrul. Reprinted by permission of Viking Penguin, Inc. For an elaboration of this thesis of a national power elite, see the following: C. Wright Mills, *The Power Elite* (New York: Oxford University Press, 1956); G. William Domhoff, *Who Rules America?* (Englewood Cliffs, NJ: Prentice Hall, 1967); and Michael Parenti, *Democracy for the Few*, 2nd ed. (New York: St. Martin's Press, 1977).

46. This material is from Newfield and DuBrul, 75–108. See also Joe R. Feagin, *The Urban Real Estate Came: Playing Monopoly with Real Money* (Englewood Cliffs, NJ: Prentice Hall, 1983).

47. Newfield and DuBrul, 76.

48. See Robert Caro, *The Power Broker: Robert Moses and the Fall of New York* (New York: Vintage, 1975).

49. For an elaboration of this thesis, see Charles Beard, *An Economic Interpretation of the Constitution of the United States* (New York: Macmillan, 1919).

50. Max Ferrand (ed.), *Records of the Federal Convention* (New Haven, CT: Yale University Press, 1927), quoted in Parenti, 53.

51. Quoted in Parenti, 56.

52. C. B. Macpherson, *The Real World of Democracy* (New York: Oxford University Press, 1972), Chapter 1.

53. Parenti, 56.

54. Ibid., 57–58.

55. Weinstein and Wilson, 430.

56. Parenti, 51.

57. Cited in Matthew Josephson, *The Robber Barons: The Great American Capitalists, 1861–1901* (New York: Harcourt Brace and World, 1962), 352.

58. The following is taken from V. O. Key, Jr., *Southern Politics* (New York: Vintage, 1949), Chapter 26.

59. Ibid.

60. Howard Ball, "Mississippi's Voting Wrongs," *Washington Post,* January 26, 1982, A-19.

61. Benson, 171; reprinted by permission of the publisher.

62. Victor Lasky, *It Didn't Start with Watergate* (New York: Dial Press, 1977), 122.

63. Benson, 172 (originally appeared in *Los Angeles Times,* August 8, 1976, 1, 24).

64. Lasky, 199–223.

65. "More Mississippi Mud," *Newsweek,* January 30, 1984, 32. For historical examples of the use of slander in political campaigns, see John S. Lang, "Political Invective: It's Not What It Used to Be," *U.S. News & World Report,* July 16, 1984, 86–87.

66. See Frank H. Jonas (ed.), *Political Dynamiting* (Salt Lake City: University of Utah Press, 1970).

67. These examples are from Frank Mankiewicz, *Perfectly Clear: Nixon from Whittier to Watergate* (New York: Quadrangle, 1973), 39, 45, 51–52.

68. Ibid., 52–53.

69. Ibid., 54–55.

70. Cited in David W. Adamany and George E. Agree, *Political Money* (Baltimore: Johns Hopkins, 1975), 4.

71. Stu Bishop and Bert Knorr, "The Moneymen," in *Big Brother and the Holding Company: The World Behind Watergate,* ed. Steve Weissman (Palo Alto, CA: Ramparts Press, 1974), 211–12.

72. Benson, 177.

73. Ibid., 179.

74. Ibid., 181–83.

75. See also David Wise, *The Politics of Lying* (New York: Vintage, 1966), xi–xiv.

76. This section on Watergate is based on D. Stanley Eitzen, *Social Problems* (Boston: Allyn & Bacon, 1980), Chapter 2.

77. Wise, ibid., x–xi.

78. See also xi–xiv; "The Tangled Web They Wove," *Newsweek,* December 2, 1974, 32–37; "Four Key Convictions in the Watergate Affair" *U.S. News & World Report,* January 13, 1975, 15–17; William A. Dobrovir, Joseph D. Gebhardt, Samuel J. Boffone, and Andre N. Oakes, *The Offenses of Richard Nixon* (New York: Quadrangle, 1973); Theodore H. White, *Breach of Faith: The Fall of Richard Nixon* (New York: Atheneum, 1975); and John Dean, *Blind Ambition* (New York: Simon & Schuster, 1976). For a sociological analysis of Watergate, see Jack D. Douglas, "Watergate: Harbinger of the American Prince," in *Official Deviance,* ed. Jack D. Douglas and John M. Johnson (Philadelphia: Lippincott, 1977), 112–20.

79. See, for example, Len Colodny and Robert Gettlin, *Silent Coup: The Removal of a President* (New York: St. Martin's Press, 1991); Peter Dale Scott, "From Dallas to Watergate: The Longest Coverup," in *Assassinations, Dallas and Beyond: A Guide to Cover-ups and Investigations,* ed. Peter Dale Scott et al. (New York: Random House, 1976), 357–76; and David Scheim, *The Mafia Killed President Kennedy* (London: W. H. Allen, 1988), 297–326.

80. Benson, 3.

7

Political Deviance

Criminologists interested in political crimes have traditionally concentrated on acts by individuals and organizations against the government, that is, attempts to change the political system through violating the law. Although these political acts are important to understand, this exclusive focus neglects those crimes perpetrated by the government against the people. The purpose of this chapter is to attempt to right this imbalance by focusing on the deviance of the political elite (see also Chapter 6).[1] Political deviance is an omnibus concept, including a number of practices. Under this rubric are the numerous forms of political corruption noted in Chapter 6, as well as the consequences of the government's bias in favor of business that negatively affects the powerless.

This chapter catalogues additional political acts that are deviant. Specifically, we examine deviance in the domestic and foreign spheres. On the domestic level, we consider (1) the secrecy and deception used by government officials to manipulate public opinion; (2) the abuse of power by government officials and agencies; (3) political prisoners; and (4) official violence, as manifested in police brutality and the use of citizens as unwilling guinea pigs. On the international level, we will focus on two illegal warlike acts: clandestine intervention and war crimes.

Domestic Political Deviance

Secrecy, Lying, and Deception

The hallmark of any democracy is the consent of the governed based on a reliable flow of information from the government. Unfortunately, a number of mechanisms serve to thwart this principle in U.S. society.[2] One common technique used to withhold information is the presidential exercise of *executive privilege*. The doctrine of executive privilege is the constitutionally questionable belief that the president and his staff cannot be made to testify and that presidential documents cannot be examined without the president's permission. The argument given for this immunity is that such information might compromise national security. However, the more realistic effect is that executive privilege allows the executive branch to withhold information from the courts and Congress, not to mention the general public.

Executive privilege has been used several times in recent U.S. history:[3]

- **Item:** President Truman refused to turn over to the House Un-American Activities Committee a Federal Bureau of Investigation report on a government scientist.
- **Item:** In 1963, General Maxwell Taylor declined to appear before the House Subcommittee on Defense Appropriations to discuss the Bay of Pigs invasion.
- **Item:** In 1972, the Securities and Exchange Commission refused to give certain information to the House Interstate and Foreign Commerce Subcommittee concerning its investigation of ITT.
- **Item:** In 1973, President Nixon refused to surrender the White House tape recordings to Special Prosecutor Archibald Cox.

Another method used to stonewall is to designate information as memoranda. The following is an example of a secret memo from Assistant Secretary of Defense Daniel McNaughton to Secretary Robert McNamara:

> 70 percent [of the reasons for fighting in Vietnam are] to avoid a humiliating U.S. defeat (to our reputation as a guarantor), 20 percent, to keep South Vietnam (and the adjacent territory) from Chinese hands, 10 percent to benefit the people of South Vietnam [with] a better, freer way of life.[4]

What would've happened had these goals been made public?

> Would Congress have authorized a major war and more than 50,000 U.S. combat deaths for these goals? Would the American people have supported a war for these goals? And if not, was an American President justified in going to war for them anyway? More importantly, was an American President justified in concealing these goals and our own acts of provocation while he was, in fact, making a unilateral decision to go to war?[5]

Most likely, the people would not have supported the war if they had known about the government's goals. Realizing this, President Nixon (who broadened the war from Johnson's policies) attempted to suppress publication of the Pentagon Papers, which would have revealed the true U.S. intentions and behaviors. In addition, the weight of the government's force was brought to the prosecution of those who had leaked the Pentagon Papers

(Daniel Ellsberg and Anthony Russo). The government even went so far as to offer the judge in that case the directorship of the Federal Bureau of Investigations (FBI) while the case was being heard.[6]

Officials can also deceive the public by the "you did not ask me the right question, so I did not give you the right answer" game.[7] As an example, when Richard Helms was director of the Central Intelligence Agency (CIA), he was asked before Congress if his agency had been involved in Watergate. His reply was no. Much later, when it became known that the CIA had lent equipment to the Watergate burglars and concealed the laundering of checks used in the cover-up, Helms was reminded of his previous answer. He explained that he had not been asked the right question, for he had assumed that the original question meant involvement in the actual break-in at Democratic headquarters.

Although all the above tactics work to deceive the public, none is more onerous than outright lying by government officials, which has occurred many times in recent U.S. history.[8]

- **Item:** In 1954, Secretary of State John Foster Dulles said that Americans were not involved in the coup in Guatemala that deposed the regime of leftist President José Guzman, even though the operation was financed, organized, and run by the CIA.
- **Item:** In 1960, a U.S. spy plane, flown by a CIA pilot, was shot down over the Soviet Union. Although the United States had been using U-2 planes to spy on the Soviets for the preceding four years, officials denied the incident, saying that the United States had not violated Soviet air space.
- **Item:** In 1961, the CIA, under President Kennedy, organized an invasion of Cuba at the Bay of Pigs. Yet, when the Cubans charged in the United Nations that the United States was behind the operation, Ambassador Adlai Stevenson responded that no U.S. personnel or government planes were involved.
- **Item:** In 1963, the United States supported but officially denied its involvement in the coup against South Vietnam President Ngo Dinh Diem.
- **Item:** In 1964, President Johnson used an incident in which U.S. ships were allegedly shot at in the Tonkin Gulf to give him a free hand to escalate the war in Vietnam. Congress was deliberately misled by the official representation of the facts.[9]
- **Item:** President Johnson praised U.S. Asian allies for sending supposed volunteers to fight in Vietnam when in fact our government had paid Thailand and the Philippines $200 million each to make this gesture.
- **Item:** President Nixon and his advisors told the U.S. public that the neutrality of Cambodia had not been violated when the United States had already conducted 3,600 bombing missions in that country over a

five-year period. To carry out this deception, the U.S. government falsified the death certificates of Americans who died in Cambodia.

- **Item:** U.S. military and government officials in the Vietnam War deliberately underestimated enemy troop strength to provide the illusion of military progress.[10]
- **Item:** In February 1976, George Bush, then director of the CIA, said, "Effective immediately the CIA will not enter into any paid or contractual relationship with any full-time or part-time news correspondent accredited by any U.S. news service, newspaper, periodical, radio, or television network or station." At the time of this announcement, the CIA employed about fifty members of U.S. media organizations and kept twenty-five journalists on the payroll, despite official pronouncement to the contrary.[11]

In 1994, the CIA was haunted by a series of miniscandals involving fraud and corruption by its own agents.[12]

- An agent stationed in Venezuela knowingly several shipments of cocaine into the United States. At the time, the agent was romantically involved with a Drug Enforcement Agency (DEA) official.
- In the mid-1980s, an FBI investigation revealed that CIA contract officers were illegally shipping arms back into the United States. The agents were dismissed but never prosecuted.
- The CIA spent more than $13 million to spirit its agents out of Ghana after one of its secretaries revealed the agents' identities to her lover.
- The CIA has lost all of its Iranian agents twice in the last fifteen years. The first time occurred in 1979 when the U.S. embassy was taken over by Iranian revolutionaries. This episode probably cost Jimmy Carter his bid for reelection. The second loss occurred in the late 1980s and is still going on. Since 1988, Iranian authorities have hunted down at least thirty Iranians who spied for the CIA. The CIA knew of this threat to their own agents, but the officer in charge of operations in Iran ignored numerous warnings of the impending danger. Most of these spies were tortured and executed for lack of proper protection.
- One agent working in Moscow was personally trained by the director of operations there. However, the agent had a criminal record involving assault with a deadly weapon and drug abuse problems. When these were revealed, he defected to Russia, with numerous CIA secrets.
- Finally, consider the case of agent Aldrich Ames, who sold intelligence secrets to the Russians for years and was paid some $2 million for doing so. Ames and his wife spent large sums of money overtly, buying a $540,000 house and a $40,000 Jaguar. Nevertheless, their treasonous activities went undetected by the CIA for years.

In addition to these examples, we must remember cover-ups of CIA involvement in the takeover of the Allende government in Chile, the attempted whitewashing of the sheep deaths in Utah because of an unintended release of chemicals used in biological warfare, the denial by Attorney General John Mitchell that ITT had offered $400,000 to underwrite the 1972 Republican National Convention, and so on. Cover-ups, lies, and secrecy by the government certainly run counter to the long-standing philosophical commitment of the United States to an open system in which the public is included in the decision-making process. Thomas Emerson, Yale law professor, alleges that secrecy in a democratic society is a source of illegitimate power, for several reasons.

1. When the people are assumed to be the master and the government, the servant, it makes no sense that the master should be denied the information upon which to direct the activities of the servants.
2. Each branch of government has its constitutional role to play and for one branch to withhold information from another undermines the whole principle of checks and balances.
3. Secrecy denies the individual due process, which demands that the citizen be furnished all the information upon which his or her destiny rests.[13]

Of course, at times, the public must be kept in the dark. The question, though is, when is secrecy legitimate? The burden of proof lies with those imposing the secrecy. The key is whether the intentional tampering with the free flow of public information is more beneficial to the public interest than disclosure.[14]

The determination of whether the public is better served by secrecy or disclosure is difficult to assess because one can argue that the public interest is *always* paramount, regardless of the situation. For example, most Americans believed the actions of Daniel Ellsberg were wrong when he disclosed the secrets of the Pentagon Papers. Thus, the secret leaker was deemed guilty, while the secret keepers were innocent because the public interest required secrecy in these militarily sensitive matters. Others, in contrast, perceived Ellsberg as a hero, one with courage enough to reveal the errors of the establishment. In this view, the secret keepers were guilty and the secret leaker was honored because public policy in Vietnam was against the public's interest.

David Wise has bluntly summarized the secrecy problem:

> With its control over information supported by an official system of secrecy and classification, the government has almost unlimited power to misinform the public. It does so for various reasons. The government lies to manipulate

public opinion, to generate public support for its policies, and to silence its critics. Ultimately, it lies to stay in power.[15]

The CIA has also had a long history of involvement with drug traffickers. On August 18, 1996, the *San Jose Mercury News*[16] published a front-page story claiming that

> [F]or the better part of a decade, a San Francisco Bay Area drug ring sold tons of cocaine to the Crips and Bloods street gangs of Los Angeles and funneled millions in drug profits to a Latin American guerrilla army run by the U.S. Central Intelligence Agency.
> This drug network opened the first pipeline between Colombia's cocaine cartels and the black neighborhoods of Los Angeles.... The cocaine that flooded in helped spark a crack explosion in urban America...and provided the cash and connections needed for L.A.'s gangs to buy automatic weapons.

The army's financiers, who met with CIA agents both before and during the time they were selling the drugs in Los Angeles, delivered cut-rate cocaine to the gangs through a young south-central crack dealer named Ricky Donnell Ross. Unaware of his suppliers' military and political connections, "Freeway Rick," a dope dealer of mythic proportions in the Los Angeles drug world, turned the cocaine powder into crack and wholesaled it to gangs across the country. The cash Ross paid for the cocaine, court records show, was then used to buy weapons and equipment for a guerrilla army named the Fuerza Democratica Nicaraguense (Nicaraguan Democratic Force) or FDN, the largest of several anticommunist groups commonly called the *Contras*.

The fact that the CIA aided drug traffickers in the 1980s was confirmed by a number of sources, including *The Nation* magazine, which argued the fact that the "government turned a blind eye to Contra drug trafficking has long resided in Washington files."[17]

Likewise, an investigative report by Peter Kornbluh confirmed that

> [U]sing the Freedom of Information Act, the National Security Archive obtained the declassification of thousands of pages of secret White House documents, regarding the Contra war.... Those records revealed a sad and shocking truth: U.S. officials—White House, National Security Council and CIA—not only knew about and condoned drug smuggling during the Contra operations, but in some cases collaborated with, protected, and even paid known dope traffickers who were deemed important players in the Reagan administration's obsessed covert effort to overthrow the Sandinista government in Nicaragua.

"This is a scandal," Kornbluh claimed, " and it is a scandal that demands a full accounting."[18] According to Project Censored, Congress, in 2000, refused to hold any public hearings on the question of CIA–Contra–cocaine links, acting more secretively than the CIA itself.[19]

The Contra–CIA drug trafficking link is a symptom of several much more widespread conditions. First, the CIA has been a major force in international drug trafficking for decades:

- **Item:** In France in 1950 the CIA recruited Corsican gangsters, the Ferri-Pisani family, to break a strike by dockworkers. The workers had refused to ship arms to Vietnam (where France was then at war). Corsican gangsters assaulted picket lines of communist union members and harassed union officials. In return for stopping the strike, the Ferri-Pisani family was allowed to use Marseilles as a shipping center for heroin.

- **Item:** For more than thirty years the U.S. government supported opium production in Southeast Asia's Golden Triangle by providing arms, military support, and protection to corrupt officials—all in the name of anticommunism, of course. This relationship began in the 1950s, after the Chinese Communists defeated Chiang Kai-shek's Nationalist Chinese army (the Kuomintang) in 1949. The CIA helped the Kuomintang regroup and settle in Burma's Shan states, bordering on China. The Shan area is a rich source of opium poppies. The CIA even helped smuggle the heroin out of Laos on its own airline, Air America. The CIA was aided in this project by American Mafia members whose lucrative Cuban market had dried up after Fidel Castro ousted the corrupt dictator Fulgencio Batista. (The story of Air America was made into a movie starring Mel Gibson in the 1980s.)

- **Item:** In the 1970s the Kuomintang's Cholon (Chinese Mafia) began producing injectable heroin and importing it into Vietnam. It has been estimated that 100,000 American soldiers in Vietnam had become addicted to heroin by 1974.

- **Item:** The CIA also aided its Southeast Asian drug producers by establishing money-laundering facilities for them in Australia. The Nugen Hand Bank was established by a number of ex-CIA agents and U.S. military officers. William Colby, former director of the CIA, was hired as the bank's lawyer. The bank was involved in numerous illegal activities, including a scheme to defraud U.S. oil workers in Saudi Arabia of their wages.

- **Item:** Other incidents link U.S. government agencies to drug trafficking by the Nicaraguan Contras in the 1980s. The Medellín cocaine cartel paid the Contras $10 million to allow its agents safe passage through Contra-held territory, with the full knowledge of the CIA. The Enterprise operation established by Lieutenant Colonel Oliver North and Admiral John Poindexter provided airplanes to the Medellín cartel in

1984–1985. The cartel paid the Enterprise for use of planes, landing strips, and labor to load drug shipments. The proceeds were allegedly used to buy arms for the Contras.

- **Item:** In 1985, the CIA supplied arms to the Afghans under General Hekmatyar. The CIA aided the Mujahedin (holy war fighters) after the Soviet army invaded Afghanistan to prop up the communist regime it had installed there. Hekmatyar and his army promptly went into the heroin business, and by 1988 they had 100 to 200 heroin refineries just across the border in Pakistan. By the late 1980s, heroin from these Southwest Asian nations accounted for about 50 percent of the European and American heroin supplies.[20]

Scandals involving the CIA and drug traffickers are symptomatic of an age in which elite deviance in both government and business has become an institutionalized feature of global capitalism.

Abuse of Power by Government Agencies

Watergate revealed that the highest U.S. leaders had conspired, among other things, to win an election by using such illegal means as dirty tricks, burglary of opponents, and soliciting of campaign funds by threats and bribes. But these White House transgressions, which we examined earlier in some detail, are only one expression of illicit government intervention. In this section, we focus on the deviant actions of government agencies in several key areas.

Many government abuses have occurred under the guise of internal security. Domestic surveillance is one example. Government agencies have a long history of surveilling citizens.[21] The pace quickened in the 1930s and increased further with the communist threat in the 1950s. Surveillance reached its peak during the height of antiwar and civil rights protests during the late 1960s and early 1970s. The FBI's concern with internal security, for example, dates back to 1936, when President Roosevelt asked FBI Director J. Edgar Hoover to investigate domestic communist and fascist organizations in the United States.[22] In 1939, as World War II began in Europe, President Roosevelt issued a proclamation that the FBI would be in charge of investigating subversive activities, espionage, and sabotage and that all law enforcement offices should give the FBI any relevant information on suspected activities. These directives began a pattern followed by the FBI under the administrations of Presidents Truman, Eisenhower, Kennedy, Johnson, Nixon, Ford, Carter, Reagan, and Bush.

The scope of these abuses by the FBI, the CIA, the National Security Agency (NSA), and eighteen other federal agencies engaged in surreptitious surveillance is incredible.[23] Indeed, many questionable acts against U.S. citizens have been performed in the name of national security.

- **Item:** From 1967 to 1973, the NSA monitored the overseas telephone calls and cables of approximately 1,650 U.S. citizens and organizations, as well as almost 6,000 foreign nationals and groups.[24]
- **Item:** Between 1953 and 1973, the CIA opened and photographed nearly 250,000 first-class letters in the United States.
- **Item:** As director of the CIA, William Colby acknowledged to Congress that his organization had opened the mail of private citizens and accumulated secret files on more than 10,000 Americans.[25]
- **Item:** Over the years, the FBI has conducted about 1,500 break-ins of foreign embassies and missions, mob hangouts, and the headquarters of such organizations as the Ku Klux Klan and the American Communist Party. [26]
- **Item:** During the last five years of the Reagan administration, the FBI spied on numerous U.S. citizens and groups that opposed the administration's Central American policies. The groups under surveillance included the Committee in Solidarity with the People of El Salvador, the Southern Christian Leadership Conference (SCLC), the Maryknoll Sisters, and the United Automobile Workers.[27]

These are but a few examples of government abuses against its citizens. To make the point clearer, we will describe in greater detail two nefarious (but representative) government campaigns: (1) the FBI's vendetta against Martin Luther King, Jr., and (2) the FBI's campaign to nullify the effectiveness of the Socialist Workers Party (SWP).

The FBI campaigned to destroy civil rights groups. The most infamous example was the attempt to negate the power of Martin Luther King, Jr. King had been openly critical of the bureau's ineffectual enforcement of civil rights laws. This apparently led the director, J. Edgar Hoover, to label King "the most notorious liar in the U.S." and to launch a vendetta against him.[28] From 1957, when King became prominent in the Montgomery bus boycott, the FBI monitored his activities under its vague authority to investigate subversives. The more powerful King became, the more the FBI pursued him.

King was indexed in the files as a communist; as a result, he was to be imprisoned in the event of a national emergency. This charge against King was based on the allegation that two of his associates in the SCLC were communists.

Because Hoover had convinced Attorney General Robert Kennedy of the possible link between King and the communists, Kennedy authorized wiretaps of King's phones, which continued for the next two years. Kennedy did not know, however, that the FBI planned to use the wiretaps to discredit King.

The FBI's efforts to neutralize or even destroy King were intensified with King's increasing popularity, as exemplified by his "I Have a Dream" speech before 250,000 in Washington, D.C., in August 1963. King was thus characterized in an FBI memo: "He stands head and shoulders over all other Negro leaders put together when it comes to influencing great masses of Negroes. We must mark him now…as the most dangerous Negro of the future of this Nation from the standpoint of Communism, the Negro and national security."[29]

The efforts then escalated to include physical and photographic surveillance and the placement of illegal bugs in King's living quarters. Tapes of conversations in a Washington hotel were used by the FBI to imply that King engaged in extramarital sexual activities. The FBI used these tapes, which may or may not have been altered, to dishonor King. At the very time King was receiving great honors including the Nobel Peace Prize, *Time* magazine's "Man of the Year" award, and numerous honorary degrees, the FBI countered with briefings, distribution of the tapes to newspeople and columnists, and congressional testimony about King's supposed communist activities and questionable private behavior. The FBI even briefed officials of the National Council of Churches and other church bodies about King's alleged deviance. The smear campaign against King reached its zenith when the FBI mailed the tapes to the SCLC offices in Atlanta with a covering letter suggesting that he commit suicide or face humiliation when the tapes were made public on the eve of the Nobel award ceremonies in Sweden.

Summing up the sordid affair, Halperin and his associates editorialized as follows:

> The FBI had turned its arsenal of surveillance and disruption techniques on Martin Luther King and the civil rights movement. It was concerned not with Soviet agents nor with criminal activity, but with the political and personal activities of a man and a movement committed to nonviolence and democracy. King was not the first such target, nor the last. In the end we are all victims, as our political life is distorted and constricted by the FBI, a law enforcement agency now policing politics.[30]

This comment is critical of the FBI and justifiably so. Clearly, the FBI's tactics were illegal, whether King was a communist or not. And that is a moot point because King was not a communist. In testimony before a Senate committee, the FBI's assistant deputy director, James Adams, was asked by Senator Frank Church if the FBI ever found that King was a communist. Replied Adams, "No, we did not."[31]

Another example of an FBI vendetta against a nonexistent threat involved the SWP, a small, peaceful, and legal political group. This party became the target of FBI abuses because it supported Castro's Cuba and worked for racial integration in the South. For these transgressions, the FBI kept the SWP under surveillance for thirty-four years. FBI documents have revealed that, in one 6½-year period in the early 1960s, the agency burglarized the offices of the party in ninety-four raids, often with the complicity of the New York City Police Department. Over this period, FBI agents photographed 8,700 pages of party files and compiled dossiers totaling 8 million pages.[32] The FBI tried to destroy the party by sending anonymous letters to members' employers, by working to keep the party's candidates off the ballot, and by otherwise sabotaging political campaigns. Informants were also used to collect information about the political views of the organization.

Several points need to be made about these FBI activities. Obviously, they were a thorough waste of time and money. As one observer put it, "If they had devoted tens of thousands of man-hours to pursuing true criminals, say those involved in organized crime they might have served the public interest as they were meant to."[33] Most important, the FBI's tactics not only were illegal but were directed at an organization that was working legally *within the system.*

> Just as the FBI's illegal assumption of the authority to investigate subversive activities led to illegal methods, the failure of those methods to produce evidence that could be used to take legal action against radical and liberal political movements led to further lawlessness: achieve efforts to destroy them. In October, 1961, for example, the FBI put into operation its "S.W.P. Disruption Program." The grounds for this program, as a confidential Bureau memorandum described them, were that the Socialist Workers Party had been "openly espousing its line on a local and national basis through running candidates for public office...." The memorandum is astonishingly revealing about the political sophistication of the FBI. If these Socialists were openly espousing their line by running candidates for public office, including the Presidency, these activities weren't illegal. And if their support for the civil-rights movement was subversive, then so was that of many millions of Americans.[34]

Some justice was finally served when the SWP sued the FBI for violation of civil rights. This, too, was accomplished by working legally within the system.

Finally, it is important to recognize that the government's violation of the rights of its citizens was not just an aberration of the Nixon years. For instance, illegal wiretaps were commonplace during the Roosevelt and Truman years. Although bugging declined during the Eisenhower administration, it rose sharply during the Kennedy and Nixon presidencies. And under President Reagan, illegal wiretaps reached an all-time high.[35] This increase can be attributed in part to the Electronic Communication Privacy Act of 1986, which deleted from the federal wiretap law the need for authorization of government surveillance.

Political Prisoners

In 1978, when he was ambassador to the United Nations, Andrew Young commented publicly that the United States was guilty, as were other nations, of having political prisoners. Young's accusation was widely denounced by politicians and editorial writers, many of whom saw such wild statements as reason enough for the ambassador's ouster. Andrew Young, however, was correct. Exactly what is meant by *political prisoner?* The key is that a political prisoner is prosecuted by the criminal justice system because of his or her political activities.[36] McConnell describes this concept:

> Socrates, Charles I and Patty Hearst, despite their widely varied times, circumstances and beliefs, shared the common characteristic that at a certain time in their lives they were placed on trial because of behavior found reprehensible by the political elite of their day, for activities thought highly prejudicial to the welfare of the state, and tried in legal proceedings from which a large political element and an inflamed public opinion could not be severed. And they were tried, moreover, by bodies seeking to foster official values or notions of public policy which the victims repudiated.[37]

Three factors are central to our distinction of political prisoners. First, political repression begins with the assumption that the law serves the interests of those with the power to make and enforce it. The law, therefore, is a tool by which the powerful retain their advantages. They do this by legally punishing those who threaten the status quo.

Second, although political criminals and other criminals may both pose a threat, the former are considered a direct threat to established political power. [38]

> If the members of a ruling elite believe a particular individual or group to be imminently hostile to the prevailing pattern of value distribution, and if they activate the criminal process against him (or them) for that reason, what results is a political trial. Additionally, if members of the ruling elite feel someone seriously intends to alter the way in which the government distributes those values, and if the elite activates the criminal process against them for that reason that, too, constitutes a political trial.[39]

Third, political criminals do not perceive themselves as animals but as people who have violated the law out of a set of convictions to create a better society. Thus, they see the system and its agents as the criminals and the enemy.

Of course, according to our view of political prisoners, acts such as assassination, treason, mutiny, and conspiracy to overthrow the government are examples of dissent by perpetrators who will be punished by the legal system. Throughout U.S. history, groups that were oppressed resorted to various illegitimate means to secure the rights and privileges that they believed were justly theirs. The revolutionary colonists used acts of civil disobedience and finally eight years of war to accomplish their goals. Native Americans have fought the intrusions of white settlers and systematic suppression by the

U.S. government. And other groups, such as farmers, slaveholders, WASP (white Anglo-Saxon Protestant) supremacists, ethnic and racial minorities, and laborers, have at times broken the law in efforts to change what they considered an unfair system. Although these are extremely important, we will concentrate here on the efforts by dissenters during the Vietnam War to change the government's course, as well as the governmental efforts to silence these critics.

The Vietnam War was never formally declared by Congress.[40] It escalated from presidential decisions and commitments that were camouflaged from the public. In effect, the United States had taken a side in an Asian civil war without the consent of the people. Even if this consent had been given, it would have been achieved through the manipulation of events and information by our leaders, as we know now. Because of the uniqueness of our involvement in this war, many young men refused to serve. Some became fugitives from the law by hiding in the United States or by fleeing to other countries. Others accepted imprisonment. Some 20,000 Americans of all ages refused to pay all or part of their taxes because the money would be used to support a war that they considered illegal, immoral, and unjust. As a result, they risked harassment by the Internal Revenue Service and possible imprisonment.

At one demonstration before the Oakland induction center in 1965, one David Miller set fire to his draft card, saying, "I believe the napalming of villages to be an immoral act. I hope this will be a significant political act, so here goes."[41] He was arrested and later sentenced to two and one-half years in prison. This started a rash of similar protests that the establishment considered a threat to its power. At one rally, the Reverend Sloane Coffin, Dr. Benjamin Spock, and two others announced that they would henceforth counsel young men to refuse to serve in the armed forces as long as the Vietnam War continued. They were arrested for conspiracy, convicted, and sentenced to two years' imprisonment for treason.

One of the most infamous political trials of this era involved the Chicago Eight.[42] In 1968, a year of ghetto riots and the assassinations of Martin Luther King, Jr., and Robert Kennedy, Congress passed the Rap Brown Amendment (Brown was chairperson of the Student Nonviolent Coordinating Committee [SNCC] at the time), which nearly outlawed interstate travel by political activists. In the summer of that year, the Democratic National Convention was held in Chicago. Because Hubert Humphrey, a hawk on Vietnam, was the leading nominee, thousands of youths flooded Chicago, bent on protesting the war and venting their anger against what they perceived as an unresponsive political leadership. They protested and the police reacted violently, adding to the volatility of the situation.

Months later, when Richard Nixon took office and John Mitchell became attorney general, the federal government issued indictments against individuals believed to be the leaders of the Chicago riots: David Dellinger,

Rennie Davis, Tom Hayden, Abbie Hoffman, Jerry Rubin, Lee Weiner, John Froines, and Bobby Seale, soon to be known collectively as the Chicago Eight. These persons were charged with conspiracy to cross state lines with intent to cause a riot (violating the Rap Brown law). Together, they represented various kinds of dissent, such as radical pacifism, the New Left, political hippies, academic dissent, and black militance. The case was heard in the U.S. District Court in Chicago, Judge Julius Hoffman presiding.

Many knowledgeable observers, including former Attorney General Ramsey Clark, felt that the trial was a political gesture by the new Nixon administration to demonstrate a no-nonsense policy against dissent. The conspiracy charge made little sense because the actions of the defendants and their constituencies were uncoordinated. Moreover, Bobby Seale, an alleged coconspirator, knew only one of the other defendants.

The Chicago Eight trial was a symbolic showcase for the defendants as well. Because of their disrespect for the system, the defendants refused to accept the traditional role.[43] Instead of allowing the system to keep them quiet while the long judicial process wound down, the defendants acted so that their actions would be headline news. Thus, they continually challenged the judiciary's legitimacy. Sternberg has characterized their rationale as follows:

> The argument that the court is illegitimate rests on the defendants' analysis and condemnation of the existing situation in the United States. They see themselves as political prisoners trapped by a power structure of laws created by societal groups hostile to their interests. The court is both an agent for these groups and institutions most significantly, monopoly, capitalism, racism, colonialism, the military–industrial complex, and incipient fascism, and also an oppressive power group in its own right. Although defendants may vary somewhat in the rank or order of their targets, all are in agreement that the criminal court's allegiances are squarely with the oppressor groups and directly hostile to the powerless classes in American society.[44]

As a result of their disrespectful behavior toward the court, Judge Hoffman found the defendants and their lawyers guilty of 159 contempt citations and sentenced them to jail for terms ranging from sixty-eight days to four years and thirteen days. In addition, each defendant was found guilty of inciting a riot, receiving a sentence of five years in prison and a $5,000 fine. However, all were acquitted of conspiracy. Before the sentences were passed, each defendant was allowed to make a final statement. The speech by Tom Hayden captured the essence of the problem from the perspective of the accused:

> Our intention in coming to Chicago was not to initiate a riot…it was to see to it that certain things, that is, the right of every human being, the right to assemble, the right to protest, can be carried out even where the Government chooses to suspend those rights. It was because we chose to exercise those rights in Chicago…that we are here today.… We would hardly be notorious

characters if they had left us alone in the streets of Chicago last year.... It would have been testimony to our failure as organizers. But instead we became the architects, the master minds, and the geniuses of a conspiracy to overthrow the government. We were invented. We were chosen by the government to serve as scapegoats for all that they wanted to prevent happening in the 1970's.[45]

Daniel Berrigan, himself a political prisoner, has discussed his concern for the direction of the government and the need for dissent.

Indeed it cannot be thought that men and women like ourselves will continue, as though we were automated heroes, to rush for redress from the King of the Blind. The King will have to listen to other voices, over which neither he nor we will indefinitely have control: voices of public violence and chaos. For you cannot set up a court in the Kingdom of the Blind, to condemn those who see; a court presided over by those who would pluck out the eyes of men and call it rehabilitation.[46]

More recently, the sanctuary movement has raised the issue of political prisoners, highlighting the conflict between law and morality. This movement is composed of liberal religious groups that provide shelter, transportation, and other aid to illegal immigrants who have fled to the United States to escape tyranny in their native countries of El Salvador and Guatemala. The U.S. government prosecutes persons who aid these refugees because they disobey the law by harboring an illegal immigrant. These individuals argue that they are simply showing humanitarian concern for the suffering. Moreover, they argue, if they were providing shelter to those fleeing communist countries (e.g., Cuba or Nicaragua), the government would treat them as heroes. But since they give sanctuary to those fleeing governments that are friendly to the United States (but nonetheless repressive), they are treated as criminals. Hence, these individuals are political prisoners.

Official Violence

We do not usually think of government actions as violent. Most often, violence is viewed as injury to persons or property. We make this distinction because the powerful, through the lawmaking process and control of communication, actually define what behavior is violent. In this section, we examine instances of what we have called *official violence*, including overt acts by the government and subtle ways that the system operates to do harm.

Consider, for example, the violence perpetrated against minorities throughout U.S. history according to official government policy. The government supported slavery. The government took land forcibly from the Native Americans and for a time had an official policy to exterminate them. During World War II, Japanese Americans were relocated in detention camps, causing them great losses of property and wealth. The law itself has helped to cause violence against minority groups. Amnesty International, in its study of the death penalty in the United States, concludes:

> There is strong evidence of racial discrimination in the application of the death penalty up to 1967, especially in the southern states. About two thirds of offenders executed there from 1930 to 1967 were black, although they constituted a minority of the population. In some individual states, an even higher proportion of those executed were black. The greatest disparities were in rape cases, in which the death penalty was imposed almost exclusively on blacks, usually in cases involving white victims—405 (or 89 percent) of the 455 prisoners executed for rape after 1930 were black.[47]

This is a historic problem. Former Attorney General Ramsey Clark commented on this disparity in sentencing some twenty years ago: "There can be no rationalization or justification of such clear discrimination. It is outrageous public murder, illuminating our darkest racism."[48] The system also injures when reforms that would adequately house, clothe, feed, and provide medical attention are not instituted. Carmichael and Hamilton describe how this phenomenon does violence to minority members.

> When white terrorists bomb a black church and kill five black children, that is an act of individual racism, widely deplored by most segments of the society. But when in that same city, Birmingham, Alabama, five hundred black babies die each year because of the lack of proper food, shelter and medical facilities, and thousands more are destroyed and maimed physically, emotionally, and intellectually because of conditions of poverty and discrimination in the black community, that is a function of institutional racism.[49]

Of the many forms of official violence, we consider two in some detail: police brutality and the use of citizens as unknowing guinea pigs.

Police Brutality.   What is or is not classified as police brutality depends on one's placement in the hierarchy of power. An act is perceived as violent if it challenges existing arrangements. Thus, what a victimized group may perceive as police brutality is viewed by those in power as the legitimate enforcement of law and order.[50] Police are legally permitted to carry weapons and use them against citizens. This unique power results occasionally in citizens being killed by their law enforcement officers. Five times as many citizens as police are killed in these shoot-outs.[51] Also, the killings appear to be selective by the social characteristics of the victims. For example, research has shown that very few women are killed by police (0.8 percent), whereas a disproportionately large proportion of nonwhite males are killed (49.6 percent of all males killed).[52] Put another way, statistically, the number of shooting deaths of African Americans and Hispanic Americans by police is ten to thirteen times higher per 100,000 population than that of white Americans.[53] These data support the charge of police brutality that is so often heard from minority communities.

The use of deadly force by police varies greatly from community to community. For instance, recent data show that each year more than 2 persons per 100,000 die at the hands of the police in New Orleans, a rate nearly twenty-seven times as high as that in Sacramento, California.[54]

Four of the most publicized instances of police brutality are (1) the Chicago police's treatment of civil rights demonstrators at the 1968 Democratic convention; (2) the Ohio National Guard's firing of sixty-one shots that killed four college students and wounded nine at Kent State University in 1970; (3) the killing of forty-three inmates at Attica Prison in 1971; and (4) the 1991 beating of a black motorist, Rodney King, by Los Angeles area law enforcement officers.

Let's examine the Attica incident. The Attica case is noteworthy because the revolt was a result in part of a raised consciousness among the prisoners that they were in jail for political reasons.[55] They tended to think of themselves as political prisoners and as victims rather than as criminals for two reasons:

1. As members of largely African American or Hispanic ghettos, they were acutely aware of the inequities of society.
2. They were especially aware of the ways the criminal justice system singled them out unfairly.

Many factors caused the inmates' rage, but one was particularly symbolic: The corrections staff did not include one African American or Puerto Rican American. The primary concern of the all-white staff from rural western New York state was that the inmates "knew their place." This typical attitude clashed with the inmates' view that they were victims rather than criminals, which resulted in a rising level of tension as inmates increasingly refused to adhere to the demands of the corrections officers.

Under these conditions, a spontaneous riot occurred after an incident, with 1,281 inmates eventually controlling four cell blocks and forty hostages. Negotiations took place over a four-day period, with the prisoners demanding twenty-eight prison reforms and amnesty for the uprising. Governor Nelson Rockefeller was convinced that the revolt was led by revolutionaries, and he refused to negotiate. As he told the commission investigating the Attica incident:

> One of the most recent and widely used techniques of modern-day revolutionaries has been the taking of political hostages and using the threat to kill them as blackmail to achieve unconditional demands and to gain wide public attention to further their revolutionary ends.... [T]olerated, they pose a serious threat to the ability of free government to preserve order and to protect the se-

curity of the individual citizens. Therefore, I firmly believe that a duly elected official sworn to defend the Constitution and the laws of the state and nation would be betraying his trust to the people he serves if he were to sanction or condone such criminal acts by negotiating under such circumstances.[56]

Thus came the decision to retake the prison by force. The time had come to reassert the sovereignty and power of the state over the rebels. A full-scale assault was launched, and in fifteen minutes the state police had retaken the prison at a cost of thirty-nine dead and eighty wounded, the bloodiest one-day encounter between Americans since the Civil War, with the exception of the American Indian massacres of the late nineteenth century.

Although the charge of police brutality is often made, it is seldom punished. Few of the officers involved in fatal cases of brutality have ever been indicted for murder. Some have been suspended from the force, while others have been tried for lesser crimes (such as justifiable homicide or manslaughter) and then been acquitted or given light sentences.[57]

The Use of Citizens as Guinea Pigs.   Nazi Germany is often cited as a horrible example of a government's disregard for human life. Among the Nazis' crimes was medical experimentation on human subjects. For example, Josef Mengele, the infamous Nazi doctor known as the angel of death, conducted a variety of inhumane experiments using the Auschwitz inmates as subjects. Included in Mengele's so-called medical experiments were sewing together three-year-old twins, back to back, and injecting dye into infants' eyeballs.

The United States has also used unwilling and unknowing subjects in potentially dangerous medical experiments. One case that clearly rivals Nazi Germany for its contempt for the human subjects was conducted by the U.S. Public Health Service. Beginning in 1932, doctors under the auspices of the Public Health Service began observing 400 African American male syphilis patients in Macon County, Alabama. The patients did not know they had syphilis; rather, they were told that they had "bad blood." The purpose of the study was to assess the consequences of not treating the disease. So during the forty years of the experiment the men were not treated; their pain was not even alleviated. When the men's wives contracted syphilis, again, they were not treated. And when their children were born with congenital syphilis, they, too, were not treated.[58]

Also consider this example: From 1946 to 1963, between 250,000 and 300,000 soldiers and civilians were exposed to radiation during 192 nuclear bomb tests. Among the tests conducted by the Army was one that assessed the resultant psychological effects on soldiers who observed an atomic blast four times the size of the bomb dropped on Hiroshima from a distance of two miles. The Army wanted to determine whether soldiers could perform battlefield assignments after being exposed to such an explosion. These exposed soldiers suffered severe, long-term negative effects from this experiment, yet the government has been unwilling to accept blame for the higher than usual incidence of leukemia and cancer. Instead, the government has tried to suppress scientific research findings linking low-level radiation exposure to medical problems. In addition, many of the medical records of the men exposed have mysteriously disappeared.[59] In August 1986, the Veterans Administration deliberately shredded thousands of case records of military personnel who had been exposed to nuclear radiation since the 1940s.[60]

Federal agencies also conducted radiation experiments on human subjects from the mid-1940s until the 1970s. The House Energy and Commerce Subcommittee on Energy Conservation and Power reviewed Department of Energy documents and concluded that U.S. citizens were tested as nuclear calibration devices to measure the biological effects of radioactive material. Some of the participants did so knowingly, but others were unaware of the purpose of the test. A number of experiments were cited in the report.[61]

- **Item:** From 1963 to 1971, x-rays were applied to the testes of 131 inmates at Oregon and Washington state prisons.
- **Item:** Between 1953 to 1957, twelve terminal brain tumor patients at Massachusetts General Hospital, most of them comatose or semicomatose, were injected with uranium.
- **Item:** Radioactive iodine was deliberately released into groundwater seven times from 1963 to 1965 at the Atomic Energy Commission's National Reactor Testing Station in Idaho. Experiments that followed include having seven people drink milk from cows that had grazed on contaminated land and placing people in pastures during radiation release.
- **Item:** In the early 1960s, twenty elderly adults were fed radium or thorium at the Massachusetts Institute of Technology.

In the late 1970s, declassification of government documents revealed that U.S. people had been subjects in 239 open-air bacteriological tests conducted by the Army between 1949 and 1969. The objectives of these tests were to investigate the offensive possibilities of biological warfare, to understand the magnitude of defensing against biological warfare, and to gain data on the behavior of biological agents as they are borne downwind. During one of these tests, San Francisco was blanketed with poisonous bacteria known as *Serratia*, which cause a type of pneumonia that can be fatal. One hospital treated twelve persons for *Serratia* pneumonia, and one victim died.[62]

Finally, in 1994, the Department of Energy revealed that more than fifty separate experiments were done on unknowing subjects between the 1940s and the 1980s. These experiments involved exposure to radiation:

- Ninety-five previously secret nuclear bomb tests took place at a Nevada test site.

- Pregnant women scheduled for therapeutic abortions were injected with radioactive iodine 131 to test the effects of radiation on aborted fetuses.
- In 1946, six laboratory employees were given plutonium-contaminated water to drink to test plutonium absorption.
- As late as the 1980s, subjects were exposed to radioactive isotopes at government weapons laboratories. The extent of consent obtained has not been made public.
- To date the federal government has spent $3.7 million just to learn more about the extent of radiation testing on unknowing human subjects since 1945 and will probably spend a total of $24 million just to document searches on its own experiments.[63]

Another example of the exposure of Americans to potentially dangerous chemicals without their knowledge or consent was the behavioral-control experiments conducted by the government after World War II.[64] For thirty-five years, various government agencies used tens of thousands of individuals to test several mind-control techniques: hypnosis, electronic brain stimulation, aversive and other behavior-modification therapies, and drugs. Many of the subjects in these experiments were volunteers, but many others were not. Throughout U.S. history, one government agency in particular, the CIA, has proved its disregard for the rights of citizens in its quest for national security.

- **Item:** Documents revealed in the 1950s under the Freedom of Information Act show that, during the height of the Cold War, the CIA developed knockout substances and incapacitating agents. The pool of subjects used to develop these compounds consisted of terminal cancer patients, who had no idea that they were being used as guinea pigs.[65]
- **Item:** In 1953, a CIA scientist slipped LSD into the after-dinner drinks of scientists from the Army Chemical Corps. The drug had an especially adverse effect on one of these persons. He experienced psychotic confusion and two days later leapt to his death from a hotel window. The CIA withheld these facts from the victim's family for twenty-two years.[66]
- **Item:** The CIA hired prostitutes in San Francisco to give their customers drugs. The behavior of the victims was then observed through two-way mirrors and heard through hidden microphones.
- **Item:** The CIA administered LSD to borderline underworld "prostitutes, drug addicts, and other small timers who would be powerless to seek any sort of revenge if they ever found out what the CIA had done to them."[67]

> Agents working on the project would randomly choose a victim at a bar or off the street and, with no prior consent or medical pre-screening,

would take the individual back to a safe house and administer the drug. For many of the unsuspecting victims, the result was days or even weeks of hospitalization and mental stress.[68]

- **Item:** In 1996, it was learned that U.S. troops serving in the Persian Gulf in 1991 were exposed to ammunition composed of depleted uranium (DU). In one case, the 144th Army National Guard Service and Supply Company performed battlefield cleanup for three weeks, without protective clothing or knowledge of what they were handling. At least 40,000 DU rounds were fired by U.S. troops in Kuwait. DU is linked to many illnesses, including cancer, birth defects, and so-called Gulf War syndrome. For six years the Pentagon denied that U.S. troop exposure to DU and other dangerous chemicals in the Gulf was in any way related to Gulf War syndrome.[69] However, a 1997 investigation found that the CIA knew in the mid-1980s that Iraqi bunkers (attacked in the 1991 Gulf War by U.S. soldiers) contained stored chemical weapons. The CIA failed to warn military commanders clearly enough to avert possible exposure of U.S. troops. In June 1996, the Pentagon disclosed that several hundred, possibly even thousands, of soldiers may have been exposed to sarin and other toxic agents because Iraqi weapons were blown up in a bunker at Khamisiyah. The Pentagon had denied for five years that any U.S. soldiers had been exposed. The Pentagon claimed that information about the Khamisiyah bunker had been lost.[70]

These examples demonstrate the arrogance of the CIA, a government agency that is willing to victimize some of its citizens to achieve an edge in its battle against U.S. enemies. Some would argue that this behavior, so contrary to life in a free society, is more characteristic of the enemy.

International Crimes

Crimes by the government are not limited to those directed at its citizens. War is an obvious example of one government's willful attempt to harm citizens of another country. Other government acts short of war, including trade embargoes, arms sales, colonial arrangements, and the like, are also harmful to others. In this section, we discuss two other types of crimes perpetrated by the U.S. government against other nations: intervention in domestic affairs and war crimes.

U.S. Intervention in the Domestic Affairs of Other Nations

How would the United States respond if foreigners assassinated the president? What if foreign agents tried to influence the outcome of an election? Or what if a foreign power supported one side in a domestic dispute with money and weapons? Obviously, Americans would not tolerate these attempts by outsiders to affect U.S. domestic affairs. Such acts would be interpreted as imperialistic acts of war. The irony, of course, is that we have and continue to perpetrate such acts on other countries as part of U.S. foreign policy.

The number of clandestine acts of intervention by the U.S. government is legion. Evidence from Senate investigating committees has shown, for example, that, over a twenty-year period, one government agency, the CIA, was involved in more than 900 foreign interventions, including paramilitary operations, surreptitious manipulation of foreign governments, and assassinations.[71] We limit our discussion here to several well-known cases of CIA involvement in foreign assassinations. In 1975, the Senate Select Committee on Intelligence reported on the activities of the CIA over a thirteen-year period. The publication of this report occurred over the objections of President Gerald Ford and CIA Director William Colby. The reason for their fears was obvious: The government was embarrassed for citizens to find out that the CIA was actively involved in assassination plots and coups against foreign governments.[72]

- **Item:** Between 1960 and 1965, the CIA initiated at least eight plots to assassinate Fidel Castro, prime minister of Cuba. The unsuccessful attempts included applying instantly lethal botulinium toxin to a box of Castro's cigars, hiring the Mafia to poison him, and presenting him a gift of a wet suit (for skin diving) treated with a fungus.
- **Item:** In 1975, the Senate Select Committee on Intelligence found strong evidence that CIA officials had planned the assassination of Congolese (Zaire) leader Patrice Lumumba and that President Eisenhower had ordered his death.
- **Item:** The United States was implicated in the assassination of Dominican dictator Rafael Trujillo, South Vietnam's President Ngo Dinh Diem, and General Rene Schneider of Chile.
- **Item:** In 1985, CIA Director William Casey arranged for the assassination of Sheikh Mohammed Hussein Fadlallah, a Lebanese Shiite Muslim leader, in coordination with Saudi Arabian intelligence. During the assassination attempt in Beirut, eighty innocent people were killed when a car bomb exploded.[73]

The CIA's actions are contrary to U.S. principles in fundamental ways. Aside from supporting regimes notorious for their violation of human rights (see Chapter 5), the United States, which based its independence on the people's right to self-determination, is now actively involved in manipulating foreign governments to achieve its own will. The infusion of money in foreign elections, the use of propaganda, assassination attempts, and the like are all contrary to the guiding principle of the Monroe Doctrine, that is, self-determination of peoples, which we invoke readily when other nations intrude in the affairs of state in any Western Hemisphere nation.

War Crimes

War crimes can be interpreted in three ways. According to the first view, crimes in war are illogical, war is hell, anything goes. The only crime, from this position, is to lose. A second view is that war crimes are acts for which the victors punish the losers. The winners denounce the atrocities committed by the enemy while justifying their own conduct. Thus, the Germans and Japanese were tried for war crimes at the conclusion of World War II, but the United States was not, even though it had used atomic bombs to destroy two cities and kill most of their inhabitants. For even if one assumes that the bombing of Hiroshima was necessary to bring an early end to the war (a debatable assumption), the bombing of Nagasaki two days later was clearly an unnecessary waste of life. A third view of war crimes is one that applies a standard of morality to war, applicable to winners and losers alike. The chief U.S. prosecutor at Nuremberg, Robert Jackson, summarizes this interpretation: "If certain acts in violation of treaties are crimes, they are crimes whether the United States does them or whether Germany does them, and we are not prepared to lay down a rule of criminal conduct against others which we would be unwilling to have invoked against us."[74]

We will use this last view in our examination of war crimes. And, in doing so, we will see that throughout history nations, including the United States (examples include the oppression of Native Americans and the 1900 counterinsurgency campaign in the Philippines),[75] have been guilty of war crimes. Since the government, the media, and the schools traditionally remind us of the heinous acts of our enemies throughout history, we will focus on the war crimes perpetrated by the United States, limiting the discussion to the Vietnam experience. The principle we will apply is the definition of war crimes established by the Nuremberg tribunal (Principle VI, b):

> Violations of the laws of customs of war which include, but are not limited to, murder, ill-treatment or deportation to slave-labor or for any other purpose of civilian population of or in occupied territory, murder or ill-treatment of prisoners of war or persons on the seas, killing of hostages, plunder of public or private property, wanton destruction of cities, towns, or villages, or devastation not justified by military necessity.[76]

The Vietnam War provides many examples of U.S. actions in clear violation of this principle.

Indiscriminate Shelling and Bombing of Civilians. The enemy in the Vietnam War, the National Liberation Front, was difficult to fight because it was everywhere. It was often impossible to distinguish allies from enemies. Thus, in strategic terms, the entire geographical area of Vietnam was the enemy. As Roebuck and Weeber have observed, "In order to 'save' Vietnam from Communism, it was therefore necessary to destroy the entire country."[77]

As a result, civilian villages were bombed in the enemy region of North Vietnam and in South Vietnam, as well. The amount of firepower used was unparalleled in history.

> From 315,000 tons of air ordnance dropped in Southeast Asia in 1965, the quantity by January–October, 1969, the peak year of the war, reached 1,388,000 tons. Over that period, 4,580,000 tons were dropped on Southeast Asia, or six and one-half times that employed in Korea. To this we must add ground munitions, which rose from 577,000 tons in 1966 to 1,278,000 tons in the first eleven months of 1969.[78]

Perhaps the most significant (and certainly the most infamous) bomb used by the United States was napalm, a jellylike, inflammable mixture packed into canisters and dropped from aircraft. This mixture of benzene, gasoline, and polystyrene is a highly incendiary fluid that clings. It is an antipersonnel weapon that causes deep and persistent burning.

> Napalm is probably the most horrible anti-personnel weapon ever invented. The point of a weapon in war is to put an enemy out of action, and that is most readily and permanently accomplished by killing him; but civilized nations have tried not to induce more suffering than is necessary to accomplish this end. Napalm, in its means of attack, in its capacity to maim permanently and to induce slow death, is a particularly horrifying weapon. That its use in Vietnam has involved many civilians, peasant families in undefined villages has magnified the horror.[79]

The most infamous incident of the war was the March 1968 massacre at Song My (also known as My Lai). Under orders from their superiors, U.S. soldiers slaughtered more than 500 civilians.[80] The troops had been told to destroy all structures and render the place uninhabitable. They killed every inhabitant, regardless of age or sex, encountering no opposition or hostile behavior. In Operation Cedar Falls, 30,000 U.S. troops were assigned the task of destroying all villages in a forty-square-mile area. In this and other operations, groups of soldiers known as "Zippo squads" burned village after village.

> The intensely cultivated flat lands south of the Vaico Oriental River about 20 miles from Saigon are prime "scorched earth" targets. U.S. paratroopers from the 173rd Airborne Brigade began operating there last weekend. They burned to the ground every hut they saw. Sampans were sunk and bullock carts were smashed. The 173rd laid their base camp among the blackened frames of burned houses. Within two miles of the camp not a house was left standing....

Every house found by the 173rd was burned to the ground. Every cooking utensil was smashed, every banana tree severed, every mattress slashed.... Thousands of ducks and chickens were slaughtered....Dozens of pigs, water buffalo and cows were destroyed. A twenty-mile stretch along the Vaico Oriental was left scorched and barren.[81]

Ecocide.   A variation on the scorched-earth policy just noted was the use of anticrop chemicals. The Air Force sprayed defoliants on 100,000 acres in 1964 and 1,500,000 acres in 1969. Herbicides were used to destroy foliage that hid the enemy, as well as the crops that fed the Vietcong soldiers and their civilian supporters.

Almost 11 million gallons of Agent Orange were sprayed in Vietnam from 1961 to 1970, even though it was one of the most toxic chemicals known.[82] The results of this campaign were devastating in a number of ways.

1. Timber, a major crop in South Vietnam, was destroyed and replaced by bamboo, generally considered a nuisance.
2. The mangroves in swamp lands were killed, negatively affecting shellfish and migratory fish, major sources of protein for the Vietnamese.
3. Vast areas of soil eroded.
4. Toxic substances such as 2,4,5T were ingested by humans and animals, which may lead to birth abnormalities.[83]

Gaston has summarized this catastrophe of U.S. war strategy: "After the end of World War II, and as a result of the Nuremberg trials, we justly condemned the willful destruction of an entire people and its culture, calling this crime against humanity genocide."[84]

In addition to ecocide, U.S. conduct in Vietnam killed a sizable portion of the population. Entire villages of people were killed. Thousands more were killed in bombings. The enormous tragedy of this is seen in data supplied by the Senate Subcommittee on Refugees, which estimated that, from 1965 to 1969, more than 1 million refugees were killed and 2 million were wounded by the U.S. armed services.[85]

In sum, U.S. strategy in the Vietnam civil war served to shatter the whole society, from its ecology to village life and to life itself. Daniel Ellsberg has called this "the violent destruction of a patterned society."

Conclusion

In this chapter, we have catalogued many overt and horrifying forms of political deviance. We also observed the ultimate irony: The United States, a country that takes pride in calling itself a free and open society, has sponsored repressive government organizations that, in the name of national security, operate to make society anything but free and open. Thus, it seems that to protect the national interest means to punish dissent and manipulate foreign governments. Somehow, the FBI, the CIA, and other such agencies have come to believe that it is necessary to break the law in order to protect the system. In so doing, their actions reap the very results that they wish to abolish. Supreme Court Justice Louis Brandeis has summarized this, saying, "For to break some laws in order to enforce other laws is not to fight anarchy and terrorism but to create them."[86] Harris concurs:

> In a government of laws, existence of the government will be imperiled if it fails to observe the law scrupulously.... Our government is the potent, the omnipresent teacher. For good or for ill, it teaches the whole people by its example. Crime is contagious. If the government becomes a lawbreaker, it breeds contempt for the law; it invites every man to become a law unto himself; it invites anarchy. To declare that in the administration of the criminal law the end justifies the means, to declare that the government may commit crimes in order to secure the conviction of a private criminal would bring terrible retribution.[87]

Critical Thinking Exercise 7.1:
The CIA's Higher Immorality

This chapter is largely about the abuses committed by the CIA since its inception in 1947.[88] Among the abuses documented here are the following:

1. *Immorality of covert actions and a lack of oversight of covert operations.* CIA officials have failed to tell their own boss, the director of central intelligence (DCI), the truth. The DCI found that plans for covert action were rarely scrutinized formally and their approval was given informally. CIA misdeeds have been supported by Congress, which has neglected oversight responsibilities.
2. *Reckless excesses.* The CIA's past attempt to humiliate Castro "by trying to get his beard to fall off—is something that only someone whose level of maturity had not advanced beyond kindergarten could have dreamed up." The CIA "is also secretive—sometimes foolishly so.... Even newspaper clippings have been stamped 'secret.'"[89]
3. *Deviance by CIA agents.* One common form of fraud is when CIA personnel claim that they have paid a local agent and actually have kept the money for themselves.
4. *Corrupt personnel.* New recruits are sought for their character and loyalty, yet recruits are asked to spend their lives in false identities.
5. *Perversion of democratic principles.* The CIA has sabotaged the democratic processes of other countries, sometimes by overthrowing legally and

democratically elected leaders, sometimes by outright assassination, including (at times) hiring organized crime figures to engage in such work.
6. *Illegal domestic spying.* The CIA has opened the mail of U.S. citizens going to or coming from communist nations.
7. *Experimenting with LSD without subjects' consent.* Such experiments resulted in at least one suicide.
8. *Illegal investigative methods.* Wiretapping the telephones of newsmen to learn about their sources and conducting illegal break-ins and installing wiretaps while investigating CIA employees have been carried out.
9. *Laundering of money.* The CIA has laundered its money at the Nugan Hand Bank, the Bank of Credit and Commerce International (BCCI), and various S&Ls, sometimes in cooperation with organized crime (see Chapter 2).

Are these deviant practices something that is merely an outgrowth of Cold War necessities, or are they built into the structure of the CIA and its organizational culture? To answer this question, go to Infotrack II or another online data-based site, and read stories about the CIA's scandals since the Cold War's end (1989).[90] Does the CIA continue to suffer scandals like those mentioned above? If so, do the scandals in question fit into any of the above categories? Are there any deviant acts committed by the CIA since 1990 that do not fall into these categories? What do you think is causing the CIA's deviance in the post–Cold War era?

Endnotes

1. For other sources emphasizing government deviance, consult the following: Julian Roebuck and Stanley C. Weeber, *Political Crime in the United States: Analyzing Crime by and against Government* (New York: Praeger, 1978); Alan Wolfe, *The Seamy Side of Democracy: Repression in America,* 2nd ed. (New York: Longman 1978); David Wise, *The American Police State: The Government against the People* (New York: Vintage, 1978); Charles E. Reasons, *The Criminologist: Crime and the Criminal* (Pacific Palisades, CA: Goodyear, 1974); Amitai Etzioni, *Capital Corruption* (New York: Harcourt, Brace, Jovanovich, 1984); James W. Coleman, *The Criminal Elite,* 3rd ed. (New York: St. Martin's Press, 1993); and Michael Parenti, *The Sword and the Dollar: Imperialism, Revolution, and the Arms Race* (New York: St. Martin's Press, 1989).
2. The discussion here is limited to the federal government, especially the executive branch. However, attempts to deceive the public are found at all levels of government. For examples of cover-ups, secrecy, and the like at other levels, see Seymour M. Hersh, *Cover-up* (New York: Random House, 1972); Peter K. Manning, "The Police: Mandate, Strategies, and Appearances," in *Criminal Justice in America: A Critical Understanding,* ed. Richard Quinney (Boston: Little, Brown, 1974), 170–200; Mike Royko, *Boss: Richard J. Daley of Chicago* (New York: E.P. Dutton, 1971); and Joel Henderson and David R. Simon, *Crimes of the Criminal Justice System* (Cincinnati, OH: Anderson, 1994).
3. Norman Dorsen and John H. F. Shattuck, "Executive Privilege: The President Won't Tell," in *None of Your Business: Government Secrecy in America,* ed. Norman Dorsen and Stephen Gillers (New York: Viking, 1974), 27–60.

4. Cited in Paul N. McCloskey, Jr., *Truth and Untruth: Political Deceit in America* (New York: Simon & Schuster, 1972), 54.

5. Ibid.

6. Michael Parenti, *Democracy for the Few*, 3rd ed. (New York: St. Martin's Press, 1980), 157.

7. Anthony Lewis, "Introduction," in *None of Your Business: Government Secrecy in America*, ed. Dorsen and Gillers, 3–24.

8. The examples in this section are taken from David Wise, *The Politics of Lying: Government Deception, Secrecy, and Power* (New York: Random House Vintage Books, 1973).

9. See also "The 'Phantom Battle' That Led to War," *U.S. News & World Report* 23, July 1984, 56–67.

10. Walter Schneir and Miriam Schneir, "How the Military Cooked the Books," *The Nation*, May 12, 1984, 570–76.

11. David Corn, "The Same Old Dirty Tricks," *The Nation*, August 27, 1988, 158.

12. The following examples are taken from John Walcott and Brian Duffy, "The CIA's Darkest Secrets," *U.S. News & World Report*, July 4, 1994, 34–47. That a conservative magazine such as this one blew the whistle on the CIA is a good indication that the agency has finally fallen into the disrepute its critics have warned of for the last thirty years.

13. Thomas L. Emerson, "The Danger of State Secrecy," *The Nation*, March 30, 1974, 395–99. See also Arthur S. Miller, "Watergate and Beyond: The Issue of Secrecy," *The Progressive* 37, December 1973, 15–19.

14. Itzhak Galnoor, "The Politics of Public Information," *Society* 16, May/June 1979, 20–30.

15. Wise, *The American Police State*, 40.

16. Gary Webb, "America's 'Crack' Plague Has Roots in Nicaragua War," *San Jose Mercury News*, August 18, 1996, A-1.

17. See *The Nation*, October 21, 1996, 4.

18. Peter Kornbluh, "Special to the *Baltimore Sun*," November 18, 1996.

19. Peter Phillips and Project Censored, *Censored 2000: The Year's Top 25 Censored Stories* (New York: Seven Stories), 108.

20. See David R. Simon with Joel Henderson, *Private Troubles and Public Issues: Social Problems in the Postmodern Era* (Houston, TX: Harcourt Brace, 1997), 15–16.

21. For a history of the government's monitoring of its citizens, see Alan Wolfe, "Political Repression and the Liberal Democratic State," *Monthly Review* 23, December 1971, 18–38; Donald B. Davis, "Internal Security in Historical Perspective: From the Revolution to World War II," in *Surveillance and Espionage in a Free Society*, ed. Richard H. Blum (New York: Praeger, 1972), 3–19; "It's Official: Government Snooping Has Been Going On for 50 Years," Intelligence Activities and the Rights of Americans: *Book 11*, Report 94–755, April 26, 1976, 1,120, in *Corporate and Governmental Deviance*, ed. M. David Ermann and Richard J. Lundman (New York: Oxford University Press, 1978), 151–73.

22. This brief history of the FBI is taken from Richard Harris, "Crime in the FBI," *The New Yorker*, August 8, 1977, 30–42.

23. T. R. Young, *Political Surveillance, Inequality and the Democratic State* (Red Feather, CO: Red Feather Institute, September 1981), 1.

24. "Project Minaret," *Newsweek*, November 10, 1975, 31–32.

25. U.S. Senate, Select Committee to Study Governmental Operations with Respect to Intelligence Activities, Intelligence Activities, *Book 11*, 156. See also "Who's Chipping Away at Your Privacy," *U.S. News & World Report*, March 31, 1975, 18.

26. "The FBI's 'Black-Bag Boys,'" *Newsweek*, July 28, 1975, 18, 21.

27. See "G-Men at It Again," *The Progressive* 52, March 1988, 9; "Events the FBI Watched," *First Principles* 13, February/March 1988, 3; and Philip Shenon, "FBI Papers Show Wide Surveillance of Reagan Critics," *New York Times*, January 28, 1988, A-1, A-8.

28. The following account is taken from several sources: Morton H. Halperin et al., *The Lawless State: The Crimes of the U.S. Intelligence Agencies* (New York: Penguin, 1976), 61–89;

"The Truth about Hoover," Time, December 22, 1975, 14–21; and "Tales of the FBI" and "The Crusade to Topple King," *Time*, December 1, 1975, 11–12.

29. U.S. Senate, Final Report of the Select Committee to Study Governmental Operations with Respect to Intelligence Activities, "Dr. Martin Luther King, Jr., Case Study," in *Intelligence Activities and the Rights of Americans: Book 111* (Washington, DC: U.S. Government Printing Office, 1976), 107–98; (cited in Halperin et al., 78).

30. Halperin et al., 89.

31. Quoted in "The Crusade to Topple King," 11.

32. The evidence presented on the FBI's campaign against the SWP is taken from Harris; Associated Press release, March 29, 1976; and "Monitoring Repression," *The Progressive* 41, January 1977, 7.

33. Harris, 40.

34. Ibid.

35. Ronald J. Ostrow, "Electronic Surveillance Hits New Highs in War on Crime," *Los Angeles Times,* December 18, 1983, 1–4.

36. Charles Goodell, *Political Prisoners in America* (New York: Random House, 1973), 3–13.

37. W. H. McConnell, "Political Trials East and West," in *The Sociology of Law: A Conflict Perspective,* ed. Charles E. Reasons and Robert M. Rich (Toronto: Butterworth, 1978), 333.

38. We will consider political crimes only in the narrow sense of crimes against the establishment. We are sympathetic, however, with the view expressed by Alexander Liazos:

"Only now are we beginning to realize that most prisoners are political prisoners—that their criminal actions (whether against individuals, such as robbing, or conscious political acts against the state) result largely from current social and political conditions, and not the work of 'disturbed' and 'psychotic' personalities" (p. 108).

In this view, then, all prisoners are political in the sense that they became criminals as a result of struggling against the inequities of society. See Alexander Liazos, "The Poverty of the Sociology of Deviance: Nuts, Sluts, and Perverts," *Social Problems* 20, Summer 1972.

39. Theodore Becker (ed.), *Political Trials* (Indianapolis, IN: Bobbs-Merrill, 1971), xi–xii.

40. Much of this account is based on Goodell, 126–59.

41. Quoted in ibid.130.

42. The following account is based primarily on David J. Danelski "The Chicago Conspiracy Trial," in *Political Trials,* ed. Theodore Becker (Indianapolis, IN: Bobbs-Merrill, 1971), 134–35. We have used this case as representative of many others from the same time period. For other illustrations of the existence of political trials and political prisoners, see the following trial accounts: for the vendetta against the Black Panthers, Tom Hayden, *Trial* (New York: Holt, Rinehart and Winston, 1970); the trials of the Berrigans, Daniel Berrigan, *The Trial of the Catonsville Nine* (Boston: Beacon Press, 1970); and the trial of the Wilmington 10, Jack Anderson, "U.S. Is Cited for Human Rights Violations," *Rocky Mountain News,* December 11, 1978, 61. For general statements on political criminals, see Judith Frutig, "Political Trials: What Impact on America?" *Christian Science Monitor,* August 27, 1976, 16–17; Goodell; and Becker.

43. See David Sternberg, "The New Radical–Criminal Trials: A Step Toward a Class-for-Itself in the American Proletariat?" cited in Quinney, 274–94.

44. Sternberg, 281.

45. Quoted in Danelski, 177.

46. Berrigan, x–xii.

47. Amnesty International, *United States of America: The Death Penalty* (London: Amnesty International Publications, 1987), 10–11.

48. Ramsey Clark, *Crime in America: Observations on Its Nature, Causes, Prevention and Control* (New York: Simon & Schuster, 1970), 335.

49. Stokely Carmichael and Charles V. Hamilton, *Black Power: The Politics of Liberation in America* (New York: Random House, 1967), 4.

50. See Jerome Skolnick, *The Politics of Protest* (New York: Ballantine Books, 1969), 3–8.

51. Arthur L. Kobler, "Police Homicide in a Democracy," *Journal of Social Issues* 31, Winter 1975, 163–84.

52. U.S. Public Health Service data, quoted in ibid., 164.

53. Paul T. Takagi, "Abuse of Authority Is a Very Explosive Situation," *U.S. News & World Report,* August 27, 1979, 29.

54. Reported in David A. Wiessler, "When Police Officers Use Deadly Force," *U.S. News & World Report,* January 10, 1983, 59.

55. The following is taken from the New York State Special Commission on Attica, *Attica, The Official Report* (New York: Bantam, 1972), excerpted in *Official Deviance,* ed. Jack D. Douglas and John M. Johnson (Philadelphia: Lippincott, 1977), 186–94.

56. Quoted in New York State Special Commission on Attica, 193.

57. Michael Parenti, *Democracy for the Few,* 4th ed. (New York: St. Martin's Press, 1983), 154.

58. J. H. Jones, *Bad Blood* (New York: Free Press, 1981).

59. H. L. Rosenberg, "The Guinea Pigs at Camp Desert Rock," *The Progressive* 40, June 1976, 37–43.

60. "Project Censored," *Editor and Publisher* 120, June 13, 1987, 20.

61. Reported in Jill Lawrence, "Americans Served as Guinea Pigs for Radiation Testing," *Fort Collins Coloradoan,* October 25, 1986, A-10.

62. Norman Cousins, "How the U.S. Used Its Citizens as Guinea Pigs," *Saturday Review,* November 10, 1979, 10. See also United Press International release, December 4, 1979.

63. See *San Francisco Chronicle,* June 28, 1994, A-4; and *New York Times,* June 28, 1994, A-6.

64. See W. H. Bowart, *Operation Mind Control: Our Government's War against Its Own People* (New York: Dell, 1978); and John Marks, "Sex, Drugs, and the CIA," *Saturday Review,* February 3, 1979, 12–16.

65. M. A. Lee, "CIA: Carcinogen," *The Nation,* June 5, 1982, 675.

66. Bowart, 87–91.

67. Marks, 12–16.

68. Halperin et al., 52.

69. B. Messler, "Pentagon Poison: The Great Radioactive Cover-up," *In These Times,* May 26, 1997, 17; and Peter Phillips and Project Censored, *Project Censored, 1997* (New York: Seven Stories, 1997), 47–51.

70. Art Pine, "CIA Knew of Chemical Weapons in Iraq Bunker Military," *Los Angeles Times,* April 10, 1997, A-1.

71. Roebuck and Weeber, 82.

72. The following list is taken from "CIA Murder Plots Weighing the Damage to U.S.," *U.S. News & World Report,* December 1, 1975, 13–15; and "The CIA's Hit List," *Newsweek,* December 1, 1975, 28–32.

73. Haynes Johnson, "Casey Circumvented the CIA in '85 Assassination Attempt," *Washington Post,* September 26, 1987, A-1. For other examples, see David Corn, "The Same Old Dirty Tricks," *The Nation,* August 27, 1988, 158.

74. Quoted in *War Crimes and the American Conscience,* ed. Erwin Knoll and Judith Nies McFadden, (New York: Holt, Rinehart and Winston, 1970), 1.

75. For information regarding U.S. treatment of Native Americans, see Bruce Johansen and Roberto Maestas, *Wasi'chu: The Continuing Indian Wars* (New York: Monthly Review Press, 1979); and Dee Brown, *Bury My Heart at Wounded Knee: An Indian History of the American West* (New York: Bantam, 1972). For information regarding U.S. involvement in the Philippines, see Stuart C. Miller, "Our My Lai of 1900: Americans in the Philippine Insurrection," *Trans-action* 7, September 1970, 19–28; and Telford Taylor, *Nuremberg and Vietnam: An American Tragedy* (New York: Bantam, 1971), 173–74.

76. Cited in Knoll and McFadden, 193. See also William Thomas Mallison, "Political Crimes in the International Law of War: Concepts and Consequences," in *Crime and the Inter-*

national Scene: An Inter-American Focus, ed. Freda Adler and G. O. W. Mueller (San Juan, Puerto Rico: North-South Center Press, 1972), 96–107.

77. Roebuck and Weeber, 70.

78. Gabriel Kolko, quoted in Knoll and McFadden, 57.

79. George Wald, in Knoll and McFadden, 73.

80. See Taylor, 122–53; and Richard A. Falk, "Song My: War Crimes and Individual Responsibility," *Trans-action,* January 1970, 33–40.

81. Associated Press release, quoted in Edward S. Herman, *Atrocities in Vietnam: Myths and Realities* (Philadelphia: Pilgrim Press, 1970), 84.

82. Arthur W. Gaston, quoted in Knoll and McFadden, 69–72.

83. See Dennis Bell, "Agent Orange Health Hazards Known Years before Viet Use," *Denver Post,* February 3, 1985, 8-A; and Carolyn Pesce, "Vets Put Agent Orange on Trial," *USA Today,* May 7, 1984, 3-A.

84. Knoll and McFadden, 71.

85. Quoted in ibid., 82.

86. Harris, 35.

87. Ibid.

88. Brian Francis Redman, "Mother Earth," http://www.connix.com/~harry/cia-kess.htm.

89. Ronald Kessler, *Inside the CIA* (New York: Simon & Schuster, 1992).

90. See, for example, R. W. Baker, "CIA: Out of Control," *Village Voice,* September 10, 1991 for one analysis of the CIA's recent abuses.

8

Understanding Elite Deviance

Why Elite Deviance?

- **Item:** On October 23, 1989, Charles and Carol Stuart were on their way home from a Boston hospital childbirth class. When Charles pulled the car over, allegedly to check some problem, he pulled a gun on his wife (who was eight months, pregnant) and shot her at point-blank range. Initially, Stuart told police his wife had been killed by a black gunman. Two months later, Charles confessed that he shot his wife because he stood to collect hundreds of thousands of dollars in life insurance, with which he could realize his American Dream of owning a restaurant.[1]
- **Item:** In 1987, a poll was taken of 200,000 college freshmen by the American Council on Education. Of those polled, 76 percent said that it was very important to be financially well-off. Twenty years earlier, only 44 percent of freshmen held such materialistic views. In 1976, 83 percent of respondents felt it important to develop a philosophy of life. In 1987, only 39 percent of students expressed such a wish. A 1990 report by the Carnegie Foundation for the Advancement of Teaching complained of a breakdown of civility on the nation's college campuses. Especially alarming was an epidemic of cheating by students, racial attacks, hate crimes, and rapes on campus. Studies at the University of Tennessee and Indiana University found a majority of students at each campus admitted to submitting papers that were written by others or copying large sections of friends' papers.[2]
- **Item:** Elite universities, including Stanford, Harvard, MIT, Cal Tech, and others, have all recently had scandals involving the unlawful expenditure of research funds. Some of the illegal purchases included country club memberships, yachts, going-away parties for administrators, and flowers.

The problem that runs through these examples has many names: "social breakdown,"[3] "social disintegration," the rise of "the morally loose individual,"[4] instrumental and expressive "wilding," and the "ethical crisis of Western civilization."[5] Whatever one chooses to call it, the problem of moral decline is a major cause of elite deviance as well as many other types of deviant behavior.

Elite Deviance and the Sociological Imagination: A Paradigm for Analysis[6]

We began our discussion of elite deviance with a look at the power structure of American society. The power elite model was developed by C. Wright Mills in the 1950s.[7] As our examination reveals, a great deal of evidence exists to support this notion of interrelated corporate, media, political, and military elites. Further, in Chapter 2, we explored the existence of the so-called higher immorality, that set of deviant practices that Mills claimed goes on in elite circles. Again, our examination demonstrated case after case of the higher immorality that has taken place since Mills wrote in the 1950s. We have also noted how the nature of the higher immorality has changed, with scandal now an institutionalized phenomenon within the executive office of the president, Congress, and the National Security State's intelligence apparatus. What remains is to account for the theoretical causes of elite deviance.

Again, we turn to one of Mills's conceptions, the sociological imagination.[8] The sociological imagination is a paradigm, a model for looking at social reality, in this case social problems such as elite deviance. Paradigmatic models can be used to develop a number of scientific theories. "What is important," Mills notes, "is the fact that neither the correctness nor the inaccuracy of any of the specific theories necessarily confirms or upsets the usefulness of the adequacy of the models. The models can be used for the construction of many theories."[9]

Thus in this chapter we will first lay out the paradigm for constructing a theory of elite deviance and then proceed to make various theoretical statements derived from the model.

The paradigm raises questions regarding three levels of social analysis. These include:

1. *The macro level of analysis.* Here we explain how the institutional structures and the cultural values the of a given society contribute to elite deviance.
2. *The immediate milieux.* Here we must explain how the immediate environment of everyday life, especially the structure and characteristics of the bureaucratic organizations in which people work, contribute to the planning and commission of acts of elite deviance.

3. *The individual level.* Here we must explain how individual personality characteristics of elites and those in their employ figure in the planning and commission of acts of elite deviance. Specifically, how do issues of character structure and alienation contribute to the commission of elite deviance?

We begin with an analysis of macro-level concerns, specifically values and institutional structures.

Elite Deviance and American Values: The American Dream

Messner and Rosenfeld[10] argue that the causes of crime lie within the same values and behaviors that are usually viewed as part of the American version of success. The American Dream is defined as a "broad cultural ethos that entails a commitment to the goal of material success, to be pursued by everyone in society, under conditions of open individual competition." The power of the American Dream comes from the widely shared values that it includes:

1. *An achievement orientation:* This includes pressure to "make something" of oneself, to set goals and achieve them. Achieving material success is one way personal worth is measured in America.[11] While this is a shaky basis for self-esteem, it is nevertheless true that Americans view their personal worth much like a stock, one that rises or falls with the realization of moneymaking.
2. *Individualism:* This refers to the notion that Americans possess not only autonomy but also basic individual rights. Americans make individualistic decisions regarding marriage and career choices, religion, political outlook, and probably thousands of other issues. The result is that individualism and achievement combine to produce anomie because fellow Americans often become rivals and competitors for rewards and status. Intense personal competition increases pressure to succeed. Often this means that rules about the means by which success is obtained are disregarded when they threaten to interfere with personal goals. The case of Charles Stuart, described above, offers an extreme example of anomie and the American Dream.
3. *Universalism:* This includes the idea that the American Dream is open to all. Universalism means that the chances of success and failure are possibilities that are open to everyone. Fear of failure is intense in America and increases pressure to abandon conformity to rules governing proper conduct in favor of expedience.
4. *The "fetishism" of money:* Money has attained an almost sacred quality in American life. It is the way Americans keep score in the game of success, and, as noted, there are no rules that tell us when enough is enough. What

is stressed in the American Dream is ends over means. As Elliott Currie[12] notes in his discussion of a market society, the pursuit of private gain has become the organizing principle for all of social life. Charles Derber[13] argues that, during the Reagan–Bush era, increasing inequality, along with an ethic of "greed is good," combined to give the American character an element of narcissism. Narcissism is a personality disorder, a mental illness, characterized by distorted self-love and, most important, selfishness coupled with a lack of guilt. The Reagan–Bush ideology of self-reliance stimulated large numbers of upper-world crooks to engage in a quest for power, status, and attention in a "money culture." The result was an unrestrained quest for personal gain.

Sociologist Robert Merton pointed out more than a half century ago that the great contradiction of American culture concerned its stress on winning and success but a lack of opportunity to achieve such success. A portion of this contradiction is due to what sociologist Emile Durkheim[14] described as anomie, a social situation in which norms are unclear. Success in America has no official limits; the private accumulation of wealth is without "a final stopping point."[15] No matter what their income level, most Americans want about 50 percent more money (which, of course, becomes 50 percent more once it is achieved).

Achieving success via force and fraud has always been considered smart, so smart that for a number of decades our culture has lionized gangsters. Beginning with Al Capone, we have come to admire Mafia dons who do not hesitate to take shortcuts to success. Thus *People Magazine*'s 1989 cover story on Gambino family godfather John Gotti pictured the don as so tough that he could punch his way through a cement block. A multimillionaire, with plenty of charisma, *People* noted, Gotti is also a loyal family man, who has never cheated on his wife. The fact that he personally has murdered a number of rivals is talked of as largely an occupational requirement.

Merton[16] also noted that crime "is a very common phenomenon" among all social classes in the United States. A study of 1,700 middle-class New Yorkers in 1947 indicated that 99 percent of them admitted to committing crimes violating one of New York's forty-nine criminal offenses, for which they could have been imprisoned for at least a year. Moreover, 64 percent of the men and 29 percent of the women reported committing felonies. A 1991 survey by Patterson and Kim also showed a high percentage of Americans engaging in criminal behavior (summarized in Chapter 1). Thus, one of the myths about crime is that America is divided into two populations, one law-abiding, the other criminal.

Social critic James Adams,[17] who coined the term "the American Dream," once remarked that many people coming to America's shores were relatively law-abiding before they arrived here. People "were made lawless by America, rather than America being made lawless by them." It has been

American elites who have served as role models (examples) to ordinary people. Thus elite deviance provides an excuse for nonelites to engage in crime without feeling guilty. Elite deviance also sends the message that it is stupid not to commit crime if one has the opportunity. Many a drug dealer and street gang member have remarked that they are just doing what the Rockefellers, Carnegies, and other robber barons did in the nineteenth century—establishing monopolies.

Aside from the values associated with the American Dream, elite deviance is also related to the social structure of American society.

Social Structure: The Dominance of Elite Institutions

The *structure* of American society is that of a mass society. A *mass society* is characterized by a capitalistic economy dominated by huge multinational corporations. Corporate elites (owners and managers) frequently take temporary positions in government and its military establishment. In the United States, the economic institution has always taken precedence over other institutions in American life. This has immense implications for the nature of America's social problems.

America is the only nation in the history of the world whose founding creed involved the inalienable right to pursue happiness. The American concept of happiness has always involved the unlimited accumulation of profit and property, and the goal of making money has been widely accepted as the definition of happiness and success, a central feature of what is called the American Dream.

So important has the goal of accumulating wealth, of achieving the American Dream, become that profit in America has frequently taken place without the restraints placed on capitalist economies in other nations. In the United States, attempts to regulate the excesses of business have been criticized as government interference, or "socialism."

Second, other institutions in American life have had to accommodate the needs of business. Thus, most people go to college, not because they are fascinated by learning but because it leads to a middle-class occupation afterwards. America has always been the most anti-intellectual nation in the Western world—precisely because its primary definition of success involved making money. Thus colleges and universities offer evening and weekend programs, many of them in business, because people's jobs take precedence over the needs of educational and other institutions. The requirements of work also take precedence over the needs of family life. The United States remains the only advanced industrial democracy without paid family leave, without national health care, without an extended family vacation policy precisely because the needs of business are given precedence over everything else in the American institutional order. Moreover, despite all the political rhetoric about the importance of the American family, it is nearly impossible to support a family in this country if parents are unemployed.

Government, too, has historically been subservient to the needs of business. Now that the government is a central part of the economy, the primary responsibility of modern government is not to provide for the needs of its citizens but to ensure economic growth. Much of American foreign and defense policies are about protecting the holdings of multinational corporations, not ensuring that human rights and democracy are encouraged in other nations. As discussed in Chapter 5, the United States has a long history of supporting oppressive regimes that are friendly to American business interests. Moreover, American government at all levels grants generous subsidies, tax breaks, loans and loan guarantees as well as government contracts to American businesses in the hope of stimulating economic growth. This is one reason that American federal government has spent more than $4 trillion on defense since 1947, much of it on expensive weapons systems. For all these reasons it is now more appropriate to speak of a political economy in which political and economic activities have become interrelated in a myriad of ways.

Likewise, elite deviance often requires the explicit coordination of a number of bureaucratic institutions in order to be planned and executed yet remain undetected and unpunished. Thus, in the Farben case the Nazi government participated in selling slave labor to a chemical firm for the purpose of building synthetic chemical plants. Similarly, throughout this book, we have cited numerous additional examples, illustrating how elite deviance involved interorganizational cooperation.

- **Item:** For years, government and business groups have employed organized crime to perform illegal and unethical acts. In the early 1960s, the Central Intelligence Agency (CIA) hired Mafia members to assassinate Fidel Castro. Mafia-generated drug money is routinely laundered through banks in Miami, often with the bankers' full knowledge.[18]
- **Item:** In Chapter 5, we described the cozy relationship between Pentagon employees and defense industry consultants. Promises of positions in the defense industry for retiring Pentagon employees sometimes resulted in providing insider information to defense contractors.
- **Item:** In Chapter 2, we described further episodes of Mafia–CIA ties in money laundering through a variety of savings and loans. In Chapter 7, we noted the possible ties between CIA and Mafia personnel in execution and cover-up of the assassination of President John F. Kennedy. In Chapter 9, we explore more fully the implications and history of this so-called secret government.[19]

These examples show that elite deviance often involves links between business, government, and, at times, other institutions, such as organized crime syndicates. And because of these interorganizational ties, elite deviance has a great chance of going undetected and unpunished (or at least lightly punished). As we have discussed, economic elites regularly participate in political processes involving candidate selection, monetary contributions to candidates and parties, and lobbying. This means that elites have great influence over the content and character of the law. As a result, many acts that might otherwise become crimes are prevented from becoming illegal in the first place. Thus, Hoffman-LaRoche, a drug company, successfully kept amphetamines out of federal control by paying a Washington law firm three times the amount of the annual budget of the Senate subcommittee seeking legislation for tighter controls. Moreover, when elite deviance is made illegal, it is often treated quite differently from nonelite deviance. For instance, a number of the environmental protection laws require corporations to monitor the pollution levels at their own factories. Other laws only address breaking regulations per se, and what happens as a result of the infraction is ignored. For example, in England, a company was found to be responsible for an accident that resulted in the deaths of five workers. The firm was prosecuted for not properly maintaining or inspecting the equipment; it was not charged with the deaths of the workers. Such laws focus on intention in order to substantiate guilt, which makes it virtually impossible to prove fault in the case of worker injury or fatality.[20] Under these circumstances, it is little wonder that many acts of elite deviance constitute violations of civil or administrative law rather than criminal law. Moreover, the penalties for such violations, barring a serious public outcry or a request by elites themselves for government regulation, tend to remain relatively lenient.

Other institutions in American life have been penetrated by the language, ethics, and requirements of American business. Terms such as "bottom line" and "cash flow" have become part of everyday language. Many politicians believe the way to solve the problems of government is to run government like a business. Thus, in 1992 Ross Perot ran for president promising to bring the principles that had made him a billionaire businessman to bear on governmental problems. Moreover, many individuals from the private sector are appointed to cabinet-level positions in America.

The causal links between the macro-level variables of the American Dream and institutional dominance by the political economy are depicted in Figure 8.1. Two possible hypotheses related to the sociological imagination paradigm follow from this macro-level theory:

1. Rates of elite and nonelite deviance are not constant. They wax and wane in response to changes in the American value system and changing institutional conditions. Thus both elite and nonelite deviance will be higher in those historical periods when there is more emphasis placed on the values associated with the American Dream than in periods when the culture emphasizes values such as community, teamwork, and spirituality.

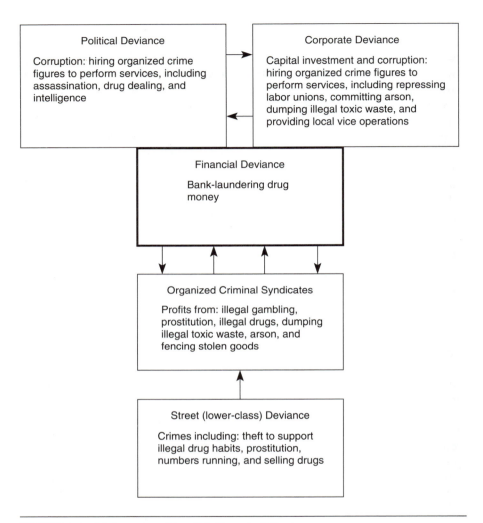

FIGURE 8-1   *Links among Tangible Forms of Deviance*

2. Likewise, now that the government has become a central part of the economy, and that the ethics of business now dominate governmental institutions, both corporate crime and political scandals will occur at the same time and frequently be interrelated.

Rates of deviance are influenced not only by macro considerations but by organizational considerations as well.

Characteristics of Bureaucratic Structures

We agree with Braithwaite and others that elite deviance is explained by examining the nature of the actors' roles within an organization, as well as the bureaucratic structures (characteristics) that shape such roles.[21] Bureaucracy, as a form of social organization, possesses certain structural characteristics that account for both its amoral ethical nature and potential to generate acts of great harm.

Modern bureaucracies are characterized by several things, including these qualities: (1) centralization of authority, (2) creation of specialized vocabularies and ideologies, and (3) fragmentation and routinization of tasks. Each of these characteristics in turn often produces a number of social and psychological processes, all of which help create the environment for elite deviance.

Centralization of Authority

Obedience to elite authority is of central importance to the study of organizations and the deviance they commit. Orders, decisions, and plans that are unethical or illegal are often carried out by underlings, in part because they feel they have no choice; they feel powerless to disobey, regardless of the intent of the order. Examples of such cases are numerous and include the massacre at My Lai, Watergate, and the General Electric price-fixing case of 1961.

Surprisingly, those who seem most powerless include both those "far removed from the centers of power and...those relatively close."[22] Thus, while such perceived powerlessness is usually characteristic of the lower-middle and lower classes, Kelman found a striking degree of such conformity among high-level military officers and bureaucratic functionaries, as well. Kanter and Kanter and Stein have discussed the existence of widespread feelings of powerlessness at both top and middle levels of organizations.[23] However, the empirical aspects of such powerlessness and its relationship to organizational and interorganizational deviance remain understudied. We do know that conformity among those in the higher circles of the power elite results for a variety of reasons.

One important structural condition that perpetuates elite deviance is the massive centralization of power in the hands of the elite themselves. Such centralization tends to guarantee the conformity of underling bureaucrats, either corporate or governmental, for two reasons. Because they possess such overwhelming power, elites can often secure nonelite cooperation by giving direct orders to engage in deviant acts. Refusal to conform to such directives may result in severe sanctions for potential dissidents, including being fired, court-martialed, blacklisted, demoted, or not promoted. Still other sanctions might include transfer to a less desirable assignment or geographic location or forced early retirement.[24]

Thus, the distinction often made between those deviant acts committed by workers for their personal enrichment and those committed on behalf of their employer is misleading. That is, given the centralization of power in organizations, acts committed on behalf of an organization often involve personal rewards for nonelites, as well as the threat of sanctions for noncompliance with elite directives. Moreover, people who occupy positions in bureaucratic organizations play roles for which they have been trained. As such, they are acutely aware that as people they are replaceable, interchangeable parts, mere occupants of bureaucratic positions.[25] This is certainly a dehumanizing realization for the individuals involved. Nonetheless, such conformity is the rule rather than the exception.

Quite clearly, much conformity is due to feelings of powerlessness. However, no organization operates by the threat of sanction alone. Elite authority, especially that of a national president or an upper corporate manager, is obeyed in large measure because it is recognized as legitimate. Such authority is seldom questioned. This legitimacy is part of another aspect of elite deviance, the higher immorality. As we discussed in Chapter 2, the higher immorality includes many forms of deviance that are not considered to be particularly wrong by the elites who engage in them (for example, antitrust violations). A number of social psychological factors account for elite approval of such deviance.

Specialized Vocabularies and Ideologies

From a social–psychological perspective, the higher immorality consists of a subculture that forms at the top of bureaucratic organizations. A small group of power holders tends to develop precepts and customs delicately balanced between conventional and criminal (deviant) behavior, as well as objectives that may be obtained through both deviant and nondeviant means. Part of this subculture of elite behavior consists of norms and sentiments that make deviance permissible. That is, deviant acts are filtered through a sanitizing, ideological prism, which gives them the appearance of not being criminal or deviant.[26]

Part of this sanitizing ideology involves the adoption of special vocabularies of motive. According to Mills, "It is an hypothesis worthy of test that typical vocabularies of motive for different situations are significant determinants of conduct."[27] A number of recent case studies of elite deviance report the construction of an elaborate vocabulary designed to provide both motive and neutralization of guilt.[28] Janis made this observation of the Johnson administration's Vietnam policy group:

> The members of the group adopted a special vocabulary for describing the Vietnam war, using such terms as body count, armed reconnaissance, and surgical strikes, which they picked up from their military colleagues. The

Vietnam policy makers, by using this professional military vocabulary, were able to avoid in their discussions with each other all direct references to human suffering and thus to form an attitude of detachment similar to that of surgeons.[29]

Likewise, the Nazi SS, in their extermination of the Jews, adopted such a vocabulary in dealing with "the Jewish problem." Special language rules were adopted: Terms such as *special treatment* and *clearing up fundamental problems* were utilized as euphemisms for mass murder.[30] Moreover, such vocabularies are symptomatic of the alienation, stereotyping, and dehumanization involved in elite deviance (also see the following section).

A final aspect of the vocabulary of motives involves a series of mechanisms specifically designed to neutralize guilt. While such mechanisms are found in almost all deviant subcultures, in the case of the elite, their adoption is more direct and absolute because the elite themselves have generated and established the ideology of deviance, as discussed earlier. When applied to elite deviance, the general ideology of deviance becomes interlaced with a number of guilt-reducing rationalizations.

1. *Denying responsibility:* The rationalization here is that what went wrong was not the organization's fault. Mechanical malfunctions in the workplace resulting in employee deaths are termed "accidents." Likewise, consumers are blamed for their ignorance in "misusing" products that cause harm. Or blame may be shifted to other officials or organizations, as when businesses blame a problem on a lack of government regulations.

2. *Denying victimization/dehumanization:* This guilt-reducing mechanism functions to convince interested parties that no real person was, or is being, victimized. Such denials usually take one of two forms. The first may be *object-directed dehumanization;* it involves the perception of others as statistics or commodities in a vast numbers game. People are no longer perceived as human beings but as a portion of a less than human collectivity (for example, the enemy, the market, the competition, or the government).

Janis has described the presence of a second denial mechanism at work in elite circles. Termed *groupthink,* it refers to "a mode of thinking that people engage in where they are deeply involved in a cohesive in-group, where the members' striving for unanimity overrides their motivations to realistically appraise alternative courses of action."[31] Groupthink reduces individual capacity for moral judgment, enhancing the formation of stereotyped thought by in-group members. Thus, during the Vietnam era, members of the Johnson inner circle of policy makers created stereotypes portraying the poor of the world as wanting to take from the rich and espousing Asian disregard for human life. The Vietnamese were also the subject of racial stereotypes developed by U.S. troops, who used terms like *mooks, gooks, slopes,* and *dinks* and described the people as barbaric and uncivilized, deserving of ruthless slaughter.

3. *Authorization/higher loyalties:* Another rationalization technique, termed *authorization*, stems directly from the legitimacy of elite power. Authorization is an ideological device involving the creation of some transcendent mission whereby elites stake claim to supposedly higher purposes that are clearly outside legal and ethical boundaries. In the case of government, such purposes usually relate to the national interest, executive privilege, fighting the communist menace or other foreign threat. In the case of corporate deviance, such notions usually involve meeting profit targets or protecting the interests of the stockholders. Such amoral justifications have been propagated for decades by conservative social critics. Milton Friedman, for example, has long argued that businesses possess virtually no social responsibility for their acts.

> There is one and only one social responsibility of business—to use its resources and engage in activities designed to increase its profits so long as it stays within the rules of the game...[and] engages in open and free competition, without deception or fraud.... Few trends could so thoroughly undermine the very foundations of our free society as the acceptance by corporate officials of a social responsibility other than to make as much money for their stockholders as possible. This is a fundamentally subversive doctrine. If business people do have a social responsibility other than making maximum profits, how are they to know what it is?[32]

Such statements can easily be interpreted to mean that any profit-making behavior in which businesses engage is morally acceptable, as long as no laws are broken.

4. *Condemning condemners:* This mechanism is used to handle critics of deviant behavior. Namely, attention is diverted away from the real issue and focused on another topic or even the critics themselves. For instance, corporations often attack proposals involving further government regulation as being opposed to free enterprise. Governments, in turn, often view critics of civil rights abuses or war crimes as "communist sympathizers."

These neutralization techniques, along with an official ideology of deviance accepted by general society, ensure that elites may commit deviant acts without guilt or damage to their respectable self-images. Moreover, underlings will come to share these ideological visions and adopt the Adolf Eichmann excuse of elite authorization ("only following orders").

Finally, these ideological constructions allow elites to attribute real deviance and crime to the lower classes, thus mystifying themselves as to their own deviance and misdirecting perceptions of the distribution of societal harm in general. The dimensions of such harm are even greater when committed by organizations because of the nature of modern organizational life.

Fragmentation and Routinization

Decisions to commit deviant acts—even murder—are carried out within established routines. Such routines not only involve filling out forms, reports, and schedules. Indeed, a number of scholars maintain that the large, complex nature of modern organizations encourages deviance, for two reasons: (1) specialized tasks involve the same routines, whether they are deviant or legitimate; and (2) elites both discourage being informed of scandals within organizations by lower functionaries and hide acts of elite deviance from functionaries and the public.[33]

Related to the specialization of tasks found in modern organizations is alienation, which denotes "a mode of experience in which the person experiences himself or herself [and other people] as alien."[34] Within bureaucratic organizations, alienation is manifested partially through distance. For example, workers engaged in producing dioxin never witnessed the effects of the chemical on the residents of Love Canal in Niagara Falls. Similarly, pilots serving in the Vietnam War convinced themselves that they were bombing geographic targets on maps, not killing civilians in their homes. In modern society, technology has produced a world of such extreme distances that victimization becomes impersonal.

Image Construction and Inauthenticity

Front Activities

The centralization of power and fragmentation of tasks in large organizations create still another important aspect of elite deviance: a world of image construction that masks acts of deviance behind a smokescreen of *"front"* activities.

A number of scholars have commented on the subject of front activities involved in elite deviance.[35] Yet the term is vague and has come to include everything from making deceptive or false statements about a deviant act (or series of acts) to creating pseudo-events and phony crises by news media, public relations firms, and governmental agencies.[36] Quite simply and directly, front activities may be described as management via image manipulation.

During the Watergate era, for example, a number of commentators observed that the White House staff felt that the basic problem was successfully managing public opinion.[37] And during the Carter era, White House staffers commonly complained that the confidence gap between the White House and the public was due to an image problem.

The use of front activities to camouflage deviance is a common and accepted practice of virtually all types of bureaucratic entities. Turk believes that lying within government agencies is "a routine tactic" and that its use is limited only by expediency.[38] Such lying is accompanied by many front activities: (1) providing only the information requested by investigating officials or citizens; (2) destroying or conveniently misfiling incriminating items before they have to be produced; (3) fragmenting information so it appears incomplete and out of sequence; and (4) depicting deviant acts as the work of "bad apples" or even past leaders. Another common ploy is to deny access to information on the basis of "need to know," "national security," or other justifications to hide embarrassing secrets.[39]

The discussion in this chapter has centered around the structural causes of elite deviance. A central portion of this discussion has emphasized that the causes and consequences of elite deviance are hidden from, even mystified by, both elites and nonelites, victimizers as well as victims. This mystification of elite deviance via an official ideology and a host of guilt-neutralizing techniques and front activities has serious implications for those who occupy positions in bureaucratic hierarchies. The alienation and dehumanization that characterize elite deviance produce a condition that has been described as *inauthentic*.[40] As an objective social condition, inauthenticity refers to maintaining overt positive appearances despite the presence of negative underlying realities.[41] Within powerful organizations, inauthenticity is indicated by the amount of resources spent on various front activities as the organization tries to convince workers, clients, and the general public of its positive attributes in the face of negative, often tightly held secrets.

Given these central variables regarding modern organizations, bureaucratic concerns may be hypothesized to cause elite deviance in a number of respects:

- *Hypothesis:* The more centralized authority is within an organization, and the more secrecy, the more elite deviance will be committed.
- *Hypothesis:* Organizations that engage in one type of elite deviance (for example, price-fixing or environmental law violations) will also tend to engage in other types of elite deviance (for example, sexual harassment or other civil rights violations).
- *Hypothesis:* Organizations that engage in high levels of inauthentic front activities (for example, public relations and image-enhancing advertising) will also be engaging in high levels of deviant activity.

Finally, it is likewise important to understand the types of personality traits that are likely to characterize individuals who engage in deviant acts within organizations.

Elite Deviance and "Individual" Characteristics

Certain people who work in organizations also possess unique personality characteristics that lead them to engage in deviant acts of various kinds. Presthus has noted that one type of personality is particularly successful in making it to the top of bureaucratic organizations.[42] Such an individual exudes charisma via a superficial sense of warmth and charm. He or she is able to make decisions easily because matters are viewed in black-and-white terms. This requires the ability to categorize and thus dehumanize individuals as nonhuman entities for the purpose of making decisions concerning layoffs, firings, plant closings, and advertising campaigns.

Clinard's study of managers of large corporations found that those executives likely to engage in acts of organizational deviance were often recruited from outside the companies they administered.[43] These executives were interested in getting publicity in financial journals, showing quick increases in profits, and moving on to higher positions within two years.

Recent studies of work alienation demonstrate that people with such high extrinsic needs also tend to be workaholics, displaying what are called type A personality characteristics. Such traits involve "free floating hostility, competitiveness, a high need for socially approved success, unbridled ambitions, aggressiveness, impatience, and polyphasic thought and action" (trying to do two things at once).[44] Such persons also frequently exhibit the lowest scores on mental health measures in such studies. Thus, victimizers in elite deviance often turn into victims, in a sense, dehumanizing both their victims and themselves.

Finally, there is evidence that, within single organizational hierarchies, many of the same people who execute deviance on behalf of the organization also commit acts against it for their own personal gain. In a Canadian study, Reasons noted that supervisory personnel accounted for approximately two-thirds of the business dishonesty over the last decade.[45] Furthermore, within the organizations that commit deviant acts, those individuals who participated were likely to engage in acts of deviance for personal gain against their employers. This may be true because such employees resent being asked to engage in deviant acts and thus strike out against their employers in revenge. Or perhaps, having demonstrated their corrupt moral nature to their employees, such organizations invite acts of deviance against themselves by providing an untrustworthy role model. Again, we come to a similar conclusion regarding conformity within bureaucratic organizations.

One useful concept in explaining the deviant behavior of some individuals is *attachment disorder,* a condition that affects 30 million children in the United States.[46] These children are frequently the victims of incest, abuse, and neglect. They are unable to bond—to become attached—to other human beings. As children, they often strangle animals, start fires, try to drown their playmates, steal, lie, and inflict physical damage on other people's belongings.

The symptoms associated with attachment disorder involve severe forms of inauthenticity and dehumanization. Disordered children do not treat themselves or other people as human beings with needs for love and recognition. Consequently, the symptoms of disordered children reflect extreme forms of alienation:

- They are self-destructive. Disordered children often stab themselves with knives and exhibit no fear of dangerous heights or other risky situations (such as reckless driving or robbing convenience stores). In adulthood, these people become the salespeople who sell unsafe used cars, the bosses who steal their subordinates' ideas, the consumers who fail to pay their debts, or the serial killers (such as Ted Bundy and Charles Manson).
- They exhibit phoniness (personal inauthenticity). Attachment-disordered children have no idea how to relate to other people. Consequently, they tend to behave insincerely when expressing love or other emotions. They tend to be perceived as untrustworthy and come across as manipulators. One parent of an attachment-disordered child remarked that it was like living with a "robot."[47]
- Stealing, hording, and gorging of food and possessions are common among attachment-disordered children. Not knowing how to form attachments to other people, disordered children experience severe unmet emotional needs. As a substitute for needs involving love and human contact, disordered children often steal and hoard items such as food, even if they are not hungry.
- Conning behavior is also common. Acts of deception take place in both childhood and adulthood. As children, disordered persons often fein helplessness, act loving or cute, smart or beguiling—whatever suits their need at the time to obtain what they want. In adulthood, such behavior may manifest itself as fraud and con games.
- A final symptom of attachment disorder involves what is termed "crazy lying."[48] Such children lie even under the most extreme circumstances, especially when they are caught directly in the act of misbehaving. Crazy lying means that lies will be told even when such behavior is obvious.

Organizational Conditions and the Production of Deviant Personalities

It is much too facile to argue that elite deviance is caused by deviant personalities, people who were predisposed to deviant acts before they arrived at the organization's doorstep. Reality, unfortunately, is a good deal more complicated and much more interesting than this. There are instances when organizations can and do influence workers to commit deviant acts. Such motivations are frequently associated with the presence of alienation within organizations.

Thus Boston University professors Donald Kanter and Philip Mirvis[49] have substantiated that alienation is surprisingly widespread in America. In their analysis of a national sample of data, about half of their respondents agree with the statement that "most people are only out for themselves and that you are better off zapping them before they do it to you."[50] Among their most important findings are that many people in America now take a cynical approach to the work they do, and that this cynicism extends from the very top to the lowly bottom of the American occupational structure.

At the zenith of corporate America are so-called "command cynics." These are senior managers who see themselves in a corporate jungle. They believe that their advancement has been an outcome of Darwinian logic, which holds that since they are on top, those beneath them must be "weak, naive, inept, or just plain dumb." Command cynics also hold that everyone has his or her price, and everyone can be had.

Beneath the "command cynics" are the "administrative sideliners," middle managers and upper-level government bureaucrats who view human nature as being cold and uncaring, and who have no genuine concern for people, except as means for their own ends. Next is a group of young game players, self-absorbed professionals who became visible symbols of the greed and narcissism of the 1980s. What these self-centered people have in common is willingness to do whatever it takes to move up the bureaucratic ladder. Kanter and Mirvis referred to them as "porcupine quills," people who take pleasure in putting others down as they climb to the top of corporate or government hierarchies.

In the middle levels of the bureaucratic layers of business and government sit so-called "squeezed cynics," usually the sons and daughters of skilled factory workers and working-class clericals. This once upwardly mobile working-class group has been made cynical by the loss of manufacturing jobs and the decline of heavy industry. The jobs they once expected to give them security have been sent overseas, automated, or completely eliminated. They are now downwardly mobile Americans. They have lost faith in the American Dream, and their cynicism stems from a belief that their careers have reached a dead end. These sad people are hard-bitten cynics, who believe they cannot trust anyone at work or in business, and that "expecting anyone to help you makes you a damn fool."

White-collar workers often suffer from self-estrangement and other feelings of alienation associated with inauthenticity, previously discussed. One of the most interesting studies in this regard is Jan Halper's *Quiet Desperation*.[51] Dr. Halper is a humanistic psychologist and organizational consultant. She interviewed 4,126 Fortune 500 executives, middle managers, and other professionals; she also intensely interviewed and provided free therapy to a subsample of executives.

To advance in their firms, these men must go along, sacrificing for the sake of their careers and companies. What Dr. Halper discovered was that a large proportion of these successful men were self-estranged, cut off from their feelings, wishes, wants, and needs. Their socialization both within their families and at work has taught them to deny their feelings, and to conform to the demands of job and family. Halper found that a large portion of these men, almost two-thirds, are tired of being dutiful, loyal employees, with no control over their jobs. Many suffer from reactions to denying their feelings for so long. Depression, feeling out of control, and other stress reactions are common. Some commit suicide.

Moreover, many of these men suffer the ill effects of not knowing who they are. They confuse the roles they play with who they are as people. Often they see themselves as a group of titles: "hero, breadwinner, lover, husband, father, warrior, empire builder, or mover-and-shaker."[52] Relinquishing a role or two, through dismissal, retirement, or divorce, often leads to an identity crisis in which they feel they are nothing without the identities they have lost.

The credo these men are taught is that they are responsible for others' needs over and above their own. Often they avoid thinking about their own needs in order not to feel anticipated guilt, feeling they have violated the male credo. Despite their considerable accomplishments in many cases, a large number of these professionals suffer from low self-esteem. Frustrated at work, not intimately related to their wives, many of these men lead rich fantasy lives, preferring to see themselves as what they want rather than who they really are. No matter how successful they are, many feel that they have not achieved success.

Most of these men also suffer from numerous contradictions. One of the most common among the executives is that they feel forced to demonstrate that they are both tough and nice guys at the same time. Halper found that 57 percent of managers don't delegate authority because they fear giving up control over decisions. As a result, many feel great stress over being constantly responsible for what takes place inside their firms. Related to this control over decision making is the fact that many corporate executives Halper interviewed find it difficult to trust their fellow employees. Moreover, this distrust between workers increased in the 1990s. This is because of the massive layoffs that have taken place in recent years in corporate America. No job seems safe anymore. Frequently, those not laid off feel the guilt, irritability, fatigue, and stress that come with being left on a job that requires more effort.

People have made a tacit bargain with the capitalist system, exchanging their work time for escapist consumption and leisure. Alienation at work is soon transformed into reification in the marketplace. It is often rendered in a reluctant, incomplete, and psychologically stressful manner. Moreover, such conformity is related to a number of types of more personal deviance, even among elites themselves. This is especially true when front activities fail and organizations are implicated in deviant acts. For instance, Eli Black, chairman of United Brands, committed suicide when it was revealed that his company was involved in a bribery scandal designed to hold down taxes on bananas. Similarly, Japanese executive Mitsushiro Shimada killed himself when his company was proven to be involved in the Grumman bribery scandal.[53] We can conclude then that if official ideologies of deviance were fully accepted, embarrassed organizational elites would probably not resort to such desperate acts.

Taken together, this body of evidence leads to the following hypotheses:

- *Hypothesis:* Those individuals likely to engage in acts of elite deviance will tend to exhibit weak attachments to friends, family, and co-workers. Elite deviants are thus likely to suffer from all of the symptoms that accompany attachment disorder, including the ability to freely lie and manipulate and the inability to delay any sort of gratification.
- *Hypothesis:* Organizations headed by people suffering from alienation and attachment disorder will likely be "polyoffenders." As we have seen with General Electric (Chapter 3), corporations that commit deviant acts in one area (for example, defrauding the government in defense contracting) will likely commit deviant acts in other areas (for example, ecological crime).

Links between Elite Deviance and Nonelite Deviance

Another critical aspect of elite deviance often overlooked when the subject is confined to so-called corporate criminality or political deviance involves the mutually dependent (symbiotic) relationship between certain types of elite and nonelite deviance. This point stems from an additional aspect of the sociological imagination that holds that society, as Mills put it, is "a network of rackets."[54] Such rackets arise because of institutional contradictions, permanent conflicts within social structures.[55] One of these contradictions concerns the relationship between elite and nonelite deviance. This symbiotic relationship exists on two levels: tangible (involving money, products, and/or services) and symbolic (involving the construction of ideological and social structural variables).[56]

Tangible Links

The tangible links between elite and nonelite deviance are represented in Figure 8.1. As the figure shows, the great bridge between elite and nonelite deviance is organized crime. Profits from the activities of organized criminal syndicates are made from various types of street crime—including prostitution, illegal gambling, selling drugs—which include moneys obtained by burglars and robbers who need to support drug habits. Such proceeds, totaling some $150 billion in annual gross revenues, generate an estimated $50 billion in net profits, profits that must be reinvested in order to grow.[57] At times, such profits have been invested in partnership ventures with legitimate corporations, as when Pan Am and Mafia interests opened gambling resorts in the Caribbean following Castro's expulsion of the Mafia from Cuban casinos.

Likewise, business dealings between organized crime and legitimate corporations include the use of racketeers to suppress labor unions and the laundering of Mafia drug funds through banks and other legal enterprises. In addition, there are numerous financial links between organized criminal syndicates and the government, from campaign donations of Mafia moneys to outright bribery of politicians (not to mention the infamous activities of the CIA).

Finally, as mentioned above, numerous legitimate and illegitimate financial links exist between political and economic elites: political lobby groups, government contracts, bribery, and corporate efforts to influence governmental behavior overseas. This is not to say that all legitimate corporations working with legitimate politicians are also automatically linked to organized criminal syndicates. It is merely to say that such three-way links do exist. And obviously, many of the links between legitimate corporations and Mafia-owned businesses are of a customer–retailer nature. This includes phone calls made by bookies using AT&T lines, Mafia-owned automobile dealerships, syndicate influence in the legitimate gambling industry (for example, Las Vegas and Atlantic City), and relationships between the Mafia-dominated Teamsters Union, legitimate corporations, and politicians. (See Chapter 9 for further examples.)

Symbolic Links

As discussed in Chapters 1 and 2, the most powerful U.S. elites have access to the nation's great socializing institutions, especially the mass media and the schools. Such access has been utilized in part to create an ideological view of deviance. This view holds that the U.S. crime problem is the fault of a supposedly dangerous lower class that is criminal in nature, deserving of its poverty and moral inferiority, and in need of increased social-control measures by the state. Such deviants are typically viewed as the products of certain individual pathologies (for example, "evil, subculture of poverty"). The notion that justice is blind in its fairness—ignoring race, class, and power—is completely overlooked.

Because many people in the United States are convinced that the deviance of the powerless is a greater harm to society than that of elites, both moral indignation and financial resources are focused there. This further serves to convince elites of their own moral superiority, reaffirming that their acts do not constitute the real deviance of common criminals. Thus, the official (elite) ideology of deviance serves to convince elites of the rightness of their own conduct, even if unethical or illegal. It also serves to keep the attention of law from the deviance of elites, focusing instead on the apprehension, processing, and punishing of so-called street criminals.

Finally, the official ideology of deviance gives rise to a situation in which the deviance of the powerless reinforces the inequality between the powerless (nonelites) and powerful (elites). This occurs in part because the victims of nonelite street criminals are disproportionately members of the same powerless lower class. Such deviance tends to keep the lower class divided within itself, destroying any sense of community that might result in a united lower-class movement for social change.

For its part, the deviance of elites has both direct and indirect impacts on the deviance of nonelites. First, elites, under certain circumstances, may order relatively powerless people to commit deviant acts. We observed this in the Farben case, where the cruel Capos were ordered to oversee the slave-labor inmates of Nazi concentration camps. Second, as we have already noted, elite deviance often has a trickle-down effect, providing a standard of ethics and behavior by which nonelites can justify their own deviant acts. Finally, elite deviance often victimizes nonelites financially and in other ways. Such exploitation serves to reinforce the inequalities of power and wealth that are in large measure responsible for this symbiotic relationship between elite and nonelite deviance. To understand the causes of elite deviance, one must first understand the symbolic and symbiotic dimensions of the structure of wealth and power, in U.S. society and elsewhere.

Elite Deviance and Victimization

A great deal of attention has been paid by sociologists in recent years to the effects of class, race, gender, and age on human behavior. Nowhere are these variables more relevant than in the study of the victims of elite deviance. Consider the following.

- **Item:** In 1993, a Defense Department report stated that 83 women and 7 men were assaulted during the 1991 Tailhook Association Convention at the Las Vegas Hilton. (The association's members are present and former Navy fliers.) The 300-page report was based on more than 2,900 interviews. The report said that victims were "groped, pinched, fondled," and "bitten" by their assailants and that oral sex and sexual intercourse performed in front of others contributed to a "general atmosphere of debauchery."[58] Ultimately, Navy Secretary John Dalton asked for the removal of Admiral Frank Kelso, chief of naval operations, and three other admirals were censured. Then 28 other admirals and 1 marine general received letters of caution.[59] None of the officers involved ever went to prison.

- **Item:** In November 1996, an Army sexual misconduct scandal broke at the Army's Aberdeen Proving Ground, Maryland, where company commander Captain Derrick Robertson was charged with rape, violation of the Ordnance Center and School Regulation that prohibits improper student/cadre relationships, conduct unbecoming an officer (fraternization), adultery, obstruction of justice, and related charges. Robertson was a company commander. Staff Sergeants Nathaniel Beach and Delmar Simpson, both drill sergeants, were arraigned on a variety of charges, including rape, forcible sodomy, adultery, and obstruction of justice. As part of the investigation, the Army established a 1-800 number for receiving calls from victims, parents, and anyone with information pertaining to the sexual misconduct investigation.[60]
- **Item:** In April 1997, a former drill instructor was convicted of raping six trainees.[61] The Aberdeen Proving Ground incident was the most serious case arising from a sexual deviance scandal that spread to U.S. military bases worldwide. The same drill instructor had already been sentenced to thirty-two years in prison for having consensual sex with eleven trainees, a violation of Army rules.
- **Item:** Immediately following the former drill sergeant's conviction, General John Longhouser, the Aberdeen Proving Ground's base commander, announced his retirement, admitting he had had an adulterous affair in 1992, while separated from his wife. The general reportedly became the subject of a Pentagon inquiry after an anonymous tip was received over a telephone hot line, established because of the charges leveled at Aberdeen drill sergeants. Other sexual harassment complaints were leveled against Air Force Lieutenant Kelly Flinn, the Air Force's only female bomber pilot. Flinn was given a general (less than honorable) discharge and forced to resign from the service. The incident touched off national debate over a sexual double standard wherein women charged with sexual misconduct are forced to resign under less than honorable conditions while males charged with similar behavior simply retire without penalty.

  The debate intensified when Air Force General Joseph Ralston, vice chairman of the Joint Chiefs of Staff, admitted to an adulterous affair, but President Clinton refused to accept his resignation, noting that he wanted the general to become his new top military advisor. Likewise, retired Sergeant Major Brenda Hoster accused the Army's highest-ranking enlisted man, Sergeant Major McKinney, of grabbing her and demanding sex during a business trip. Hoster made her charges public after learning that Sergeant McKinney had been appointed to a panel investigating sexual misconduct in the Army.

As usual, the Tailhook scandal and the 1997 Army sexual harassment scandals are symbolic of a much more widespread condition. In March 1994, four women serving in the military told a House committee that sexual harassment in the military is very common and that complaints about it often go unheeded. While stronger harassment rules have been issued by all branches of the armed services, and sensitivity training initiated, the female personnel claim that complaints of sexual harassment are met with disdain, ostracism, and in some cases transfer to a dead-end job.[62]

Sexual harassment has long been part of the organizational culture of the military, but it is certainly not limited to the armed services. Such harassment is most heavily centered in male-dominated occupations and organizations, and its toleration depends on the behavior of the elites in charge. If vigorously opposed, harassment can be overcome. The same is true of the denial of civil liberties to gays, more than 10,000 of whom have been forcibly discharged from the U.S. military in the last thirty years, and there exist many forms of institutional discrimination against homosexuals and lesbians in American life.[63]

Moreover, the Tailhook scandal points up one additional facet of organizational life, but this time the organization concerns the discipline of criminology itself. Recent publications have pointed out that women, as victims of "white-collar crime," have gone unstudied, as indeed all such victims have. As this book has pointed out for a decade, many of the victims of international corporate dumping are women and children, but their victimization does not stop there:

- In 1991, twenty-five people were killed in a fire in a North Carolina chicken processing plant. More than 75 percent of the victims were female in a plant where doors were locked to prevent workers from stealing chickens.
- The Dalkon Shield intrauterine birth control device, which caused sterilization, infections, and death in some women, created a scandal that victimized women, as did Ovulen, an oral contraceptive, information about the dangerous side effects of which was withheld by its manufacturer, Searle Company. Likewise, carpal tunnel syndrome (atrophy of thumb muscles) primarily affects assembly-line workers and typists, who are mainly female. The same is true for conditions related to the use of video display terminals in offices, which can cause a variety of neck, back, and shoulder problems, as well as eye strain and carpal tunnel syndrome. Likewise, in the textile industry, women make up from 62 to 89 percent of the workers in certain occupations that incur the risk of contracting "brown lung" disease from exposure to cotton dust.[64]

Finally, the elderly suffer very high rates of victimization from white-collar crimes, especially scams (confidence games) and frauds.

- **Item:** More than 10,000 elderly residents of Arizona alone are victims of fraudulent auto repairs and other consumer frauds, situations that exist nationwide.[65]
- **Item:** The elderly are among those prone to cons by televangelist hucksters. In 1990, Reverend Jim Bakker received a forty-five-year prison sentence (later commuted) for mail fraud and related offenses when he misappropriated moneys supposedly raised to support his PTL ("Praise the Lord") ministries. Bakker's $150-million-a-year "Church" was well connected to the Reagan and Bush administrations, as well as to large corporations. One firm, Wedtech (later bankrupted in a scandal involving defense contracting fraud), paid thousands to silence Jessica Hahn, a secretary who was forced to engage in sex with Bakker and an associate. Many of the people who mailed money to Bakker were elderly, some of whom went without heat during the winter, and whose only incomes were their Social Security checks.
- **Item:** The elderly's cost of living continues to rise faster than that of other consumers. This is because the elderly spend a higher proportion of their incomes on medical care and shelter than do other groups. Throughout the 1980s, a special consumer price index (cpi) for the elderly rose 19.5 percent compared with an 18.2 percent cpi rise for nonelderly persons living in urban areas.[66]

All these examples point to the fact that the most powerless people in American society and around the world are the leading victims of elite deviance of all kinds, and part of their continuing victimization includes a lack of attention to this serious social problem.

Constructionist and Objectivist Positions on Elite Deviance

Throughout this book, we have presented a view of elite deviance that is admittedly controversial. Rather than take a safe position, involving only white-collar criminal acts, we have argued for a definition that encompasses both illegal and immoral acts. But, one may ask, whose morality is to be used as a basis in deciding what may be termed elite deviance?

In general, two answers may be offered to this question. First, there is the constructionist position, which views all deviance as acts occurring in a particular context: a given historical period, a specific culture, and even an isolated situation within a specific culture.[67] Thus, a murder committed during peacetime may become a heroic act in war. But not all societies condone all wars or even war in general.

In this chapter, we have stressed the importance of reality as a social construction in our discussion of the official elite ideology of deviance.[68]

This official ideology has several negative effects: (1) it blinds both elites and nonelites to the greater harms generated by elite deviance; (2) it focuses attention and resources on the less harmful deviance of the powerless; and (3) it serves as a basis for guilt-reducing rationalizations used by powerful individuals engaged in deviance. We have also examined the question of who possesses the power to construct such definitions or, conversely, to prevent competing definitions of deviance from being constructed. Finally, we have assessed the harmful consequences that follow from defining deviance in this way.

A central problem with the constructionist position is that it treats all moral positions as relative, denying the existence of any absolutes, including reality of human pain and suffering.[69] Erich Goode's argument in his otherwise excellent text, *Deviant Behavior*, is characteristic of the constructionist view on this point. Like most constructionists, he argues that human suffering is nothing but a social construct, thus implying that there is no human suffering until such misfortunes are officially defined as such. Moreover, just because new practices (such as various human rights violations) come into existence, and old ones (such as slavery) disappear, does not mean that the pain of physical injury or death, or theft, or rape, or any other practice that causes suffering is less real. Goode also seems determined to limit the definition of elite deviance to violations of human rights, thus overlooking all our discussions of the higher immorality, the interrelated nature of deviance, and the like.

Ideologically, the constructionist position is safe because it easily excuses one from taking sides and advocating solutions, which leads to the implicit acceptance of the dominant ideology concerning social problems, including various forms of deviance. Thus, the constructionist position supports the stance that nothing matters, which for us is unacceptable.

An alternate position is that of the objectivists, which holds that there are moral absolutes regarding social problems.

> There are social structures that induce material or psychic suffering for certain segments of the population; there are structures that ensure the maldistribution of resources within and across societies;…there are corporate and political organizations that waste valuable resources, that pollute the environment, that are imperialistic, and that increase the gap between the "haves" and "have nots" globally and societally.[70]

The objectivist (or normative) approach, unlike that of social constructionism, argues for the adoption of moral imperatives and human needs that are universal and ahistorical. To describe violation of these norms by elites as "wrongs," "deviance," or "social problems" is merely to state such universals using another label. Stated in the positive, such universals provide a coherent view of basic human needs that may serve as a foundation for policies designed to address the causes and consequences of the types of deviance we have described in this book. Among these basic needs are essential physical requirements (food, clothing, shelter, and medical care), as well as a host of nonmaterial needs, including the basic human rights discussed in Chapter 5. (Others are discussed in the Epilogue.)

More important, however, is the realization that dangers are involved with adopting any set of basic "rights," "wrongs," and "shoulds," or causes and solutions. Objections can be offered to any position, as seen in the following examples.

1. The only reason most of the examples that make up this book are here is because they constitute what Simon believes to be deviance. He's just being self-righteous.

This charge is profoundly untrue! The examples in this book constitute a case-by-case series of deviant acts that have offended the sensibilities of many leading social critics, muckrakers, and social scientists. The ethical foundation rests on the same moral principle on which the Judeo-Christian and many other non-Western ethical systems are founded: namely, the Golden Rule, which holds that one should treat others as he or she would like to be treated. What society would sanction the behavior related in this chapter's examples? Even I. G. Farben's use of slave labor would have been disapproved of by the mass of the German people had they known about it and been free to render a judgment.

2. How dare you speak of the salaries of corporate executives, war crimes, antitrust violations, and pollution as if they all constitute equal wrongs? All you do is open up a Pandora's box! Now virtually anything elites do can be considered deviant by someone writing on the subject. As a result, the issue of criminal elite deviance is lost in the process.

Such an argument ignores the fact that we have introduced a standard by which to measure deviance: harm, including physical loss (death and injury), financial loss, and the destruction of public trust. Our argument is not that all deviant acts cause the same kind and degree of harm. Instead, we find that such acts—whether technically criminal or not—are harmful in some way. For instance, the three-martini lunch and other special privileges given elite executives cause harm by furthering massive federal deficits, as wealthy individuals and corporations legally evade paying taxes. In addition, citizens lose faith in taxation, thus destroying public trust. Those $3,000-per-day executive salaries and perks further contribute to many social inequalities, which are in turn related to many social ills, including crime at all societal levels. So yes, not all the wrongs we discuss are of equal dimension. Nonetheless, they remain wrongs and are symbolic and symptomatic of still greater problems.

3. Calling some practices "deviant" when they are not considered to be so by those who commit them is irrational. Practices such as corporate dumping, even if dangerous, are still legal and justified by those individuals involved. They have their reasons. Your approach completely rules out any understanding of the people involved.

Yes, and juvenile delinquents, Nazis, I. G. Farben executives, rapists, and all other criminals have their reasons, too. Deviant individuals erect ideologies and rationalizations to reduce the guilt they feel. Further, they feel that what they do is quite rational, according to their own value systems.

Still, just because corporate dumping in foreign countries is profitable and legal does not make the harm it causes any less serious than the harm to those who lose their lives to pesticide poisoning or suffer birth defects due to faulty contraceptives. And the fact that the victims of dumping are not Americans should not matter; they are still human beings. Calling such behavior "rational" misses the point. The harm is intrinsically real and empirically measurable, as this book documents.

Moreover, the rational pursuit of profit may not be as rational as we sometimes think. Practices such as corporate bribery actually have very negative consequences for many of the companies and officials involved. Therefore, in the long run, they may be viewed as irrational.

It is impossible to account for every individual rationale when trying to define elite deviance. So instead, should we limit our definition to include only criminal acts? Doing so would be unfortunate. Many great harms would go neglected—harms that, if properly understood, would aid in our knowledge of how and why elite deviance works.

Conclusion

The discussion in this chapter has analyzed how rationalizations for elite deviance are constructed and maintained through the use of front activities, and how they fail due to the emergence of scandal and opposing beliefs. Based on this analysis, we conclude that elite deviance is understandable from the deviant's perspective. In addition, we feel that elite deviance is empirically testable. To establish such empiricism, the following hypotheses must be verified:

1. *Hypothesis:* Public distrust and alienation are increased by elite acts that are considered to be immoral/unethical, as well as by those that are clearly illegal.

2. *Hypothesis:* Major corporations involved in scandals (such as pollution or dangerous working conditions) are likely to suffer from distrust among their employees, the result of which will be deviance: stealing from the workplace, absenteeism, and perhaps drug and alcohol abuse.

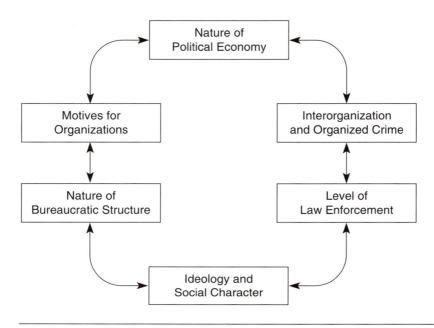

FIGURE 8-2 *Interrelated Causes of Elite Deviance*

3. *Hypothesis:* Employees asked to participate directly in acts of organizational deviance may comply with such directives. But in some cases, especially when scandal occurs, intense psychological strain will result in acts of personal deviance (for example, drug addiction, mental illness, suicide) and resentment against the organization (causing white-collar crime).

Each of these hypotheses may be tested via interviews, as a number of studies attest.[71] Thus, we see little incompatibility between our so-called ideological stance and the canons of empirical science. The fact that elite deviance is empirically testable is one of the major strengths of our view of deviance.

The discussion in this chapter has illustrated the complexity of the subject, elite deviance. It is quite clearly a product of our complex society, as a number of forces work together to provide the motive, the opportunity, and the structure necessary for deviance to occur (see Figure 8.2).

Perhaps the most basic cause of elite deviance is the structure and internal workings of the contemporary political economy. Assigning structural causes requires one to examine solutions that are structural, as well. Not to include solutions in a text such as this does little more than contribute to the feelings of powerlessness and alienation that already plague U.S. society, not to mention much of social science. Not to propose such changes would be, we feel, intellectually dishonest. Unfortunately, we find that a double standard operates in this area. On the one hand, when so-called objective social scientists offer reformist solutions to the problems plaguing society, their work is labeled as "policy study," "social policy," "foreign policy," or some other pseudoscientific label. Most important, it is believed to be unbiased, scientific, and value free. On the other hand, when anyone proposes change that involves the basic distribution of wealth, power, and private property, the work is labeled as "utopian," "unscientific," "social criticism," or even "subversive."

In response to this arbitrary approach to social problems, we suggest that the time for labels is past. To avoid making proposals leaves students with a sense of hopelessness and fatalism that merely serves to perpetuate such problems. To label our approach as being more ideologically biased than reformist is to deny the pluralistic nature of the U.S. political and intellectual landscape. However, to criticize our beliefs as being utopian does us great honor, for we, with Kenneth Keniston, hold that positive utopian visions are essential as a source of hope in an increasingly cynical, alienated, and negative world.[72]

Critical Thinking Exercise 8.1: Elite Deviance and the Sociological Imagination _____

Write a short paper (three to five pages, double-spaced) stating your opinion in response to the following questions. *Be sure to make a copy of your paper. What's important now is your impressions of the issues raised here.*

1. *Social problem.* Select a magazine or newspaper article about a topic currently in the news—a murder in a high school, say, or an indictment of a politician on corruption charges, a kidnapping, a terrorist bombing incident, or a shoot-out between rival drug gangs. Does the article's topic indicate a more widespread problem in America? What types of harm result from this socially patterned problem? Consider the following dimensions of the sociological imagination.

A. *Contradiction.* What are the institutional contradictions surrounding the problem? For example, do some institutions in American society approve of drug use, either legal or illegal, while other institutions condemn it? What contradictions are inherent in American institutions that may cause the problem you selected?

B. *Historical epoch.* What events in the recent past have raised concern about this problem?

C. *Immediate milieu.* To what extent is this problem a part of your immediate environment? For example, do you know other students who abuse alcohol or illegal drugs? Has someone ever attempted to sell you illegal drugs? Have you experienced any direct contact with the problem you chose to analyze?

D. *Personal troubles.* Have you or members of your family experienced problems with the issue you chose? Are any of your friends experiencing problems with it? If so, what sorts of trauma have you experienced because of this social problem? Is the problem resolvable within your immediate environment, or do you believe that some larger effort is necessary—perhaps a private effort in your local community, or governmental legislation, or public service education by the mass media? If so, what kinds of efforts do you believe are necessary to rid your everyday life of this problem?

Endnotes

1. Charles Derber, *Money, Murder, and the American Dream: Wilding from Wall Street to Main Street* (New York: Faber & Faber, 1992), 8. This is one of the most important books on American social character in a generation.
2. Ibid., 101.
3. See the Winter 1991 issue of *Dissent.*
4. See Robert Nisbet, *The Present Age* (New York: HarperCollins, 1988).
5. Leslie Lipson, *The Ethical Crisis of Civilization* (Newbury Park, CA: Sage, 1993).
6. The following is based in part on David R. Simon, *Social Problems and the Sociological Imagination* (New York: McGraw-Hill, 1995).
7. See C. Wright Mills, *The Power Elite* (New York: Oxford University Press, 1956).
8. See C. Wright Mills, *The Sociological Imagination* (New York: Oxford University Press, 1959), Chapter 1ff, for an extended discussion of this point.
9. See C. Wright Mills, *Images of Man: The Classic Tradition in Sociological Thinking* (New York: Braziller, 1960), 3.
10. S. Messner and R. Rosenfeld, *Crime and the American Dream* (Belmont, CA: Wadsworth, 1994), 6.
11. See, on this point, Karen Horney, *The Neurotic Personality of Our Time* (New York: W. W. Norton, 1938); Erich Fromm, *Escape from Freedom* (New York: Avon, 1966); and David Riesman, *The Lonely Crowd* (New Haven, CN: Yale University Press, 1950).
12. Elliott Currie, "The Market Society," *Dissent*, Winter 1991, 255–58, elaborated in a speech "The Market Society" at the 1994 meeting of the Academy of Criminal Justice Sciences, Chicago, Illinois.
13. Derber.
14. See Emile Durkheim's classic, *Suicide* (New York: Free Press, 1966).
15. Robert Merton, "Social Structure and Anomie," in *Theories of Deviance*, 4th ed., ed. S. Traub and C. Little, (Itaska, IL: Peacock Publishers, 1994), 114–48.
16. Merton, 116.
17. James Ring Adams, *America as a Business Civilization* (New York: Holmes and Meier), 44.
18. See, for example, P. Lernoux, "The Miami Connection," *The Nation*, February 18, 1984, 186–98; and P. Lernoux, *In Banks We Trust* (New York: Anchor/Doubleday Press, 1984).
19. Bill Moyers, *The Secret Government: The Constitution in Crisis* (Berkeley: Seven Locks, 1988).
20. Steven Box, *Crime, Power, and Mystification* (London: Tavistock, 1983), 58–60.

21. John Braithwaite, *Corporate Crime in the Pharmaceutical Industry* (London: Routledge and Kegan Paul, 1984), 26.

22. H. Kelman, "The Social-Psychological Context of Watergate," *Psychiatry* 39, Winter 1976, 308; and H. Kelman, "Violence without Moral Restraint: Reflections on the Dehumanization of Victims and Victimizers," *Journal of Social Issues* 29, Fall 1973, 25–61.

23. R. M. Kanter, *Men and Women of the Corporation* (New York: Basic Books, 1977), 189–205; and R. M. Kanter and B. A. Stein (eds.), *Life in Organizations* (New York: Basic Books, 1979), 80–96.

24. On this point, see J. Glass, "Organizations in Action," *Journal of Contemporary Business,* Autumn 1976, 91–111.

25. M. D. Ermann and R. J. Lundman (eds.), *Corporate and Governmental Deviance: Problems of Organizational Behavior in Contemporary Society,* 2nd ed. (New York: Oxford University Press, 1982), Chapter 1; and M. MacCoby, *The Gamesman* (New York: Simon & Schuster, 1976), 230.

26. Based on Box, 54–57.

27. C. Wright Mills, "A Diagnosis of Our Moral Uneasiness," in *Power, Politics, and People,* ed. I. L. Horowitz (New York: Oxford University Press, 1963), 445.

28. G. Sykes and D. Matza, "Techniques of Neutralization: A Theory of Delinquency," *American Sociological Review* 22 , May 1957, 664–70.

29. I. Janis, "Groupthink among Policy Makers," in *Sanctions for Evil,* ed. N. Sanford and C. Comstock (San Francisco: Jossey-Bass, 1971), 73.

30. H. Arendt, *Eichmann in Jerusalem: A Report on the Banality of Evil* (New York: Viking, 1964).

31. I. Janis, *Victims of Groupthink* (Boston: Houghton Mifflin, 1972), 9. For more on dehumanization, see V. Bernard et al., "Dehumanization," in Sanford and Comstock 102–24; and T. Duster, "Conditions for Guilt Free Massacre," also in Sanford and Comstock, 25–36.

32. Milton Friedman, *Capitalism and Freedom* (Chicago: University of Chicago Press, 1972), 133. For an interesting elaboration, see James W. McKie (ed.), *Social Responsibility and the Business Relationship* (Washington, DC: Brookings, 1974).

33. See M. Silver and D. Geller, "On the Irrelevance of Evil: The Organization and Individuals Action," *Journal of Social Issues* 34, Fall 1978, 125–36; D. Vaughn, "Crime between Organizations: Implications for Victimology," in *White-Collar Crime: Theory and Research,* ed. G. Geis and E. Stotland (Beverly Hills: Sage, 1980), 87; R. C. Kramer, "Corporate Crime: An Organizational Perspective," in *White-Collar and Economic Crime,* ed. Wickman and T. Dailey, (Lexington, MA: D.C. Heath, 1982) 75–94; and E. Smigel, "Public Attitudes toward Stealing in Relationship to the Size of the Victim Organization," *American Sociological Review* 21, February 1956, 320–47.

34. E. Fromm, *The Sane Society* (New York: Holt, Rinehart and Winston, 1955), 111.

35. R. Barnet, *The Roots of War* (Baltimore: Penguin, 1972); Mills, *The Power Elite,* 354–56.

36. D. Boorstin, *The Image: A Guide to Pseudo-Events in America* (New York: Harper & Row, 1961).

37. For an analysis of conservative, liberal, and socialist reactions to Watergate, see D. R. Simon, "Watergate as a Social Problem," paper presented at the meeting of the Society for the Study of Social Problems, August 1978.

38. A. Turk, "Organizational Deviance and Political Policing," *Criminology* 19, February 1981, 231–50.

39. B. Bernstein, "The Road to Watergate and Beyond: The Growth and Abuse of Executive Authority Since 1940," *Law and Contemporary Problems* 40, Spring 1976, 57–86.

40. M. Seeman,"Status and Identity: The Problem of Inauthenticity," *Pacific Sociological Review* 9, Fall 1966 and 67–73; B. Baxter, *Alienation and Inauthenticity* (London: Routledge Kegan Paul, 1982); A. Etzioni, "Basic Human Needs, Alienation, and Inauthenticity,"

American Sociological Review 33, December 1968, 870–84; and A. Etzioni, "Man and Society: The Inauthentic Condition," *Human Relations* 22, Spring 1969, 325–32.

41. W. Plasek, "Marxist and Sociological Concepts of Alienation: Implications for Social Problems Theory," *Social Problems* 21, February 1974, 316–28; and D. Schweitzer, "Contemporary Alienation Theory and Research," in *Sociology, the State of the Art,* ed. T. Bottomore et al. (Beverly Hills: Sage, 1982), 68.

42. R. Presthus, *The Organizational Society,* rev. ed. (New York: St. Martin's Press, 1978).

43. M. B. Clinard, *Corporate Ethics and Crime: The Role of Middle Management* (Beverly Hills: Sage, 1983), 136–38.

44. R. N. Kanungo, *Work Alienation: An Integrated Approach* (New York: Praeger, 1982), 157.

45. C. Reasons, "Crime and the Abuse of Power: Offenses beyond the Reach of the Law," in *White-Collar and Economic Crime,* ed. P. Wickman and T. Dailey (Lexington, MA: D.C. Heath, 1982), 59–72.

46. R. Keough, *Attachment Disorder* (New York: Dell, 1993).

47. Keogh, 56.

48. Ibid., 55.

49. Donald Kanter and Philip Mirvis, *The Cynical Americans* (San Francisco: Jossey-Bass, 1989).

50. Ibid., 34.

51. Jan Halper, *Quiet Desperation: The Truth about Successful Men* (New York: Warner Books, 1988).

52. Ibid., 66.

53. B. Fisse and J. Braithwaite, *The Impact of Publicity on Corporate Crime* (Albany, NY: SUNY Press, 1983), 240.

54. Mills, *Images of Man,* 17.

55. See Simon, *Social Problems and the Sociological Imagination,* Chapter 2, for a detailed analysis.

56. See A. Thio, *Deviant Behavior,* 2nd ed. (Boston: Houghton Mifflin, 1988), 88–96; and Box, Chapter 1.

57. This argument is based primarily on Box, Chapter 2. For a related perspective, consult the following: D. C. Smith, "White Collar Crime, Organized Crime, and the Business Establishment: Resolving a Crisis in Criminological Theory," in Wickman and Dailey 23–38; D. C. Smith, "Paragons, Pariahs, and Pirates: A Spectrum Based Theory of Enterprise," *Crime and Delinquency* 26, January 1980, 358–86; and S. Terreberry, "The Evolution of Organizational Environments," *Administrative Science Quarterly* 12, March 1968, 590–613. For estimates, see J. Cook, "The Invisible Enterprise," *Forbes,* September 29, 1980, 60–71.

58. *World Almanac and Book of Facts* (Mahwah, NJ: Funk & Wagnalls, 1994), 52.

59. *New York Times,* October 1993, A-1, A-8.

60. Army News Service, November 8, 1996.

61. Associated Press, April 29, 1997.

62. *New York Times,* March 10, 1994, A-1, A-11.

63. See John D'Emilio, "All That You Can Be," *The Nation,* June 7, 1993, 806–08; and W. Blumfield and Diane Raymond, *Looking at Gay and Lesbian Life,* ed. (Boston: Beacon Press, 1993), 252–54, for a discussion of institutional homophobia.

64. See, for example, Jerg Gerber and Susan Weeks, "Women as Victims of Corporate Crime: A Call for Research on a Neglected Topic," *Deviant Behavior* 13, 1992, 325–47.

65. See "60 Minutes," July 10, 1994, first segment.

66. Gerber and Weeks, 325ff.

67. The following discussion is based, in part, on D. Stanley Eitzen, "Teaching Social Problems: Implications of the Objectivist-Subjectivist Debate," paper presented at the 1984

meeting of the Society for the Study of Social Problems, San Antonio, Texas, August 23–26, 1984.

68. See Erich Goode, *Deviant Behavior,* 5th ed. (Upper Saddle River, NJ: Prentice-Hall, 1997), 354–56, for a constructionist critique of the position discussed here.

69. See David Simon, *Private Troubles and Public Issues* (Fort Worth, TX: Harcourt Brace, 1997), Chapter 1.

70. Eitzen, 7.

71. Clinard, 136–38; and Fisse and Braithwaite, 240.

72. See Kenneth Keniston, *The Uncommitted* (New York: Dell, 1965), Chapter 2.

9

The Scandalization of America

The Higher Immorality in an Era of Greed

Between 1860 and 1920, the United States suffered only two major crises involving corruption on the federal level. This amounts to about one scandal every fifty years. However, beginning in 1963 with the investigation into the assassination of President Kennedy, the American federal government has experienced repeated scandals. The scandals themselves are serious social problems, causing all manner of social harm.

- **Item:** When President Kennedy was assassinated in Dallas, Texas, on November 22, 1963, a cover-up of the investigation into the crime was personally ordered by President Johnson, Assistant Attorney General Katzenbach, and Federal Bureau of Investigation (FBI) Director Hoover. They allegedly felt that communist elements from either Cuba or the Soviet Union (or both) might be involved and feared a war would result. These officials agreed that the public must be convinced that Lee Harvey Oswald acted alone in killing the president. This was President Johnson's motive in setting up the Warren Commission in December 1963. Moreover, the Warren Commission did indeed find that Oswald had acted alone in killing the president, and that Dallas nightclub owner Jack Ruby had acted alone in killing Oswald (who at the time was surrounded by nearly 200 armed law enforcement officers) in the Dallas Police Station.

    Subsequent investigations into the crime by the House Special Committee on Assassinations (HSCA), 1975–1978, found numerous inconsistencies in the case. The HSCA found that President Kennedy "was probably assassinated as a result of a conspiracy."[1] Likely suspects included members of organized crime.[2] The HSCA concluded that Mafia bosses Marcello of New Orleans and Trafficante of Florida had the "means, motive, and opportunity" to assassinate the president, and/or that anti-Castro activists may have been involved.

Within the decade, a disturbing body of writing has emerged, raising questions about conspiracies in the killings of major political and civil rights leaders of the 1960s. These questions continue to tear at the soul of many Americans who look fondly upon the Kennedy era as a time of high public confidence and optimistic notions of progress and human concern. As noted in Chapter 1, conspiracy theory is extreme in its tone and incorrect in its substance. However, this does not mean that conspiracies do not happen. The issue becomes a matter of evidence either for or against conspiracy. Today, the evidence for conspiracy cannot be ignored.

- **Item:** Several studies have examined the notion that President John F. Kennedy was assassinated by the Marcello crime family of New Orleans. Carlos Marcello, now in federal prison, supposedly ordered the murder in an attempt to stop then Attorney General Robert Kennedy's efforts to deport Marcello to Costa Rica. There is also evidence that former Teamsters Union President Jimmy Hoffa, later imprisoned by Robert Kennedy, and Mafia family boss Santos Trafficante, solicited by the Central Intelligence Agency (CIA) in 1961 to assassinate Premier Castro of Cuba, were in on the conspiracy. In 1977, the HSCA found that these mobsters had "the motive, means, and opportunity to murder the president."[3] The committee's chief counsel, Robert Blakey, concluded: "The mob did it.… It's an historical fact."[4]

- **Item:** Marcello also allegedly ordered associate David Ferrie to Dallas immediately after the assassination. Ferrie supposedly gave orders to Marcello family associate Jack Ruby to kill the president's accused assassin, Lee Harvey Oswald. Ruby did in fact murder Oswald on national television two days after President Kennedy was killed. Oswald also had longstanding ties to the Marcello family through his uncle, a bookie, for whom Oswald worked during the spring and summer of 1963, just preceding the assassination.[5] Telephone records document numerous phone calls between Ruby, top Marcello aides, Florida mobster Trafficante, and convicted Teamsters boss Hoffa just prior to Oswald's murder.

- **Item:** FBI head J. Edgar Hoover knew about the Mafia conspiracy but covered it up to protect the bureau from criticism for its failure to investigate the case. Robert Kennedy was allegedly blackmailed into keeping quiet about Mafia involvement because Hoover had secret files on the Kennedy brothers showing their involvement in CIA plots to kill Castro, as well as President Kennedy's sexual dalliances with Marilyn Monroe and Mafia moll Judith Exner.[6]

- **Item:** It has also been alleged that the Mafia was responsible for the 1968 murders of presidential candidate Robert Kennedy and civil rights leader Martin Luther King, Jr., and the 1965 murder of black activist Malcolm X. For example, it has now been established that thirteen shots were fired at Robert Kennedy on June 5, 1968, five more than "lone" assassin Sirhan Sirhan's eight-shot revolver held, and the fatal bullets came from the rear, not from the front, where Sirhan stood in relationship to Kennedy. Separate examination of all fired bullets demonstrated that two .22-caliber guns were involved. Moreover, Sirhan had ties to the Mafia. He worked on the Carona horse-breeding farm, run by Frank Donneroummus, a convicted criminal and associate of the farm's part owner, Mafia member Mickey Cohen. Cohen was also an associate of Marcello and other mobsters implicated in President Kennedy's assassination. FBI Director Hoover consistently argued against the very existence of a Mafia in the United States. Thus, he denied the possibility of conspiracy in any of these assassinations, most likely to protect the bureau.

Journalist Bill Moyers has commented on the assassination of President Kennedy and the work of the CIA and related agencies (the secret government):

> The accusations linger; the suspicion of a dark, unsolved conspiracy behind Kennedy's murder. You can dismiss them,…but since we know how our secret government had planned for Castro, the possibility remains: Once we decide that anything goes, anything can come home to haunt us.[7]

Some of the most thorough research done on President Kennedy's assassination has been the investigation by physicist David Lifton. Over more than fifteen years, Lifton has painstakingly examined all forensic, autopsy, and photographic evidence available. He has drawn several conclusions.

1. Following the assassination, the president's body was brutally and surgically altered and the photos of it falsified so as not to show bullet entry holes in the back of his head, which was blown apart. Testimony by many doctors, nurses, and others who attended the president, as well as the original photos of his body, all document rear head wounds. The opening for the tracheotomy done on the president was also enlarged to cover up a wound to his throat. Kennedy's body also contained some unexplained abrasions and a "clip" device in his skull, which was designed to reattach the back of his head to the rest of his skull. This was done to hide the fact that the bullets that killed him came from more than one direction and were thus the work of more than one assassin. Lifton also found evidence that a bullet was surgically removed from the rear of Kennedy's head.[8]

2. The autopsy pictures and x-rays of Kennedy's body were never examined by the Warren Commission, which was established by President Johnson to investigate the assassination. Moreover, the Warren Commission was led to believe, by FBI Director Hoover and Assistant Attorney General Katzenbach, that Oswald acted as lone gunman, despite massive evidence to the contrary. Proof of Oswald's identity, gathered by the CIA, was also suppressed by various officials, including ex-CIA head Allen Dulles, himself a Warren Commission member.[9]

In 1977, the HSCA found that the killings of President Kennedy and Martin Luther King, Jr., were probably due to conspiracies, and that the FBI, CIA, and other government agencies had deliberately withheld evidence from the Warren Commission.[10] Certainly, only legitimate government agencies had the level of access to Kennedy's body necessary for the surgical alterations that were made.[11]

Considerable circumstantial evidence implicates the CIA in President Kennedy's assassination. The CIA was upset that the Kennedy administration had refused to launch further covert operations against Cuba following the attempted assassination of Castro and the failed CIA-backed Bay of Pigs invasion. What's more, many of the government agents involved in Watergate were also in Dallas the day Kennedy was shot. Some of these agents played roles in the Iran–Contra scandal (see later section) and other CIA-related covert operations as well, including the secret war in Cambodia in the early 1970s.

Perhaps the most thought-provoking issues in considering why the CIA would have killed Kennedy surround the Vietnam War and covert operations. The Kennedy administration was actively planning withdrawal of all U.S. military personnel from Vietnam, which angered the CIA. Likewise, Kennedy's order for the CIA to cease paramilitary (covert) operations during peacetime also met with strong disapproval. Not surprisingly, U.S. involvement in the Vietnam War escalated dramatically within a month after President Kennedy's assassination. Clearly, in many ways, the course of U.S. history was violently altered. The country would never be the same.

The precise nature of the conspiracy as related to the actual assassination, and those persons or organizations that were involved, was never determined, and, consequently, numerous theories have been advanced. Between 1966 and 1993, more than 600 books and 2,000 articles were written about the Kennedy assassination. The dominant view in these writings is that government agencies killed their own president. They did this because the president was going to make peace with the Soviet Union and end the Cold War. There is also speculation that Kennedy was going to disengage the

United States from its involvement in Vietnam. The JFK assassination is important in that it marks not only the first major postwar scandal but the beginning of a drastic decline in public confidence in government agencies and politicians.

Following President Kennedy's death, the United States escalated its presence in Vietnam. As previously discussed, the Vietnam War was loaded with a number of scandalous incidents that divided American public opinion and, ultimately, contributed to public distrust in government. Vietnam was followed by the Watergate scandal, which caused public trust to decline even further.

Watergate

The Watergate-related crimes committed by government officials represent acts of official secrecy and deception taken to the extreme.[12] They demonstrate forcefully and fearfully just how far away from the democratic ideal the U.S. political system had moved at the time and how close it was to approaching totalitarianism. In the words of David Wise:

> Watergate revealed that under President Nixon a kind of totalitarianism had already come to America, creeping in, not like Carl Sandburg's fog, on little cat feet, but in button-down shirts, worn by handsome young advertising and public relations men carrying neat attache cases crammed with $100 bills. Men willing to perjure themselves to stay on the team, to serve their leader. It came in the guise of "national security," a blanket term used to justify the most appalling criminal acts by men determined to preserve their own political power at any cost. It came in the form of the ladder against the bedroom window, miniature transmitters in the ceiling, wiretaps, burglaries, enemies lists, tax audits, and psychiatric profiles. It is not easy to write the word totalitarian when reporting about America, but if the word jars, or seems overstated, consider the dictionary definition: "Of or pertaining to a centralized government in which those in control grant neither recognition nor tolerance to parties of differing opinion."
>
> And that is very close to what happened, for, as we learned from the Watergate investigation, the enormous power of the government of the United States, including the police power and the secret intelligence apparatus, had been turned loose against the people of the United States, at least against those who held differing opinions, against the opposition political party, and the press.[13]

The Watergate investigation revealed a number of criminal and undemocratic actions by President Nixon and his closest advisors.[14]

- **Item:** Burglars, financed by funds from the Committee to Re-elect the President, broke into and bugged the headquarters of the Democratic party in the Watergate apartment complex. These individuals were paid hush money and promised executive clemency to protect the president and his advisors.

- **Item:** Burglars also broke into the office of the psychiatrist of Daniel Ellsberg, the person who leaked the Pentagon Papers to the press. These papers, of course, were instrumental in showing the public how it had been systematically deceived by a series of presidents during the long Vietnam War. While the trial was in session, the White House offered the judge in the Ellsberg case the possibility of his being named director of the FBI.
- **Item:** President Nixon's personal attorney solicited money for an illegally formed campaign committee and offered an ambassadorship in return for a campaign contribution. Money gathered from contributions, some illegally, was systematically laundered to conceal the donors. Much of this money was kept in cash so when payoffs occurred, the money could not be traced.
- **Item:** President Nixon ordered secret wiretapping of his own aides, several journalists, and even his brother. Additionally, he had secret microphones planted in his offices to record clandestinely every conversation.
- **Item:** John Mitchell, attorney general of the United States, participated in preliminary discussions about bugging the Democratic headquarters. He even suggested that one means of gaining information about the Democrats was to establish a floating bordello at the Miami convention.
- **Item:** The president's men participated in a campaign of dirty tricks to discredit various potential Democratic nominees for president, including the publication and distribution of letters—purporting to come from Senator Muskie—claiming that Senator Jackson was a homosexual. The White House also requested tax audits of administration opponents.
- **Item:** The White House used the CIA in an effort to halt the FBI investigation of Watergate. The director of the FBI even destroyed vital legal evidence at the suggestion of the president's aides.
- **Item:** President Nixon offered aides H. R. Haldeman and John Erlichman as much as $300,000 from a secret slush fund for their legal fees after they were forced to resign.
- **Item:** The president and his advisors, using the cloak of national security, strongly resisted attempts by the special prosecutor, the courts, and Congress to get the facts in the case. Various administration officials were found guilty of perjury and withholding information.
- **Item:** When the president, under duress, did provide transcripts of the tapes or other materials, they had been edited.
- **Item:** The president, on television and in press releases, lied to the U.S. public, over and over again.

This infamous list of discretions comprises a tangled web of activities that posed a significant threat to the democratic political system of the

United States. All the efforts were directed at subverting the political process so that the administration in power would stay in power, regardless of the means. There was a systematic effort to discredit enemies of the administration, to weaken the two-party system, and to control the flow of information to citizens.

Although the Nixon administration was guilty of these heinous acts, we should not assume that Nixon was the first U.S. president to be involved in such chicanery. Watergate was no aberration. Rather, it was a startling illustration of government practices that have been significant throughout U.S. history.

Moreover, there is ample evidence of various linkages between the Watergate scandal and other major American scandals since 1963, including the Iran–Contra affair.[15]

Iran–Contra

In 1987, news broke concerning what was to be the most damaging scandal of the Reagan administration, the so-called Iran–Contra affair. The root of the scandal involved the diversion of funds from profits on missiles sold to the Iranian government. The profits were diverted to the Nicaraguan Contras, a counterrevolutionary force virtually created by the CIA.[16] At first the entire episode was blamed on Marine Lieutenant Colonel Oliver North, with virtually all high-ranking officials of the Reagan administration claiming they were "out of the loop" concerning any knowledge of the events. Subsequent investigations and trial testimony, however, pointed to a massive cover-up by White House aides and others.

North's 1989 trial revealed that at a 1984 national security group meeting composed of Vice President Bush, the Joint Chiefs of Staff, several cabinet officers, and President Reagan, a discussion of Contra aid based on solicitation of "third" parties (foreign governments) took place. This was adopted as a strategy of getting around the Boland Amendment that forbid further military aid to the Contras. President Reagan personally solicited the largest contributions for Contra aid from foreign nations, and a number of Latin American governments were requested to cooperate by falsifying arms sales transactions so knowledge that the weapons were for the Contras could be hidden. Those nations agreeing to falsify such documents were promised increased U.S. foreign aid.

Both illegal arms sales and illegal solicitation of funds were orchestrated by a secret group, the Enterprise, set up apart from the CIA and other governmental agencies to ensure secrecy. The Enterprise was composed of retired military and intelligence personnel, arms dealers, and drug smugglers.[17]

Actually, the North trial was part of a cover-up that began when President Reagan appointed the Tower Commission to look into his handling of

Irangate. In the end, the commission reported that President Reagan had been unaware of what was going on around him and that his management style was based on his being removed from decision making. The Tower Commission also found that the Iranian arms sale was mismanaged by various members of the Reagan White House staff. Reagan had told the Tower Commission that he was unaware that North and the other Reagan appointees to the National Security Council (NSC), including Admiral John Poindexter and Colonel Robert McFarlane, had been aiding the Contras. But it was North who was first tried for creating an organization known as the Enterprise in order to execute the arms deal. Along with retired Air Force General Richard Secord and Iranian-born businessman Albert Hakim (both of whom are awaiting trial), North was charged with, among other things, making a profit from the sale of government property.

This was actually a trivial charge, considering that North could have stood trial for lying to Congress and perhaps even treason. Despite later remarks made about his lack of involvement, in 1987, President Reagan told the press that he had definitely been involved in the decision to support the Contras. In fact, North's trial revealed Reagan's direct involvement in Contragate. President Reagan was prevented from testifying at North's trial because classified information was withheld by the very government prosecuting North.

Early Involvement with Iran

There is evidence that the Iran–Contra episode was rooted in two incidents that involved George Bush, who was then vice president. According to a recent documentary, vice-presidential nominee Bush went to Paris before the 1980 election to meet with Iranian officials.[18] At the time, the Iranians were holding some eighty American hostages, who had been kidnapped from the U.S. embassy in Teheran by Iranian revolutionaries. The American hostages were a crucial issue in the 1980 U.S. presidential election, in which the Republican Ronald Reagan sought to unseat Democratic President Jimmy Carter. In 1980, Bush allegedly offered the Iranians arms to delay release of the American hostages until after the election in November. Had the hostages been released prior to the election, such an "October Surprise" surely would have increased Carter's chance of winning.

Tremendous controversy still surrounds this affair. In early May 1991, Gary Sick, former Ford appointee to the NSC, claimed that it was Reagan campaign manager and subsequent CIA Director William Casey, not Vice President Bush, who met in Washington, D.C., in late February or early March 1980 with Jamshid Hashemi, an Iranian arms dealer.[19] Hashemi himself has admitted to meeting with Casey and two additional U.S. aides in Madrid in July 1980 and Paris in October 1980. He claims the outcome of the meetings was initial U.S. shipments of tires for Iranian fighting vehicles via Israel. Similar claims have also been made by former Iranian President

Bani-Sadr.[20] Interestingly, a former CIA operative, Richard Brenneke, claimed in sworn testimony in 1988 that he met with Casey, Iranian Manucher Ghorbanifar, Israeli and French intermediaries, and Donald Gregg (then a CIA officer attached to the NSC).[21] Gregg went on to become Vice President Bush's aide and is suspected of involvement in Operation Black Eagle, another scandal predating the Iran–Contra affair.

The possibility that George Bush attended the Paris meeting still exists,[22] but most observers now feel that Casey made the deal. Casey was also likely the man who arranged for the theft of President Carter's debate-briefing papers in October 1980.[23] There were calls for a congressional investigation into the October Surprise incident, but no such calls have yet arisen for a similar look into Operation Black Eagle.

Diverting Funds to the Contras

While this may have been the beginning of arms sales to Iran, the idea of diverting funds to the Contras did not take place until after the 1980 election, when President Reagan and CIA head William Casey actually created the Contras. The first illegal operation to aid them took place in 1983, once again involving George Bush. From 1983–1986, Bush was involved in Operation Black Eagle, the purpose of which was to find a way around the Boland aid prohibition. Black Eagle was run out of Bush's office by CIA agent Donald Gregg, a longtime friend from the days when Bush was head of the CIA. Gregg and other operatives negotiated an arrangement with Panamanian dictator Manuel Noriega, whereby Panamanian airfields and front companies would be made available to Black Eagle operatives in exchange for Panamanian use of Black Eagle cargo planes. In fact, the planes were used to smuggle cocaine and marijuana into the United States at the behest of Colombia's Medellin cartel. "Several of those involved in the operation were aware that Bush and Donald Gregg knew about Noriega's use of Black Eagle for drug running and that nothing was done to stop it."[24] It was also learned that General Noriega had dossiers and videotapes about Vice President Bush's role in the Black Eagle project. Black Eagle itself was part of a plan to defy the first Boland Amendment, which Congress had passed in order to stop aid to the Nicaraguan Contras. Between October 1984 and October 1986, Congress acted further to prohibit aid to the Nicaraguan Contras by passing additional Boland Amendments. In response, the Reagan administration launched what ultimately became the Iran–Contra affair. Along with the Iran–Contra operation, involving Lieutenant Colonel North and Enterprise, there was also a further resupply effort whereby planeloads of Colombian cocaine were flown to Costa Rican farmlands owned by John Hull, CIA/NSC liaison to the Contras. Hull claimed in 1984–1985 to have received $10,000 a month from the NSC. The cocaine in question belonged to Pablo Escobar and Jorge Ochoa, two major Medellin cartel figures, whose business accounts for 80 percent of the cocaine smuggled into the United States each year. Once off-loaded at Hull's ranch, the drugs were shipped by sea and air to the United States. Hull was paid by the Medellin traffickers in return for the labor and facilities supplied for the operation. The proceeds Hull was paid allegedly went to buy arms for the Contras. In other cases, the Contras smuggled drugs directly, possibly purchasing them from the Medellin cartel. The drugs were again flown to Hull's Costa Rican ranch, where they were swapped for arms.[25]

The Scandal: Contragate

The selling of arms to Iran and the diversion of funds from such sales to the Nicaraguan Contras were accomplished by setting up a private supply operation using a company owned by retired Air Force General Richard Secord. Secord's American National Management Corporation has been involved in other covert operations besides Contragate, including providing logistical support for the military elite's Delta Force commandos and short-term secret airlift operations.[26] In fact, it appears as though the Iran–Contra operation was conceived by Secord as part of a meeting on special operations held in March 1983 at the National Strategy Information Center at Georgetown University. The meeting was attended by a number of CIA officials, military officers (including North), Secord associate Ted Schackley (later involved in Contra shipments himself), and Carl Channel (used by North to raise private funds to buy weapons for the Contras and to raise money illegally for candidates supporting the administration's Contra policy). Secord's philosophy of the NSC's role is expressed in his master's thesis, written in the late 1970s at the Naval War College, in which he spoke of the need to circumvent Congress and the bureaucracy in setting up covert operations and argued that the NSC would be a likely place to attempt such circumvention.[27]

The Nugan–Hand Bank Affair

Another scandal involving Secord and others associated with Contragate involves the Nugan–Hand Bank. This bank, set up in Australia by a host of former U.S. military officers and ex-CIA agents, hired as one of its attorneys former CIA Director William Colby. Subsequently, bank personnel were involved in a scheme to defraud U.S. civilians working in Saudi Arabia of their wages, which were deposited with bank officials ostensibly for the purpose of investment. The bank has also been involved in laundering drug money and in a smuggling operation that included former CIA agent Thomas Clines, associate of another former CIA operative, and Edmund Wilson, who is now serving a prison sentence for selling arms to Libya's Premier Muammar Kaddafi. In his Nugan–Hand dealings, Clines was involved in selling Philippine jeeps to Egypt and was convicted of submitting $8 million in false vouchers to the Department of Defense. Another Nugan–Hand arms sale involved Edmund Wilson directly, along with bank employee Bernie Houghton, a businessman with CIA and U.S. military connections in Australia since 1967.[28]

The Iran–Contra Conspiracy—"Operation Polecat"

At the State Department, the Iran operation was described as "Operation Polecat" because they thought it stank so much. George Bush at first lied and claimed that he had been "out of the loop" and unaware of Iran–Contra activities. Even though, as vice-president, Bush headed a *Vice President's Task Force on Terrorism,* which urged that it was futile to make deals with hostage-takers, he later admitted that he was aware of the hostage deal but did not admit to knowledge of diversion of funds to the Contras. Ironically, by violating their own rules and dealing for hostages, the Reagan–Bush team proved their own point. Such secret operations released three hostages but encouraged the taking of more.

The entire cover-up—lying to Congress and hiding of evidence—had been intended to protect Ronald Reagan from possible impeachment. In June 1992, Special Prosecutor Walsh indicted former Secretary of Defense Caspar Weinberger in order to attempt to prove a conspiracy to cover up Reagan's involvement. The charges were that Weinberger had lied to Congress and obstructed justice, based upon entries in his diary.

Finally came the "Christmas Eve Massacre" (December 1992) in which lame duck President George Bush issued pardons to most of those convicted or under investigation claiming that they "did not profit or seek to profit from the conduct," that they were acting in what they believed to have been the national interest, and that the Iran–Contra investigation represented an unnecessary "criminalization of policy differences." Bush did not pardon Secord, Hakim, and Clines, who were convicted in Iran–Contra and whose motivations appeared to be more of a mercenary nature. The pardons left Lawrence Walsh little choice but to close down the probe.

The message sent by George Bush in issuing the pardons was that government officials are free to violate the law whenever they believe their behavior is for the good of the country, even if it is in violation of the Constitution.

Connections and Conspiracies

A shocking set of additional Central American connections runs through the Contragate affair and involves such groups as the World Anti-Communist League (WACL), whose membership includes another of the Contragate arms dealers, former U.S. General Singlaub, who was part of the North/ Secord Enterprise venture. WACL's Latin American affiliate, known as CAL, possesses direct links to Bolivian officials involved in cocaine smuggling and now convicted ex-Nazi turned drug trafficker Klaus Barbie. Barbie is reputed to have supplied the CIA with a list of KGB agents operating in Latin America and organized a meeting, with CIA approval, of the Condor Group, made up of intelligence officials from right-wing regimes in Argentina, Chile, and Bolivia. Barbie was also a security consultant to Roberto Suarez, a major cocaine dealer and producer.[29] WACL members form Guatemala, Taiwan, and Argentina have been represented in Washington by former White House aide Michael Deaver, who lobbied for U.S. military aid. The Guatemalan and Argentine officials represented by Deaver have been tied to death squads in those nations. Also among CAL's members is D'Aubuisson, organizer of El Salvador's death squads. Finally, it is known that the Argentine affiliate of the WACL was responsible for the deaths of Archbishop Romero and twenty-eight other liberation advocates in Latin America. Moreover, the former Argentine interior minister has been tied directly to Paraguayan cocaine trafficking. In turn, Paraguayan intelligence chief Pastor Coronel, coordinator of local death squads, is a partner of Corsican drug smuggler Augusto Ricord, who is linked to the Gambino Mafia family in New York.[30]

The Contras themselves have recently been the study of an investigation by a human rights organization mandated by Congress as a condition of military aid. The investigating body cited twenty-two abuses of human rights by Contra troops between December 1985 and June 1987, including the execution of eight Sandinista prisoners, forced recruitment of Nicaraguan Mennonites, the killing of Baptist relief workers and a Catholic social worker, the abduction of Sumo Indians, the killing of three civilians, and the kidnapping of two civilian women.[31]

A Latin American drugs/arms connection also involves the Contras. Colombian cocaine cartel launderer Ramon Milian-Rodriguez recently testified in front of a congressional committee on narcotics that he funneled nearly $10 million to the Contras via CIA operative Felix Rodriguez in order to gain favor with Drug Enforcement Agency and CIA operatives. Rodriguez (aka Max Gomez) helped oversee the supplying of the Contras in the Enterprise operation.[32]

Other reports of a Contra cocaine link are disturbing.

- **Item:** A cable message from the U.S. ambassador to Costa Rica (Tams) to Lieutenant Colonel North dated March 27, 1986, noted that "Popp" Chamorro, a Contra leader on the Costa Rican border, was allegedly involved in drug trafficking. North aide Robert Owen also testified that a plane delivering rocket-launching equipment to the Contras, secured by the CIA, was involved in drug running. The company hired by the CIA had a long history of cocaine smuggling, according to Owen.[33]
- **Item:** Perhaps most disturbing is the alleged episode concerning Tom Posey, head of the Alabama-based Civilian Military Assistance Group that aided in supplying weapons to the Contras. One Contra operative,

Jesus Garcia, has testified that Posey hatched a plot to assassinate the U.S. ambassador to Costa Rica and blame it on the Sandinistas in an effort to draw the United States into a direct military confrontation in Latin America.[34]

Contragate and the Changing Nature of American Power and Corruption

As power has become more and more concentrated at the federal level and as the economy itself has become more militarized (see Chapter 5), the nature of corruption has changed. What is not generally appreciated about this prevalence of corruption is what it reveals about the structure of power in American society.

Contragate, the Wedtech scandal, former White House employee Michael Deaver, and the problems of Jackie Presser and the Mafia-linked Teamsters Union all seem totally unrelated at first glance. Yet a deeper look reveals a disturbing pattern of interaction among officials of the executive branch of the U.S. government, former CIA agents turned businessmen, organized crime figures and drug traffickers, and large corporations.[35]

Wedtech, now bankrupt, was linked to Attorney General Edwin Meese, who was accused of securing a large defense contract for Wedtech at a time when he owned stock in the company. By further coincidence, Lieutenant Colonel Oliver North belongs to the Officers of Christian Fellowship and the Full Gospel Businessmen's Association—groups that provided funds that helped launch the careers of right-wing preachers Jim Bakker and Pat Robertson.[36]

Other links show a disturbing pattern of relationships.[37]

- **Item:** Wedtech paid Robert Wallach, attorney for and close friend of Attorney General Meese, $1 million in stocks and cash. In 1982, Meese's intervention on Wedtech's behalf obtained a $32 million Army contract.
- **Item:** Wallach used his ties to Meese to intervene in a scheme involving building a billion-dollar pipeline from Iraq to the Gulf of Aqaba and alleged payoffs to the Israeli Labor Party. Meese also solicited the aid of NSC advisor Robert McFarlane, who saw the project as a method of balancing the advantages to Iran in the Contragate arms-for-hostages deal, which he and Oliver North masterminded.
- **Item:** International arms dealer Adnan Khashoggi, involved in financing the Irangate arms sale, is now under investigation by a New York grand jury for allegedly assisting Ferdinand and Imelda Marcos in transferring hundreds of millions of dollars' worth of Manhattan real estate and art objects to Khashoggi in order to keep the Philippine gov-

ernment from obtaining them. Khashoggi and the Marcoses were indicted for fraud but later acquitted.

- **Item:** Francis D. Gomez of the Washington public relations firm International Business Communications, which was used by Lieutenant Colonel North to funnel funds raised by Carl Spitz to the Contras, was also serving, at $21,000 per month, as the Washington representative of Impulso Turistico y Financiero. Impulso was also used by General Manuel Noriega to perform certain tasks in the United States.
- **Item:** Noriega, while in the employ of the CIA at $200,000 per year, aided North and Secord in support of the Contras in violation of the Boland Amendment. At the same time, Noriega also supplied arms to M-19, a Colombian left-wing terrorist organization aligned with the Medellin cocaine cartel. In turn, Noriega contributed to the organization of Lyndon LaRouche, found guilty in 1988 of credit card swindling. Noriega was tried for drug trafficking in Miami and convicted.

Characteristics of Contemporary Scandal

All of the scandals listed above share a number of common characteristics:

1. They were all the result of secret actions of government agencies (especially the FBI, CIA, executive office of the president) that were either illegal or unethical and caused severe physical, financial, and/or moral harm to the nation. All have taken place since the passage of the National Security Act of 1947, which institutionalized the most secretive aspects of what President Eisenhower termed the military–industrial complex, and C. Wright Mills characterized as the power elite and higher immorality (as described in Chapters 1 and 2). The key here is that organizations with immense resources—not merely corrupt individuals—were involved in criminal acts and their cover-up.

2. All the episodes discussed were the subject of official government hearings or investigations, some of which were nationally televised. Despite official investigations, the original causes of most of these scandals remain unknown. Thus motives for President Kennedy's assassination, the reason(s) for the Watergate break-in, and the possible involvement of Vice President Bush, President Reagan, and CIA Director Casey in planning the Iranian arms sales and diversion of funds to the Contras remain matters of heated debate. Indeed one of the hallmarks of the official investigation of modern scandal is that the investigations tend to become part of the scandals themselves, leaving unanswered questions concerning the causes of and mysterious events surrounding scandals to linger.

Unanswered questions characterize scandals both large and small. Consider the Bush administration, which left office with a host of unanswered questions concerning its deviant activity. According to Hagan and Simon:[38]

- **Item:** Brett Kimberlin, while serving time as a federal prisoner for drug offenses, was on two separate occasions placed in detention and *incommunicado* from the media in order to silence him. Kimberlin claimed that in the early seventies he frequently sold marijuana to Dan Quayle, then a law student and later to be vice president. During the 1988 presidential campaign, Kimberlin was invited twice by reporters to discuss these charges. In both instances, before he could speak, he was put into detention by order of J. Michael Quinlan, then director of the Federal Bureau of Prisons. This was unprecedented—never before had a bureau director isolated an individual inmate. A report issued by Senator Carl Levin (D, MI) and chairperson of the Subcommittee on Oversight of Government Management concluded that Kimberlin was silenced for political reasons. According to one source, the Drug Enforcement Agency (DEA) had informed the Bush campaign that it had a file on Quayle alleging cocaine use. The truth or falsity of these allegations remains a mystery.
- **Item:** The Inslaw case charges that the U.S. Department of Justice, beginning during the Reagan administration, stole proprietary software from the Hamiltons and tried to force their small company out of business in order to pirate its software and sell it for the benefit of Reagan cronies. Two court cases have ruled in favor of the Hamiltons and against the Justice Department. The software that they had developed that was the subject of dispute was PROMIS (Prosecutor's Management Information System), which enabled the computerization of law enforcement and criminal justice system files. The Hamiltons' defense attorney, Elliot Richardson, discovered that Inslaw's lucrative contracts and software had been planned to be passed on to then Attorney General Meese's friends. Further intrigue was added to the Inslaw case when, in 1990, a free-lance writer Danny Casolaro mysteriously "committed suicide" while hot on the trail of what he described as an outlaw intelligence operation behind Inslaw. The Inslaw matter remains unresolved to this day.

3. Moreover, numerous unanswered questions concerning events within each scandal remain shrouded in mystery. What was Lee Harvey Oswald's true identity? Why did Jack Ruby, in front of more than 200 armed officers, shoot him? Did the Nixon White House hire Arthur Bremmer to assassinate George Wallace in 1972? Why was the FBI the first agency to meet Dorothy Hunt's airplane following its bombing? Did the 1980 Reagan campaign arrange an "October surprise" of its own that eventually became the Iran–Contra scandal? These and many other questions await answers.

4. Recent political scandals, especially Iran–Contra and the savings and loan episode, interrelate, not only to each other but to other types of crime and deviance as well. As mentioned earlier, the secret government is a product of the National Security Act passed in 1947.

Almost immediately, intelligence agencies began classifying documents and budgets (see "The Pentagon's 'Black' Budget" case study in Chapter 5) and engaging in covert operations using a bewildering collection of personnel: ex-Nazis, Mafia gangsters, arms dealers, right-wing extremists, corrupt politicians and bureaucrats, and current and former CIA and military officials. By 1963, the secret government had become a force unto itself. Since then, it has been linked to every major scandal at the federal level in U.S. domestic and foreign affairs.

- **Item:** Virtually every member of the Watergate break-in team (the "plumbers") was involved in the failed CIA Bay of Pigs invasion, the idea for which belonged to then Vice President Richard Nixon. One Watergate team member, Frank Sturgis, was also part of the CIA–Mafia plot to assassinate Fidel Castro in the 1960s.[39]

  Sturgis also knew and had dealings with Lee Oswald, the alleged lone assassin of President John F. Kennedy, as did former CIA agent E. Howard Hunt and many other CIA employees. Watergate burglar Bernard Barker was also involved with Jack Ruby, who killed Oswald several days after his arrest. Ruby was also tied to an anti-Castro group in New Orleans that had links to the New Orleans Marcello crime family, which was implicated in 1977 by the House Assassinations Committee in the killing of President Kennedy. Both Hunt and Sturgis participated in a plot to mislead investigators concerning Oswald's real identity.[40]

  Sturgis was also linked to Mafia gambling operations in Cuba from 1959 to 1961. Indeed, there is evidence that the hush money paid by the Nixon administration to the Watergate team was obtained from the Mafia and paid in part to keep the burglars from revealing their participation in the CIA–Mafia attempt to kill Castro. Interestingly, eleven former members of the Warren Commission were hired by Watergate defendants, including President Nixon, as defense attorneys.[41]

- **Item:** President Nixon, for his part, had long-standing ties to organized crime and the secret government. Nixon and close friend Bebe Rebozo invested in the Mafia-linked Keyes Realty Company, of which Watergate burglar Eugene Martinez was vice-president. The loan for the investment came from Arthur Dresser, an associate of mob financier Meyer Lansky, and another suspected plotter in the Kennedy assassination,

Teamsters boss Jimmy Hoffa. Rebozo was also a partner in the Mafia-financed Resorts International Paradise Casino, profits from which were skimmed by organized crime.[42]

- **Item:** There are also some fascinating links between the Watergate and Iran–Contra scandals, most of which center around Reagan CIA Director and former Nixon Securities and Exchange Commission (SEC) head William Casey. In 1970, Casey was a partner in an agribusiness called Multiponics; the firm filed for bankruptcy in 1971. Another partner in the business was Carl Biehl, associate of Mafia boss and suspected Kennedy assassin Carlos Marcello since the 1950s. Casey also represented a New Jersey waste disposal company, SCA, in 1977. SCA, according to New Jersey state police intelligence, had deep ties to organized crime. Two close Casey associates, Max Hugel and William McCann, men whom Casey sponsored for Reagan administration appointments, were also closely linked to organized crime.[43]

- **Item:** The Reagan administration also had numerous links with organized crime. Jacky Presser, the Teamsters Union head, was used as an informant for the FBI at the same time he was under investigation for defrauding the union's pension fund. Presser, long linked to the Cleveland Mafia, was later named as a special economic advisor by Reagan. Presser advised the Reagan team, including George Bush, to select two appointees with ties to organized crime: as labor secretary, Ray Donovan, who was later twice indicted for Mafia-linked union activity, and as a Labor Department official, Roy Brewer, who was former head of the Mafia-dominated stagehands union and a friend of Reagan's since his days as president of the Screen Actors Guild (1940s–1950s).

- **Item:** Another close Reagan associate with Mafia ties was Senator Paul Laxalt (R, NV). Laxalt and his brother invested in a Carson City, Nevada, casino, Ormsby House, with partner Bernard Nemerov, who had a long association with the Mafia. Laxalt was also instrumental in the 1971 Nixon decision to commute the prison sentence of Jimmy Hoffa. Hoffa mysteriously disappeared, however, just before he was to testify concerning his knowledge of the assassination of President Kennedy. Laxalt was Reagan's campaign manager in 1976, 1980, and 1984 and was nearly nominated for vice president.[44]

Thus there is an emerging body of evidence that much of what is mistakenly called the American "street crime" problem is actually part of a complicated network of relationships among criminals and organizations at all strata of society (see Chapter 8).

5. The episodes in this chapter also contain numerous examples of what William Chambliss has described as "state organized crime,"[45] which stems from the need of nations for legitimacy, which is rooted in the rule of law.

Some laws, however, conflict with other needs of nations, especially the need to accumulate wealth. Chambliss explored the origins of state-organized crime in European nations' support for piracy in the New World between 1400 and 1800. In the modern era, state-organized crime involves institutionalized practices discussed in depth in this book: namely, state-sponsored drug and arms smuggling; assassinations of foreign leaders (with the cooperation of organized crime syndicates); illegal surveillance of U.S. citizens; illegal drug experimentation on unsuspecting subjects by the CIA; and the illegal harassment of dissidents by the FBI. While Chambliss's concept of state-organized crime constitutes both a useful theory and typology of deviance by governmental elites, it does not include the possibility of either assassination of domestic officials or what has been termed "state-supported corporate crime,"[46] wherein the state and private corporations cooperate in the commission of criminal acts (see Chapter 8). The many unanswered questions concerning the secret government's involvement in assassinations and scandals (e.g., the killings of President Kennedy, Martin Luther King, Jr., Robert Kennedy, and Malcolm X; the 1972 attempt on the life of Democratic presidential candidate George Wallace; and the BCCI scandal) lead us to conclude that the discipline of criminal justice has neglected this topic for far too long. Indeed, the CIA has trained more police forces around the world than virtually any other agency of U.S. government, yet it is almost never mentioned in criminal justice and law enforcement texts. Obtaining a working knowledge of the motives for, and depth of, state-organized and state-supported corporate crime is essential to understanding elite deviance—as well as how the overall political economy of the nation functions. For example, Chambliss claims that not all governmental agencies are likely to engage in state-organized crimes—usually just the more secretive ones. The CIA, FBI, DEA, and various intelligence agencies are in ideal positions to engage in such acts. Indeed, these agencies have repeatedly obstructed justice in the name of secrecy.

- **Item:** The CIA and FBI covered up the crimes of former employee and Cuban exile Ricardo Morales, who, on CIA orders, bombed a Cuban airliner in Venezuela, killing seventy-three people.[47]

While the activities of the secret government constitute a crucial topic, it is also a challenging one. It will require innovative research strategies as well as new theories about the nature of the American political economy and culture. Moreover, there are problems with validity in such research. Considering the secrecy of the organizations and the emotional nature of the issues involved, this is hardly surprising. But what may hang in the balance is the very freedom Americans have come to associate with democracy.

The Study of Elite Deviance

What implications do these examples hold for elite deviance theory, methodology, and policy?

The power elite of which C. Wright Mills wrote so eloquently has taken on dimensions that might surprise him. Not only are corporations, politicians, and military officials interlinked with Mafia figures, international narcotics smugglers, and small-time street criminals, but the CIA seems to regularly employ a vast array of drug dealers, arms smugglers, and ex-military and ex-CIA officials in its covert operations. Contragate, it would appear, is the tip of an iceberg, the dimensions of which are currently unknown. We must await further revelation by whistle-blowers, investigative journalists, and perhaps even enemies of the United States who stand to gain from such an exposé. In any case, the American power elite is clearly more structurally and morally complex than Mills initially proposed.

"Most criminologists tend to separate white-collar crime and the explanations for it from the organizational context and the political economy of which it is a part."[48] Specific goals, such as profit and power, often create situations wherein values conflict and deviant and/or criminal activity becomes an acceptable means of achieving such goals.[49] Situations that have the potential of bringing considerable harm are perpetrated in the pursuit of organizational goals by persons who would be reluctant to commit such acts outside their organizational roles. Indeed, as Montagu and Matson note, the new face of evil in the world wears the mask of everyday normality precisely because evil is now committed without feelings of shame, guilt, or other moral recognition. Instead, elites commit acts of great harm, often without knowing they are doing anything wrong.[50]

Moreover, scholars have studied crime in general and white-collar crime in particular on a type-by-type and case-by-case basis. This approach stems from the individualistic bias built into the legal apparatus of Western society. Overlooked, however, are the links among different types of crime as well as among various scandals.

Conclusion

The discussion in this chapter has not been in the methodological tradition of social science. It has been devoid of the representative samples and empirical testing that characterize mainstream research. Clearly, the study of elite victimization and organizational behavior is in an embryonic state in terms of description and classification of events. Moreover, even when and if genuine testable propositions are put forth, traditional social science methodology will be of little use in much of the undertaking, for several reasons.

(1) Much of the information about this field of study is secretive. It does not lend itself to observation, survey, variation of experimental design, cost-benefit analysis, or other traditional methodology that has been used in social science research. (2) Much of the information available is often intentionally deceptive. That is, false records, fronts, and other devices are created to hide exactly what must be studied. There is also a legitimized value system, a profit motive, and a desire for self-preservation that support and encourage elite deviance. (3) The behavior to be examined involves both individuals and organizations, thereby not allowing for a clear unit of analysis. Movement from individual to social structural conditions and from informal to formal groups is the rule rather than the exception, once again making traditional social science research methods implausible.

Do these methodological difficulties leave us unable as social scientists to accomplish systematic study? We contend that they do not, although it seems clear that such study will require new research standards and tools. Finally, contrary to the independent or separate traditional conceptualizations in this field, we argue that three behaviors in this area—namely, corporate (organizational) crime, corporate (organizational) deviance, and behaviors that are legitimate but socially harmful—are intricately related to the extent that to study them independently would provide an inaccurate picture. White-collar crime at the individual level is an important component in this field of inquiry, due to the individualistic nature of our criminal justice system. That is, behaviors at the organizational level can be understood structurally, and reducing them to individual incidents of criminal behavior distracts from the structural understanding. Thus, Contragate was about one presidential administration's attempt to circumvent laws that proscribed what it wanted to do. Yet individuals have been indicted and convicted, not the entire administration or even its leaders. Another crucial issue is the nature of the evidence gathered in support of whatever propositions may be put forth. Validity problems loom large in research of this nature because much of the information gathered comes from private memos, government cables, and testimony given by people who may all have personal axes to grind. Perhaps the only solid evidence comes in the form of criminal conviction, as documented by court transcripts and files of law enforcement agencies. And on occasion, confidential information is leaked to the media and reveals what would have otherwise remained suppressed or distorted. These incidents are rare, but the evidence they provide can be substantiated by interviews with remaining role players. Regardless of how information is obtained, validity problems will remain, calling into question whether the study of elite deviance falls within the purview of social science. This is a question that those who study and work in sociology, political science, and criminal justice must decide for themselves. Indeed, this promises to be an issue in the debate over the definition and scope of elite deviance. For our part, we do not see how those disciplines that call themselves the social sciences can avoid the study of behavior that is so prevalent and demonstrably harmful—not only to American society but to the entire world.

Critical Thinking Exercise 9.1:
Scandal: The Hidden Dimensions _____

This chapter began with a discussion of some of the characteristics of modern scandal on the federal level. One of the most interesting aspects of contemporary scandal concerns lingering questions that remain the subject of controversy and debate. For example, after more than twenty-five years, we still do not know why the Nixon administration decided to bug the Democratic National Committee headquarters in the Watergate apartment complex. This and many other unanswered questions are the subject of this exercise.

Select one of the following scandals:

- Watergate
- Iran–Contra
- Inslaw
- The savings & loan scandal
- Iraqgate

Look up articles about any one of the above scandals. Then write a paper answering the following questions:

1. What remains unknown concerning the causes of the scandal?
2. What other scandalous events are speculated about by writers as occurring during the scandal? For example, some people have speculated that the Nixon administration hired Arthur Bremmer to assassinate George Wallace during the 1972 election campaign.
3. What reforms are proposed to prevent such scandals from taking place in the future?

Endnotes _____

1. Anthony Summers, *Conspiracy* (New York: Paragon House, 1980), 14.
2. Select Committee on Assassinations of the U.S. House of Representatives, Volume IX (Washington, DC: 1979), 53.
3. Ibid.
4. Dan Moldea, *Dark Victory: Ronald Reagan, MCA, and the Mob* (New York: Viking, 1986), 234–35.
5. See, for example, John Davis, *Mafia Kingfish: Carlos Marcello and the Assassination of John F. Kennedy* (New York: Signet, 1989), 258–303; David Scheim, *The Mafia Killed President*

Kennedy (London: W. H. Allen, 1988), 288–94, also published in the United States as *Contract on America* (New York: Kensington, 1988); and Allen Friedman and Ted Schwarz, *Power and Greed: Inside the Teamsters Empire of Corruption* (New York: Watts, 1989), 184–87.

6. See Jack Beatty, "Jack Be Nimble: A Question of Character," *Los Angeles Times Book Review,* June 23, 1991, 1, 13; and Davis.

7. Bill Moyers, *The Secret Government: The Constitution in Crisis* (Cabin John, MD: Locks Press, 1988), 44.

8. David S. Lifton, *Best Evidence: Disguise and Deception in the Assassination of John F. Kennedy* (New York: Carroll and Graff, 1988), 703–8.

9. Scheim, 208–11; and Davis, 290–95.

10. Scheim, 210.

11. See L. Fletcher Prouty, *The Secret Team: The CIA and Its Allies in Control of the United States and the World* (Englewood Cliffs, NJ: Prentice-Hall, 1973), 416–17; and Robert Groden and Harrison Livingston, *High Treason: The Assassination of John F. Kennedy and the New Evidence of Conspiracy* (New York: Berkeley Books, 1990), especially 273–465.

12. This section on Watergate is based in part on D. Stanley Eitzen, *Social Problems* (Boston: Allyn & Bacon, 1980), Chapter 2.

13. David Wise, *The Politics of Lying* (New York: Vintage, 1966), x–xi.

14. See also ibid., xi–xiv; "The Tangled Web They Wove," *Newsweek,* December 2, 1974, 32–37; "Four Key Convictions in the Watergate Affair," *U.S. News & World Report,* January 13, 1975, 15–17; William A. Dobrovir, Joseph D. Gebhardt, Samuel J. Boffone, and Andre N. Oakes, *The Offenses of Richard Nixon* (New York: Quadrangle, 1973); Theodore H. White, *Breach of Faith: The Fall of Richard Nixon* (New York: Atheneum, 1975); and John Dean, *Blind Ambition* (New York: Simon & Schuster, 1976). For a sociological analysis of Watergate, see Jack D. Douglas, "Watergate: Harbinger of the American Prince," in *Official Deviance,* ed. Jack D. Douglas and John M. Johnson (Philadelphia: Lippincott, 1977), 112–20.

15. See, for example, Len Colodny and Robert Gettlin, *Silent Coup: The Removal of a President* (New York: St. Martin's Press, 1991); Peter Dale Scott, "From Dallas to Watergate: The Longest Coverup," in *Assassinations, Dallas and Beyond: A Guide to Cover-Ups and Investigations,* ed. Peter Dale Scott et al. (New York: Random House, 1976), 357–76; and Scheim, 297–326.

16. Moyers.

17. The following account of North's trial is based on Theodore Draper, "Revelations of the North Trial," *New York Review of Books* 27, August 17, 1989, 5:59. In June 1991, most of the charges against North were overturned on appeal. The charges on which he was convicted (e.g., making a profit from the sale of government property) failed to address the real harm of the Iran–Contra affair (e.g., usurping Congress's constitutional powers in foreign policy, lying to Congress, and perhaps even treason).

For evidence on this point, see *Coverup* (Los Angeles: The Empowerment Project, 1988); Abbie Hoffman and Jonathon Silver, "An Election Held Hostage," *Playboy* 9, September 1988, 7ff.; Christopher Hitchens, "Minority Report," *The Nation,* September 19, 1988, 192–93; and *Los Angeles Times,* June 23 , 1991, A-1.

18. ABC News, "Nightline," 1995.

19. *Los Angeles Times,* June 23, 1991, A-1.

20. Ibid.

21. See "Octoberfuss," *The New Republic,* May 13, 1991, 7–8; ABC News, "Nightline," June 19, 1991; Kevin Phillips, "Political Scandals Brew—Is This Bush's Watergate?" *Los Angeles Times,* May 12, 1991, M-1, Mb; and "Bush Absence Fuels Hostage Deal Rumors," *San Diego Union,* May 11, 1991, A-1, A6.

22. Joseph Persico, *Casey: From the OSS to the CIA* (New York: Viking, 1990), 193.

23. Ibid., 196–98.

24. M. Waas, "Two Roads to a Cover-up," *Village Voice,* July 14 , 1987, 29.

25. See Gil Geis, "From Deuteronomy to Deniability," *Justice Quarterly,* March 1, 1988, 1–32.

26. M. Miller, *The Founding Finaglers* (New York: McKay, 1976), 350.

27. M. Hosenball and M. Isadorff, "One Big Scandal," *The New Republic,* April 4, 1988, 12–15.

28. J. Kwitney, "Crimes of Patriots, " *Mother Jones* 16, August/September 1987, 15–23.

29. See Scott, "Beyond Irangate," *Crime and Social Justice* 6, Summer, 25–46.

30. Ibid., 40ff. See also William Safire, "Iraqgate Giveaway," *New York Times,* May 20, 1993, A-13. The following examples are based on the discussion in Frank Hagan and David R. Simon, "Elite Deviance in the Bush Era," *The Justice Professional,* in press, 1997.

31. *San Diego Union,* July 29, 1987, A-11.

32. James Mills, *The Underground Empire* (New York: Dell, 1987), 138ff.

33. *The Los Angeles Times,* June 29 , 1987, A-4.

34. See *The Nation,* June 13 , 1987, 786.

35. See Moyers.

36. J. Ridgeway and K. Jacobs, "Onward Christian Soldiers," *Village Voice,* March 17, 1987, 32ff.

37. Hosenball and Isadorff, 12–15, is the source of these examples.

38. Hagan and Simon.

39. Ridgeway and Jacobs, 32ff.

40. For discussion of possible CIA involvement in the Kennedy assassination, see Jim Marrs, *Crossfire: The Plot That Killed Kennedy* (New York: Carroll and Graff, 1989), 181–210; Peter Dale Scott, "From Dallas to Watergate," *Government by Gunplay: Assassination Conspiracy Theories from Dallas to Today,* ed. Sid Blumenthal and Harvey Yazijian (New York: Signet, 1976), 113–29; and Davis, 400–17.

41. Scheim, 296–97 and Moldea, 294–96.

42. Scheim, 316–17.

43. See Gary Potter et al., *Organized Crime* (Upper Saddle River, NJ: Prentice Hall, 1997), 238ff, for a detailed analysis of Nixon's ties to the Mafia.

44. Scheim, 39. A movie presentation of some of these events is found in Francis Coppola's *The Godfather Part III* (1990).

45. W. Chambliss, "State-Organized Crime," *Criminology* 27, 1989, 183–98.

46. Ron Kramer, "State-Supported Corporate Crime," presented at the 1991 meeting of the Society for the Study for Social Problems, Cincinnati, Ohio, August 1991.

47. Chambliss, 185ff.

48. M. D. Ermann and R. Lundman (eds.), *Corporate and Governmental Deviance,* 4th ed. (New York: Oxford University Press, 1993), 3ff.

49. Chambliss 185ff.

50. A. Montagu and F. Matson, 185ff. *The Dehumanization of Man* (New York: McGraw-Hill, 1983).

Epilogue: Economic Democracy

A Proposal to Transform Society

As long as there are social problems in U.S. society, we cannot be content with the status quo. The dominant theme of this book is that the source of these problems is the structure of society. Thus, any real solution must require that the system change fundamentally. We believe that for changing the basis of the existing system the capitalist economy is the key.

The economy must be changed so that people, rather than profit, are paramount. And the economy must be changed to achieve a reasonably equitable distribution of goods and services. We agree with Mortimer Adler's conception that "economic justice and equality are...akin to political justice and equality...as the politically democratic state is the politically classless society, so the economically democratic state is the economically classless society."[1] Thus, economic equality consists of all people having and none wanting essential material possessions, although not everyone would have like amounts of economic necessities. Adler argues that economic democracy is not antithetical to democracy but is instead a necessity required to guarantee true democracy. We agree.

Although absolute equality is utopian, the economic system can be changed to eliminate the upside-down effect, by which the few benefit at the expense of the many, and to ensure jobs for all with a reasonable wage and the assurance of adequate housing, food, and medical care. There is no excuse for a society such as ours to allow some of its citizens to live in squalor, be poorly fed, have inadequate medical attention, and be objects of contempt from other citizens. A final change needed for our economic system is greater regulation of business activity in accord with central planning to achieve societal objectives and meet the needs of a future characterized by shortages, ecological threats, and worldwide population pressures.

In this Epilogue, we propose an economic system that makes the most sense to us for an economic democracy. Other proposals may also help to solve the problems endemic to the contemporary United States. We should, however, be aware that all social systems, regardless of their economic and political underpinnings, will have social problems. Utopia literally means nowhere. Thus, we do not assume that this system will be perfect. There will be unanticipated problems. But the fear of unknown problems should not deter our willingness to work for social change to reduce or even eradicate current problems. Also, we reject the proposition that just because a utopia is impossible to attain, we should not try to approximate perfection. We believe that the call to change society to eliminate current problems is the most important call any patriot can answer. What follows is our plan for change. We challenge you to work your way through it, find the flaws, and propose alternative planks to the platform or entire new schemes to achieve the goal of "a more perfect Union."

Basic Assumptions

Let's begin by enumerating the assumptions that must guide our search for a possible solution to the elite deviance that plagues contemporary U.S. society. Foremost is the assumption that these problems will be alleviated only through altering the social structure, not by altering so-called problem persons. This assumption does not deny that some individuals are pathological and need personal attention. But attending to these individuals only attacks the symptoms of the problem, not the disease itself. The basic premise is that elite deviance is endemic to our social system.[2]

A second guiding assumption in our search for a solution to elite deviance is that the system must be fundamentally changed. Cosmetic changes or even genuine reforms are likely to fail because they are based on the political–economic base that is the source of many social problems. As Parenti has observed, "As long as we look for solutions within the very system that causes the problems, we will continue to produce cosmetic, Band-Aid programs. The end result is shameful public poverty and shameless private wealth."[3]

In short, the U.S. economic system, state-supported capitalism, is the source for many of our elite deviance problems. Capitalism and the government that accompanies it have no fundamental commitment to remedying social ills.[4] Instead of a commitment to a more equitable distribution of resources, capitalism promotes competition, with the victors widening the gap between themselves and the losers. Tax reforms are instituted to encourage profits rather than to solve problems of unemployment and low wages. Inflation, rather than unemployment, is viewed as the culprit. Suburbanites may work in the city, but they do everything possible to avoid paying taxes that will help the city to eliminate its fiscal woes. The current wave of reducing taxes, government services, and government intervention, while aimed at government waste, also reflects the lack of humane concern for those who are less fortunate, which characterizes capitalists.[5] For capitalism and the highly competitive individuals it engenders create a me-first mentality. According to Parenti:

> Contrary to the view of liberal critics, the nation's immense social problems are not irrational offshoots of a basically rational system, to be solved by replacing the existing corporate and political decision-makers with persons who would be better intentioned and more socially aware. Rather, the problems are rational outcomes of a basically irrational system, a system structured not for the satisfaction of human need but the multiplication of human greed.[6]

A third assumption is that the level of the current U.S. social problems will only be magnified further by the conditions of the future unless the politicoeconomic structure is changed significantly. International tensions in the future will be heightened by scarcity, pollution, and the ever increasing gap between rich and poor nations. Domestically, the future holds similar problems, as well as increased unemployment, deeper economic cycles, urban blight, and problems of racism, ageism, and sexism. Will societies propelled by the profit motive increase or lessen these international and domestic problems?

Although capitalism was instrumental in bringing the United States to its present level of affluence and power (at the expense of labor, minorities, and the Third World), the organization and needs of capitalism are not appropriate for a world of scarcity, overpopulation, ecological disasters, and vast inequities. The future does not hold promise unless competition gives way to cooperation, individual choice is superseded by the needs of society, uncoordinated efforts are supplanted by democratic (not bureaucratic) planning, and economic advantages are spread more evenly throughout society.

Our final assumption is that any attempt to make significant changes in society will be resisted by those in positions of power and wealth (the elite) in current society. Those who benefit by the present arrangement will naturally favor stability, law and order, and other practices that guarantee their advantages. On the other side are those who favor change because they are disadvantaged by the existing system. Thus, the basic problem of implementing change is that "those who have the interest in fundamental change have not the power, while those who have the power have not the interest."[7]

We assume that change will only occur with the emergence of a mass political movement that is a coalition of the poor, the disadvantaged blue-collar worker, and the increasingly impoverished middle class. The formation becomes all the more probable as the current economy and polity become less effective at meeting contemporary problems.

Finally, the United States itself is now beleaguered by a host of domestic social problems; solutions to them will require the application of resources and costly planning. Consider the following observations from former diplomat Leslie Gelb and physics professor Alvin Saperstein:

- **Item:** The richest 2.5 million Americans now earn as much as the bottom 100 million Americans, making inequality a central and potentially divisive future issue.
- **Item:** Between 30 and 40 million Americans live in poverty.
- **Item:** Half of American children in urban primary schools will drop out before graduation.
- **Item:** The number of Americans who do not have health insurance is roughly equal to the population of Central America, approximately 40 million people.
- **Item:** More than 50 percent of the students in U.S. science and engineering schools are now foreign born. A recent math test was given to a national survey of eighth-graders. Results showed that only 14 percent had even seventh-grade math skills; none demonstrated a readiness to begin advanced math procedures. In comparison to thirteen-year-olds from five advanced nations, U.S. students scored last in math.
- **Item:** Two-thirds of federal spending on research and development goes into weapons systems. More research is needed in areas such as energy and alternative fuels, alternative resources, food supplies, drug abuse, contraception, and medical care delivery.[8]

In short, there are real and pressing human deprivations in American society that demand a reordering of priorities.

General Principles

Given these assumptions, which we believe reflect reality, what is the best solution? As a prologue for further discussion and realizing that we cannot foresee all possible angles, let us elaborate on the features of the political–economic form for U.S. society that would make the necessary structural changes to alleviate the problems that are part of the current politicoeconomic system. This is *economic democracy* (also called *social democracy*).

The three fundamental themes of economic democracy are democratism, egalitarianism, and efficiency.[9] Authentic economic democracy must be democratic. Representatives must be answerable and responsive to the wishes of the public that they serve, which means that public officials, whether in the political or economic spheres, must be accountable for their actions. Elite deviance is, above all, a problem of poor accountability.

> Unaccountability pervades American life—not merely the Presidency, not merely the rest of government, but all public and private institutions that exert substantial power over us and, inevitably, over future generations.... Accountability, if it means anything, means that those who wield power have to answer in another place and give reasons for decisions that are taken.[10]

The problem for present-day U.S. society is that the democratic goal of the people having the ultimate power is not realized. As Parenti has charged, "'Democracy,' as it is practiced by institutional oligarchs, consists of allowing others the opportunity to *say* what they want while the oligarchs, commanding all institutional resources, continue to *do* what they want."[11]

Democratic relations must also be found throughout the social structure: in government, at work, at school, and in the community. Along with the election of officials responsive to public opinion and the disappearance of authoritarian relations, democracy entails the full extension of civic freedoms to protect individuals and groups from the arbitrariness of officials.[12]

The second principle of social democracy is *egalitarianism*. The goal is equality: equality of opportunity for the self-fulfillment of all, equality rather than hierarchy in making decisions, and equality in sharing the benefits of society. Thus, economic democracy requires a fundamental commitment to achieving a rough equality by leveling out the gross inequities in income, property, and opportunities. This means that arbitrary distinctions, such as sex, age, race, and ethnicity, no longer serve as criteria for oppressing or for forcing certain categories of persons into limited opportunities.[13]

A major issue is whether the goal is equality of *opportunity* or equality of *outcomes*. Equality of opportunity is a necessity of economic democracy, whereas equality of outcome is probably impossible to attain in a complex society. The key is a leveling of the advantages so that all receive the necessities (food, clothing, medical care, living wages, sick pay, retirement benefits, and shelter). But an absolute equality of outcomes is very likely an unattainable goal, given unequal endowments, motivations, and the like. Moreover, the efforts to approximate this goal would require the imposition of the tightest controls on society and thus very likely be destined to fail.

A third feature of people's capitalism is *efficiency*. This refers to the organization of the society to provide, at the least possible individual and collective cost, the best conditions to meet the material needs of the citizens. Production of necessary goods must be ensured, as well as the distribution of the goods produced, and the services offered must be planned and managed. But this is true of all types of economies. The key method to accomplish economic efficiency for economic democracy is the substitution of public for private ownership of the means of production. The people own the basic industries, financial institutions, agriculture, utilities, transportation, and communication companies. The goal is to serve the public, not to make profit, as is the case in capitalism. Economic democracy, compared to capitalism, will likely have lower prices, greater availability of necessary goods and services, better coordination of economic endeavors, and better central planning to achieve societal goals, such as protecting the environment, combating pollution, saving natural resources, and developing new technologies.

A proposal by former President Gerald Ford, former Vice President Nelson Rockefeller, and the late Senator Henry Jackson illustrates a fundamental difference between the present state-supported capitalism and people's capitalism. This group proposed that taxpayers subsidize the huge development costs of new energy technologies (e.g., refining of shale oil, gasification of coal) and then, once perfected, turn over the benefits of these technologies to private corporations. This tactic allows the public to take all the risks, whereas private corporations wait for the right time to take over the enterprise for their own profit, at the expense of the public. If the socialist principle were applied, the people would collectively take the risks but then reap the benefits, too.[14]

A fundamental argument of the socialist credo is that private corporations work in opposition to human needs. In the search for profit, private corporations have withheld supplies to contrive shortages, colluded with competitors to keep prices abnormally high, encouraged extraordinary and wasteful military expenditures, polluted the environment, and encouraged wasteful consumptive patterns. Moreover, capitalism encourages unemployment. As Harrington has argued, "Sustained full employment is a threat to corporations. For when there is full employment, the labor market tightens up, unions become more combative, and wages tend to rise at the expense of profits."[15]

To summarize, social democracy, or economic democracy, is a politico-economic form of organization dedicated to full human equality, cooperation, participatory democracy, and meeting of human needs. Admittedly, these goals are idealistic. But the closer that U.S. society approaches them, the more social problems such as poverty, racism, sexism, exploitation, unemployment, and human misery will be minimized. To the degree that these goals are achieved, elite deviance is reduced.

The Planks of a Social Democratic Platform

A number of fundamental changes must be made to bring about social democracy. Let's begin with the central problem of capitalist corporate control of the economy for private gain.

1. *Reorganizing large corporations to meet public needs.* The major corporations present the primary obstacles to social justice. The primacy of profit means that these huge organizations resist social goals. They are not concerned with their role in unemployment, pollution, and the perpetuation of poverty. The curbing of pollution reduces profits. High labor costs at home force company officials to move their operations overseas or to another part of the country, where costs are lower. Supposedly competing corporations in a shared monopoly continue to raise prices, even during economic downturns, which contributes to the problem of stagflation. The greed of corporate officials and owners inclines them to use and abuse natural resources without regard for conservation. This greed also encourages them to produce and market unsafe and unhealthy products.

At one time, economic activity was the result of many decisions made by individual entrepreneurs and the heads of small businesses. Now, a handful of corporations have virtual control over the marketplace. The decisions made by the boards of directors and the management personnel of these huge corporations, determined solely by the profit motive, affect employment and production, consumption patterns, wages and prices, the extent of foreign trade, the rate of natural resource depletion, and the like.

Economic democracy requires that the decisions made by corporations be in the public interest. However, the public interest will not be primary unless there is democracy within these corporations and the boards of directors are composed of owners and representatives of the workers and the public. Representatives of the workers are important to democratize the workplace and improve the morale and material conditions of the workers. The public must also be represented on the boards so that the decisions of the organizations will take into account the larger public issues of pollution, use of natural resources, plant location, prices, and product safety. These moves from economic oligarchy to industrial democracy represent a monumental shift from the present arrangement.

Economic democracy can be achieved in a number of ways. First, all major corporations could be required to have a certain proportion of public and employee representatives on their boards of directors as a condition for doing business in interstate commerce.[16] Another procedure would be that every year the corporation would add a number of worker and public representatives, depending on the profits of the previous year. This would mean in effect that, after fifteen or twenty years, the corporation would be controlled by the workers and public representatives. A final example of how industrial democracy could be accomplished would be for the government to insist that, with each subsidy given to the company, a proportion of the company's stock be given to the workers and the public. Thus, in return for tax breaks, low-interest loans, loan guarantees, and the like, the owners of the corporation would lose some of their control. As an example, in 1980 the government agreed to prop up the ailing Chrysler Corporation with loan guarantees of $1.5 billion. Under a plan to bring about economic democracy, the government could have agreed to this proposal in return for a percentage of Chrysler's stock, say 30 percent. Such a plan would give the public a return for its risk capital and the social management of the corporations for the public good.

One question raised about social democracy involves individualism, as we know it. A socialist society is generally perceived as one in which the group smothers the individual personality, prohibiting the use of individual initiative to start businesses. Neither assumption need be true. One plan to promote individualism is to nationalize only those companies that possess or are soon likely to possess a great amount of assets (e.g., $100 million). Small companies could still be owned by groups or individuals. Similarly, large apartment complexes, supermarkets, and department stores could be purchased by government and run cooperatively by local community groups.

2. *Establishing democratic ownership of certain industries.* We propose that the utilities, owners and processors of natural resources, transportation, banks, and credit institutions should be nationalized to ensure the adequacy of services, to plan for the social good, and to minimize business cycles.

The irony of the present capitalist system stems in part from its bouts with economic crises: inflation, unemployment, depression, and the like. To end the vicious swings of business cycles and to provide rationally for the needs of all, economic planning is necessary. Community needs, regional needs, and national needs would all be balanced against each other at succeeding levels of government. But this planning, like all other decisions in this regard, would be done democratically by boards of elected representatives at each governmental level. Many such bodies already exist today, but their roles are largely advisory. Thus, we do not see ourselves merely adding another layer of bureaucracy with this proposal. Rather, we propose to provide a democratic mechanism that would make the most humane and rational use of human and natural resources.

Such planning would also apply to wages, prices, monetary supplies, and interest rates. Presently, these decisions are already made by business-dominated groups such as the Federal Reserve Board. The question of economic planning, in the estimation of many, is not if it will be done, but who will do it, big business or the people? For people to have a democratic voice in economic matters requires a democratization of banking and credit, as well as production.

Finally, we would nationalize all major defense contractors whose prime client is the government. These companies are currently subsidized by the government; they take no risks but make enormous profits. The nationalization of these companies would reduce Pentagon waste significantly, increase efficiency, and eliminate the current sham of government subsidies to profit-making businesses.[17]

3. *Maintaining a democratic government.* Government control, governmental planning, and the nationalization of industries will not accomplish socialist goals unless accompanied by true democracy.

> Where the government owns or directs the means of production, the crucial question is: Who owns the government? There is only one way for the majority to "own" the government: through a political democracy which allows them to change its policies and personnel and which assures minorities, not only civil liberties to try and become a majority, but technical and financial means to exercise that liberty as well. So democracy is thus not simply central to the political structure of economic democracy; it is the guarantee, the only guarantee, of the people's economic and social power.[18]

This quote makes two important points. First, the lack of democracy found in communist countries means that they are not socialist. Second, if democracy at the national level is missing under economic democracy, then we will likely repeat a fundamental problem of contemporary U.S. society, that is, collusion between the government and the economic elite.

4. *Legislating a progressive income tax without loopholes.* A perennial issue in U.S. politics is the structure of the income tax laws. We have examined many of the loopholes that make for this disgrace, but little has been done to correct the situation. We believe that little will ever be done until a mass democratic movement brings about change in such laws. Again, the tax system is a key mechanism by which the rich retain their wealth. Numerous studies reveal that the middle class and the poor pay higher percentages of their incomes in taxes than do the rich.[19]

The problem socialists face concerning tax reform is that the average person is taught that socialist reforms mean heavier taxes for the non-wealthy, but this need not necessarily be the case. What is being proposed here is no less than a truly progressive income tax, one that would require those with the highest incomes to pay the highest percentages in taxes. Thus, 100 percent of the money over a certain amount (to be determined democratically) would be taxed. Under the current system, a number of millionaires pay no income taxes. Under the proposed system, such people would still be comfortable yet pay their fair share.

5. *Legislating an inheritance tax with sufficient controls.* We have seen that the power and wealth of elites rest in part on the special tax advantages that they have been granted. The heart of these advantages is the ability to transfer wealth from one generation to the next through inheritance and tax-exempt foundations. Our proposal would not end inheritance altogether, but it would prohibit the amassing of huge fortunes, which makes elite rule possible.

The amount that a given individual or family would be allowed to inherit would have to be determined democratically. The money raised by the imposition of such taxes would go to pay for the various social projects and programs deemed necessary for a universal decent standard of living. Such standards are already regularly set by the federal government and are not difficult to determine.

6. *Implementing a program of progressive income redistribution.* The goal of this plank is to eliminate the misery associated with poverty. All citizens would, under this proposal, be provided with cradle-to-grave insurance, paid for entirely from income and inheritance taxes. In addition, everyone would be guaranteed adequate housing, an acceptable standard of health care, and a sufficient standard of living. As the Democratic Socialist Organizing Committee has stated, "Socialist democracy, we believe, would make it increasingly possible for the free provision of the necessities of life. That should be done as soon as possible with medicine; eventually, it should extend to housing, food and clothing."[20]

This program would also guarantee full employment for its workers. The societal commitment to full employment is crucial. The typical criticism of full employment concerns the incentive to work. Socialists are often accused of favoring measures that would reward people for not working, but this proposal might not be for the able-bodied who refused to work. This proposal would be coupled with one that legally required U.S. society to provide full employment. The wages and programs mentioned above would go to those unable to work, as well as to all who did work. Not everyone would earn the same amount of money, but the great inequalities of income that plague U.S. society would be reduced.

In addition, this program would guarantee annual income approximately equivalent to trade-union wages. Thus, there would be no need for welfare from the state to those who were unemployed because there would be no unemployment. As for those who refused to work, we believe that there are very few such people in society. Studies demonstrate that the number of people on welfare, yet able to work, constitutes less than 25 percent of welfare recipients. The studies done concerning various groups of poor show that they are virtually unanimous in demonstrating a willingness and need to engage in useful labor.[21] The problem with capitalism is that it has always required a pool of cheap labor to exploit, and it has created unemployment during economic crises. We believe that decent wage and fringe benefits, together with full employment, are the most rational and humane ways of guaranteeing a decent standard of living for all.

7. *Implementing an expanded program of social construction.* In providing full employment, there are always questions about the kind of work that people will do: Will such jobs be meaningful? Will they be undertaken voluntarily? We believe that there is a great deal of work that urgently needs to be done but that has a low priority due to the profit motive that dominates U.S. capitalism. For instance, the need for low-cost housing is immense, with the cost of homes beyond even families at the median income level. Moreover, four out of ten U.S. families live in apartments. Many people, especially those of modest means, would like to own a house but cannot afford one. Aside from housing, there are energy needs that can be urgently met by converting to power from the sun, wind, and tides, a step that would provide millions of new jobs.[22] Employment in construction and related trades is often erratic because of weather and market conditions. This industry contains many who would prefer steady work at a decent standard of living. In providing full employment, we believe that there are enough unmet and important needs in this nation to assure everyone who wants a job a freely chosen position. Aside from social construction, we envision more teachers for special education and reductions in class sizes at all levels. We also foresee the cre-

ation of many jobs for people who wish to represent community interests at all levels of government.

8. *Implementing national indicator planning.* Unlike the current system, for which private, profit-maximizing corporations are the planners of the economy, we propose a system for which the primary goal of economic activity is the public good. National indicator planning would use monetary, import, resource allocation, and other controls to direct production into more useful channels, redistributing income and wealth in favor of the lower classes. The present system requires that government policy making benefit the corporations. These trickle-down solutions disproportionately benefit the elite and are therefore not only unfair but inefficient.[23] For example, the government is faced periodically with the problem of finding a way to stimulate the economy during an economic downturn. The socialist solution would be to spend federal money through unemployment insurance, government jobs, and housing subsidies. In this way, the funds go directly to those most hurt by shortages, unemployment, inadequate housing, and the like. The capitalist response, however, is to advocate subsidies directly to business, which, they claim, will help the economy by encouraging companies to hire more workers, add to their inventories, and build new plants. To provide subsidies to businesses, rather than directly to needy individuals, is based on the assumption (faulty, we contend) that private profit maximizes the public good.

9. *Developing a national ecological plan compatible with the overall economic plan.* We live in an age in which the environment is threatened daily by hazardous chemicals, nuclear waste, and a host of air and water pollutants. We believe that decisions concerning nuclear power and the dumping of hazardous materials should be made by the people who will be most affected by such events. We have provided ample evidence that the pollution problem in the United States is primarily a problem involving the priorities of capitalism, that is, profits. We believe that only a system that does not depend on profit, economic growth, and the continuous use and depletion of resources can practice conservation. Such conservation must be carefully planned in a way that balances human needs with environmental quality. Again, we feel that this is best accomplished through the widest democratic participation.

Michael Lerner has written about economic and ecological planning in a democratic socialist state. He envisions each home being equipped with a voting device that is attached to the phone or television set.[24] After issues have been debated in the media and at community meetings, the wishes of the public could be recorded and presented to elected public officials at local, regional, and national levels (each of whom would face a recall election anytime 10 percent of the registered voters signed a petition to that effect). In addition, groups would also have the power to put a given issue on the political agenda.

Signatures of 1 percent of the voting population in the relevant area would give the group the right to (1) write its own proposal to be put directly to the people, and (2) air its views on the media (it would be given more time than any single position normally is, on the grounds that its view had not previously been given exposure in the usual debates on relevant issues).[25]

Lerner has further suggested that there would be an elected executive branch at all levels, but its decisions could easily be put to the voters for approval. In Lerner's scheme, the planning required for production and ecology, while complex, would be democratic.

Each work unit and each consumer entity would submit its ideas and desires to a community board which would try to adjust them into a coherent whole, then resubmit the adjustments back to the populace for approval. Thereafter, they would be submitted to a regional board that took all the ideas and tried to develop a regional plan, which itself would be sent to a national board, which would try to adjust the regional plans. The last step would be to send the plan back to everyone for approval.[26]

Lerner has argued that equally complex planning is already done by the Department of Defense and other governmental units. However, the people consulted now are the heads of corporate boards, not working-class people. The decisions made by such boards reflect, of course, the wishes of the decision makers. Lerner has also argued that it would be necessary to vote on the components as well as the totality of plans and that one aspect of any plan would be the economy of the local community in which it is generated.

Such planning would be oriented toward overcoming some of the root causes of certain types of elite deviance. Instead of being based on planned obsolescence, all goods would be designed to last as long as possible. This would eliminate much waste and pollution and would save energy, as well.

10. *Implementing a tax policy that would discourage private overseas investment and development of multinational corporations.* We suggest that the United States does not need a multinational empire. Rather, its best hope lies in the promotion of a peaceful, stable, and prosperous world. This is best accomplished by policies designed to end poverty, famine, and political instability in the Third World. Such humane policies would also end the unpopular opinion concerning "ugly American" and "Yankee imperialism" in much of the Third World. In addition, these policies will return many jobs to the United States that have been exported by multinationals in recent years. To accomplish these goals, stringent measures should be provided to curb and then liquidate the great multinational corporations. Moreover, private investment by U.S. corporations overseas should be discouraged through an appropriate tax policy. These things cannot be accomplished overnight and will require a transition period to minimize the disruption of the U.S. economy. We do, however, believe such a conversion is both possible and prudent.

Implementing Economic Democracy

Now that we have characterized how economic democracy ought to work, let's deal with some of the practical problems and questions that always seem to arise in any serious discussion of how it might be implemented.

To begin, the essence of economic democracy is a cooperative spirit among the people. Yet, for some reason, it is commonly believed that people are naturally sinful, aggressive, and self-seeking. In this perspective, competition is natural, and long-range cooperation is impossible. If this postulate is accurate, then the goal of economic democracy will always elude human societies. The question then is whether human beings in groups are capable of long-range cooperative relationships in which the needs of the group supersede the needs of the individual.

The U.S. experience is so competitive that we easily assume such competition is natural. Virtually all aspects of American life involve competition, whether in school or on the job, in organizations, or in activities such as sports, music, and dating. However, there is ample evidence from anthropological studies to show that societies like the Zuni have individuals who are group centered. The members of these societies never attempt to outdo one another, and they accept this sacrifice for the accomplishment of group goals as natural.[27] The conclusion derived from studies like this is that people in societies can be taught to be competitive or cooperative. There is no necessary obstacle to the possibility that Americans could be taught from infancy to work for group goals rather than strive for individual achievement at the expense of others. In short, human nature is really social nature shaped by the society in which the individual lives.

In a related issue, it is often argued that economic democracy runs contrary to human nature because our needs are met by society, whether we work or not. The assumption is that massive inequalities are necessary to motivate citizens to work and avoid a class of lazy welfare recipients. Motivation in socialist countries could be achieved in several ways, without using the repressive tactics of a totalitarian regime. The first would be to socialize citizens to work for the good of the community. Evidence from many experiments with communes shows that the successful ones developed an ideology that the members of the community shared. In a group sharing a common ideology, informal sanctions can be used to achieve conformity among potential deviants.

All societies have members who vary in talent, achievement, and motivation. The problem for a socialist society is how to reward excellence. This could be done through nonmaterial satisfactions, such as honors, responsible community functions, or some extra material benefits. The extra material benefits must be kept in check within a socialist economy, however, so that the private accumulation of wealth is confined within tolerable limits. The permissible maximum, for example, could be twice the median income, with the guaranteed minimum being half the median income. Such a plan would allow everyone the necessities and the personal choice to work for some additional benefits.[28]

Another motivational problem is how to get people to do society's dirty work. After all, if all our basic needs are met, why should anyone do dangerous or menial jobs? Capitalist countries solve this problem of job allocation by paying extra money in the case of hazardous jobs or, in the case of demeaning work, having an underclass (usually minorities) whose opportunities are so limited that they have little choice but to cooperate. A socialist country could see that these necessary tasks are done either by appealing to persons on ideological grounds to give a period of time for these societal duties or by conscripting youth to do the necessary work of society as a kind of societal tax that they owe as citizens. Just as in the time of war, able-bodied persons (male and female) would owe, say, two years of service to their society. A problem that plagues all existing socialist systems (but is not limited to them) is massive bureaucratization. The more the economy is controlled by the government, the greater the problem of inflated stateism, which translates into the twin problems of inefficiency and centralized power. The problem of inefficiency can be addressed through the constant monitoring of procedures and administrators, with the people affected having the power to redress grievances and change inadequate procedures.

The other problem emanating from excessive bureaucratization, centralized power, is especially crucial, for if it is not solved, the goal of economic democracy will be unachievable. This is the problem of the so-called socialist countries with totalitarian regimes. The group that gains power tends to stay in power and sees its goals as those needed by the society. This illustrates the strong organizational tendency labeled the "Iron Law of Oligarchy" by Robert Michels.[29]

Although this probability plagues social organizations, under certain conditions, it does not occur, that is, where democracy prevails.[30] By definition, a democracy exists where at least two political parties regularly compete for office and control alternates periodically. The chances of this happening are maximized when (1) the citizens have a strong interest, concern, and commitment to the society; (2) the subunits (communities, states) are relatively autonomous units forming a federation; (3) the leaders get few special perquisites of office, making them little different from the masses in material rewards; and (4) dissent and innovation are allowed.[31] Admittedly, the problem of the emergence of a self-serving power elite is an especially dangerous issue for socialist countries. Therefore, these societies must institutionalize forms of democratic control at all levels, using the insights provided above. The key is to control power, making it both concentrated and dispersed. The citizens must be ever diligent to counter oligarchic tendencies, and there must be constitutional avenues for the control of the controllers.

Another practical problem facing any socialist society is the high cost of providing minimal benefits to all members. The semisocialist countries of Western Europe have extremely high taxes to level material differences and provide the necessary services. Also, it is charged, societies will experience ruinous inflation if they increase expenditures for social services.

In the United States, there are at least two basic ways that money could be raised for increasing social programs without too great an adjustment. One source of money would come from paring the inflated military budget. The question is how much the current year 2001 $300 billion budget could be reduced without endangering the safety of the society. This question quickly divides liberals and conservatives. Nonetheless, we believe that it is safe to say that if objective observers (e.g., those outside the military, those in business without military contracts, and those public officials outside districts with huge military expenditures) examined military expenditures carefully, they would find numerous military bases that should be closed, redundancy in weapons systems, too many highly paid officers, and a too expensive pension system. Obviously, if the appropriate cuts in the military budget were made, the savings could be deployed elsewhere to meet social needs.

A second and even more lucrative source of money to finance increased social programs would be to eliminate tax expenditures, the money that the government could collect but chooses not to. Most of these tax breaks go to the upper-middle and upper classes. "There are enormous savings to be made in these areas simply by following in fact the principle we now honor in the breach: that those best able to pay should bear their share of the tax burden."[32]

Finally, there is the question upon which all else hinges: How could an economic democracy develop in U.S. society? If the corporate rich are powerful and control the governmental apparatus (including the ability to repress dissent, the media, and the universities), how are the fundamental changes in the structure that are necessary for economic democracy to occur? And who will be included in a social movement bent on making these social changes?

The obvious candidates are those most oppressed by capitalism, the poor, minorities, women, the aged, and the working class (including white- and blue-collar workers). These categories, however, have historically failed to cooperate in a common venture to change the system. They have not developed the class consciousness that Marx envisioned because of racial antipathies and other prejudices, because of their own self-doubt, and because of their belief in the viability of the current politicoeconomic system. They tend to believe that the opportunities available in society will eventually pay off for them or their children. They believe that capitalism is responsible for our greatness and will meet the challenges of the future successfully. In short, persons in these social categories have not seen that they are oppressed. Ironically, they accept the system that works to their disadvantage. Thus, they adhere to beliefs damaging to their interests, what Marx termed *false consciousness.*

Elite Deviance and Economic Democracy

Most certainly, some will view these proposals for economic democracy as being too radical, fearing that such change would undermine the capitalist system that has given U.S. society the wealth and power that have, in the minds of many Americans, proved U.S. superiority in the world. For such critics, the nature of capitalism is not the issue at hand. Such critics accept the distribution of power and wealth as given and believe that solutions to the problems of elite deviance (defined by them as white-collar crime) merely require a series of legal reforms designed to fine-tune an otherwise useful and just social order.

In the past few years, a multitude of schemes has been put forth designed to deal with corporate crime. In fact, so many of these schemes have been proposed that only a brief summary can be given here. Basically, such proposals say more about the faults of the current system than they do about the chances of accomplishing meaningful inroads against the problem of corporate crime. Fisse and Braithwaite have devoted an entire volume to the impact of publicity on corporate offenders.[33] After examining thirteen of the most celebrated cases of corporate crime in the last fifteen years or so, the authors conclude that the only adverse impact such publicity had was nonfinancial, including the loss of individual and corporate prestige, declining morale, distraction from job goals, and humiliation in the witness box for corporate executives. At times, reforms within corporations were instituted following the revelation of scandal. However, according to the authors, these reforms were initiated largely to convince the government not to prosecute offending companies. What is truly needed, claim these researchers, is more effective means of publicizing corporate wrongdoing. Numerous recommendations have been made, including the following:

- Use qui tam suits by consumer groups, which would allow for private prosecution of corporate offenders.
- Relax contempt laws to allow good-faith press comments on matters pertinent to trials.
- Provide immunity from prosecution for voluntary corporate disclosure.
- Require official governmental inquiries into corporate reactions to scandal, particularly those concerning changes in corporate policies.
- Require corporate disclosure of risks of serious harm.

- Promote international exposure of irresponsible corporate practices, including international consumer information networks, investigative journalism, and an international complaint forum.
- Use publicity paid for by corporations as part of the punishment inflicted on offending corporations.
- Use formal publicity following trials to convey information to the public concerning corporate offenses and the consequences of noncompliance with the judgments laid down.
- Initiate presentence or probation orders against offending corporations, requiring disclosure of organizational reforms and disciplinary action undertaken as a result of the offenses in question.[34]

Aside from the use of publicity, other reform-oriented students of corporate deviance have advocated these measures:

- Declare occupational disqualification for corporate offenders.[35]
- Use fines, imprisonment, and rehabilitation more extensively in punishing convicted corporate executives.
- Appoint certain members of boards of directors of convicted companies to represent the public interest through a Federal Corporation Commission. Their tasks would be to ensure that laws are being complied with, to oversee the environmental impact of future actions by convicted corporations, to oversee mandated reforms, and to implement judgments against the corporation.
- Deny insurance coverage to companies lacking adequate systems of information concerning internal wrongdoing.
- Designate a specific corporate official to be charged with the preparation of all raw data concerning violations and disclosure thereof.
- Provide inspectors to oversee enforcement of federal regulations.
- Offer protection and rewards to whistle-blowers.
- Establish an exchange program between officials in both business and government.[36]

Conklin has also developed a scheme of corporate criminal law reforms.[37] These reforms fall into two broad categories: (1) those that deal specifically with laws and practices relating to crimes committed by corporations and (2) those that deal specifically with the corporation's internal structure for decision making and rewards. In many ways, the proposals for corporate criminal law reforms amount to a get-tough policy regarding corporations that commit crimes. Such proposals include but are by no means limited to the following:

1. The consolidation of existing consumer protection agencies and/or the sharing of information among such agencies should be promoted. This

would make obtaining evidence of fraud easier than it is now. Geis has proposed that such agencies infiltrate corporations suspected of committing crimes for delicate undercover work.[38]

2. A mandatory replacement or refund system should be established through which consumer loss resulting from merchant or corporate dishonesty would be reimbursed from tax revenues.

3. An annual report of business crimes by government, like the *FBI Uniform Crime Reports,* should be developed. Perhaps, suggests Geis, we should establish a list of the ten most wanted white-collar criminals.

4. Agencies that are designed to regulate corporate practices should have administrators who either are given fixed terms (perhaps coinciding with that of the president) or are removed from the control of the executive branch and made responsible to either Congress or the federal courts.

5. Companies and executives found guilty of wrongdoing should be required to make a public confession, which is done in countries such as Germany.

6. Corporate accountability to both stockholders and the public should be increased, perhaps through the practice of federal chartering. Under this proposal:

   a. Corporations whose gross assets (including those of subsidiaries) exceeded $100,000 would be required to obtain a federal license to engage in interstate business.

   b. Detailed information on the financial affairs of the corporation, including dealings with foreign firms, would have to be supplied periodically to the Federal Trade Commission (FTC).

   c. Diversification "incidental to the business in which it is authorized to engage," as well as ownership of the stock in other companies, would be forbidden. (This rule would be prospective only, leaving existing relationships unchanged.)

   d. Any proposal altering the existing rights of shareholders, as well as any financial dealings between the corporation and the officers and directors, would have to be fully disclosed to the shareholders.

   e. Directors could not be employed by or have a financial interest in a competitor but would have to have a financial interest in their own corporation.

   f. Any corporation in violation of antitrust laws or one that discriminated by sex, employed child labor, or refused to bargain collectively could lose its federal license and hence its right to do interstate business.

   g. Penalties would range from nominal fines for a thirty-day period during a violation of the license to 1 percent of the book value of the capital stock or assets per month to actual revocation of the license following hearings by the FTC and an action instituted by the attorney general in any district court.[39]

Walter Adams has proposed extending federal chartering regulations to include any industry with assets in excess of $250 million or any corporation that ranks among the eight top producers in an industry where eight firms control 70 percent or more of a market. Under Adams's plan, chartered firms would be prohibited from the following:

1. Acquiring the stock, assets, or property of another company
2. Granting or receiving any discrimination in price, service, or allowances, except where such discrimination can be demonstrated to be justified by savings in cost
3. Engaging in any tie-in arrangements or exclusive dealerships
4. Participating in any scheme of interlocking control over any other corporation[40]

In addition, such firms would be obligated to do the following:

1. Perform the duties of a common carrier by serving all customers on reasonable and nondiscriminatory terms.
2. License patents and know-how to other firms on a reasonable royalty basis.
3. Pursue pricing and product policies calculated to achieve capacity production and full employment.[41]
4. Allow those who blow the whistle on corporate crime to keep as reward up to half the fine(s) levied in court against the corporation reported (the 1899 Rivers and Harbors Act already contains such qui tam action clauses; they could be extended to include other types of corporate criminality).[42]
5. Eliminate the nolo contendere plea and pass reforms that clearly specify the extent of liability of both corporate executives and the corporations for which they work in various situations.
6. Prohibit executives from working in their profession following conviction of wrongdoing and release from prison.
7. Encourage business to develop better internal controls through the use of audits and accounting procedures that make it more difficult to conduct secret and illegal financial transactions.

The other major thrust of liberal reform concerns changing the corporate structure itself. The following proposals take modest steps toward economic democracy. However, as Hacker has commented, "None…call for so drastic a transformation as proposed by Marx and Engels (*The Communist Manifesto*).… The implications inherent in these essays should not be minimized. Put very simply, they will be fought at every stage by organizations having the skills, resources, and experiences for this kind of struggle."[43]

Thus, some liberals are not hopeful about even modest reforms concerning corporate conduct and corporate structure. Still, critics like John Flynn do have some interesting suggestions:

1. The corporation's constituency should be redefined. Under this plan, employees would be given a voice in the running of the corporation's affairs. Workers would provide a check-and-power balance against corporate management.
2. The Kelso Plan should be implemented to give workers a second income. Under this plan, corporate capital formation would take place through the purchase of stock to an employee stock ownership trust, which is paid credit on future corporate dividends. The plan requires the corporation to pay dividends based on net earnings to the employee stockholders. The goal here is to redistribute the wealth in part, as well as to give employees a shareholder's status in the company for which they work.
3. Finally, measures should be provided to end the influence of large amounts of corporate funds in political financing, to require corporate disclosure of ownership, and to initiate antitrust actions to break up both vertical (within one industry) and horizontal (across different industries) monopolies by huge corporations (without nationalization).[44]

Thus, liberal proposals to remedy the ills of corporate crime employ a combination of criminal justice reform and further democratization of the corporation itself.

In part, these proposals assume that democracy, when extended to the corporation and the workplace, will work to overcome the undemocratic effects of the maldistribution of wealth and political power. Liberals believe that it is possible to do this using nonradical reforms.

There are a number of problems with these suggestions. First, each in its own way represents a tacit acknowledgment that corporate crime is out of control. This conclusion is understandable, considering the secrecy that surrounds corporate crime (hence the need for publicity), the lack of punishment that results (hence the need for experimental techniques such as occupational disqualification), and the lack of resources that are committed to fight it (hence the suggestion for more government inspectors). Many of these reforms are compatible with the framework for economic democracy incorporated above. But by themselves, none aims at the root cause of corporate crime: the system of political economy that makes crime both profitable and even necessary.

There is a fundamental distinction between the liberal, reformist approach to white-collar crime and our own. Liberal students of the subject view corporate criminality as a function of "bad apples," including supposedly criminogenic industries, amoral managers, and unethical companies.[45] Such students are careful to point out that the fault is not that of the system of corporate capitalism itself. In defense, they assume that there are large corporations and entire industries in which corporate deviance is either rare or virtually nonexistent. Thus, it is not the business system that is at fault but a few of its bad apples.

We feel that this argument is based on very unreliable evidence; no such assumption is warranted. First, the bad-apple theory is based almost solely on official statistics concerning corporations that are charged with and convicted of criminal wrongdoing. However, this is misrepresentative because it does not count those corporations that victimize workers, consumers, or the public at large yet never get caught. There are no victimization surveys that estimate the actual rate of corporate offenses. We do not study the incidence of corporate crime like we study street crime. Therefore, we cannot accept at face value any theory based on unreliable evidence.

Second, between 1970 and 1979, 11 percent of the largest 1,000 U.S. corporations were convicted of at least one illegal act (and this estimate is low). Imagine for a moment that, between 1970 and 1979, 11 percent of the adult population of the United States had been convicted of some illegal offense and sentenced to prison. As a result, approximately 12 million people would be placed in a prison system that is overcrowded with a mere 0.5 million inmates. At such a point, liberals and conservatives alike would call crime an epidemic- institutionalized phenomenon in U.S. society. However, when the same level of corporate crime is discussed, the problem is not considered to be as serious.

There is also the question of just how much deviant behavior has to occur before it is considered to be an institutionalized practice. We can find no simple answer. If we examine both the illegal and unethical practices that we have described in this book, there is plenty of evidence to indicate that virtually all sectors of the corporate economy and federal government engage regularly in deviant behavior. At the very least, a great deal more research needs to be done. For the moment, we reiterate that we find no credible evidence whatsoever in support of the bad-apple view of white-collar criminality.

Second, the reforms mentioned above deal only with corporate criminality. Barely, if ever, do reforms address the interdependent nature of corporate, political, and organized criminal deviance (as discussed in Chapter 8). While corporate crime is a major factor in elite deviance, it is certainly not the only problem in need of resolution. Elite deviance is deviance between and within organizations. No matter how many corporate executives, politicians, and organized crime leaders are sent to jail, the organizations of which they were a part continue on.

Third, reformist suggestions fail to deal with many of the social problems created by the organizational society in which we live: environmental pollution, the threat of nuclear war, inflation, unemployment, poverty, economic development in the Third World, racism, sexism, the decay of the U.S. economic infrastructure, government deficits, alienation in the workplace, street crime, and cost overruns in defense weapons systems contracting. None of these problems is dealt with when the focus is placed on corporate criminality alone.[46]

Finally, elite deviance includes more than just criminal acts. Ethical values and moral principles are created, shaped, and accepted as part of ideologies precisely because of the great power and wealth held by elites. We stand with the National Conference of Catholic Bishops in asserting that "the time has come for...[an]...experiment in economic democracy: the creation of an order that guarantees the minimum conditions of human dignity in the economic sphere for every person."[47]

We believe that corporate morality flies in the face of such dignity and that such dignity is achievable only through a fundamental democratic restructuring of society.

Sources

The following is a list of articles, books, and organizations relating to the issues raised in this Epilogue.

Publications

BankCheck. 1847 Berkeley Way, Berkeley, CA 94703. World Bank and IMF activities and opposition campaigns. Web site: http://www.irn. org.

The Ecologist. c/o M.I.T. Press, Journals, 55 Hayward St., Cambridge, MA 02142. Europe's leading journal on social and environmental issues; emphasizes the effects of globalization and grassroots resistance movements. E-mail: theecologist@gn.apc.org.

Multinational Monitor. P.O. Box 19405, Washington, DC 20036. Reports on corporate activity, emphasizing accountability, trade, worker health, indigenous rights, environment, and consumer issues. Web site: http://www.essential.org.

Third World Resurgence. Third World Network, 228 Macalister Road, 10400 Penang, Malaysia. Deep analysis of North–South economic, social, and environmental issues from perspectives of Southern activists and governments.

Books

Barlow, Maude, and Bruce Campbell. *Straight through the Heart: How the Liberals Abandoned the Just Society.* HarperCollins, New York, 1995. Documents Canadian Liberal Party's dismantling of the world's most effective social welfare programs.

Barnet, Richard J., and John Cavanagh. *Global Dreams: Imperial Corporations and the New World Order.* Simon & Schuster, New York, 1994. How 200 companies are weaving webs of production, consumption, finance, and culture, leading to social, environmental, and political disintegration.

Bello, Walden, with Shea Cunningham and Bill Rau. *Dark Victory: The United States, Structural Adjustment, and Global Poverty.* Pluto Press, London, 1994. Reports on multilateral development banks and their effects on the poor.

Cobb, Clifford, Ted Halstead, and Jonathan Rowe. "If the GDP Is Up, Why Is America Down?" *Atlantic Monthly,* October 1995. Blistering critique of gross national product (GNP) and other current economic measurements and suggests new measurements that account for social and environmental effects.

Daly, Herman E. "The Perils of Free Trade." *Scientific American,* November 1993. The inherent flaws of free trade; why it cannot possibly promote equity or ecological sustainability.

Daly, Herman E., and John B. Cobb, Jr. *For the Common Good: Redirecting the Economy Toward Community, the Environment, and a Sustainable Future.* Beacon Press, Boston, 1994. Critique of current economic theory and practice; promotes alternative economic values for sustainability, not growth.

Heredia, Carlos A., and Mary E. Purcell. *The Polarization of Mexican Society: A Grassroots View of World Bank Economic Adjustment Policies.* The Development GAP 1994. Study of the effect of World Bank policies on Mexico's small farmers and the urban poor.

Korten, David C. *When Corporations Rule the World.* Kumarian Press, Washington, DC, 1995. How the rules of the global economy were created by and for transnational corporate gain while devastating the environment and social equity; also offers a relocalizing strategy.

Mander, Jerry, and Edward Goldsmith. *The Case against the Global Economy.* Sierra Club Books, 1999. Forty-three authors present comprehensive analyses of globalization's effects, the corporations and theories that drive it, and some ideas for localizing alternatives.

Raghavan, Chakravarthi. *Recolonization: GATT, the Uruguay Round, and the Third World.* Third World Network, New York, 1990. Analysis of the latest round of global trade talks.

Rifkin, Jeremy. *The End of Work.* G. P. Putnam's, New York, 1994. Scary study of how new technologies are destroying jobs in industry, agriculture, and the service sector globally.

Shiva, Vandana. *Monocultures of the Mind: Perspectives on Biodiversity and Biotechnology.* Third World Network, 1993. Analysis of effects of new technologies on Third World cultures.

Wallach, Lori, Peter Cooper, Chris McGinn, et al. "NAFTA's Broken Promises: The Border Betrayed." *Public Citizen,* January 1996. Examines environment and health decline of the U.S.–Mexico border in NAFTA's first two years.

Organizations

Council of Canadians. 904-251 Laurier Ave. W., Ottawa, Ontario K1P 5J6, Canada. Leading battler against NAFTA; works to safeguard Canada's social programs and the environment and advocates alternatives to free trade.

Development Group for Alternative Policies (D-GAP). 927 15th St. NW, 4th Floor, Washington, DC 20005. Brings Southern grassroots voice into international economic policy making. Web site: http://www.igc.apc.org/dgap.

Earth Island Institute. 300 Broadway, Suite 28, San Francisco, CA 94133. Environmental group that has led resistance to GATT challenge of Marine Mammal Protection Act and other wildlife issues. Publishes excellent journal. Web site: http://www.earthisland.org/ei/.

Fifty Years Is Enough: US Network for Global Economic Justice. 1025 Vermont Ave. NW, Suite 300, Washington, DC 20005. International coalition challenging the World Bank–IMF economic model. E-mail: wb50years@igc.apc.org.

Friends of the Earth. 1025 Vermont Ave. NW, Suite 300, Washington, DC 20005. Leading environmental group that campaigns against globalization and current economic policies. Web site: http://www.foe.org.

Global Exchange. 2017 Mission St., Suite 303, San Francisco, CA 94110. Books and publications on globalization; builds links between international organizing efforts. E-mail: globalexch@igc.apc.org.

Institute for Agriculture and Trade Policy. 1313 5th St. SE, Suite 303, Minneapolis, MN 55414. Pioneer campaigner and publisher against NAFTA and GATT and for preservation of small and indigenous farms. Web site: http://www.iatp.org/iatp.

Institute for Food and Development Policy (Food First). 398 60th St., Oakland, CA 94618. Think tank and publisher supporting citizen action on issues of food, poverty, development, and globalization. E-mail: foodfirst@igc.apc.org. Web site: http://www.netspace.org/hungerweb/FoodFirst/index.htm.

Institute for Local Self-Reliance. 1313 5th St. SE, Suite 306, Minneapolis, MN 55414. Develops alternative economic and technological policies for local production, consumption, and political control. Web site: http://www.ilsr.org.

Institute for Policy Studies. Working Group on the World Economy, 1601 Connecticut Ave. NW, Washington, DC 20009. Progressive think tank that produces books, studies, articles, and films on globalization and strategies for citizen responses. E-mail: ipscomm@igc.apc.org.

International Forum on Globalization. P.O. Box 12218, San Francisco, CA 94112. New alliance of activists from twenty countries presenting public education events and publications against globalization. E-mail: ifg@igc.org.

International Labor Rights Fund. 110 Maryland Ave. NE, Suite 101, Washington, DC 20002. Pioneered international worker rights through legislative, consumer, corporate, labor, and social charter strategies. E-mail: laborrights@ igc.apc.org.

International Society for Ecology and Culture. 850 Talbot Ave., Albany, CA 94706. Workshops and publications on counterdevelopment strategies, antiglobalization, and preservation of local cultures.

People-Centered Development Forum. International alliance seeking sustainable and equitable community-based economies. Web site: http://iisd1.iisd.ca/pcdf.

Program on Corporations, Law, and Democracy. P.O. Box 806, Cambridge, MA 02140. Educational programs on corporate dominance; organizing strategies for challenging corporate charters. E-mail: poclad@aol.com.

Public Citizen/Global Trade Watch. 215 Pennsylvania Ave. SE, Washington, DC 20003. Policy development; organizing and legal action on issues of trade and food safety, public health, the environment and democracy.

Rainforest Action Network. 450 Sansome St., Suite 700, San Francisco, CA 94111. Focuses on the threats that global trade rules pose to tropical and temperate forests and to native peoples. E-mail: rainforest@ran.org. Web site: http://www.ran.org/ran/.

Redefining Progress. One Kearny St., 4th Floor, San Francisco, CA 94108. Think tank challenging economic assumptions and measurements that ignore social and environmental costs. E-mail: info@rprogress.org.

Sierra Club. 85 2nd St., 2nd Floor, San Francisco, CA 94105. Mainstream environmental group opposing GATT and NAFTA. Web site: http://www.sierraclub.org.

Southwest Network for Environmental and Economic Justice. P.O. Box 7399, Albuquerque, NM 87194. Grassroots organization of people of color promoting regional strategies on environmental degradation and corporate behavior.

Endnotes

1. Mortimer J. Adler, *Haves without the Have-Nots: Essays for the Twenty-First Century on Democracy and Socialism* (New York: Macmillan, 1991), xi.

2. For elaboration on this point, see the following: James M. Henslin, "Social Problems and Systemic Origins," in *Social Problems in American Society,* 2nd ed., ed. James M. Henslin and Larry T. Reynolds (Boston: Holbrook, 1976), 375–81; William Ryan, *Blaming the Victim,* 2nd ed. (New York: Pantheon, 1977); and Michael Parenti, *Power and the Powerless* (New York: St. Martin's Press, 1978).

3. Michael Parenti, *Democracy for the Few,* 3rd ed. (New York: St. Martin's Press, 1980), 314.

4. Ibid.

5. Also see Vernon E. Jordan, Jr., "The New Minimalism," *Newsweek,* August 14, 1978, 13.

6. Parenti, *Democracy for the Few,* 314.

7. Ibid., 312.

8. Leslie Gelb, "Memo for Mr. Bush," *Seattle Times,* August 21, 1991, A-20; Alvin M. Saperstein, "Decaying from Within," *Detroit Free Press,* June 12, 1990, 7-A; and *Detroit Free Press,* June 7, 1991, 1-A, 6-A.

9. Ralph Miliband, "The Future of Socialism in England," in *The Socialist Register 1977* (London: Merlin, 1977), 38–50. See also Samuel Bowles and Herbert Gintis, *Schooling in Capitalist America: Educational Reforms and the Contradictions of Economic Life* (New York: Basic Books, 1976), Chapter 11.

10. M. Mintz and J. Cohen, *Power Inc.* (New York: Viking, 1976), iii.

11. Parenti, *Power and the Powerless,* 203.

12. Michael Harrington, *Socialism* (New York: Saturday Review Press, 1979), 8–9.

13. Richard C. Edwards, Michael Reich, and Thomas E. Weisskopf (eds.), *The Capitalist System,* 3rd ed. (Englewood Cliffs, NJ: Prentice Hall, 1986), 517ff.

14. Miliband, 42–43.

15. Michael Harrington, "How to Reshape America's Economy," *Dissent* 23, Spring 1976, 122.

16. Ibid.

17. Ibid., 22.

18. Michael Harrington, cited in "We Are Socialists of the Democratic Left," a statement of principles by the Democratic Socialist Organizing Committee (1978), 2.

19. See, for example, R. Parker, *The Myth of the Middle Class* (New York: Liveright, 1972); Phillip Stern, *The Rape of the Taxpayer* (New York: Random House, 1973); and J. Turner and C. Starnes, *Inequality: Privilege and Power in America* (Pacific Palisades, CA: Goodyear, 1976).

20. Harrington, "We Are Socialists of the Democratic Left," 3.

21. For a detailed review of such studies, see C. H. Anderson and J. R. Gibson, *Toward a New Sociology,* 3rd ed. (Homewood, IL: Dorsey Press, 1978), 170–76.

22. See the program for economic conversion designed to shift the United States toward a peacetime economy, available from SANE, Washington, DC.

23. Michael Harrington, "The Socialist Case," *Center Magazine,* July / August 1976.

24. Cable television in Columbus, Ohio, currently provides an interactive system through which individuals can instantaneously record their preferences in a central computer.

25. Michael Lerner, cited in M. Edwards et al. (eds.), *The Capitalist System,* 2nd ed. (Englewood Cliffs, NJ: Prentice Hall, 1978), 535. For more complete information, see Lerner, *The New Socialist Revolution* (New York: Dell, 1973).

26. Edwards et al., 536.

27. See Ruth Benedict, *Patterns of Culture* (New York: Mentor Books, 1934).

28. See Henry Pachter, "Freedom, Authority, Participation," *Dissent* 25, Summer 1978, 296.

29. Robert Michels, *Political Parties,* trans. Eden and Cedar Paul (New York: Free Press, 1966). See also Max Weber, *The Theory of Social and Economic Organization* (Glencoe, IL: Free Press, 1947).

30. See Seymour Martin Lipset, Martin Trow, and James C. Coleman, *Union Democracy: The Internal Politics of the International Typographers Union* (Garden City, NY: Doubleday Anchor, 1962).

31. Anthony M. Orum, *Introduction to Political Sociology: The Social Anatomy of the Body Politic* (Englewood Cliffs, NJ: Prentice Hall, 1978), 259–60.

32. Harrington, "How to Reshape America's Economy," 122. See also Robert M. Brandon et al., *Tax Politics* (New York: Pantheon, 1976).

33. B. Fisse and J. Braithwaite, *The Impact of Publicity on Corporate Offenders* (Albany, NY: SUNY Press, 1983).

34. Ibid., 243, 312.

35. M. F. McDermott, "Occupational Disqualification of Corporate Executives: An Innovative Condition of Probation," *Journal of Criminal Law and Criminology* 73, Summer 1982, 604–41.

36. C. D. Stone, *Where the Law Ends* (New York: Harper & Row, 1975), 133–60.

37. J. Conklin, *Illegal But Not Criminal: Business Crime in America* (Englewood Cliffs, NJ: Prentice Hall, 1977), 104.

38. *Current Perspectives on Criminal Behavior: Original Essays in Criminology,* ed. A. Blumberg (New York: Knopf, 1984), 130ff.

39. R. Nader, "The Case for Federal Chartering, in *Taming the Giant Corporation,* ed. R. Nader and M. Green (New York: Grossman, 1973).

40. W. Adams, "The Antitrust Alternative," in Nader and Green, 130–50.

41. A. S. Miller, "The Courts and Corporate Accountability," in Nader and Green, 198–214.

42. Ibid., 146–47.

43. A. Hacker, "Citizen Counteraction," in Nader and Green, 182–97.

44. J. Flynn, "Corporate Democracy: Nice Work If You Can Get It," in Nader and Green, 94–111.

45. See, for example, M. B. Clinard and M. Yeager, *Corporate Crime* (New York: Macmillan, 1980); and M. B. Clinard, *Corporate Ethics and Crime: The Role of Middle Management* (Beverly Hills, CA: Sage, 1983).

46. For an excellent discussion of how the alienating nature of capitalism itself relates to many of these conditions, see J. Wildeman, *Social Problems in America: Alienation and Discontinuity* (New York: Irvington, 1983).

47. *New York Times,* November 12, 1984, B-10.

Name Index

Abramo, Don, 81
Ackerman, Frank, 88*n*.40
Adamany, David W., 231*n*.70
Adams, James Ring, 241, 266, 292*n*.17
Adams, Sam, 41*n*.6
Adams, Walter, 337, 344*n*.40
Adler, Mortimer, 319, 343
Adonnis, 76
Agnew, Spiro, 197–198
Agree, George E., 231*n*.70
Alfonsin, Raul, 185
Allain, Bill, 222
Allen, Gary, 44*n*.62
Allende, 236
Altman, Robert, 54
Altman, Roger, 18
Ames, Aldrich, 235
Ames, Oakes, 203
Amick, George, 202, 229*n*.1, 229*n*.3,
    229*n*.6–7, 229*n*.12, 229*n*.14–16,
    229*n*.18–19
Anastasia, Albert, 77
Anders, William, 56
Anderson, C. H., 343*n*.21
Anderson, Jack, 109, 119*n*.69,
    193*n*.61–62, 193*n*.64, 197, 260*n*.42
Andreotti, Giulio, 79
Arendt, H., 293*n*.30
Armas, Castillo, 186
Aubuisson, Roberto d', 185, 186, 307
Azima, Farhad, 52

Bagdikian, Ben, 43*n*.47
Baird, Zoe, 7
Baker, Peter, 41*n*.1
Baker, R. W., 262*n*.90
Bakker, Jim, 286, 308
Baldridge, J. Victor, 90*n*.133

Balkan, S., 42*n*.24, 86*n*.2
Ball, Howard, 220, 231*n*.60
Bani-Sadr, 304
Baraheni, R., 193*n*.59
Barber, James David, 193*n*.76
Barbie, Klaus, 307
Barker, Bernard, 311
Barlett, Donald, 88*n*.38–39, 88*n*.41
Barnet, Harold, 45*n*.99–100
Barnet, R., 293*n*.35
Barnouw, Erick, 43*n*.41
Barr, (Attorney General), 223
Bass, Robert, 50
Bates, James, 87*n*.17
Batista, Fulgencio, 82, 238
Beach, Nathaniel, 284
Beard, Charles, 230*n*.49
Beatty, Jack, 317*n*.6
Beaty, Jonathan, 87*n*.18
Bebe, Herman, 52
Becker, Theodore, 260*n*.39, 260*n*.42
Behar, Richard, 90*n*.111
Bell, Dennis, 262*n*.83
Benedict, Ruth, 344*n*.27
Ben-Horin, Daniel, 156*n*.75
Benny, Jack, 115
Benson, George C. S., 228, 229*n*.1–3,
    229*n*.5, 229*n*.11, 229*n*.13, 229*n*.20,
    230*n*.41–43, 231*n*.61, 231*n*.63,
    231*n*.72–74, 231*n*.80
Bentsen, Lloyd, 18, 27
Bequai, August, 89*n*.81–82, 89*n*.90
Bergen, Candice, 115
Bernard, V., 293*n*.31
Bernstein, B., 293*n*39
Berrigan, Daniel, 246, 260*n*.42, 260*n*.46
Best, Michael H., 148, 157*n*.97–99
Biehl, Carl, 312

Subject Index

Subject Index **365**

leaked information to, 315
power elite and, 14, 15, 16, 20, 23–24
trivial coverage, 74
underreporting, 103–104
mass society, 267
Mattel, 132
Meat Inspection Act (1906), 32, 126
Medellín cartel, 238–239, 304, 305, 309
Medicaid, fraud, 92, 114
Medicare fraud, 50–51, 92, 114
Medicare Anti-Kickback Statute, 114
mergers, 69, 70–71, 73, 94–95, 97
Merrill Lynch, 81
Mexico, 79–80, 83, 177
Microsoft, 71
military elite, 14, 47
military-industrial complex, 29, 73, 158,
160–174, 190–191, 267, 309
budget, 160, 161, 162, 164, 170, 333
defense contract practices, 164–170
defense policy consequences, 170–172
origins, 160–163
as triangle, 162–163
waste, 324, 326
MILSTAR, 168
mining industry, 136, 144–146
MITLAMP complex, 161, 162
M-19, 309
Mobil, 97
money, fetishism of, 265–266, 267
money laundering, 28, 31, 92, 99, 234
CIA, 238, 268
of drug money, 268, 270, 282, 305
international, 51–54, 79, 80–82, 173
of political contributions, 225, 227, 301
monopoly, 33, 36, 76–77, 100, 105, 121, 201
antitrust laws and, 70, 71, 73
China state tobacco, 173
corporate deviance and, 91, 93–100
horizontal/vertical, 338
shared, 94, 96–98, 100, 104, 115, 324
Monroe Doctrine, 253
Monsanto Chemical Co., 152–153
Montgomery bus boycott, 240
Montgomery Ward, 112
moral harms, 35
multinational corporations (MNC), 158,
162, 174–191, 267, 268

tax policy to discourage, 330–331
U.S. policy and, 179, 180, 185, 188–190
Multinational Monitor study (1992), 93
MX missile guidance system, 169
My Lai massacre, 255–256, 271

napalm, 255
narcissism, 266, 279
NASDAQ, 81
National Advertising Council, 23
National Aeronautics and Space
Administration (NASA), 161, 162
National Association of Broadcasters,
132
National Association of Feed Chains, 32
National Association of Manufacturers,
24, 32
National Commission on Product
Safety, 121
national ecological plan, 329–330
National Highway Traffic Safety
Administration (NHTSA), 124
national indicator planning, 329
National Institute for Occupational
Safety and Health (NIOSH), 138
nationalization, 325, 326, 338
National Liberation Front, 254
National Rifle Association, 26
national security, 37, 226–227, 233, 257,
276, 300–301
National Security Act (1947), 309
National Security Agency (NSA), 158,
239–240
National Security Council (NSC),
54, 168
National Sewing Contractors, 174
Native Americans, 254
NATO, 171
Nazi Germany, 35, 62, 82, 249, 268,
273, 283
slave labor, 288–289
Nebraska Beef-Cattle King scandal, 127
new global economy, 172–174
New Left, 245
Nicaragua, 53–54, 187, 190, 237, 246,
302–307. See also Iran-Contra.
"nickel job", 169
Nigeria, 180